RUNNING AS
A WOMAN

RUNNING AS A WOMAN

Gender and Power in American Politics

LINDA WITT
KAREN M. PAGET
GLENNA MATTHEWS

THE FREE PRESS
New York   London   Toronto   Sydney   Tokyo   Singapore

The Free Press
A Division of Simon & Schuster Inc.
866 Third Avenue, New York, N.Y. 10022

First Free Press Paperback Edition 1995

Printed in the United States of America

printing number

1 2 3 4 5 6 7 8 9 10

Library of Congress Cataloging-in-Publication Data

Witt, Linda.
   Running as a woman : gender and power in American politics / Linda
Witt, Karen M. Paget, Glenna Matthews.
      p. cm.
   Includes bibliographical references and index.
   ISBN 0-02-874069-6
   1. Women in politics—United States. I. Paget, Karen M.
II. Matthews, Glenna. III. Title.
HQ1391.U5W58 1994
320′.082—dc20   93–14615
                                                       CIP

To Jim
—LW

To Janet, Ruth, Pen, and Tim
who made being a woman in politics so incredible
—KP

To my aunt, Norma Nicolais Cook,
an important source of love and continuity in my life
To the memory of my uncle,
Wilbur Nicolais
—GM

CONTENTS

PREFACE:
THE BIRTHING OF A BOOK

This book was conceived as a result of something women do well—a friend got friends together—and it has been blessed with many midwives. The first, Josie Heath, late in 1989 introduced two old friends of hers, journalist Linda Witt and political scientist Karen Paget. The book gestated over several long lunches spent discussing the various women running for high-stakes political office in 1990—among them their mutual friend Josie Heath, who was running for the U.S. Senate from Colorado.

Change was in the air that year. The Berlin Wall had tumbled. A new phrase, "peace dividend," was all the buzz among the media and politicians. Pundits were predicting this newfound windfall would focus the public's interest on domestic issues, thus flinging open the doors of governors' mansions and the U.S. Congress to the type of candidates deemed most tied to those issues: women. The year 1990 would be, they said, "The Year of the Woman in Politics."

To the two of us enjoying those getting-to-know-you lunches, the hype seemed too reminiscent of earlier electoral cycles, of earlier raised and dashed hopes: 1984 and Geraldine Ferraro, 1972 and a big freshman class that did include Congresswoman Patricia Schroeder, Yvonne Brathwaite Burke, and Barbara Jordan but still failed to create a critical mass.

But we were sensing something new in 1990. Not numbers, but a new level of confidence among women candidates. A new sense of legitimacy and entitlement. Gone was the old defensive posture, "It doesn't matter that I'm a woman. I can do this job as well as any man." Suddenly it did matter. Women candidates were arguing they would bring different views to the process of making public policy. There was a new edge in their voices and campaign messages. And there were new kinds of women entering the arena: women whose life experiences in the varied neighborhoods of America meant new ways of seeing political issues, new ways of expressing the policy needs of women and families, and a new sense that our national government might finally even look like all our people.

Enter the third member of this team, historian Glenna Matthews, whose earlier book, *Just a Housewife—The Rise and Fall of Domesticity in America*, had given both the journalist and the political scientist new insights into the ways American women's cultural traditions meshed with politics. One of us said to the other, "You should meet . . ." and we discovered we both already were friends with Glenna. At the next lunch, as Linda and Karen began listing for Glenna the messages we were hearing in women's campaign slogans, she began explaining how they echoed the rationales American women had used, long before suffrage, to have a political voice.

When yet another friend, Lael Stegall, hosted a "book birthing" dinner party for us in Washington, D.C., early in 1991, we feasted as much on the richness and depth of some three dozen politically involved women's experiences and knowledge as on the food. It was a diverse group: some former candidates, some former campaign staffers, some just politically aware citizens. Among the "midwives" were author Celia Morris, the McCormick Foundation's Ruth Adams, Brigadier General Wilma Vaught (USAF-Ret.) and EMILY's List founder Ellen Malcolm.

When we began *Running as a Woman*, we had simple goals. The political scientist and the historian have taught various gender- and politics-related courses at the University of California at Berkeley and Stanford University, as well as elsewhere, and both felt a need for a contemporary text that would explain why women finally are beginning to succeed electorally—and what held them back for so long. As a reporter and columnist who has covered national politics since 1968 and whose special interest has been women's issues, the journalist wanted to tell the stories of the remarkable women who pioneered politics and made possible the swelling pipeline of elected women officials all across the country. What we did not understand then was how hard it would be to construct the necessary bridges to each other's disciplinary knowledge, ways of thinking, and ways of working. We accomplished it because we began as friends, and friends of friends, all philosophically committed to women's equality.

The wealth of professional experience and insight each of us brought from our respective disciplines led us much further than we had imagined possible, and we came to understand that the book we wanted to write could not be written by any two of us without the third. Despite our involvement in our generation's politics and more than a quarter century each as participant/beneficiary/observers of the women's movement, our knowledge overlapped only occasionally. There were times, at our weekly brainstorming sessions, when one of us would struggle to find words that might explain some new direction her own investigation had taken, only to discover that one of the others could give it a name or connect it to another scholar's thinking or at least fit another piece into the puzzle.

And there were questions that initially puzzled us. Why had women voters never flexed the electoral muscle their majority status made possible? Why is the act of running for office still, to some women, an unseemly thing for a woman to do? Why, even after the gender gap was identified, quantified, and the threat of it exploited, could no one quite explain what it was or what triggered it? And why was it that women politicians were still being asked the same absurd question that might-have-been presidential candidate Pat Schroeder had been asked in 1987— "Are you running as a woman?"—despite her droll response, "Do I have an option?"

Some of the answers we sought became clear in the failed races and few successes of 1990— a "Year of the Woman in Politics" ridiculed by many, including *New York Times* columnist William Safire. In December 1990, he sarcastically denounced women and their political record as almost predictable failures "in the land of equal opportunity, where the U.S. Mint can't get rid of its Susan B. Anthony dollars."

Women's progress is slow, he sniped, because "women of every political stripe . . . are letting down their own sexual side by not demanding more female candidates and by not supporting them when they run."

Schroeder herself has expressed similar exasperation: "After we [women] got the vote this body quaked and said we'd better start paying attention. . . . It's not like they didn't know these issues were out there . . . they just never felt they had to deal with them. But [after suffrage] they found it didn't make any difference because women didn't hold them accountable.

"We were always very timid about pushing our own issues politically, we women. We would push others' issues. The environment, civil rights . . . just not ours," she added, lamenting the "common wisdom that it is somehow tacky for women to push their own issues. . . . We honestly believe if it's right and fair, the majority will just do it."

In his summation of 1990's Year of the Woman, Safire was harsher, accusing women of a "dismaying lack of assertiveness" and wondering when they would learn, as had men, to vote with their buddies from the foxholes of shared battles.

Then came Anita Hill.

Over the course of the next year American women came to understand many of the battles we had shared, and our book, intended as an update on women in politics as of 1990, rapidly became something more. We found ourselves correspondents on the front lines of women's battle for full citizenship. In closing the gaps in our understanding of an issue or an era—or even of the would-be First Ladies' Cookie War—we found new ways of thinking and interpreting events.

Schroeder's 1987 response to this nation's odd perplexity at the mere possibility that one of its foremost congressional representatives—by chance also a daughter, wife, mother, Harvard-trained lawyer, and one of its most competent female citizens—might actually be "running as a woman" encapsulates the history of and core dilemma for America's political women. Her response was also an expression of the feminist hope that women finally might have achieved a right their brothers had always taken for granted: The right to be full citizens. The right to be persons whose gender—and all the biological and cultural traditions that word implies—is no barrier to life, liberties, happiness, and the fulfillment and purpose that can come from serving one's country.

Would that we could end this book secure in the knowledge that women now do have the option to be women wherever their lives, talents, and goals beckon them. Would that the question, "Are you running as a woman?" had ceased to be asked because it is, as it always has been, ridiculous on its face. It is as ridiculous as presuming a candidate for office will be in favor of, or "better on," issue Y because her chromosomes are X. It is as ridiculous, particularly, as asking a candidate, because she is a woman, if she could be "man enough" to declare war, forgetting that all candidates need to be strong enough to fight for peace and share responsibility for families, society, our planet, and human dignity everywhere.

To the extent that we are optimistic about the future, it is because of the women we have met during the research for this book—most in person, but some only through their too-brief mention in the history books. One of them, the very first woman to serve in the U.S. Senate, was a senator for just one day, November 21, 1922. Rebecca Latimer Felton was then 87 years old, an artifact of the nineteenth century and a product of an anti-Semitic, anti-Catholic, rigidly segregated South. At best she is flawed heroine, yet in some ways she was quite a modern political woman. She had been an activist: a temperance veteran and a "progressive" newspaper columnist. She had been a political daughter, stumping the state with her father as a child, meeting every president since Grant. As a political wife she had even managed her husband's campaigns, long before respectable "ladies" did such things. And she was a suffragist, a savvy one at that.

When Georgia's governor appointed her to finish the term of a senator who died in office, it was an obvious sop to the brand new women's vote. Congress had already adjourned that session. The appointment was merely symbolic. Yet Felton demanded to be treated seriously. She pleaded unsuccessfully with President Warren G. Harding to call a special session. When women throughout the country echoed her plea and petitioned him to reconsider, Harding suddenly found it politically expedient to call a special session for other reasons—no gender gap imperative existed at that time. Felton, although assumed to be too elderly and frail to make the arduous journey to Washington, nonetheless did so, then was forced to cool her heels for a day and a half in the Capitol's corridors while the Senate debated whether to allow a woman in. Once sworn in, she asked for the floor.

With the speech she proceeded to give—the first by any American woman on the U.S. Senate floor—this white-haired old lady put her fellow Senators on notice that, while she might be the first, she would not be the last of her gender in Congress, and when her sisters would follow, she declared, "I pledge you that you will get ability, you will get integrity of purpose, you will get exalted patriotism, and you will get unstinted usefulness."

Many colleagues and friends have supported this project with everything from bed and breakfast to financial contributions (Lisa Goldberg of the Revson Foundation, Nancy Woodhull of the Freedom Forum, and Jim Browne of the Tides Foundation). Many read early drafts and found encouraging words. We would particularly like to thank Jane Mansbridge, Margaret Gordon, Ethel Klein, Jane DeHart, John Snetsinger, Helen Kelley, Loni Hancock, Raymond Smock, the Women's Research Group and the Beatrice Bain Scholars at the University of California at Berkeley, the Institute for Historical Study, Beth Rashbaum (who cheerily promised to shoot us if we didn't finish the book), our guardian agent

Felicia Eth (who kept us on course), and editor Susan Arellano (who told us on Day One that the project "was far richer than even you now know.")

Ruth Mandel, Sue Carroll, and the other wonderful scholars and staff at Rutgers' Center for the American Woman and Politics let us sojourn with them early on and helped us at every turn. The Great Falls, Montana, chapter of Women in Communications gifted us with a pristine out-of-print and hard-to-find copy of Jeannette Rankin's biography. Political veterans Jane Danowitz, Linda DiVall, Celinda Lake, Ellen Malcolm, Sharon Rodine, and Harriett Woods were generous with time and resources. San Francisco's Women's Campaign Research Fund organized a series of breakfasts with women in politics—serendipity that saved us much travel time and money. Linda's column editors (especially Shirley Ragsdale in Muskogee, Pamela Moreland in Marin County, Mike Oakland and Dean Schacklett in Olympia, David Pollak in San Jose, and Sid Hurlburt of *USA Today*) not only encouraged but kindly suffered column after column on some aspect of the status of women in politics in the 1990s. We also benefited from the enthusiasm and library sleuthing of Jennifer Steen and Barbara Newcombe here and Letitia Wells in Washington, D.C.

Our own mothers (Enid Witt, Maxine Eggert, and Alberta Ingles) got into the act, showering us with clippings, as did our daughters (Amy Witt Leroux and Karen Matthews). Linda's husband Jim Marsh provided Frequent Flyer bonuses as well as broad technical support, and he and Karen's son Tim Enwall performed miracles when the PCs weren't speaking to the Macintoshes.

Beyond the dozens of formal interviews that served as the basis for this book, many far less structured moments, in elevators and "ladies" rooms, over coffee, and in cars and airports between appearances with the hundred-plus women we met, gave us a deeper understanding of our subject—the American political woman.

Again and again, when the "conference call" came that the Senator's or Congresswoman's aide had warned us "will have to cut short this interview," the Senator or the Congresswoman invariably waved the interruption away and continued talking—often for more than an hour beyond the time the aide had scheduled.

We were touched when Senator Nancy Kassebaum spoke so knowledgeably, and appreciatively, of the contributions made by Kansas pioneer women, a love the women and men of her staff acknowledged by each creating a piece for a Kansas quilt for her Senate office wall.

Another treasure: hearing then 90-year-old Senator Margaret Chase Smith express her delight at her first snowmobile outing a few weeks earlier, then receiving a note from her—on rose-engraved paper—with an insightful afterthought on our discussion about her fight for equal opportunity for military women: "It was because of the nurses and what I saw them doing in the Pacific in the 40s that caused me to make the fight. I was right. . . and hope time will prove it was well for all of us."

One moment that stands out, and one we undoubtedly will repeat again and again to bolster sagging spirits whenever we or a sister begin to lose hope that the women of America will learn to stick together, work across race and class lines together, and count on one another to create a new future and fight our common battles: Attorney General Janet Reno, after being introduced to a wildly cheering overflow crowd at the National Women's Political Caucus's July 1993 national convention, let everyone in on a secret. Her nomination had happened so fast, she confided, that the embattled White House staff didn't know—and wondered out loud—if women's groups would support her. "I didn't know, so I called an old friend of mine, Ann Lewis. . . . The next thing I knew Harriett Woods was quoted in papers saying 'Why not Janet Reno?' That afternoon, at my meeting with the President, he said 'Well, I see you have the support of women.'"

But the most stunning and thought-provoking moment came in late 1991: In the foyer of the Texas governor's mansion, a place replete with macho trappings that evoke every myth of the West, Governor Ann Richards was working a crowd of political women from across the nation when she spied and made a special point of singling out and welcoming Native American Wilma Mankiller, principal chief of the Cherokee Nation.

How might our nation's history have been different if those two women had had those two jobs a hundred years earlier? How will our nation be different when women are fully equal citizens and officeholders?

1

Breaking Ground

The Evolution of Citizenship

" **W**ho had more influence on the '92 election: Saddam Hussein or Anita Hill?" asked Maryland senator Barbara Mikulski, playing to the enthusiastic crowd that had gathered to celebrate the victories of new women senators.

"Anita Hill," they cried. The correct answer was never in doubt on this evening of November 10, 1992.

Again, Senator Mikulski called out the question. And again the crowd at the Democratic Women's Club roared back "Anita Hill."

Mikulski belted out the question one more time. As if on cue, Anita Hill, whose testimony on sexual harassment before an all-male Senate Judiciary Committee had created a wave of political action by women, entered the room. Hill's soft-spoken acknowledgment of the applause— and of her role in history—was lost in the pandemonium that followed her entrance.

In the space of one year, Anita Hill had become a symbol of women's status in American life and, in particular, their exclusion from the halls of power. Virtually all the women who ran for the U.S. Senate used references to Anita Hill in their campaign literature and direct mail solicita-

1

tions as a symbol of that exclusion. She had sparked the most unprecedented mobilization of women voters since they had won the vote in 1920, and she was now receiving accolades for the boost she had given to the newly elected female senators.

Prior to the November elections—just a few days before this celebration—women had been a mere 2 percent of the 100-member U.S. Senate, and about 6 percent of the 435-member House of Representatives. Since the late 1960s, their minuscule representation had been increasing at a slow but steady rate. Before Anita Hill, there was little reason to think that the change in the 1992 elections would be anything other than incremental.

Early in the election cycle, women candidates feared that the U.S. war with Iraq would dominate the 1992 presidential and congressional elections, as it had the November elections of 1990. That election year had been proclaimed the Year of the Woman, but women candidates for Congress saw their electoral hopes dashed with the invasion of Kuwait on August 3, 1990. The return of old worries of war and military preparedness shifted hopes that the post–cold war peace would allow for attending to domestic problems. Polling data indicated that foreign affairs and defense issues did not play to women candidates' strengths in the same way domestic issues of health care and the economy did.

A singular event had changed the expected dynamics of women's campaigns in 1992, and it changed the answer to Mikulski's question from Saddam Hussein to Anita Hill: President George Bush nominated Clarence Thomas, Federal Appeals Court Judge of the Washington Circuit and former director of the Equal Employment Opportunity Commission (EEOC) to the U.S. Supreme Court. Despite some argument over his judicial qualifications and protests over his conservative political positions, offset for some by his status as an African-American, Thomas seemed destined to be confirmed by the U.S. Senate.

No one was prepared for what happened next. On National Public Radio, Nina Totenberg reported confidential information that an unknown Oklahoma University law professor named Anita Hill, who had worked for Thomas at the EEOC, had given closed-door testimony to the Senate Judiciary Committee accusing him of sexual harassment, and that the Judiciary Committee had chosen not to pursue her charges. *Newsday*'s Timothy Phelps reported the same story, also from undisclosed sources. Soon, the news ripped through the rest of the media.

News reports that the charges were not taken seriously infuriated women on Capitol Hill. Before noon on October 8, an impromptu delegation of Democratic congresswomen marched en masse from the House of Representatives to the U.S. Senate to demand an investigation of Hill's allegations. With Barbara Boxer (California) and Patricia Schroeder (Colorado) in the lead, they banged on the door of the Senate Democratic Caucus room, only to be told they were "strangers" who could not come in. The picture of these angry women charging up the Capitol stairs in a formation that evoked images of planting the flag atop Iwo Jima appeared on television and on the front page of major newspapers. It was an unprecedented display of anger, a frontal assault on the virtually all-male Senate.

Within a very short time, an embarrassed Judiciary Committee overturned its decision and agreed to extend the confirmation hearings. Anita Hill, who had been willing to speak to the Judiciary Committee staff only on the basis of confidentiality, reluctantly agreed to testify publicly before the full committee. For several days in October, the American public was riveted to these hearings. Women rarely brought charges of sexual harassment against powerful men, and none had ever done so on television. The traditional October preoccupation with baseball was suspended as viewers tuned in.

The televised hearings produced and sustained another image that proved even more politically potent in the long run than the Iwo Jima image of angry congresswomen. The sight of the Senate Judiciary Committee members, all male, all white, grilling Anita Hill as if it were her history that was on trial drove home to American women their absence from the U.S. Senate. "It was like free advertising for the Women's Campaign Fund," said Jane Danowitz, head of the organization that had spent twenty years helping women climb the electoral ladder with the hope of someday reaching the Senate.

Though Thomas was ultimately confirmed, the depth of the rebellion created by Anita Hill's confrontation with the men on the Judiciary Committee became quickly evident. Seasoned activists snapped into action. More important, women who had never been politically active were also aroused to action. Grandmothers, mothers, and daughters discussed their own episodes of sexual harassment. For many older women, memories often deeply buried came to life. Collectively, women convened public speak-outs to dramatize the pervasiveness of sexual harassment and to overcome the shame and silence that accompany such experiences. The extent of the outpouring surprised almost everyone.

More women than ever before decided to run for political office, many as a direct result of the Thomas/Hill hearings. By April 30, 1992, over 213 women had announced they would seek, or consider seeking, their party's nomination for the House of Representatives or the U.S. Senate.[1] While more women announced for office at every level of government, the most dramatic change was the number of women declaring their candidacies for the U.S. Senate, the highest legislative office in the land and, short of the presidency, the most difficult elective office for women to obtain.

Jean Lloyd-Jones, state senator from Iowa who decided to challenge Charles Grassley for the U.S. Senate, said, "I never, ever thought I would run for higher office." Lynn Yeakel from Pennsylvania, who had never held public office, said it just "pushed people like me over the line." She announced she would take on Republican senator Arlen Specter, whose aggressive, prosecutorial role on the Judiciary Committee had especially angered women. Yeakel had considered running for office before, "but it took the image of seeing those men making those decisions and controlling our future to get me to do it."

Carol Moseley-Braun, the recorder of deeds for Chicago's Cook County, said she "started getting calls" about challenging Thomas supporter Illinois senator Alan Dixon. The hearings for Moseley-Braun were decisive: "I would not have run for the Senate had the Senate not gone on television."

Senate candidates Dianne Feinstein and Barbara Boxer of California, who had announced before the hearings, found their campaigns "jump started" by an outpouring of money and volunteers. Other candidates experienced a similar surge of support. By early spring of 1992, twenty-two women had announced their candidacies for the U.S. Senate. In 1990, by contrast, only eight women had run.

Bipartisan organizations such as the Women's Campaign Fund (WCF) and the National Women's Political Caucus (NWPC), whose previous efforts to raise money for women candidates might best be described as painstaking, found their contributions doubling, even tripling, with little or no effort. The pro-choice and Democratic EMILY's List (for Early Money Is Like Yeast) enjoyed an astronomical rise in membership and donations. Within one year, it became the largest political action committee (PAC) in the country, growing from 3,000 to 23,000 members, and from $1.5 million in 1990 contributions to $6 million in 1992. Republican women formed a new organization called WISH, short for Women in the Senate and the House, patterned after EMILY's List. At the state level, new statewide fund-raising networks and informal "lists" seem to spring up overnight.

The Anita Hill effect on women's political chances seemed confirmed when, in rapid succession, Carol Moseley-Braun defeated the incumbent senator Alan Dixon in the Illinois Democratic primary, and Lynn Yeakel beat out four men, including Pennsylvania's incumbent lieutenant governor, to win the right to challenge Senator Arlen Specter.

During the primary, Yeakel had not minced words about her real target. She ignored her primary opponents and focused her campaign ads on Specter. Showing him questioning Anita Hill, Yeakel asked, "Did this make you as angry as it made me?" In roughly one month's time, Yeakel rose from an unknown with no name recognition to victory in the primary. Yeakel's achievement occurred in a state traditionally inhospitable toward women candidates. No woman had ever before been elected to Congress from Pennsylvania, and women had never been able to claim more than 7 percent of the state legislative offices.

A month or so after Yeakel's victory, the unthinkable happened in California. Not one, but two women candidates beat their male primary opponents to become candidates for the U.S. Senate. An anomaly had caused two Senate seats to be open in the same year. Former San Francisco mayor Dianne Feinstein had announced for one. Marin County congresswoman Barbara Boxer had announced for the other. A firm conviction of just about every observer of politics was that California's voters would never elect two women. They were not only the "wrong" sex, they both hailed from northern California, the less populous region of the state, and they were both Jewish. But in June 1992, shortly after the Moseley-Braun and Yeakel victories, both California women won their primary races.

By the end of the primary season, 106 women had survived their primaries to run in the general election for Congress, and 11 women had won Senate nominations. Along the way, these women candidates had knocked out longtime incumbents, heir apparents, and other political veterans.

Media attention focused on women candidates with unprecedented intensity. The possibility of women voters exercising the clout inherent in their status as a 54 percent majority of the voting population was debated on television, in newspapers and magazines, on talk shows, and even in a made-for-television movie called *Majority Rule,* which depicted the election of the first woman president. All this focus and energy became wrapped up and labeled with the perennial slogan, the Year of the Woman.

For nearly twenty years, ever since the women's movement began to encourage more women to seek public office, "Year of the Woman" had become a shorthand way to refer to the possibility that women candidates would do well.[2] In fact, Jane Danowitz of the WCF had been through so many cycles of raised expectations and dashed hopes, and was so weary of answering the same set of questions, that, long before Anita Hill precipitated another round, she had dubbed all of the 1990s as the "Decade of Women."

This time, however, the increased participation and victory of women who ran and were elected in November seemed a confirmation of the slogan. Senate representation tripled, to 6 percent, while women increased their numbers in the House by nearly 70 percent, from twenty-nine women to forty-eight, raising the percentage of women to 10 percent overall.[3] Included in these figures were many "firsts." Carol Moseley-Braun was the first African-American woman to win a statewide race in any state of the union, let alone to the U.S. Senate. Georgia and North Carolina also sent African-American women to Congress for the first time. The state of Virginia elected its first woman. Nydia Velázquez from New York City became the first Puerto Rican congresswoman and Lucille Roybal-Allard from Los Angeles the first Mexican-American.

The symmetry of the long political season that was born in front of the Judiciary Committee was completed with the appointments of Moseley-Braun and Feinstein to the same committee that had grilled Anita Hill.

Was 1992, in fact, the Year of the Woman? Many activists thought so.

"A revolution . . . twenty years in the making," declared Ruth Mandel, director of the Eagleton Institute's Center for the American Woman and Politics at Rutgers University, underscoring the effort it took to produce these successes. Mandel cited the many factors, in addition to Anita Hill, that coalesced in 1992 to propel women candidates into office. A wave of public sentiment against incumbents, along with reapportionment, had created more open or "winnable" seats. Not since 1948 had there been so many turnovers in Congress.

"Opportunity met readiness," said Jane Danowitz. The growing pool of women officeholders is "laying the base for years to come. When all's said and done, 1992 is not a one-night stand."

Even Eleanor Smeal, president of the Fund for a Feminist Majority and a past president of the National Organization for Women (NOW), who had helped found a woman's party the summer before, called 1992 a "real breakthrough." She argued that the rate of growth was more significant than the actual numbers.

But not everyone agreed the Year of the Woman was a success, or even a valid construct. Skepticism came from several quarters.

Veteran feminist leader Gloria Steinem was one who minimized the hoopla surrounding the Year of the Woman. "It's bullshit. It will only be the Year of the Woman when we have 50 percent [women represented] in Congress and in the Senate, and we can stop talking about the Year of the Woman."[4]

Others, including President Bush and Senate Republican Minority Leader Robert Dole, questioned the validity of the construct itself, viewing the Year of the Woman as media hype that favored liberal Democratic candidates, who far outnumbered their Republican counterparts. Nationally syndicated columnist Mona Charen echoed and defended Bush's views in a column shortly before the November election. She said of Democratic Senate candidates Patty Murray, Carol Moseley-Braun, Lynn Yeakel, Dianne Feinstein, and Barbara Boxer, "I hope *all* of them lose." The Year was "claptrap," treading on the "tiresome theme" that "estrogen alone would mark an improvement in the Senate."[5]

Was it really a breakthrough year for women? Do the 1992 victories suggest more victories in the future, or were they flukes? How much progress have women really made? What advances their entry into politics and, conversely, what holds them back? Were women advocating that they be elected simply because they were women? Did women voters put them into office? Are female politicians developing a new ease in exercising power?

These are some of the key questions that shape this book, and they must be answered in three different ways. One is to understand the election cycle of 1992 in terms of its own dynamic—the factors unique to this election cycle. The second is to differentiate between those factors and trends that have been developing over the last twenty years. The third approach, and perhaps the most important to a deeper understanding, is placing these trends in a long-term historical context.

The "opportunity" highlighted by Jane Danowitz in her classic aphorism was the sheer number of seats, open or available, that created an unusual chance for newcomers in general. In the last several decades, most incumbent officeholders who sought reelection were elected, making the political system inhospitable to newcomers. Every ten years, after the census is taken, congressional boundary lines are reviewed or redrawn in every state. Some states lose population and, therefore, have reduced representation in the House of Representatives, while other states gain seats. After the 1990 census, for example, Montana lost one House seat while California gained seven. Whether the number of seats is increased or decreased, the effect on incumbent officeholders is a kind of fruit basket upset, since most district lines undergo some kind of change.

In 1992 the effects of reapportionment were accompanied by a fierce wave of anti-incumbent sentiment. Voters were disposed to "throw the bums out." Some veteran politicians decided to retire rather than risk primary opposition or defeat. Some seemed as disgusted as the voters at the inability of Washington to make a dent in our major social and economic problems, and announced their retirement. The outcome was the creation of many more genuinely fluid races in which the results were not at all predetermined. The number of open seats, positions without an incumbent officeholder, was four times higher in 1992 than in 1990. In the House alone, 91 of the 435 seats were open.

Reapportionment and voter anger, however, would not have resulted in so many women candidates if women had not been preparing themselves through years of office-holding experience. This "readiness," to which Danowitz refers, meant that not only did women take advantage of the increase in open seats, but more women were willing to challenge incumbents as well.

Ellen Malcolm, founder of EMILY's List, whose fund-raising support was a major determinant in the success of Democratic women in 1992, said her organization supported thirty-five challengers compared with six two years before. EMILY's List backing is hard for women candidates to obtain unless they really have a chance to win. In 1992, Malcolm says, challengers simply had more "viability" than they had had in previous years, although she cautions against expecting these large numbers in the future.

"The reality is, the whole system will close up again." Not only will the political environment be altered, but "the bums will be gone," she said. Malcolm estimated that approximately thirty seats will be open in 1994, roughly 7 percent of all seats compared with 20 percent in 1992. That means a return "to the tough old days of 1988 and 1990, when there were very few realistic opportunities to elect women to the House, because we are constantly thwarted by the power of incumbency."[6]

Malcolm might have added that the power of incumbency was not entirely absent in 1992. While more congressional seats turned over than in any election cycle since 1948, the incumbency return rate was 93 percent for House seats and 85.2 percent for Senate seats. In California's congressional races, the rate was over 97 percent, confirming political analysts' long-documented conclusion that voters who say they are disgusted with politicians in general like their own representative.

Beneath these dynamics lie deeper changes that helped create the breakthroughs of 1992, and they are likely to persist. The changes, so visible in 1992 and still in progress, are a product of the subtle and cumulative changes in women's campaigns and voter attitudes that have been occurring over the last twenty years or so.

"Women's campaigns are different from men's campaigns," says Celinda Lake, one of the few consultants to specialize in women's campaigns. She joins more traditional consultants who believe women's campaigns are different but who see the difference as a kind of "add on" to men's campaigns. Republican consultant John Deardourff believes that women's campaigns carry "an extra strategic burden," regardless of precisely how these differences are conceived or managed by individual consultants.[7] Over the years, a number of differences that pose specific campaign problems for women have been identified. These range from marital status—either the presence *or* the absence of a husband—to children, credentials, and the ability to put across campaign messages.

Children, for instance, immediately evoke the image of woman as mother, which can swamp other aspects of her background or career. Motherhood may be revered within the family, but it has not been considered an experience or a credential for holding political office. Having children at home often resulted in charges of child neglect even if, as some candidates found, the children in question were nearly grown. Over the years, many women have dealt with this particular "strategic burden" by waiting until their children were adults before running for a high-visibility office or one far away from home base.

A male candidate's children were presumed to be an asset, evidence of his success as a family man, and hardly a problem for the campaign. And plenty of men have run for office over their wives' objections without fear that their ambition might become a campaign issue.

Husbands have been only slightly less of a problem in campaigns than children. If she were married, a candidate's husband needed to show his active support so that voters would know she was running with his permission. A visible and supportive husband also was prima facie evidence that family obligations, considered by many voters a woman's primary obligation, were being fulfilled. Democratic campaign strategist Michael Berman remembers Geraldine Ferraro's first campaign for Congress in 1978: "How did she prove that John Zaccaro was not pissed off at her and was not about to throw her out? And the answer was: they took poor John, who could have cared less and was delighted with her and supported her more than any man I have ever met, and they trotted him around for six weeks in Queens."[8]

Unmarried women, who didn't face the problem of permission, were advised to find a male escort for campaign events, perhaps a brother, uncle, or grown son, in order to avoid any sexual innuendo or hint of impropriety.

Women candidates agonized over decisions, often small ones, that rarely troubled male candidates. No male candidate worried that a trip to his barber would make him appear frivolous. But Geraldine Ferraro, desperate for a haircut before her interview with Walter Mondale for the vice presidency, worried about just that in 1984.

Adding to the "strategic burden" of women's campaigns, and less easily managed, were voters' perceptions of women in general. Certain images of women are specific to particular historical periods, while others ignore time's passage. Sometimes the same characteristic can be perceived as either negative or positive, depending on the situation. For instance, images or characteristics associated with motherhood, so valued in the context of family, lack authority when they are projected into the public. In a campaign for political office, images of a nurturing female generated concern that women might not be tough enough to handle the rough-and-tumble realm of politics.

Even issues can develop a gender flavor and become classified as "hard" or "soft." A favorite tactic of women candidates is deliberately to choose a hard issue, such as crime or finance, to emphasize during a campaign to demonstrate the candidate's toughness. Conversely, regardless of their actual position, women are usually perceived by voters as sympathetic to the softer issues of education or health. The John Muir cartoon shows how issues have always been gendered. John Muir, a nineteenth-century pioneer "environmentalist," is depicted in a woman's apron. Attitudes such as Muir's were regarded as "sissy" ones.

In 1992, however, polls indicated that women candidates were pulling away from some of these traditional disadvantages. Characteristics that had worked against women candidates in the past were being reevaluated by voters and seen in a more positive light. Voters believed women were likely to be familiar with household budget issues, making them "fighters" for the middle class. On some issues, particularly health care, voters were giving Democratic women a huge (thirty plus) point advantage over men.[9]

Some issues, such as finance and war, which called for skills more associated with men, continued to be a problem for women. When these

Bancroft Library, University of California, Berkeley

issues dominated campaigns, women had a harder time convincing the electorate that they had the skills and experience necessary to making decisions in these areas. Lake found one other potential glitch in the more favorable views of women candidates: Even when voters thought their hypothetical woman was the superior candidate, they were not sure a woman could win. The finding raised the possibility that voters might feel a vote for any woman would be wasted.

Women's previous exclusion from politics, however, was seen as an asset in a period when voters were disgusted with incumbent politicians and searching for new voices. Voters were looking for people who were not part of the existing mess, and women, by definition, were outsiders.

A convincing indication that candidates were sensing changes in voter attitudes came from a woman who had been winning—and losing— political races since 1969, California's U.S. Senate candidate Dianne Feinstein.

Feinstein stood on the stairway of her spacious home in Presidio Heights, San Francisco, several months after her primary victory, and told a friendly group of delegates to the annual convention of the California Women's Political Caucus: "This is the first time I feel that running as a woman isn't a disadvantage." She had not stated her feelings in the affirmative—she did not say that running as a woman was *an advantage* in 1992—but had used the double negative, "not a disadvantage."

If Feinstein had been understated, even cautious, in her statement, she had good reason to be. For most of her political life she had been advised, as most women candidates have been, not to run as a woman.

This advice was not, of course, a literal command to alter their biological status before they announced for public office. It was meant as strategic advice—how to overcome the burden of being female. Don't "run as a woman" meant be as "like male" as possible.

"Are you running as a woman?" is the question put to most women candidates from the time they first ran for public office. In 1991, Melinda Schwegmann, elected as Louisiana's first female lieutenant governor, echoed the conventional disclaimer: "When I decided to run, I certainly wasn't running because I was a woman. . . ." One of the few women to challenge the question itself was Congresswoman Patricia Schroeder. In 1987, Schroeder was exploring the possibility of running for president. She faced the inevitable question from the press, "Are you running as a woman?" Schroeder immediately retorted, "Do I have an option?" Whether or not individual candidates knew exactly what the question meant, most women seemed to know instinctively that a "yes" answer would spell political death.

Consultants, however, understood fully the danger of running as a woman. Three specific caveats stood out: don't call attention to yourself as female, especially through clothing that is either sexually suggestive or frilly; don't campaign on women's issues; don't think women will vote for you just because you're a woman.

These caveats contained an even more extensive list of "do's" and "don'ts." The one that caused the most trouble for women candidates, of course, was the requirement to downplay or hide their femaleness. Skirts that were too short or necklines that were too plunging suggested sexual intent, not political seriousness. For many years, women elected to office solved the problem by wearing tailored suits in dark colors. If early congressional group photos are examined, for instance, it is difficult to pick out the women. They "all looked like ushers," says former NWPC president, Sharon Rodine, of the unwritten dress code.[10]

Changes in these prescriptions have not come all at once, nor are they necessarily similar from state to state, region to region, or even race to race. But the days of the dark suits are gone, as any quick glimpse of congressional women on C-SPAN reveals. Women now are easily identifiable in their brightly colored dresses or suits—ranging from shocking pink to luminescent chartreuse. Indeed, these bright colors now seem to emphasize women's difference from men and make them stand out from the blue and banker's gray of their male colleagues.

Changes in clothing or dress may seem trivial compared with campaign strategies or policy issues, but they must be seen as emblematic of all that is female. In a campaign, clothing, like marital status or children, can become an object of intense scrutiny, capable of evoking age-old beliefs about women.

Paradoxically, these deeply held beliefs, even in their simplest form as stereotypes, have always contained built-in limits to how much a woman should follow the advice to be "like male." Voters want women to be tough and aggressive as evidence that they can handle political life, but if they are too tough or too aggressive, voters become wary. Thus, being too male can also jeopardize a woman's standing with voters.

The boundaries between being "like male" and "too male" are not always very clear, and the problem has added another layer of complexity for women who wish to run for office. One step over the line and women candidates will hear themselves described as "shrill," or "outspoken," or "power-hungry." Everyone knew what Barbara Bush meant when she said, after the George Bush–Geraldine Ferraro debate, that Ferraro was "a five-letter word that rhymes with rich."

Campaign slogans are a good indication of how women have tried to reconcile these competing stereotypes, and to see how the boundaries have changed over time. As recently as 1990, a considerable number of women candidates chose slogans, such as "Tough and Caring," to convey they were tough but not too tough. Yet these carefully crafted slogans, designed to navigate between the stereotypes, were virtually nonexistent in the high-visibility campaigns of 1992.

What was stunning about the slogans and rhetoric of 1992, in comparison with the past twenty years, was how often candidates placed the exclusion of women from power as a central theme of their campaigns. Feinstein, who two years earlier had described herself with the slogan "Tough and Caring," now used "Two Percent Is Not Enough," referring to the number of women in the Senate. On the campaign stump, as if to soften the theme just slightly, she found an image that would readily connect with ordinary voters, adding, "It may be good enough for milk, but not for the U.S. Senate." In New York, Senate primary candidate Geraldine Ferraro urged women to use their hands to seek political power rather than to rock the cradle: "It's no longer enough for women to run for office—we must *elect* more women so our hands too can be on the levers of power." In her mail solicitations, Carol Moseley-Braun drew on images of the angry congresswomen marching to the Senate: "Women Across the Country Are Willing and Ready to Strike a Blow for Opening the Doors to the U.S. Senate." In the days before Anita Hill, such bold and evocative imagery would have caused consultants to cringe.

Women were not only highlighting their exclusion from power through emphatic language, they were also violating other aspects of traditional advice. They were raising women's issues and targeting women voters, "even at the expense of men's votes," as veteran California pollster Mervin Field observed.[11]

While Field indicated surprise at how rapidly candidates were changing the old rules, women candidates had been experimenting with how to pitch women's issues for most of the last twenty years. The original advice to avoid women's issues—however a candidate might have defined them—has several origins. Historically, women were not seen as a potential voting bloc to be wooed, because there was no evidence their voting behavior was any different from male voters'. Although little actual investigation of their votes had been undertaken prior to the 1970s, what evidence there was suggested that women's votes were shaped by the usual factors of income, education, partisan affiliation, or geographical location, and not by sex. In at least two presidential elections, women slightly preferred Eisenhower to Stevenson, and Nixon to Kennedy. These preferences were not regarded as intriguing, however, because women were viewed as naturally more conservative than men, a function of their roles as wives and mothers.

Moreover, prior to 1968, women voted less often than men, so the incentive either to study their voting behavior or to mobilize it was about nil. The fact that women outnumbered men in the general population, therefore, was not thought relevant to winning elections. Differences among women seemed so self-evident that little thought was given to the notion of a female voting bloc.

When women's voting rates finally caught up with men's in 1968, and the women's movement began to generate a more intense interest in politics, analysts reminded any candidate who might be tempted to target women voters that women were just as divided as men on issues.

But women weren't just divided on issues, they were especially polarized over issues associated with the burgeoning women's movement of the late 1960s. Polling data from the 1970s indicated that campaigning on issues explicitly identified as feminist was a high-risk strategy. Support for the Equal Rights Amendment (ERA) to the U.S. Constitution, or for abortion rights, for example, was seen as feminist and therefore controversial. Among women, there was little neutral ground. Women were either strongly in favor of or strongly opposed to these measures.

Then, during the 1980s, the emergence of a new electoral variable—the gender gap—helped change the dynamics of women's campaigns. Beginning with the presidential election of Ronald Reagan, some evidence emerged that women were voting differently from men. Compared with men's votes, women had preferred President Jimmy Carter over Ronald Reagan by a statistically significant seven points. The presence of the gender gap was confirmed in the 1982 congressional campaigns. Its potential significance led directly to the selection of Geraldine Ferraro as vice presidential nominee in 1984. But the fact that the Democrats chose a woman on the ticket to help mobilize women voters did not mean they wanted her to address women's issues. The Mondale campaign staff argued strenuously against such an approach to women voters.

While there is no agreement either by candidates or voters over the definition of women's issues, abortion rights is often used as the quintessential women's issue. Advocating abortion rights was initially in the high-risk category for candidates, although that has changed over time. During the 1970s, candidates tried to avoid taking a position on abortion rights; by the 1980s, taking a stand was virtually mandatory. In 1989 alone, forty-one individuals preparing to run for reelection to the House of Representatives changed their position on abortion. So many candidates "clarified" their position that year that it became known among some observers as the "year of the flip-flops," and among those who "flipped" were some quite prominent political figures, such as Senator Sam Nunn, chairman of the Armed Services Committee, up for reelection in Georgia, and Ohio gubernatorial candidate Anthony Celebrezze. In California, state senator John Seymour, preparing to run in the Republican primary for lieutenant governor, announced he had been in a "comfortable cocoon," and unaware of what abortion rights meant to women. He now declared that an unwanted pregnancy was "almost enslavement, for God's sake."[12]

Increased popular support for abortion rights, along with the growing importance of women's votes, helped make these flip-flops possible. In a few cases, entire races were influenced by a candidate's position on abortion rights. In 1989, consultants to Doug Wilder's gubernatorial campaign in Virginia argued that Wilder's pro-choice position was decisive in his successful election. Subsequent studies confirmed the importance of abortion as an issue in races in both Virginia and New Jersey. Abortion rights is seldom the defining issue in a campaign, partly because political campaigns are rarely won or lost on a single issue.

While polling data indicate majority support for abortion rights, a careful examination of the data shows that a small percentage (seldom higher than 15 percent) support unrestricted rights. In general, majority support among both men and women diminishes as competing interests—those of parents of teenage girls or husbands—are taken into account. A key finding in the polling data is that women who support unrestricted abortion rights are seen as selfish women who put their own interests first.

Advocacy of unrestricted abortion rights requires women to depart from a long-standing tradition of putting the interests of others first, especially the interests of children and family. If a graph could be designed for women's issues, many of them could be plotted along a similar continuum of perceived selfishness—abortion simply throws the nature of the continuum into sharper relief. The more an issue invokes images of selfish women, the less support both men and women are likely to give it. By contrast, those "women's issues" that express concern for children and are in keeping with more altruistic attitudes expected of women receive more support. Collecting child support from "deadbeat dads" elicits more sympathy, for instance, than demands for publicly funded day-care centers.

Unresolved conflicts over women's roles may help explain the Republican party's attempt in 1992 to run on the theme of "family values." The more the campaign theme became specific, however, the more it backfired and was viewed as an attack on American women. When Vice President J. Danforth Quayle attacked one of television's favorite figures, Murphy Brown, for having a baby out of wedlock, he made the theme of selfishness central to his attack. When the vice president's wife, Marilyn Quayle, gave her speech at the Republican convention and referred to women's innate nature and the satisfactions of family, she invoked the themes of altruism and self-sacrifice. How did she reconcile the roles of wife, mother, and lawyer? "I chose to leave my law practice and join his [her husband's] campaigns," she said, contrasting her choice with Hillary Clinton's. Calling the promises of the women's liberation movement "grandiose," Quayle argued that "most women do not wish to be liberated from their essential natures as women."[13]

Dan Quayle, of course, found himself the target of outraged single mothers, who viewed his remarks about Murphy Brown as an attack on their status. While Quayle never exactly apologized for his statements about the Murphy Brown character, he was forced publicly to demonstrate his support for single mothers. He spent an evening with a group of Washington, D.C., single mothers, watching an episode of "Murphy Brown," an event that received full media coverage.

Similarly, Marilyn Quayle found that her keynote speech at the Republican National Convention set off a storm among women who were unable to be the stay-at-home moms Quayle seemed to suggest they should be, despite her own earlier career as a working attorney. Marilyn Quayle was also forced to publicly clarify her remarks.

While the theme of family values may not have worked for President Bush in his presidential reelection campaign, the fact that this theme touches a dominant chord with many voters illustrates how complicated feelings are about women's rights and roles. Issues of work and child-rearing join with debates over the even more controversial issues of whether women should be soldiers and priests.

The lack of resolution or agreement on women's roles affects how much mobilization of women voters can take place, or how much focus on women's issues a campaign can sustain, without risking a reaction. At what point this boundary is crossed is often unclear. Deeply polarized voter attitudes over Hillary Clinton, for instance, caused the Clinton advisers to sharply decrease her visibility during the last half of her husband's campaign.

In the last few years, women candidates have been cautiously testing these boundaries, often in innovative ways. In 1990, Texas gubernatorial candidate Ann Richards recognized the growing clout of women voters and saw a strategic opportunity that turned all the old rules on their ear, without threatening a male reaction. Ann Richards has legendary hair. It is a high coiffure with a sweep, affectionately called by some Texans the "power do," and it must be attended to regularly. Richards posed for a picture *with* her hairdresser—whose sweep was even higher than Richards'—and then sent 45,000 of these pictures on postcards to beauticians across the state of Texas. With this mailing, candidate Richards not only got her hair fixed, she openly courted two vast constituencies of women: working-class beauticians and their clientele of all classes. She turned an assumed liability, calling attention to her femaleness, into a campaign tactic to mobilize women voters.

If Richards found a gentle way to test the parameters of mobilizing women, California's two Senate candidates in 1992 took an even bolder step. In the waning weeks before the November election, Barbara Boxer slipped from a significant lead over her opponent, Bruce Herschensohn, to a point spread that might have spelled defeat. Together, Feinstein and Boxer decided upon a high-risk strategy.

In a display of political generosity, Feinstein, who was considerably ahead of her opponent, went on the stump with Boxer, drawing on some of the most feminist images available in popular culture. "Just as Cagney needs Lacey, and Thelma needs Louise," said the prospective partners from California, "Dianne needs Barbara, and Barbara needs Dianne."[14] It is hard to conceive of images more rejecting of male authority than the two film characters, Thelma and Louise.

Also in 1992, fewer candidates argued over the definition of a woman's issue than in previous years. Rather, candidates, male and female, argued over whose record on women's issues was better. Even Arlen Specter, target of Anita Hill fallout, tried to overcome this liability by highlighting his record on women's issues. He sought endorsements from powerful women to back up his claims, and some observers believe he hit pay dirt when Teresa Heinz, the widow of the late Pennsylvania senator, endorsed Specter in a television ad. Similarly, in New York, when Robert Abrams faced both Comptroller Elizabeth Holtzman and Geraldine Ferraro during the Senate primary, he conceded no advantage to them on women's issues, and argued on the merits of his record.

If, in general, women candidates had much greater freedom in 1992 to run on women's issues, or to focus on women voters, they also began to veer close to claiming a special status for themselves and their candidacies as female. As the political year unfolded, more and more women candidates would proclaim that "women are different." Women would bring a "different voice" to politics, and they cited characteristics traditionally associated with women as now constituting their special strengths in politics. Most stressed a woman's capacity for empathy. "I think women care more," said California state treasurer Kathleen Brown. "Women think horizontally. Men think vertically," said Representative Marcy Kaptur of Ohio. Congresswoman Connie Morella of Maryland argued that "women understand all issues, certainly most issues, better than men. . . " Others cited women as better listeners, or better problem solvers.[15]

Despite the pervasiveness of these new arguments, there were important nuances in the way individual women saw the significance of their differences, and the basis upon which they made such claims.

Some candidates, including Geraldine Ferraro, argued that women's specialness resided in their life experience, which was different, in most cases, from men's. "Is it any wonder that women are better on day care," Ferraro mused, "in the same way that Senator Tom Daschle, a Vietnam veteran, is better on issues of Agent Orange, or Senator Daniel Inouye is on reparations for Japanese-Americans, or that the Black Caucus is more sensitive to South African sanctions."[16]

Reporters who had covered Feinstein's comments that she was more trustworthy on abortion rights in the gubernatorial campaign in 1990 were, off the record, highly critical of her tactics: "It's as if she is saying, I have fallopian tubes, vote for me." In 1992, a similar remark, flippantly made by a Pennsylvania Democrat, that all Lynn Yeakel had going for her was that she "had breasts," generated a media maelstrom. Meanwhile, women candidates began to flip these derisive comments into positive ones. Senate hopeful Claire Sargent of Arizona suggested that "it's about time we voted for senators with breasts. After all, we've been voting for boobs long enough."[17]

This emphasis on women's differences may have given a new cast to the races in 1992; however, it sounded very familiar to historians. The debate over whether women's equality could best be achieved by emphasizing their differences from men or by stressing their similarity has characterized women's political efforts for over a hundred years. When Marilyn Quayle clarified her remarks after the Republican convention, she drew on feminist authors and contemporary scholarship to explain what she meant when she referred to "women's essential natures": "Today women don't have to dress or act like men to advance in the professional world previously dominated by men. We don't have to reject the prospect of marriage and children to succeed. We don't have to reject our essential natures as women to prosper in what was once the domain of men. It is no longer an either-or situation."[18]

The arguments that rage today over just how different women are from men, the origin of those differences, and how laws and public policies should be structured to accommodate them are the latest version of a very old debate over women's nature.

Women candidates who sell their candidacies on the basis of their differences from men may be faced with a different standard of performance as well. Just when women candidates are being freed from the old shibboleths against running as a woman, and can run simply as the women they are, they are in danger of elevating their newfound status into new liabilities. Claims of "running as a woman," which posit the superiority of being female over male, ignore some of the forces that have allowed them their new freedom. Women's votes have grown more important, not because women have suddenly become a reliable voter bloc, but because women's votes are critical to any campaign. All candidates must compete for their votes, recognize their new public policy concerns, and speak to them directly. The changes in the lives of American women, especially their entrance into the work force, are not likely to be reversed. Without these changes in women's roles, reflected in turn in changed voter attitudes, the traditional dynamic of women's campaigns would have remained unaltered.

Women's entry into the labor force vests them as never before with interest in governmental actions and policies. New strains on family life as a result of these new economic roles have generated new agenda items ranging from child care to family leave measures. Nearly 70 percent of married women who work have children, and the percentage of women who are single heads of household continues to grow.[19]

Paradoxically, perhaps, changes in the economic position of women have thrust more traditional or nonworking women's issues into the political arena as well. Legislative changes designed to extend equitable social security benefits for longtime homemakers or programs to assist displaced homemakers have shaped the congressional agenda as much as the more familiar issues of child care or reproductive rights. To suggest that a new public agenda has emerged is not to suggest that women are in agreement on specific proposals or on what it means for them in their own lives.

We must turn to history for a fuller explanation of the change in the status of American women; it can be traced through the doctrine of coverture, the legal term used to describe the original status of women at the country's founding. Derived from British common law, and carried over to the colonies, coverture meant that women were literally, and figuratively, covered by their husband's status. According to Blackstone, the British common law authority, the theoretical basis for coverture incorporated early religious principles: "By marriage, the husband and wife are one person in law; that is, the very being or legal existence of the woman is suspended during the marriage, or at least is incorporated and consolidated."[20]

The chilling phrase "civilly dead," coined by historians, meant women had no standing, or civil rights, independent from their husbands. Rights granted to single women were lost upon marriage. Married women had no separate economic authority; they could not own or buy or sell property. They could not sign their name to contracts nor could they enter into most business transactions. Procedurally, married women had no standing to either sue or be sued.

The legal or formal aspects of coverture, such as the prohibition against married women's ownership or control of property, were gradually overturned in the last two centuries as women have gained rights previously guaranteed only to male citizens. Acquiring the most fundamental components of citizenship, however, has taken far longer than many realize. Suffrage was constitutionally guaranteed in 1920, but the right to be tried by a jury of one's peers was not constitutionally guaranteed to women until 1975, when the U.S. Supreme Court so ruled. Prior to that time, a woman could be tried and convicted without there being a single woman on the jury. Women's exclusion was not a basis on which a verdict could be challenged.

An entire edifice of other laws and statutes that embodied assumptions implicit in coverture has existed throughout the life of this country and, for the most part, was left unchallenged until the recent women's movement. Legal scholar Leo Kanowitz assessed the relationship between women and legal rights in 1969, and determined that there were still vestiges of legal discrimination against married women's property rights in forty-two common law marital property states.[21]

Laws governing access to credit, or the right to live separately from one's mate, or the legal right of a married woman to retain her maiden name, are examples of laws that were overturned in the last twenty years or so. Kanowitz concluded that the sociological effects of coverture have been long-lasting and disastrous for male-female relationships. "Above all, the position of married women at common law both resulted from and contributed to a failure of men and women to see themselves essentially as human beings rather than as representatives of another sex." He attributes this failure to the fiction that husband and wife were "one," because in practice "the 'one' was always the husband, [and his] dominance was assured."[22]

Historically, single women have had more capacity to exercise civil authority than married women. However, when coverture reigned supreme, most women passed from the authority of their fathers to that of their husbands, with little or no independence between. Wedding ceremonies that require the bride to be "given" by her father to the groom vividly illustrate these older assumptions.

The legal doctrine of coverture was buttressed by religious, social, and cultural traditions that reinforced the preeminence of male authority in both civil society and the home. Affirmation of these principles can be heard in the conversations of many religious anti-abortion activists today. These activists are often explicit about the husband's role as head of the family, and his rights in matters of sexuality and reproduction. The question of obedience surfaced most starkly in 1991 when some anti-abortion activists faced a choice to commit civil disobedience in support of their beliefs, or to obey husbands who had forbidden them from taking this course of action.

The residues of these traditions, whether legal, religious, or cultural, which restricted the independent actions of women, are evident in many aspects of today's campaigns. When voters wonder whether married women candidates have their husbands' blessing to run for office, they are harkening back to this tradition of male authority and permission. When women are attacked during their campaigns for statements or actions of their pastors, fathers, or husbands, as they were as recently as 1992, they suffer the residues of a tradition that is still reluctant to view women as independent or separate from the men to whom they are related.

When Lynn Yeakel was attacked during her campaign for her pastor's comments on Israel, for her former congressman father's vote on civil rights legislation in the 1960s, and for her husband's membership in a club that excluded minorities, Yeakel herself realized the connection. "One morning I woke up and it was as if the light dawned. What [Arlen Specter] is doing to me is what people have done to women through history, and that is to define them in terms of other people in their lives, particularly men—my father, my husband, my pastor. And when I realized this, it gave me a new way to respond."[23]

Geraldine Ferraro has been twice attacked for her husband's business activities, since they, along with his ethnicity, form the basis of her alleged Mafia ties. These allegations were conceded as groundless by at least one of her major opponents after the 1992 Democratic primary, but only after the damage to her campaign was done. In 1990, early polling data for Senate candidate Josie Heath of Colorado showed that four out of five "negatives" or liabilities against her were the result of her husband's status as a corporate executive, not her positions or experience. Women candidates have been the target of issues as extraneous to their own record as whether the men they were dating were current in their child-support payments to former wives.

How better to explain the intense debate over what role a First Lady, who is both wife/mother and career woman, has generated. While we might think the *Family Circle* magazine Great Cookie Recipe contest between Barbara Bush and Hillary Clinton was a silly way to carry on the debate, the familiar legacy of coverture resonates in the circumstances that produced it. During the campaign, Hillary Clinton's off-the-cuff remark that she "could have stayed home and baked cookies" was seen as a defense of her legal career, and a slap in the face to women who did stay home. However, few voters knew of the precise circumstances that caused her to lose her temper.

As Hillary explained it, her husband had debated primary candidate

Jerry Brown, the former governor of California, the night before. During the debate, Jerry Brown had attacked Hillary Clinton's membership in a prominent law firm in Arkansas while Clinton was governor. "Conflict of interest," charged Jerry Brown, prompting Clinton, after the debate, to point out to Jerry that his father, former governor Pat Brown, hadn't given up his law practice when Jerry was governor. Hillary relates that Brown rejected any similarity between his father and her, retorting to Bill Clinton, "Well, I don't control my father." The implication was clear enough to both Clintons. Bill Clinton should have exercised his husbandly prerogative and not given Hillary "permission" to practice law when he was governor.[24]

This precipitating event was lost in the competition over whose cookie recipe, Hillary's or Barbara's, was "better." (Hillary won—her victory attributed to the fact she cooked with less fat.)

Concern over the boundary lines of Hillary Clinton's role has continued since the election. Some commentators went so far as to suggest she owed it to the American people to spell out her conception of First Lady.[25]

Whether coverture is conceived in its original legal sense or as a broader cultural phenomenon, the depth of its hold has had lasting consequences for women's entry into politics. Women have lacked two fundamental traditions necessary to running for office: financial independence, and the stature necessary to the exercise of public leadership.

After state legislatures passed married women's property acts in the nineteenth century, women were legally empowered to control inherited wealth or retain income earned by their own hand. As a practical matter, most married women remained dependent upon their husbands' income. When married women did work, chances were they deposited their earnings in a bank account held jointly with their husbands. Few women, whether single or married, were able to amass much wealth from their employment choices, given past discriminatory practices against women holding highly paid positions.

While studies have shown that women spend 70–80 percent of the family income, few have had any inclination to spend it politically, let alone on women candidates. The willingness of women to support women candidates financially, and the growth of new financial networks that reflect these new attitudes and capacities, are of very recent origin. Until the mid-1980s, most women candidates found it very tough to raise money from individual women, and the few women's organizations dedicated to support of women candidates had meager resources to allocate.

This lack of independent wealth or financial means meant that most women faced excruciating personal decisions over whether to commit family money to their own political campaigns. Such a decision often posed a wrenching choice: the children's college education or her run for Congress. While all candidates, irrespective of gender, face these decisions, it is tougher for women, who lack a tradition of leadership in the public realm. To gamble your children's future for a congressional race requires an admission of ambition historically regarded as unseemly for a women to have, let alone express.

The establishment of leadership traditions has required breaking more barriers and acquiring opportunities that go far beyond the right to vote. Women first had to establish the right to speak or lecture in public, acts respectable women were wary of committing well into the nineteenth century. The strictures against public advocacy were still so strong in the mid-nineteenth century that neither Susan B. Anthony nor Elizabeth Cady Stanton would risk her reputation by chairing the historic 1848 Women's Rights Convention at Seneca Falls, New York. Lucretia Mott's husband, James, chaired the meeting. Stanton's and Anthony's ideas might have been radical, but their public deportment was not.

What a woman risked by being too public can easily be seen in the simple phrase, a public woman. To call a woman this was to shame her by suggesting she was a prostitute. By contrast, a reference to a "public man" was a statement of respect.[26] Unaware of this history, delegates to a meeting of the National Women's Political Caucus in 1973 were astonished when the hotel clerk at the Houston, Texas, convention site would not page a woman, arguing the only women who would answer would be prostitutes.

These echoes are faint now, and women may go into most public places and engage in public advocacy without risking their "respectability." However, sexual innuendo still follows women candidates and officeholders like an ominous shadow.

If women had to establish the very right to speak in public before they could establish a tradition of public activism, historically they also had to develop a rationale for their activism based on something other than the "inalienable rights of men" that presumed equality. What better basis could be found than for women to argue their public activities were simply an extension of domestic responsibilities and their roles as mothers? By the late nineteenth century, home was one arena in which women did exercise considerable authority, and they learned this authority could be deployed in the public arena on behalf of families and children.

Earlier in the century, motherhood had provided such a basis for expanding women's access to education. Women needed some education, the argument ran, if they were to fulfill their maternal obligation to raise proper children for the new republic. Now motherhood and family responsibilities served to underpin the argument for a new role in public life.

This expansion of women's roles resulted in a burgeoning of voluntary and charitable associations, the settlement house movement, campaigns for labor laws that would protect women and children, and the temperance movement, to name a few. Relevant to the present period, all these activities had in common an unstated assumption that still lingers: women's activities and advocacy should be on behalf of others. A commitment to altruistic social action on behalf of the "less fortunate," in other words, became a dominant characteristic of women's public activity.

The form most open to women who wished to pursue these new activities was the voluntary association, a form of organization characterized by its nonpartisanship. The Women's Christian Temperance Union, led by Frances Willard, became the first organization to mobilize grassroots women on a significant scale. Willard, whose conformity to proper demeanor and dress can be seen at a glance in old photographs, became the most influential woman in the country.[27] Excluded from partisan politics, women pioneered in and preferred the nonpartisan mode of participating in politics. The first major governmental office ever held by a woman was a recognition of their efforts in this sphere. In 1876, Josephine Shaw Lowell received an appointment to the New York Charitable Commission, a position she held until 1889. By the turn of the century, as the drive for suffrage was intensifying, women had established a primary orientation toward public life that was both nonpartisan and altruistic.

The strength of this tradition helps explain why, when women actually did win the vote in 1920, they didn't immediately flood the legislatures in pursuit of political power. Most activist women chose to continue their public work through nonpartisan organizations such as the League of Women Voters or Women's International League for Peace and Freedom, rather than affiliate with the two political parties. The tradition of nonpartisan activity is often manifested today by women who express a distaste for partisan politics. It ranges from the reluctance of many women officeholders to call themselves politicians to a disdain for the compromises or "horse-trading" aspects of the legislative process.

In the next chapter we will follow the candidacies and office-holding experience of the first women who did enter partisan politics, beginning with suffragist Jeannette Rankin of Montana, the first woman elected to Congress, ending with Shirley Chisholm of New York, the first African-American woman so elected, to show how all these features of women's political history, including the lingering effects of coverture and the commitment to public altruism rather than partisan interest, affected their efforts to establish themselves as leaders.

After making these powerful historical trends manifest through the examination of individual women, we will turn to each facet of women's entry into contemporary politics. In the first of these chapters we explore how women have dealt with issues of sexuality and sexual innuendo, and how these have affected certain public policy issues.

We then examine how women have tried to combine family life and politics, fighting many psychic battles as they try to fulfill the expectations of two very different roles, one deeply embedded in and sanctioned by tradition, the other new and only partially legitimated. Then, in two subsequent chapters, we will detail how women have become fully credible candidates, at long last overcoming the historical fact, true until the mid-1980s, that most women candidates, most of the time, have run in impossible or unwinnable races. We will show that money follows credibility, and as the viability of women's campaigns has increased, so has their ability to raise the kind of money deemed necessary to run a campaign.

As we follow the women along on the campaign trial, we will look at the changes in women voters over the last few decades, and how competition for their votes has raised the status of women's issues. We then take a closer look at the strategies women candidates have used to mobilize women voters without losing the men.

Over the years, as women have tried to get their issue messages across to voters, most have felt hampered by the way the press has covered women's campaigns. We examine how women relate to the press and the way media coverage has treated women candidates differently from men. We explore how women candidates have learned from that different treatment to craft campaign messages that reach across the barriers of stereotype. Then, recognizing that not all candidates win, we explore what happens when women lose, whether they experience the loss as a personal devastation or as a step along the way to larger goals.

Finally, we examine the evidence to see what difference women are making once in office, and whether they are likely to have a transforming effect on our political institutions.

In every chapter, the echoes of the age-old debate concerning the nature of womanhood resounds, as well as the question of who women will become in the future. This debate is unresolvable. We can, however, pinpoint, with considerable precision, the historical factors that pull in one direction, with new forces that permit women to choose their own direction.

2

Creating a New Tradition

From Altruism to Self-Interest

On April 6, 1917, Jeannette Rankin, Republican congresswoman from Montana, voted to oppose American entry into World War I, one of approximately fifty representatives to make this choice. In so doing, she became the first American woman to cast a vote in Congress—and the first woman in a Western democracy to vote in a national legislature as well. Her election to Congress had been heralded by the suffrage movement, which was on the verge of achieving its victory at the national level via passage and ratification of the Nineteenth Amendment (in 1920). But then President Woodrow Wilson's increasingly bellicose stance toward German aggression revealed that a difficult and painful decision would, of necessity, be her first official act, and her female supporters fell into bitter disagreement. Some thought she should take a principled antiwar stand. Others argued that she should demonstrate her patriotic commitment and her loyalty to the flag. The focus of extraordinary attention owing to the drama of the vote as well as to her unprecedented position, she chose her antiwar principles. No doubt at least partly in consequence, she would be elected to only one other congressional term, and that term would come more than twenty years later.

In casting her antiwar vote, as well as in her demeanor and her entire career, Jeannette Rankin revealed herself to be heir to an old and honorable tradition of principled, altruistic political service, a tradition that had been forged by women throughout the nineteenth century—despite the fact that they could neither vote nor run for office. In the name of this tradition they had organized to end slavery, to control male drinking, and to humanize the emerging urban industrial society. Eventually they would win the right to vote. But almost invariably, they had been advocates for others rather than articulating clear-cut interests of their own. Moreover, they rarely mentioned the issue of power, let alone discussed how to wield it as an elected official.[1]

With the hindsight of history, it is possible to gauge how valuable this stance was to women when they first sought public influence. Motivated by compassion for slaves, women began to seek a public voice at a time, the 1830s, when coverture was so firmly embedded in the legal codes of every state that nowhere could a married woman own property in her own name, let alone exercise the other rights of citizenship. What is more, women were supposed to be silent in public meetings, if it was even legitimate for them to be there at all.[2] Playing up their disinterestedness and their altruism made it possible for women to argue that they had something unique to bring to public life, something that the whole country desperately needed. In effect, their altruistic virtue provided them with a shield to deflect potential criticism as they marched into the public arena. Historians have demonstrated that even well into the twentieth century, women called for the vote so they could clean up the cities and ennoble politics with their presence. Altruism fueled a policy agenda, created primarily by members of the settlement house network, that included maternal and child health issues, protective legislation for women workers, and laws prohibiting child labor.[3]

What this tradition lacked, however, was a recognition of the importance of power. Women typically sought to exert influence through moral suasion and education rather than in the rough-and-tumble world inhabited by the male politician, with all its partisan maneuvering. The male world might have been morally ambiguous and even corrupt—although not necessarily so—but it schooled its participants to compromise and to deliver the goods. In short, while women were creating a political identity predicated on purity, men were learning to think of politics as the art of the possible and to practice compromise in order to achieve a measure of power.

In 1916, Jeannette Rankin, whose background was in settlement house work and suffrage organizing, very much "ran as a woman," emphasizing her gender and the issues that had been developed by women's groups: an eight-hour day for gainfully employed women, prohibition, child welfare, and suffrage by federal amendment. Her platform was "radically nonpartisan," a blend of issues associated with each of the two parties.[4] But in running as a woman in the altruistic mode, she guaranteed that she would not be taken seriously as a colleague once she was elected to office—not that the all-male Congress of 1917 was likely to take her seriously in any event. She also guaranteed that she would wield no power whatsoever.

Rankin's run was anomalous, and few women would follow in her footsteps for a good many years. Although there was a tradition of female political service, there was little to prepare women for candidacy, which is an inherently egotistical act. At first, the far more likely route to officeholding for women lay through widowhood—as the "relic" of a deceased male officeholder. Achieving the vote was necessary but not sufficient to guarantee women full citizenship rights, including the right to make a realistic run for elective office. In the 1920s, many of the remnants of coverture were still legally in place—unequal access to jury service and lack of access to credit, for example—and the psychological ramifications were still powerfully present. Above all, the legacy of coverture suggested that a woman must achieve whatever public influence and power she could through the instrumentality of a man, most likely, at first, as the widow of a politician.

It is perhaps supreme irony that coverture, which generally deprived women of their rights, was the unstated rationale for many early female officeholders serving in a legislative body. The death of the male partner left his widow with authority that had previously been corporate, pertaining to the couple but with the man responsible for wielding it. His death then changed her status from one who was subject to her husband's authority to one who could wield the corporate authority directly.

In the first generation after suffrage, some two thirds of the few women to serve in Congress were there because their husbands had died while in office and their governors had appointed them to finish their late husbands' terms. Such a congresswoman struck party leaders as a useful surrogate until a male heir apparent could be designated. The unwritten rules were that the wife would finish out a term, take no initiatives of her own, and depart when a successor was in place. Mae Ella Nolan of San

Francisco, the first widow to serve in the House of Representatives, was an exemplary surrogate by these standards. Winning a special election in January 1923—her husband had died a week after his reelection to a sixth term in November 1922—she served for two years. Faithful to her pledge to carry out her husband's agenda, she then departed, saying, "Politics is man's business."

Male authority cloaked political widows with legitimacy, as well as provided legitimacy in other ways during the first decades after women could legally serve as elected officials throughout the nation. The most powerful woman in the United States in the 1920s was Belle Moskowitz, who never ran for office herself but instead served as the right-hand woman of Governor Al Smith of New York. Moskowitz can be seen as a key transitional figure between the nineteenth-century style—she was a quintessential moral arbiter—and the women to come—she hung out with the politicos. A reformer committed to good government, active in the settlement house movement, a close student of practical politics, Moskowitz came to Smith's attention during his first campaign for the governorship in 1918. He sought her help in reaching out to the new women voters—New York enfranchised women in 1917—and after he won, they formed a potent partnership. He appreciated her tact and intelligence; she liked the access to power she gained through him. Before long, she had become deeply immersed in Democratic party affairs as well as in the kind of policy advice-giving that women had already been providing behind the scenes to officeholders.

On the face of it, they were unlikely partners. Both from immigrant backgrounds, they represented quite different portions of the immigrant community. Called the Happy Warrior, Smith was Irish Catholic, gregarious, and opposed to Prohibition. The Jewish Moskowitz supported Prohibition till the late 1920s, had devoted herself to regulating dance halls so as to contain the spread of vice, and was happy to stay out of the limelight. A woman with strong views and an equally strong personality, she evidently saw her willingness to be self-effacing as the means to achieve influence over Smith, hence to achieve a genuine impact on policy.

Never a candidate, never an officeholder, Belle Moskowitz was the first American woman with daily influence on the running of a major state. Known to insiders as the person to see in Albany, she was all-but-unknown to the public. Yet Smith turned to her for advice on appointments and policy decisions, and she also became a skilled campaign operative. Sitting quietly and knitting while a meeting was under way, she would wait "for the Governor to turn to her, as he did before making any important decision and ask: 'What do you think, Mrs. M?'"[5]

Moskowitz wielded a power known to few if any of her female contemporaries and none of her predecessors, but she nonetheless believed that men and women have radically different capabilities. Indeed, she thought women "have qualities of mind peculiarly feminine, but they are not the intellectual equals of men."[6] And she believed that compassion was *the* attribute women had to offer to the world of politics. She herself was willing, however, to consort with the likes of Frank "I am the law" Hague, the famous boss of Jersey City whose machine was legendary for its reach, if it served her political ends.

The careers of Jeannette Rankin and Belle Moskowitz reveal the limits of what was possible for women in the immediate aftermath of suffrage. One was well known but utterly lacking in power. The other was unknown, content to play the role of political helpmate to a powerful man but also powerful in her own right. It should not escape notice that the woman who held office and had captured public attention was not the powerful one.

Although not a widow, the first woman to head a major congressional committee, New Jersey Democrat Mary Norton, also owed her position to a man: Boss Hague of Jersey City. Selected as a candidate by Hague and loyal to the machine, Norton, in 1924, became the first Democratic woman to be elected to the House of Representatives; the others had been Republicans. Serving in the House till 1950, she transcended her machine roots by chairing first the Committee on the District of Columbia and then the Committee on Labor in the latter stages of the New Deal.

Perhaps the definitive word on female office-holding via derived male authority came from a congresswoman/widow. In the late 1920s, Congresswoman (and widow of a U.S. senator) Ruth Hanna McCormick, fielding a question about whether she had run as a woman, responded angrily: "I didn't run for office as a woman. I ran as the daughter of Mark Hanna [a powerful Ohio senator] and the wife of Medill McCormick [an Illinois senator and also a member of the *Chicago Tribune* publishing family] and therefore equipped for office by heredity and training."[7] The widowhood route eased women into office, but once there, they were highly unlikely to think of themselves as *women* politicians, let alone defend the interests of their gender, although some of the widows would run for reelection many times. The tradition of altruism might prepare a woman politician to play up her gender, but it prepared very few to be partisan politicians, let alone to run for office. Before female candidates could run in any great numbers, run as working politicians, and run as women, a new tradition would have to be forged.

The outlook for that new tradition was far from promising in the late 1920s: Women voters had been going to the polls in far smaller numbers than the proponents of suffrage had anticipated—they would not vote at the same level as men until 1968—and a bitter division had taken place within the ranks of organized womanhood over the best approach to legislating for their gender. One wing of the triumphant suffrage movement had continued to support the protective legislation for women workers that had been advocated by the settlement house network. The other wing followed militant Alice Paul into the National Woman's Party, whose members called for passage of the newly conceived Equal Rights Amendment (ERA), an approach emphasizing women's sameness to men as opposed to protective legislation, which emphasized difference. Congress, no longer fearing women voters (as had been the case immediately after suffrage and before the women's vote had been revealed to be a paper tiger) and seeing the divisiveness, proceeded to drop what interest there had been in women's issues.[8]

Nonetheless, in the early 1940s, little more than a decade later, two women entered Congress who would both symbolize a new era and help precipitate further change: Democrat Helen Gahagan Douglas of California and Republican Margaret Chase Smith of Maine. What happened in the interim to explain these two trailblazing women officeholders, at least in part, was that the country was blessed with its first First Lady dedicated to advancing the cause of women politicians, Eleanor Roosevelt, and also its first female political boss, Molly Dewson.

By the late 1920s, a new star had emerged among women politicians, Eleanor Roosevelt. Arguably the best-known and most-respected American woman of the twentieth century, she earned fame for much more than her role as the wife of Franklin Roosevelt, president during the 1930s and early 1940s. She was a reformer close to women in the settlement house network, a teacher, a journalist, and a mentor to countless other women, and we had never had a First Lady like her before.

Franklin Roosevelt had been a rising star himself when, in 1921, he contracted poliomyelitis. Having been assistant secretary of the navy during World War I and then the Democratic party's nominee for the vice presidency in 1920, he spent much of the ensuing decade recuperating while his wife kept the Roosevelt name alive in New York Democratic circles. Although her prominence was in some measure a result of his, she was far more than his surrogate. Says her biographer Blanche Wiesen Cook of this period: "She became famous not as FDR's wife, but as a major political force to be reckoned with."[9] She spoke, wrote, and organized tirelessly.

In 1928, Franklin Roosevelt won election as governor of New York, and in 1932 desperate Americans voted him into the presidency as the man who would lead the nation out of the Great Depression. Through his wife, FDR had come to know a number of talented and highly qualified women. Moreover, Eleanor herself was not shy about promoting her friends, not because they were her friends but because she respected them and believed in their capacity to be effective public servants. The result was that during the New Deal, more women had better positions than during all previous administrations combined. By and large these women were not candidates for elective office—although Eleanor did recruit a few as candidates—but the positions they filled gave women politicians a new visibility and a new legitimacy.

No doubt the most prominent woman New Dealer other than Mrs. Roosevelt herself was Secretary of Labor Frances Perkins, the first woman to serve in the cabinet. Having risen from settlement worker ranks, Perkins was industrial commissioner of New York during FDR's governorship. He came to admire her greatly; hence, when women lobbied for her appointment to the cabinet, he proved receptive. Perkins was one of only two cabinet members to serve throughout Roosevelt's tenure; she fought for and helped to achieve progressive legislation in a number of areas, including unemployment relief, the Social Security Act, and the Fair Labor Standards Act.[10]

Less well known now, but no less remarkable then, is Molly Dewson, who has been called the nation's first female political boss. Dewson earned this sobriquet because she organized 80,000 women into the Women's Division of the Democratic party and delivered them on election day. In so doing, she earned the gratitude and respect of the male political operatives in Roosevelt's camp. There could be no tradition of self-confident and outspoken women candidates until women voters began to come through in this fashion.

Yet for all her successes, the one thing Dewson did not accomplish—any more than did the other women New Dealers—was to advance women in the party hierarchy. Using the techniques and rhetoric of the suffrage movement, she appealed to female altruism and to the desire for service and uplift. Her approach was to "keep women's activities separate from men's, make women self-supporting, and decentralize control of women's politics to the local level."[11] Belle Moskowitz was still one of the very few women to have operated on the inside of either party—as would be the case for many years to come.

In March 1947, one of Eleanor Roosevelt's protégées made a speech to the House that dramatized what the lineaments of a new tradition for women candidates and officeholders might look like. With postwar inflation imposing hardships on housewives throughout the country, Democratic congresswoman Helen Gahagan Douglas of California decided to demonstrate her concern about the lifting of wartime price controls and the concomitant disruption of family budgets. The former actress, whose flair for dramatizing social issues had helped propel her into a political career, "walked into Congress with a metal shopping basket on my arm" and started unloading a number of grocery items. "I declared that decontrol had resulted in a 50 percent increase in the cost of bread, milk, flour, eggs, fats, meat and soap. . . . The price increases were . . . gouging the consumer."[12] Her staff had seen to it that the press was on hand when she bought the groceries, and her unusual speech attracted further attention. Some of her male colleagues found all of this to be deeply irritating, and one, Republican Frank B. Keefe of Wisconsin, even tried to interrupt her while she spoke, but Douglas held her ground and refused to yield the floor. When she lambasted the Republican party for the housewife's problems, members of the Democratic leadership were as delighted as the Republicans were annoyed. Afterwards her office received a deluge of mail. All in all, it was an unusually high-profile performance for a woman.[13]

Decades later, this speech may not seem like a revolutionary act. But during a period when few women ran for office—Mary Norton was the only other Democratic woman member when Douglas arrived in the House in 1945—and when the conventional wisdom dictated that those few who did should do as little as possible to call attention to themselves or to their gender, the market basket speech was bold indeed. Douglas's impassioned plea on behalf of the housewife took it as a given that she, as a woman politician, had a special responsibility to the woman voter—to whom she was appealing over the heads of the overwhelmingly male House of Representatives. Furthermore, she was appealing not to the altruism that most women politicians invoked when speaking to their female constituents, but to women's economic self-interest: Focusing on women in the economic role of housewife/consumer, which was the position occupied by the majority in the 1940s, she spoke to women voters' concerns about inflation, just as a male politician might do in addressing men. All of this constituted a radical departure from the usual practice. Indeed, Helen Gahagan Douglas was the first woman politician of whom it could be said both that she "ran as a woman" and that she had a real impact as a working politician.

Part of the explanation for Douglas's historic contribution to a new tradition of female candidacy and office-holding may have lain with the changing context created by the New Deal, but part was also owed to her unusual background. As it happens, Helen Gahagan Douglas was used to escaping from the limitations of conventional wisdom. While a college student in New York in 1922, she appeared in a play that garnered so much attention that, unlike most aspiring thespians, she never had to submit to the tedious—and heartbreaking—rounds of auditions usually required in order to get theater work. Rather, she became a leading lady almost overnight, a supposedly impossible feat. That she was stunningly beautiful helped. Tall with classic features, she received praise from one reviewer as being not merely one of the ten most beautiful women in the country, but all ten wrapped into one. Years later, when her acting career was fading and the country was in the grip of the Great Depression, she found herself restless for a new direction in her life. Married to fellow actor Melvyn Douglas and living in Los Angeles where Douglas's film career was flourishing, she had been receiving few offers of work. With a need for something compelling to occupy her now-idle hours, she began to take an interest in the plight of California's migrant farm workers, seeking out the most knowledgeable experts, studying hard, and then giving speeches about the problem. Before long she came to the attention of Franklin and Eleanor Roosevelt. With the President and First Lady as her sponsors, and quickly on close terms with other leading New Dealers such as Frances Perkins, she enjoyed a meteoric rise in California politics. Such experiences served to give her a level of confidence, both in her political star and in her own judgment, that was extremely unusual in a woman politician.

Given this background and these reasons for self-confidence, Douglas was not shy about calling attention to her gender. The market basket speech was part of a pattern she established before she ever ran for Congress. As the Democratic national committee woman in California from

1940 to 1944 (she had not become politically active on behalf of migrant workers until 1938), she recruited female foreign policy experts to talk to women's clubs. In 1943, she waged a tremendous, and successful, battle to obtain the appointment of a woman as postmaster of Los Angeles. On the campaign trail, she was not afraid to look glamorous, thus calling attention to her sex and even to her sexuality. (Most women politicians of the era strove for a "sensible" persona.) Once in Congress, she championed a number of issues that have become known as quintessentially "women's issues," either because they pertain to female biology/social roles or because women have identified themselves with these issues over the course of the twentieth century—health care, peace, and conservation, for example. In all these ways, she "ran as a woman," but without confining herself to the old tradition of disinterested nonpartisanship. Idealistic, as her entry into politics on behalf of migrant farm workers demonstrates, she was also a practicing politician.

By the time she had won reelection to her third term in 1948 (by a huge margin), it was clear that she occupied a safe seat. This, however, had not always been the case. Although in 1944 the retiring incumbent in Los Angeles's Fourteenth District recruited her to run as his replacement, she lived outside the generally low-to middle-income district and could legitimately be called an interloper. The first time out she won election by less than 4,000 votes. But once in office she worked hard for liberal causes that appealed to the district (which was 25 percent African-American) and began to attract significant support from the labor movement and from nationally prominent black leaders. Hence the margin of safety at the ballot box that she began to receive from her constituents.

Prominent, if not always popular with her male colleagues, hard-working, beloved by labor, in constant demand as a speaker, Douglas decided to run for the U.S. Senate in 1950. The Democratic incumbent, Sheridan Downey, seemed vulnerable, and she disliked his stands on certain issues of importance to California. At this juncture, she began to draw on a women's network for help in the primary. For example, early contributions, many from outside the state, provided her campaign with a much-needed financial boost. Eleanor Roosevelt gave a fund-raising cocktail party in New York and the socially prominent Daisy Harriman did the same in Washington, D.C. Inside the state "[m]ost of the grass-roots organizers and many county heads were women."[14] The rest of the story of the senatorial campaign has become part of American political folklore: Downey withdrew, Douglas defeated publisher Manchester

Boddy in the primary—despite the fact that he red-baited her by calling her the Pink Lady because of her steady backing of liberal causes—but lost in November to Republican Richard Nixon, who made more effective use of the Pink Lady charges.

Because the 1950 campaign has gained the status of legend, most Americans who recognize the name Helen Gahagan Douglas at all do so because they remember that she had the misfortune to be one of the first victims of Nixon's smear tactics. Yet those who study her career find much that is illuminating about the possibilities for a woman politician. Responsive to the needs of her gender, she never confined her energies to those issues, serving with distinction on the House Committee on Foreign Affairs.[15] She built a solid base of support among women throughout California, as well as among influential women in other parts of the country. When she decided to move up to the Senate, she was able to mobilize these women, using what was clearly a precursor of EMILY's List, established in 1985. The advice she gave one younger woman about being a female politician is revealing about the self-confident way she saw her own role. Rosalind Wyman, elected to the Los Angeles City Council in 1953 at the age of twenty-two, recalls seeking out Douglas, who "told me . . . about being a woman, and maintaining being a woman, and not becoming hard. In other words, if you have certain characteristics, keep them."[16]

To examine her personal papers is to understand why she had so much credibility with women and with liberals. Simply put, Douglas crusaded for many of the issues that have been essential to these groups in the ensuing decades. For example, she introduced bills in the 79th, 80th, and 81st Congresses that would have allocated funds to convene a world conference on cancer research. Once identified with this issue, she and her office became a focal point for anyone in the country who had an urgent interest in a cure for cancer. Furthermore, she tried to find a way to heal the schism in progressive circles over the ERA, a schism that lasted from its introduction in 1923 until the emergence of modern feminism in the late 1960s. Indeed, her solution—to set up a commission on the legal status of women—pointed the way to Kennedy's groundbreaking Presidential Commission on the Status of Women, about which there will be more to say later.[17]

The country had changed between Jeannette Rankin's entry into Congress in 1917 and Helen Gahagan Douglas's tenure in office in the 1940s: the New Deal years of the 1930s had seen a flowering of many different liberal causes, most notably the labor movement, and millions of women had entered the work force. But it is important also to specify the precise personal sources underlying Douglas's unprecedented political career. As previously noted, unlike most women, she had prepolitical experiences that bolstered her ego and comfort level about being in the public eye. Second, with an independent career before she married, she continued to make highly independent decisions after she married. In fact, she decided to run for Congress while her husband was serving in the military overseas; he learned about the race from a newspaper account. Not much impact from coverture in this instance, it would seem. Finally, the mother of two children, she had learned to juggle her family and her career, which put her on the road for extended periods of time, before ever running for office.

More restrained in her support of women's issues than Douglas but with a much longer tenure in Congress, Margaret Chase Smith of Maine contributed to a new tradition by being the first fully credible woman U.S. senator.[18] As such, she had a profound impact on young women growing up—such as Senator Barbara Boxer of California.[19] When her husband, Congressman Clyde Smith, suffered a fatal heart attack in the midst of his 1940 campaign, she won election in his place. She was reelected several times before running successfully for the Senate in 1948, the first woman to be elected to that body who was not the widow of a senator. She served in the Senate until 1973. Today, Smith is best known for the Declaration of Conscience she issued in 1950, a pioneering attack on the methods of her fellow Senate Republican Joseph McCarthy and an act of rare courage, given the temper of the times.

Before the 1960s, her advocacy on behalf of women consisted solely of being an ardent—and effective—defender of women in military service. Evidently fearful of engaging in special pleading for her gender—"I asked for no special privileges because I was a woman"—she explains that stance today by insisting that women need to accept responsibilities as well as to claim rights.[20] While no feminist by modern standards—indeed, she explicitly repudiates the label—she must be seen as serving an important function for all would-be woman politicians by earning wide respect for her integrity and hard work. What's more, like Douglas, she stuck her neck out. Conservative in many ways, she always insisted on charting an independent course, disagreeing with her party if her conscience so dictated. That she served in Congress for more than thirty years is a powerful message to potential women candidates in itself.

Several other Republican women in Congress during these years also deserve mention for their very considerable accomplishments. In the House from 1925 to 1960, Edith Nourse Rogers of Massachusetts still holds the title of the longest-serving woman in the history of that body. Replacing her congressman husband in a special election after his death, she went on to win seventeen additional elections. Veterans' affairs, including issues pertaining to women veterans, were her special concern. Another widow, Frances Bolton of Ohio, served from 1940 to 1969. Daughter of a U.S. senator, wife of a congressman, Bolton was also the mother of a congressman, with whom she served concurrently for three Congresses. She devoted herself to championing the cause of nurses as well as to her position on the House Committee on Foreign Affairs, where she eventually became the ranking Republican. Finally, Katharine St. George of New York won election to Congress nine times, from 1946 to 1964. A first cousin of Franklin Roosevelt, but an avid Republican, she ceased campaigning for her party when FDR entered the White House in 1932. Her opposition to his third term brought her back into partisan activity. She would meet electoral success six years later. She was most noteworthy, perhaps, for her strong support of the Equal Rights Amendment.[21]

Tenacious, courageous, and dedicated public servants though these women may have been, none of them had the credentials that make a new member likely to be taken seriously by male colleagues. Most of them first achieved a seat in the House because of a male relative. Only Douglas had had a real career, although Smith had also been gainfully employed for some years before her marriage. Only Douglas and St. George had strong backgrounds in partisan activity, and Douglas's was of short duration despite its high visibility. But in 1955, a woman entered the House, Democrat Martha Griffiths of Michigan, who was destined to play a prominent role not only by promoting feminist legislation but also by enhancing the more politically viable tradition that was emerging for women candidates and officeholders. That her background closely paralleled that of a typical male member made it all the more likely that she would be able to accomplish all of this.

Born in 1912, Martha Wright graduated from the University of Missouri, married Hicks Griffiths, and then the two of them headed for law school at the University of Michigan. After finishing law school and being admitted to the bar, she practiced law in several different capacities before running for office. Losing on her first attempt to get into the state legislature, she won in 1948 and served two terms. Governor G. Mennen Williams appointed her recorder and judge of Recorder's Court in Detroit in 1953, and she subsequently won an election as judge seven months later. Having lost on her first run for Congress in 1952, she won in 1954 and stayed in that body till she decided to retire in 1974. What is impressive about Griffiths's preparation for Congress is not only the law degree and the legal career, but also her clear determination to persevere in politics no matter what, including her willingness to bounce back from an initial loss or two. Before Griffiths, none of this belonged to the female political tradition. Worth noting, too, is the fact that she today recalls an explicitly feminist motivation for her first race: an elderly Republican woman who had picketed the White House on behalf of suffrage during Woodrow Wilson's administration invited her to run for the state legislature.[22]

Once again, it is necessary to look to the way the times shaped the possibilities for Griffiths's career as well as to the personal characteristics of the woman in question. During World War II, millions of American women entered the work force, and the country has not been the same since—including its politics. Given such unprecedented numbers of gainfully employed women, it began to be possible to define women's issues in a wholly new way. This was because a critical mass of voting-age women would now need legal guarantees of fair treatment in the workplace, equal access to graduate and professional school, access to credit, and the ability to control their reproductive lives so as not to suffer from economic disaster owing to an unplanned pregnancy. There had never been a politics based on these issues, because there had never been a need for one.

For a period after World War II, there was a backlash against women and against change: The 1950s saw a glorification of family "togetherness" and the stay-at-home mom.[23] Nonetheless, women continued to work outside the home. Writing in 1964, historian Carl Degler called the war-driven changes in patterns of female employment a "revolution without an ideology." In the late 1960s the revolution acquired an ideology—feminism—and more than two decades later Americans are still trying to deal with all the developments that were set in motion as a result.

Reproductive rights have been at the center of second-wave feminism and crucial in defining a new gender-based politics. In this area changes in contraceptive practice and in public opinion happened with breathtaking speed beginning around 1960 or shortly after Martha Griffiths arrived in the House. The earlier history of this key women's issue is necessary to an understanding of women's transition from public avowals of altruism to a politics based, at least in part, on female self-interest—and to an understanding of the new possibilities for a woman candidate to run as a woman.

Historians have established that the birth rate fell throughout the nineteenth century. Families were obviously practicing some form of birth control, most likely male withdrawal, but the public discourse gave no indication that this was taking place. Needless to say, if people were not talking about contraception, they were even less likely to be talking about abortion. Yet according to the best estimates by modern historians, many thousands of women chose to terminate pregnancies in the nineteenth century.[24]

Thus, women commonly limited family size and terminated pregnancies before such matters were even remotely defined as appropriate for public discussion, let alone for consideration as public policy. (The underground nature of the subject meant that access was far from evenly distributed throughout the society.) This phenomenon is telling about the evolution of a gender-based politics, because the advocacy of reproductive rights is at odds with access to influence based on the moral authority of home and mother, or on women's greater altruism. As long as the route to influence required women to be superior to men in morality and selflessness, they could not readily advocate their right to sexual pleasure nor their right to personal fulfillment on the same basis as men. As ever more women found employment outside the home, the altruism mode became increasingly burdensome as well as less necessary. A few decades later, a profound change in attitudes toward sexuality, amounting to the diminution if not the disappearance of the double standard, contributed to the rebirth of feminism and to the shaping of new possibilities for women's issues. Simply stated, women began to give themselves permission to be self-seeking in the way men have been. This change opened the way for women to construct their public authority not as selfless social mother but as competent and credible public being with credentials roughly equivalent to those of a man, defending interests fully as legitimate as those of a man.[25]

Griffiths, the first congresswoman to possess this type of credential, was also the first to leave as her legacy a substantial body of public policy dealing with feminist issues. Her own experience with discrimination in law school plus service on the House Ways and Means Committee and on the Joint Economic Committee convinced her of the need to attack the remnants of coverture in laws governing inheritance and social security.[26] Happily, by the time Griffiths began to tackle this work, the climate for such legislation was changing, thanks to leadership from John F. Kennedy and the aging Eleanor Roosevelt.

When he took office in 1961, Kennedy was under conflicting pressures with respect to the ERA. Despite protests from labor—unions opposed the ERA because of their desire to maintain protective legislation—the Democratic party had officially endorsed the ERA in 1944. (The Republicans had endorsed it in 1940.) Over the years, the amendment had gradually begun to attract supporters beyond the original band of militants in the National Woman's Party. Yet various attempts at compromise, such as allowing protective legislation to stand, had failed. Labor still staunchly opposed the ERA in its unaltered state, and its fervent advocates refused to accept any alteration. Kennedy needed a policy dealing with legislation on women. He had appointed a strong director of the Women's Bureau, Esther Peterson, and when she asked him to appoint the first-ever President's Commission on the Status of Women, he complied. Fortunately for the prestige of the endeavor, Eleanor Roosevelt agreed to chair the commission.

Much that was positive came out of the Kennedy commission. High-powered men and women agreed to serve on it, and they gave it far more than token attention. Adequately funded to engage a good staff, the commission then galvanized a network of women's groups throughout the country to examine policy on women and to pressure each state legislature to see to it that similar commissions were established at the state level. Says historian Cynthia Harrison: "The president's commission and its state-level offspring helped to legitimate the issue of sex discrimination, made data available to support allegations that discrimination against women constituted a serious problem, drew up agendas to ameliorate inequities, raised expectations that responsible parties would take action, and, most important, sensitized a nationwide network of women to the problems women faced."[27] She also points out that this commission antedated the rebirth of feminism and even "ultimately helped to bring it about."

The commission's report, entitled "American Women" and presented to Kennedy in October 1963, embodied a carefully worded compromise about ERA. Stopping short of endorsing the amendment, the report nonetheless acknowledged that women were far from equal under the law, and that they needed remedies. The most desirable remedy would be new Supreme Court decisions that would use the Fifth and Fourteenth Amendments to the Constitution to achieve greater sex equity. Although this approach was not satisfactory to the National Woman's Party, it in fact "broke the long-standing stalemate that had hobbled concerted action on behalf of American women since the end of World War II."[28] Helen Gahagan Douglas had been right: A high-level commission was the way to end the impasse about ERA, with its paralyzing effect on legislative remedies for women's problems.

Congress enacted two extraordinary pieces of legislation at more or less the same time. After many years of lobbying by the Women's Bureau and by female labor leaders, a majority voted for the Equal Pay Act of 1963, and the following year passed Title VII of the Civil Rights Act, which proved to be extremely consequential for women as well as for African-Americans, its intended beneficiaries in the eyes of its sponsors. This was because Howard Smith, a conservative Southerner, introduced an amendment placing the word *sex* in Title VII, seemingly as a reductio ad absurdum. His speech was greeted with hilarity. Martha Griffiths, who had made a strategic decision to let a man make the initial speech on the amendment, was then ready to follow Smith with an impassioned plea for serious consideration of the issue: "When I arose, I began by saying: 'I presume that if there had been any necessity to point out that women were a second-class sex, the laughter would have proved it.' There was no more laughter."[29] Eleven of the twelve women in the House eventually spoke on that occasion. Even the reluctant feminist Margaret Chase Smith subsequently joined in behind-the-scenes maneuvering to guarantee the inclusion of discrimination on the basis of sex in Title VII.[30]

After Congress passed this landmark legislation, Griffiths worked unceasingly to ensure that the Equal Employment Opportunity Commission (EEOC), established to enforce the law, would take gender-based discrimination seriously. She made her office a rallying point for women throughout the country who felt they had been discriminated against. The formation of the first modern advocacy group for women, the National Organization for Women (NOW), came directly out of attempts to get the EEOC to take sex discrimination seriously.

As of the late 1960s, it was a stunningly new world for women and women candidates, especially a candidate who might want to pursue the strategy of running as a woman. By that time, feminism had become a genuine social movement, with hundreds of thousands of women across the country marching, demonstrating, attending consciousness-raising sessions, or making life-changing decisions. It would not take women politicians long to respond.

As a prime example, Democrat Shirley Chisholm of New York, the first African-American woman to serve in Congress, pursued a strategy in her first campaign in 1968 that represented an important and hitherto little-used component of running as a woman: She specifically targeted the women voters. With an impressive background in teaching, social work, and community activism, Chisholm served two terms in the state legislature before deciding to run for higher office. In her autobiography she explains that her Republican opponent and his campaign staff were running her down in the Brooklyn neighborhoods as "a bossy female, a would-be matriarch." One of her campaign operatives realized that this strategy might be made to backfire against the Republicans: He noticed that "for each man registered in the district there were 2.5 women." Chisholm goes on to say:

> Men always underestimate women. They underestimated me, and they underestimated the women like me. If they had thought about it, they would have realized that many of the homes in black neighborhoods are headed by women. They stay put, raise their families—and register to vote in greater numbers. The women are always organizing something, even if it is only a bridge club. They run the PTA, they are the backbone of the social groups and the civic clubs, more than the men. So the organization was already there. All I had to do was get its help. I went to the presidents and leaders and asked, "Can you help me?"[31]

By 1970 a consensus had emerged among progressive groups about the desirability of the ERA. Even labor eventually accepted the amendment, because both the courts and the EEOC deemed that Title VII had already invalidated protective legislation. Congress soon passed the amendment, and the stultifying schism ended—at least for the moment. Organized womanhood became less divided than it had been for many years.[32] In the early 1970s, Congress and various state legislatures enacted the greatest amount of public policy devoted to women's issues in American history, including Title IX of the Higher Education Act, which has been a charter of rights for women in colleges and universities, and the Equal Credit Opportunity Act. A woman candidate could now run on her intention to work for such issues, although it would be a distortion to suggest that women all jumped on the bandwagon at once.[33]

Also by the early 1970s, 44 percent of all women were gainfully employed outside the home, and the appeal to women's pocketbook interests, so bravely attempted by Douglas in her appeal to housewives in 1947, became a potentially winning strategy for a woman candidate. What's more, by the late 1960s, women were beginning to vote at approximately the same rate as men. As recently as 1960, "women's participation rate was 11 percent below that of men."[34] In 1968, women voters had comprised a slight majority of the electorate for the first time in American history.

Shortly thereafter, indicative of the new legitimacy belonging to women's issues, the U.S. Supreme Court extended the constitutional right to an abortion in the first trimester of pregnancy to all American women in its *Roe* v. *Wade* decision of 1973. At the time, many hoped that the decision would permanently resolve the issue; instead, the ensuing decades have seen a bitter debate over the morality of abortion—and ultimately over a woman's nature.[35] Is a woman motivated primarily by altruism and does abortion violate her essential nature? At the Republican National Convention in 1992, Marilyn Quayle invoked the essentialist view of womanhood with its implicit critique of reproductive rights. What makes this controversy different and less damaging to women candidates than the one over the ERA is the fact that it is not taking place within the progressive community but between progressives and conservatives. Although progressive women candidates may occasionally suffer as a result of being pro-choice, more often they benefit, because the issue mobilizes both financial support and support at the ballot box.[36] The controversy over abortion has also meant that gender-based issues have been front and center in American public life in the recent past—as opposed to their previous invisibility or marginalization.

As of late 1971, a woman candidate could benefit not only from the supportive presence of a social movement in the background, new salience for women's issues, and greater numbers of women voting than ever before, but also from the founding of a new group, the National Women's Political Caucus (NWPC), the first-ever organization with the explicit goal of encouraging women to run for elective office. In that year a number of prominent women including Democratic congresswoman Bella Abzug of New York, Congresswoman Shirley Chisholm, author

Betty Friedan, and Gloria Steinem convened a meeting, attended by some 300 women, in order to launch NWPC. Bipartisan, the caucus then set up guidelines for dealing with candidate endorsement. The sine qua nons for a woman candidate included support for the ERA, support for *Roe* v. *Wade,* and support for publicly funded child care.[37]

The women candidates elected to the House in these years—Abzug, Chisholm, and Patricia Schroeder—did not derive their public authority through the instrumentality of a man. Neither were they social mothers, as public women of the early twentieth century had been. Although the 1970s cohort was still small—there were fourteen women elected to the House in 1972 as opposed to the forty-seven in 1992—many of its members had the energy and credibility to tackle women's issues in an unprecedented way. For example, in 1977 a group founded the Congressional Women's Caucus (now the Congressional Caucus for Women's Issues). Along with certain of their colleagues in the state legislatures, these women were exploiting the new possibilities for running as a woman.

Other women candidates still hung back. For example, after her election to the House in 1980, the *New York Times* asked Republican Lynn Martin of Illinois how much women's issues meant to her. "Zip," she replied.[38] Nonetheless, over time, more and more women candidates and officeholders have been willing to be point persons for issues of importance to their female constituents. As we shall be demonstrating, it seemed that almost all women candidates in 1992 saw it as advantageous to climb on the bandwagon for women's issues.

But that does not mean that women candidates do not still confront many challenges unique to their gender. Only a woman candidate would have to face voter scrutiny on the quality of her parenting. Only a woman candidate would have to fight inner skirmishes about her ambition, about what it might do to her marriage. Only a woman candidate would have to confront painful and potentially damaging sexual innuendo.

3

Emerging from Jezebel's Shadow

Sex, Gender, and Public Policy

When Senator Margaret Chase Smith of Maine was contemplating a run for the presidency in 1964, "[n]oticeable in reading the answers to a poll . . . was the ease with which both sexes resorted to clichés: 'Woman's place is in the home.' An engineer's aide gave as his uniform answer to the question of whether he would vote for a woman for president, governor, senator, or congresswoman, 'No—I'm a man . . . ' A farmer observed: 'Men are not ready to surrender to a woman.'"[1]

That farmer's choice of words—surrender—is telling, as was this opinion of one New York political leader, reported by Martin Gruberg in his landmark 1968 book *Women in American Politics:* "Women belong in two places—at home and in bed."[2] That remark, made today in the context of any other profession—banking, the military, academia—would be recognized as a form of sexual harassment and proof of a sexually hostile environment, a concept made possible only because modern-day women began questioning the stereotypes they had inherited.

Nearly a quarter century after Margaret Chase Smith's brief candidacy, when Patricia Schroeder was contemplating running (and being referred to, with her fellow Democratic presidential hopefuls, as "Snow

White and the Seven Dwarfs"), a September 1987 *Time* magazine poll indicated she led the pack. The near 70–30 percent pro-woman split was higher than the 1964 poll on Margaret Chase Smith, in which only 55 percent said they would vote for a woman.[3] But the question still was being asked seventy years after women achieved the vote.

Politics has been exclusively a man's world. The few women who had braved it often had been the sole members of their sex or, at best, part of a tiny minority. To be comfortable in that male world and to find any acceptance at all, those individual women had to avoid calling attention to their sex. They cloaked themselves in the most modest dress possible. The widows among them took "cover" in their late husband's authority. If they were not a husband's surrogate, women might gain acceptance by claiming to speak for the downtrodden—veiling themselves in the self-lessness of their cause. Another option that did not challenge male traditions was to behave as if St. Paul's famous letter to the Corinthians—"Let your women keep silence . . ."—concerned politics not religion.

Then, even after women found their voices and gained some measure of grudging acceptance from the men, that acceptance was so tentative and specific that the chosen women found it impolitic to raise their voices, especially to raise them "selfishly," to aid or appeal to their own sex—or, it should go without saying, to run as a woman.

Meanwhile, any breach of the male-determined sexual etiquette of the public arena made a woman subject to, at best, excessive gallantry or joviality, which only thinly disguised hostility or demeaning sarcasm. Often, the punishment for the crime of being a woman was outright sexual harassment, sometimes even rape.

Political women sensed how damaging the strategies they had adopted to avoid sexual confrontation were both to their psyches and to public policy that could work for their sisters. "Until women know they can be who they are, act like they are, and sound like they are, we're not going to make any progress," predicted former New York City Council president Carol Bellamy in 1979.[4]

In other words, until Schroeder rounded up five of her female colleagues in the House of Representatives to storm the U.S. Senate to demand that a woman named Anita Hill be heard, political women's best strategy had been to hide in plain sight. And the unacceptable aspect of themselves that these political pioneers had to keep hidden was the central biological fact of their being—their sex.

Feminists have only recently begun to decipher the ways in which "sex" and "power" are linked in a patriarchal system, and yet women have always intuited that this linkage had made the world a more dangerous place for them. Despite political women's newfound bravado, their mere existence—the phenomenon of competent, powerful public women—is still for some voters a disquieting concept. In hindsight, the early strategies political women developed to simply co-exist, given age-old sexual stereotypes and prohibitions, actually may have hindered their progress, both at the polls and in public policy, to which Bellamy's insight referred.

Congresswoman Jill Long of Indiana would seem an unlikely victim of any prejudices that hamper women. She came of age in an era when women were beginning to feel they could have it all. Campaign ads have shown her atop a tractor or operating other farm machinery on her family's large farm. She is also a former professor—business administration at Valparaiso, marketing at Indiana and Purdue universities. In high school she was both a student leader and the band's drum major. One Indiana Democratic chair calls her "a modest Methodist farmer."[5] David Axelrod, former political editor of the *Chicago Tribune* and a seasoned political operative, describes her as "wholesome . . . and tough as nails" and chuckles that the Republicans in Indiana's Fourth Congressional District, former Vice President J. Danforth Quayle's old seat, "always complain 'How do you run against everybody's little sister?'"[6]

It came as no surprise in October 1991 that Congresswoman Long would be among the outraged congresswomen to speak out as the Senate Judiciary Committee's debacle regarding Anita Hill's charges against Clarence Thomas played out next door. What surprised her colleagues was what she said:

> It was not too long ago that a colleague of mine complemented me on my appearance and then said that he was going to chase me around the House floor . . . I was offended and I was embarrassed.
>
> Sexual harassment is serious. It is not funny and it is not cute, and it is certainly not complimentary. . . . [7]

In publicly discussing a pass made by a colleague, Congresswoman Long broke one of the oldest taboos in American politics. Until very recently, sex was a "hear no evil, speak no evil, see no evil" phenomenon in Washington, D.C., and the state capitals of America. Opportunities for sex were counted among the spoils of power, one of the unquestioned privileges that came with male territory. Male politicians preferred—and undoubtedly still would prefer—to describe themselves as public men, their behavior toward women above reproach and all for the public good, or at the very least beyond the purview of the press and the people. But among themselves there has been a very different attitude. Women were booty.

The late speaker of the California assembly, Jesse Unruh, came closest to publicly defining the relationship of sex, politics, and the two genders when he described "a good politician as a guy who would take [lobbyists'] money, drink their whiskey, eat their steaks, fuck their women . . . "[8] Even in the late 1970s, well into the women's movement, but before the phrase sexual harassment was commonly used, one exasperated congresswoman recounted how a male colleague in the 95th Congress (1977–79) "tried patiently to explain to her that being in Congress meant Chivas Regal, beautiful women, and Lear jets."[9]

Sex and power are so confusingly linked as to be one and the same thing in some minds—as Henry Kissinger's remark "Power is the ultimate aphrodisiac" makes clear. Untangling that knot is not only a strategic problem for the political woman but a psychological conundrum. Power is considered a masculine attribute and is suspect in a woman. Congresswoman Nancy Johnson of Connecticut openly admits that "power is something I was always very, very afraid of. It was a *word* [emphasis added] I didn't like."[10]

To men, female competition for any sort of traditionally male power is both confusing and threatening. To grant women equal power may cause men to feel less male, somehow unsexed, or at the very least out of control of their world, a situation that can be seen as the subcontext to the recurring family values debates, or the battles over equal rights amendments and a woman's right to choose whether she will remain pregnant, or the continuing claims that women in the military (or gays, for that matter) will undermine morale even though they have proved their worth.

Granting women equal political power also may feel like "surrender," as the farmer who so feared a President Margaret Chase Smith made clear. His sexually loaded insight is the key to understanding much about the nature of men's—and society's—reluctance to welcome public women. Female power equates to unseemly, even dangerous female sexuality. Any woman who ventures, or "strays," beyond societal expectations is sexually suspect. And no matter who she is in her private life— daughter, wife, mother—she is subject to special scrutiny.

Sexual behavior also has been the subject of a double standard so accepted that until recently there was no language even to describe the effect of that double standard, much less any organized effort to question the traditional, even biblical, assumptions on which it was based: namely, women are the sexual predators, their very presence in a man's space is an invitation to transgress, and men are but powerless victims.

That has not been the rhetoric of politics, of course. The rhetoric has always been rich with proclamations about protecting women and solemn discussions of the holiness of mom and apple pie. Husbandly jokes about the formidable power that women exert over them in the private sphere were perhaps the only clues to the shared male fear of the females' sexual cunning.

That esteemed person, the public man, could hardly admit, perhaps not even recognize, that despite his chivalrous words and professed respect for women—retired senator Margaret Chase Smith derided such unwanted protectors in 1990 as "the Galahads"—his attitudes and actions had very negative consequences.

In the dissonance between male proclamation and male practice we see that sex, the key element in any one person's identity and one of the most basic functions of existence, has been the weapon of choice brandished against female incursion into the public sphere. Moral superiority and modest dress—or becoming selfless, sexless untouchables—were almost too obvious initial strategies that women could embrace to battle both their exclusion from public life and the calumny attached to being biologically female.

Given the potency of the linkages between sex and power, it is no surprise that the Anita Hill episode—and the questions it raised about women's roles, women's nature, and the interactions between powerful men and less powerful women—could so profoundly shake the system. What is less obvious are the important ways it echoes this nation's very first political crisis.

Fewer than ten years after the Massachusetts Bay Colony was founded in 1630, Boston was riveted and torn by the trial and banishment of one Anne Hutchinson.[11] Three and a half centuries separate Hutchinson and Hill, but the similarities in their cases, indeed the similarity of both public inquiries to rape trials, suggests a great deal about this society's notions of womanhood.

Just as there is no evidence that Anne Hutchinson was anything but the upstanding daughter of an English clergyman, the faithful wife of a Boston merchant, and the middle-aged mother of fifteen children, there was no evidence that Anita Hill was anything but a reluctant witness whose own life, character, and deportment were without blemish. But both women embarrassed the most powerful men of their times— Hutchinson a prominent minister and the governing clergy of the colony, Hill a Supreme Court nominee and the governing party of the nation. As a result, both became the subject of bizarre and symbolic scrutiny, not of the factual or intellectual content of their ideas or testimony but of their sexuality.

Hutchinson challenged the clergy's religious views, at first privately in her own home and only among women, but eventually to "promiscuous" audiences (meaning both women and men) and then more publicly. For her unseemly behavior she was subjected to public inquisition, excommunication, exile, and more: She was labeled a Jezebel, after the wife of Ahab in the Old Testament's Book of Kings. Jezebel used her sexual powers to persuade her husband to forsake Jehovah. By the seventeenth century, Jezebel's name had come to symbolize a very specific evil: a woman whose sexuality threatened the well-being of the community. By her rebellious, unfeminine preaching, Anne Hutchinson represented female sexuality out of control, and for nearly three centuries thereafter, her name could be invoked to silence would-be activist women.

Had Anita Hill been the little boy in the fairy story who recognizes that the emperor had no clothes, she likely would have been hailed a public hero for the courage of her words. But as a woman whose testimony, however reluctantly offered, posed questions about the supposedly private actions of a public man, she was a Jezebel. It was her sexual behavior put on trial by her publicly coming forward, not that of the Supreme Court nominee who stood accused of breaking the very laws against sexual harassment that it had been his job, as chair of the Equal Employment Opportunity Commission, to uphold.

In the same way Anne Hutchinson's religious temerity caused her judges to label her "A verye dayngerous Woman," Anita Hill found herself tarred by accusers. A Yale Law School classmate named John Doggett testified imaginatively of Hill's "sexual fantasies" regarding not only Clarence Thomas but all the powerful young black male legal superstars who were her peers, including himself. Hill was labeled a perjurer by Senator Arlen Specter; a probable wanton who found inspiration for her filthy testimony in questionable books, according to Senator Orrin G.

Hatch; and a jealous woman whose unrequited longing for a relationship with Thomas had taken a vengeful turn by others on the all-male Senate Judiciary Committee.

Given the Jezebel legacy, the discomfort created by women's still relatively recent arrival in politics is understandable. For most of our history, the idea of women serving in public office was beyond merely radical, the very concept "public woman" was either an oxymoron or an epithet synonymous with "prostitute."

Because of the Jezebel legacy, virtually every life-style choice plays differently for a male politician than for a female. While the fact that these differences exist at first may seem unimportant or just "natural," they are, in fact, neither. In interviews and conversations with innumerable political women over more than two years, it became clear these differences are connected to messages about expectations and limits on both female motivation and behavior that today's voters, as well as today's politicians, internalized early in life. Sometimes the difficulties one woman encountered may have been specific to a region or to one political campaign and not at all universal, yet the feelings that individual

By permission of Mike Luckovich and Creators Syndicate

woman described shed light on the unique emotional tangles faced by other public women—again, simply because they are female not male. Even the most trivial-seeming aspects of a political woman's life, from her hemlines to her hair style, reveal clues to the more complex and constant challenge of establishing female authority and, in the long run, equal citizenship.

Tracing what political women have chosen to wear—what might seem the most trivial of her decisions related to public life—provides insight into this peculiar status. Early political women among them the New Deal's labor secretary Frances Perkins and Molly Dewson, were careful to dress in what appears now as an almost masculine version of women's attire in order to deflect further criticism of their mentors for having allowed a woman so much power. The choice of dress was undoubtedly an attempt to deflect the sexual innuendo that was certain to be used to explain the rise of a woman to such high rank. Until very recently, this asexual or male model was the rule not the exception for political women.

Jeannette Rankin, in her early campaign for suffrage in Montana, won in 1914, felt she and her army of suffragists had a "double role to play," according to her niece Mackey Brown's remembrances. They dressed and behaved accordingly: "They had to call on influential citizens like perfect little ladies, and at the same time nerve themselves up to rather brazen 'unladylike' behavior in the street at meetings. In short, they had to be both demure and aggressive. They had to appeal to the miner, the cowhand, the banker, and the saloon keeper—and their frequently antagonistic wives."[12]

A decade later, in 1923, the handful of females among newly elected Idaho legislators were warned "never carry a pocketbook or bag" or wear Flapper earrings, lest they appear frivolous. They also were cautioned not to wear skirts so short that colleagues might look at their ankles instead of listening to what was being said,[13] lest they appear sexual. Edith Nourse Rogers, Republican congresswoman from Massachusetts who succeeded her husband in 1925 and remained in the House until 1960, once remarked: "A suit blends in. It doesn't stand out like a sore thumb."[14]

The psychological constraints and history behind the uniform cloaked a delicate problem: how first to be taken seriously, not sexually; how then to overcome the stereotype of women as frilly, fussy beings; how next to assume the authority granted men virtually as a birthright and be, in camouflage if not reality, one of the boys; and, the final step on the evolutionary path to equality, to be able to be who they are and represent their own sex's particular interests. The way political women have dressed is a visual clue to what they believed was expected of them and what they felt they had to do to accomplish the task at hand. Using modest dress or a malelike uniform to overcome the temptress label was a strategy as blatant as the protective coloring a bird might evolve in the wild. The sad reality is, of course, this survival strategy reflected the compromises with femaleness and her own sense of self that the individual woman felt necessary to achieve the political goals she set herself.

The interesting insight to be gleaned from tracing women's universal concern about dress is how pervasive men's fear of distracting female sexuality must have been, and perhaps still is, and how discombobulated men have been at the threat of having women as colleagues or equals. One speech—ramblings, really—by Massachusetts's Charles Gifford, one of the more senior and most respected members of the 80th Congress (1947–49), indicates a very real confusion about what would be required in this brave new world that, that year, included a grand total of ten congresswomen.[15]

Mr. Speaker. . . . I have my anxieties about the present Congress and the future. . . . I am anxious to know what the new members will bring us. . . . As I look to my left, I see the face of a new lady member. . . . May I say to her, one of the great worries I have in Congress itself is lest we have too many of you. Although I say this in a somewhat jocular way, still I am a little serious about it.

The lady members we have today are extremely satisfactory to us. But they, like all women, can talk to us with their eyes and their lips, and when they present to us an apple it is most difficult to refuse. Even old Adam could not resist. Women have a language all their own. I do not like to particularize but I should. I see the gentlewoman from Ohio [Frances Bolton] is present. I read or listen carefully to everything she says on the floor . . . because I admire her so much I could hardly resist. I fear supporting any measure that she would propose, especially if she looked at me as such a woman can. The gentlewoman from Maine [Margaret Chase Smith] . . . never seems to have a vacant chair beside her that I could take and get acquainted with her . . . these ladies are so attractive. They are dangerous in that they may influence us too much. Suppose we had fifty of them. Seemingly, I note flirtations enough now, but what would there be with fifty of them?[16]

How to deflect this sort of attention to their sex, without seeming hostile, and, the next step, gain their colleagues' grudging acceptance has required women's attention to details no male politician could have even imagined.

Ohio Republican Frances Bolton, then a sixty-one-year-old widow and three-term veteran of the House (she assumed her husband's seat in 1940), was the congresswoman Gifford "could hardly resist." From 1940 to the end of the 1960s, the stern-visaged Bolton was the "official guardian of female deportment, cautioning other female House members about chewing gum and wearing curlers on the floor."[17]

The concern about dress is not limited to Congress. Gail Schoettler, interviewed in her second term as state treasurer of Colorado, used a consultant to renew her wardrobe after her 1988 divorce. In part, she said, it was because "being female I wanted color and style," rather than the severe, understated suits to which she had become accustomed. In part, she also admitted, it was because "I don't want to look like I'm out to grab the next man who walks by."[18]

For openly lesbian politicians, of whom there are very few—among them two San Francisco supervisors, Carole Migden and Roberta Achtenberg (who at this writing is under vitriolic attack by Senator Jesse Helms of North Carolina in Senate confirmation hearings for her appointment as Undersecretary of Housing and Urban Development)—the clothes issue is the same: how to avoid calling attention to sex and sexuality in order to establish their authority. "If it puts people more at ease because I'm in a dress at a house party. . . . then I'm going to wear a dress so they can be open to hearing me and to something they would never imagine doing: voting to put a lesbian in office," Migden explained.[19]

Widow's weeds are the only garb that appears to have guaranteed women unquestioned access to the seats of power. During her unsuccessful race for election to the U.S. Senate seat from Alabama, which she had inherited six months earlier when her husband, James, died, Democrat Maryon Pittman Allen was advised: "Wrap that widow's veil around you, baby,"[20] clearly an injunction to cling to the coverture and greater male authority that her husband could provide, even posthumously. In other words, widow's weeds would neutralize her sexually, if only briefly. They quash only temporarily the sexual innuendo that dogs women politicians. "An attractive widow serving in the 95th Congress" put it this way: "I work hard, and I don't run around with the men here. I don't flirt with anyone, and I have gained the admiration and respect of my colleagues."[21]

Among the handful of widows in the 95th Congress (1977–79) were that era's only two women senators, Maryon Pittman Allen and Muriel Buck Humphrey, and Congresswoman Corrine "Lindy" Boggs. To make the point that it is unlikely any of their male colleagues were worried about what their own dress conveyed, whether their intellectual reputations were intact, or whether anyone might condemn their manner as flirtatious, even if it were blatantly so, seems obvious.

Amazingly the problem did not stop with these women or their pre–women's movement generation, although it began to take on a slightly nuanced symbolism. A number of unlikely modern-day congresswomen have expressed anxiety about dress. Louise Slaughter, a honey-toned Southern-born Democrat elected to Congress from New York in 1986, recalls being "told to wear black so I would look more serious."[22] Barbara Boxer recalls being told to "tone down [the] California brightness."[23] Even Bella Abzug has confided that her signature hats were not a fashion statement, but her signal to male attorneys, adopted early in her law career, that she was a colleague, someone to be taken seriously, and not a secretary who, although she did not say this, might be treated as a sex object.[24] It was also a way of appropriating a form of male authority, or establishing that she as a woman had equivalent authority. But even later, as a congresswoman, formidable and feminist though she had become, Abzug admitted in her journal how she still felt it necessary to rely on her hats to signal her personal clout:

> Tonight as I was getting my hair done in the House Beauty Parlor, I was sitting under a hair dryer next to Louise Day Hicks [a Massachusetts Democrat who served one term, 1971–73] and the first thing she said to me was, "What are you going to wear tomorrow? Long or short?"
>
> I decided to wear a short dress so I could also wear a hat. I didn't want to deprive the President [Nixon] of that great event. I figured I'd let him see me in my whole regalia.[25]

Even in 1992, Senate candidate Patty Murray found her hairstyle the subject of press scrutiny—"so she got a haircut more often," her campaign consultant Beth Sullivan said, then added exasperatedly, "But when a man gets a haircut he's taking care of business. For a woman, it's vanity." Bush campaign operative Mary Matalin concurs. "Women in politics who look chic are perceived as frivolous," she told *Vogue* magazine (November 1991). "If you're pulled together that means you've been shopping . . . instead of laboring over papers . . . fifteen hours a day. . . . Besides, every woman who looks good gets hit on, and after a while they just don't want to be hassled."

But an important change: Women now strut their female uniqueness. "This hair is no accident," Ann Richards crows. "It is obvious that I am female. I have never run from being female and I suggest you not run from it either," the governor counseled a group of political women gathered in 1991 by the Women's Campaign Fund (WCF). Still, she said, it's a "drag" to worry about it.

At a San Francisco fund-raiser early in her 1992 Senate campaign, Geraldine Ferraro noted the number of women present who were wearing the same vibrant shade of red. "What did you all do, call each other up and see what to wear?" Then, when the chuckles died down, she lamented, "Imagine the men calling each other in the morning. 'Hey, are we wearing the old-school or power-red [ties] today?'" Ferraro had her audience, a group of high-powered California businesswomen, gathered in banker Fran Streets's executive dining room, in the palm of her hand and her point was well taken. Just what does a woman candidate wear to look senatorial? It is one thing to dress for success; it is another to dress as a voter expects her or his senator to dress. And for women, of course, there is the added problem of avoiding any sexual message in her attire.

The corporate women gathered in that executive dining room understood Ferraro's problem: For them, a change of power ties simply would not make the same suit do for three days of a more conventional business trip any more than a senatorial campaign. Ferraro drew laughs as she grinned and shrugged, "It's easier for the guys."

"It's easier for the guys" could be called Ferraro's First Law of Gender Politics. In interview after interview, political women expressed similar sentiments: No matter what her education, experience, proven leadership ability, or charisma, the simple fact that she is biologically different has been a potentially damaging political destiny. No one put it more succinctly than Ferraro. Not even the wonderful imagery in the rousing keynote address of Texas's Ann Richards to the 1988 Democratic National Convention said it better, though Richards certainly made clear how much easier it is for the guys: "After all," she reminded a cheering crowd, "Ginger Rogers did everything Fred Astaire did. She just did it backwards and in high heels."[26]

Richards's glib phrase also cloaked another interesting insight into female political style. Because of the particular constraints upon female behavior, women's paths to power, a subject we will deal with more directly in a later chapter, have not been as direct as those of men. Little girls seldom say they are going to grow up to be president; they express more selfless career goals, ones they have been socialized to know are acceptable for their sex. Political ambition or a "lust for power"—a telling phrase that expresses our psychological insights into the power-sex conundrum—is deemed inappropriate in women. Robert Mann, a former Illinois state senator who has backed Carol Moseley-Braun's career since the 1970s, recalled the fury she created when she attempted to run for lieutenant governor without party permission. "Carol is an ambitious woman and that's a sin in our society," he told the *Chicago Sun Times*.

Because there still are constraints to how aggressive, ambitious, or improperly power-hungry any woman may allow herself to appear, dancing backwards—consciously working toward a style that does not confront, indeed follows the lead of, male norms—has been a clever strategy to deal with a sexually hostile environment, even while it has caused many a woman politician to repeat feminist Jill Ruckelshaus's famous advice that women stop waiting to be asked to dance. Dancing backwards, or waiting to be asked to dance, or any other metaphorically expressed strategy political women have used to deflect disapproval, has direct links to the Jezebel legacy.

As Senator Barbara Mikulski explains, there is not even a best life-style option for the woman who would run for office. Whether she is Ms., Mrs., or Mommy it can be a role that has sexual connotations which trouble the voters. And yet, as 1992's early presidential contenders demonstrated, neither bachelorhood sans children (Jerry Brown) nor marriage with kids (Tom Harkin, Paul Tsongas, Bill Clinton, George Bush), nor rumors of infidelity (Bill Clinton, George Bush), nor divorce and a very public affair with a well-known actress (Bob Kerrey) will automatically discredit a male candidate. But imagine the scandal had a woman candidate and former governor been known to have allowed a male movie star to sleep over at the mansion, à la Kerrey and Debra Winger. Imagine the uproar were a sitting female governor to name a live-in friend Official State Host and then delegate the refurbishing of the governor's mansion to her semi-official First Companion à la Maryland governor William D. Schaefer's "longtime sidekick" and Official State Hostess, Hilda Mae Snoops.[27]

Being single is no protection from critical review of one's personal life.

A single woman politician, without family to provide the paternalistic equivalent of coverture, will be gay-baited, or lusted after, or pestered with questions about why she can't get a man. Or all three. In one of Mikulski's early Baltimore City Council races, her campaign manager was incredulous: "They said she was sleeping with the Black Panthers. All of them." Mikulski herself laughed when she recalled that every member of her staff and campaign was asked why she wasn't married. "So once I was asked to my face and I said, 'Cause nobody ever asked me.'"[28]

The evolution apparent in the career of veteran Montana state legislator Dorothy Bradley is a hopeful sign. She first ran for office in 1970 when she was just twenty-three. "Having led a sheltered life" had not prepared her for campaigning in country bars and facing some of the preconceptions their patrons had about women and politics:

> I ran into a serious old gentleman who questioned me on "what interesting thing I was going to do up there." Following the advice of my many helpers, I responded . . . "What interesting things would you like me to do up there?" He scratched his head, and a small smile crept across his face. "Wahl," he said, "how about an affair with the governor?"[29]

Bradley won that and subsequent races and ran for governor in 1992. An indication that women are beginning to demand they be allowed to be who they are and be free of Jezebel, Bradley flouted conventional concerns about female sexuality by openly admitting her relationship with a divorced man as well as ignoring rumors about an homosexual friend. "Voters are grownups, too," she explained. Her very narrow defeat was attributed to the voters' fear of a sales tax, not to concerns her love life or social circle posed a threat.

Bradley's experience is virtually unique among political women at her level. Just being strong, powerful, and female subjects a woman politician to speculation about her sexuality or "true womanhood," regardless of her marital or maternal status, or even her age. Witness the "outing" of Attorney General Janet Reno by a gay journalist who reportedly admitted he had only assumed, being single, she was a sexual fellow traveler. Reno denied the charge.

The advent of the religious radical right wing in the last few years has brought a new level of ugliness to these kinds of sexual attacks. When San Diegan Kathy Frasca and other concerned southern California women launched the Mainstream Voters Project (MVP) to counter "stealth" school board candidates, they were attacked in vicious anonymous leaflets. One was described as "a Democrat who wanted to be born a man but fate . . . gave her a womb instead." A Republican MVP member "is always having her 'period' . . . resulting in . . . sporadic babbling seizures." One founder was "rumored to have no vagina"; another "uses MVP to meet other women with hairy chests," the leaflets charged.

Seasoned political women have learned, have had to learn, to shrug off such accusations. When Oregon governor Barbara Roberts heard rumors she was gay during her campaign, she shrugged it off with a dry "Who has time?"[30] EMILY's List founder Ellen Malcolm recalls a 1991 conversation with a number of Democratic women candidates running for the U.S. Senate or governorships—all but one of whom were married and had children: "Every one of them had been gay-baited," Malcolm said.[31] During research for this book, a nationally known male political consultant took one of us aside and asked, in a confidential whisper, if gossip that "Ann Richards is really a lesbian" were true. Richards, the mother of four and a grandmother, has learned to laugh at these sorts of rumors. When she first ran for county office, "I told David [her former husband] when we started that he would hear that I was sleeping with every man in Travis County. What he heard was I was sweet on Sarah Weddington."[32]

Despite the persistence of such questions about powerful political women's "real sexuality," it appears in some areas that actually being gay, or at least being openly gay, no longer carries the opprobrium it once did for political candidates. No openly lesbian women have run for major offices, although two avowedly gay congressmen, Massachusetts's Barney Frank and Gerry Studds, have broken the barrier. In June 1991, New York City Council candidate Liz Abzug, the second generation of feminist New York Abzugs, revealed she is lesbian when she announced for office—only to find herself not gay-baited, but one-upped. Her gay opponent, Tom Duane, announced he was both Abzug's equal on the issues and HIV-positive. The third Democrat, schoolteacher Victor Del Mastro, declared himself a practicing heterosexual who was better on the issues. Duane won the September primary.

In more traditional campaigns in which a man and a woman are pitted against one another, for men it can be a strategic ploy to put into play questions of a woman's sexual or domestic situation. Merely having to deal with this extraneous "issue" politically disadvantages a woman. Derogatory comments about women's sexuality—their lesbianism or libertinism, or their prudishness or sexlessness, comments about their charm and attractiveness or lack thereof, references to their time of life or time of the month—all speak to whatever level of discomfort an individual voter may still feel when his or her stereotypes of appropriate male and female roles are challenged.

That discomfort with gender role shifts is revealed in male colleagues' private assessments of political women. During the Abscam trials of House members accused of taking bribes from FBI undercover agents disguised as Arab sheiks, "Secret tape recordings . . . had one male Representative referring casually to a Congresswoman whose suggested 'meanness' was a product of her ' . . . never [having] been laid.'"[33] Even EMILY's List came in for this sort of ridicule when it became a political power. The political newsletter *Pacs & Lobbies* derided it under a headline "Below the Beltway" and a subhead "Girls Will Be Girls: "There's some whining going on at EMILY's List . . . an outburst of PMS (that would be Political Money Stress, of course). . . . It came after EMILY (Early Money Is Like Yeast) endorsed Geraldine Ferraro, not Elizabeth Holtzman in New York's senatorial primary. . . . "[34]

This sort of discussion takes the sexually hostile environment as antifemale strategy one step further by questioning a woman's legitimacy: Is Politician Jane really the person she presents herself to be? Is she a true woman or some sort of deviation who can be dismissed as such? Is she tough enough to play political hardball? Or is she so tough that her malelike mannerisms will compromise her ability to get along if she is elected?

As every woman politician discovers when male colleagues or the press inject her physical or sexual attributes into the public debate, it has the effect of trivializing, even negating, the message she is attempting to articulate. In her 1990 governor's race, Evelyn Murphy was referred to in Boston's capitol hill press room and in print as "a Michael Dukakis with tits."[35] It is an old tactic: In her 1950 Senate race Helen Gahagan Douglas was labeled by Richard M. Nixon "pink—right down to her underwear."[36]

"The image of the congresswoman as a curiosity appears to have influenced the treatment she received. . . . She was patronized, condescended to, and ignored or dismissed by her colleagues," especially early on.[37] In other words, there is a corollary to the Ferraro Law on Gender

Politics: It is easier for the guys to be taken seriously. Guys belong. Men are not a curiosity.

To say that the early women in Congress suffered these indignities in silence misses the strategic effectiveness of silence as another form of dancing backwards, conforming to male expectations, gaining acceptance with a purdahlike deference, avoiding sexual conflict by not even challenging verbally, a contest men sometimes describe as "getting into a pissing match," the protocols of the sexually hostile environment.

In the Senate, Kansan Nancy Kassebaum has relied on her dual senses of irony and humor to gain the floor and speak. But she recalls that she once had to remind her colleagues on the Foreign Relations Committee, where she is a ranking member, that she would be "no Silent Hattie,"[38] a reference to Senator Hattie Caraway of Arkansas, "who seldom spoke on the Senate floor, preferring to do crossword puzzles during debate."[39]

"Silent Hattie" was only the second woman senator, and she inherited her seat in 1931 when her husband, Thaddeus, died in office, and served until 1945. "It was her misfortune to be a nice little old lady, very unassuming and quiet, thrust by a whim of the electorate into a job far beyond her capacities," journalist Allen Drury commented.[40] But Senator Caraway's own wry explanation of her reticence suggests still waters that ran somewhat deeper than Drury's derisive appraisal: "The men have left nothing unsaid."[41]

Silent Hattie Caraway might have added that the men of Congress seemed to prefer "their women" that way—"ladies" who are anything but verbal. One congresswoman exploded at a senior committee chair who would not sign a travel voucher for an expense reimbursement, and said, "'The only reason you won't sign is that I have a vagina,' [to which] the chairman is reported to have replied: 'Well, if you used your vagina more and your mouth less you might get someplace around here."[42] On another occasion, outspoken New Jersey congresswoman Millicent Fenwick so frustrated her Ohio colleague Wayne Hays, chairman of the House Ways and Means Committee, he threatened to withhold her staff's paychecks "if that woman doesn't sit down and keep quiet." (Hays is better remembered as the Democrat whose career abruptly ended after Elizabeth Ray, a striking blond clerk in his House office, told a reporter in 1976 that she did no office work for her $14,000 a year, and, moreover, could not even type.)

One political woman in the late 1940s noted that men consider government "a man's business and did not want women's intrusion," and, a more critical point, the men "never felt that a woman could speak for women"[43] and went out of their way to kill their female colleagues' efforts, even if sometimes with "kindness."

> "To the ladies, God bless them; they lend sweetness and light to our somber legislative halls" was among the choicest bouquets tossed in their direction. On one occasion Mary Norton of New Jersey was so exasperated by these comments she cried out "I'm no lady. I'm a congressman."[44]

The "exasperating" gallantry to which congresswomen traditionally have been subjected can be explained partially by the fact that the early examples, the foremost exception being Jeannette Rankin, were the recent widows of esteemed male legislators. Maryon Pittman Allen, who was appointed senator from Alabama when her husband died in 1978, wrote that she had been treated "with the greatest respect for my abilities . . . with tenderness and touching love for the wife of a fallen colleague . . . and the most splendid show of courtly manners any lady ever basked in."[45] Interestingly, however, Senator Allen followed that comment with a revealing anecdote about Senator John Tower of Texas "belting forth some of his splendid oratory" at a time when she was presiding over the Senate. "Although he was looking at me as he spoke, and I was giving him my undivided attention, John persisted in saying 'Mr. President,'"[46]

The gallantry extended a newly widowed woman who had inherited her husband's congressional seat clearly reflects the residues of coverture. One congressman, who was critical of widows succeeding their husbands, said, "Mrs.——sits there prettily and never says anything. People ignore her. She is strictly her husband's stand in. . . ."[47]

The extension of this fawning chivalry to nonwidows in Congress, or to females who are running for office, addressing a legislative body, or testifying before a congressional committee, symbolically lumps all women in with those accidental congresspersons as outsiders, not-to-be-taken-seriously candidates, or not-to-be-listened-to representatives on issues. One congresswoman said that her male colleagues treated women like tables: "If you dust them off once a day, they will be kept quite happy."[48]

One contemporary incident suggests the lingering result of this symbolic segregation of men as real political players and women as token stand-ins. During the September 1990 hearings of the all-male Judiciary Committee on the Supreme Court nomination of Judge David H. Souter, South Carolina's Strom Thurmond made headlines with his treatment of feminist witnesses: "Mr. Chairman, we have a group of lovely ladies here," he said tonelessly. "We thank you for your presence. I have no questions."[49]

The "ladies" in question included NOW president Molly Yard, feminist attorney Gloria Allred, former congresswoman Elizabeth Holtzman, and Fund for the Feminist Majority president Eleanor Smeal. (One small irony that puts Thurmond's courtly if archaic "ladies" reference into a different syntactical context and perhaps conveys some of the dissonance Yard et al. felt: That same week the International Revenue Service seized a legendary Nevada whorehouse for back taxes. Rather than close the brothel, the IRS offered the "ladies" of the night, now in Uncle Sam's employ, a better cut of their client fee as an incentive to get the ailing business back on its feet.)

The "ladies" who had come to testify against Souter read into Thurmond's remark and his abrupt dismissal of them a condescension for their sex as well as their cause. They reacted with exasperated shrugs, prompting Senator Alan Simpson of Wyoming to scold them harshly.

> Yard spoke next and by way of "apologizing" to Thurmond "if he didn't like my glances," took up Simpson's challenge . . .
>
> "We are greeted every time we come before him as, 'Ladies, you're all so attractive,'" she said, drawing snickers for her imitation of Thurmond. "Maybe you could explain to him that we would like to be treated the way you treat everybody else. You don't say to men, 'Gentlemen, you all look lovely.'"[50]

Eleanor Smeal later told reporters she felt they had been "lectured like schoolgirls. We were powerless,"[51] summing up precisely why political women have tried so long and so hard to deflect comment on their appearance, including even the awareness that they are female. No man would be so dismissed or, more importantly, could be so dismissed.

Whether Thurmond's insult was intentional or not, one reason to have gone into this relatively recent incident at such length is that the attitude it reveals is an ongoing complication in women's quest to have their authority taken seriously, how to get their legislative agenda taken seriously. If women can be so easily dismissed because of their sexuality, which, in effect, says women are to be taken seriously only by their various sexual connections to men, their public policy needs can be dismissed as well.

Congresswoman Schroeder recounts how she and other women members of the Congressional Caucus on Women's Issues went to the National Institutes of Health (NIH) early in the 1980s and pointed out how few of NIH's scientific studies included women.

"They said, 'Oh, yeah!' It was like a light went on. 'There's no need for legislation, "ladies." We are an enlightened group of scientists. We will immediately put new rules into effect.' Then in 1988 we went to the Government Accounting Office and asked how the new rules were working. It was devastating. . . . [The NIH] wasn't even using female rats in their experiments! What they had done was the typical 'pat-the-Congresswoman-on-the-head bit.'"[52]

A new breed of women political professionals increasingly has learned to work past, indeed to laugh off or see as quaint, the courtliness of a Charles Gifford type and the veiled hostility of a Strom Thurmond. The late Republican congresswoman Millicent Fenwick "often charmed her ideological adversaries" by using men's sexist remarks to her own advantage: "In a debate over equal rights for women, she once recalled, a male legislator said: 'I just don't like this amendment. I've always thought of women as kissable, cuddly, and smelling good.' Her reply was classic Fenwick: 'That's the way I feel about men, too. I only hope for your sake that you haven't been disappointed as often as I have.'"[53]

Despite women's advances, the strategic message in such "gentlemanly" political behavior is that "ladies" still do not completely belong, should not run, and may not be accepted by "the guys" if they win. This subtle message is one that male candidates hit hard, if disingenuously, in campaigns against women, and suggests another rendering of Ferraro's Law: It will be easier for the guys to get things done once in office.

The attitude that women do not, or cannot, belong is yet another expression of society's continuing confusion over the relationship between sex and power. While women did everything from modify their dress and demeanor to shut their mouths to deflect criticism for their unseemly desire to participate in the political system, those strategies have been both psychologically damaging and self-defeating. By bowing to the stereotypes, even if it was strategically savvy to do so at the time, the women themselves have helped perpetuate the voters' widely held beliefs that politics is still a dirty place, too dirty a place for a "nice girl like you." The dirty stereotypes provide the fuel that feeds the perpetual motion machine that the sexually hostile environment can become.

The dirty stereotypes worked against women getting the vote, and then for the next half century they worked against any organized attempts to back women for office. Even as late as the 1950s, the only acceptable rationale for a woman to venture into politics was to do good and clean up. "There was a hortatory tone in magazine stories aimed at getting women into politics—picturing them as 'shining Joans of Arc leading the forces of righteousness' and wielding 'the scrub brush of reform,'"[54] but not the reins of political power. The nonpartisan nature of various women's political organizations—from the League of Women Voters, founded in the 1920s, to the National Organization for Women, (NOW) in the 1960s, and the fact that it was only with the founding of the self-styled "multipartisan" National Women's Political Caucus (NWPC) in 1971 that women actually began to be recruited and encouraged to run—are the lingering result of this attitude.

Women's own discomfort with the sexual implications of the body politic's more bawdy aspects, and the mixed message—of selfishness and sin—inherent in women's quest for power compounded the problem by delaying the entrance of whole generations of women into public life. The psychologically painful legacy of this strategy is the marked ambivalence of some women politicians, even today, to describe themselves as such: "Do I feel comfortable referring to myself as a politician? I don't," former Rhode Island congresswoman Claudine Schneider admits.

The origins of the modern-day politics-is-too-dirty/women-are-too-good prejudice are easy to discern. One obvious cause was the fact that women used their presumed better-than-thou status to first get their foot in the political door—asserting, as did one author in 1870, that "Uncle Sam is an old bachelor who needs a woman's touch."[55] It was this reputation for purity that encouraged Senator A. A. Sargeant of California to introduce a suffrage amendment in 1878: "I believe that by bringing the intelligence, the virtue, the good intentions possessed by the women of America to the ballot-box, we may have better politics, less grog shops, less hells of iniquity, and an improvement in every direction."[56] The fact that some states until recent times have closed bars and liquor stores on election day is also a reflection of the fact that in the last century, before the adoption of the secret ballot, the polls were likely raucous, drunken places no properly brought-up female would dare enter. Although with suffrage polling places were moved from bars and pool halls to schools and firehouses, North Dakota still went so far as to require women to use separate ballot boxes[57] and Missouri attempted to keep women voters safe from the process altogether by requiring them to vote on pink ballots—a practice declared a violation of the secret ballot in 1920.[58]

The politics-is-too-dirty prejudice is also a reaction to our very real history of corrupt big-city machines, venal politicians, licentious polling places, and state houses that have functioned socially more like bachelor quarters or the parlors of houses of ill repute than branches of government. Indeed, Sargeant's 1878 suffrage amendment was met with scorn by Senator George Vest of Missouri, who proclaimed the vote would "unsex our mothers, wives and sisters. . . . It will turn our blessed country's domestic peace into ward assembly rooms."[59]

Politics is dirty, to which the sex scandals that dominated many 1992 races give evidence. But there was a new element of female rage in 1992 with which miscreant male politicians had to deal. Tabloid charges from a woman who claimed she had had a twelve-year ongoing affair with Arkansas governor Bill Clinton threatened briefly to derail his presidential campaign. In March, Senator Brock Adams of Washington was forced to drop his reelection bid after the *Seattle Times* devoted its Sunday front page and three full pages inside to a three-year investigation of sex charges against the senator by former staffers and other women. The women's statements alleged that he had drugged and fondled some of them and forced drunken kisses on others. One said he had raped her. Adams responded to the charges much as he had three years earlier to a young aide's similar story of having been drugged and then molested: He tried to tar his accusers with what might be called a Jezebel defense: "They are just trying to ruin my career."

At this writing, Senator Daniel Inouye of Hawaii stands accused of rape, and demands by citizens' groups for the resignation of Senator Robert Packwood of Oregon, who has been accused of sexual misconduct by more than two dozen women, have launched a Senate probe. A twenty-year-old wire service photo of one of Packwood's alleged victims shows a pretty home-state teen beauty queen, a smile frozen on her face, and her eyes wide with alarm, as she is nuzzled by the lasciviously grinning senator. It makes the young woman's feelings so clear that a sexual harassment victims' rights group could use it as a poster.

The stories told by Adams's and Packwood's accusers were a disturbing reminder of a November 1991 conversation between a woman state legislator and the authors of this book at a conference given by the Eagleton Institute's Center for the American Woman and Politics at Rutgers University. Asked why she had delayed running for office until her fifties, after a particularly promising start as a campaign volunteer when she was in college, the well-known state legislator and political activist said bluntly that her candidate, a major city's mayor who is expected to run for higher office in 1994, had raped her.

"It took me a long time to be able to face the fact," she said. "I guess I thought it had been my fault." She was eighteen at the time, and, she explained, it was only years later that she was able to admit to herself that she had not been just forcibly seduced, as a result of some unknown invitation or weakness on her part, but raped.

She could not articulate why she had felt that the rape had been her fault; she did, however, make clear what had sent her fleeing into an early marriage and the safety of housewifery, and kept her from continuing her precocious political career: The sexually predatory behavior of too many of the men in politics meant she would have risked further abuse.

When Congresswoman Jill Long revealed, during the week in which the world learned of Anita Hill and her charges, that, despite her own status as a colleague and an equal, she, too, had been a victim, she made it clear that for women, the world of politics is still a sexually hostile place. But she also made it clear that women will no longer flee from the public arena simply because they are made to feel uncomfortable and unwelcome, nor any longer will they suffer the indignities in silence and powerlessness.

Obviously, political women have come a long way from the days of pink ballots and male fears that political equality would unsex the nation's womanhood—or somehow unsex the men. But where those sorts of macho attitudes about women's place persist—and they do— even most men now realize that they are incompatible with accepting women as equals and colleagues, and incompatible with the progress Carol Bellamy predicted could only come after women were free to know themselves, be themselves, and speak for themselves. More significantly, those sorts of attitudes are incompatible with women citizens' public policy needs. In 1990, after Louisiana state representative Odon Bacque tried to introduce a bill to criminalize marital rape, the Louisiana legislature, "a bastion of good-ole-boy buffoonery" according to *The Washington Post,* literally hooted, "snickered and guffawed" him down. "With 102 men and three women in the House, they tend to have the mentality where women are considered objects and property," Bacque complained. "These men are here for three months, most of them without their wives. They tend to party and carry on and have a good time, and the whole atmosphere, to put it mildly, is not sensitive to the needs of women."[60]

The Louisiana legislature's behavior is exceptional only in its extremes. It is merely more evidence of a continuum in male response to women's attempts to participate as equals in politics. Three decades ago, when the pioneering feminist congresswoman Martha Griffiths, who served from 1955 until 1974, spearheaded the campaign to have the word *sex* included in the language of the 1964 Civil Rights Act, her colleagues "just went into roars." In a speech at the National Press Club in 1991, she recalled with outrage the stereotypical reasoning and sniggering some of the most respected men in politics used in an attempt to keep women in their place. "The mere thought of getting women civil rights was just laughable."[61]

The Civil Rights Act covered everything from voting rights and public accommodations to workplace equity. Griffiths's amendment helped create the language that has allowed us to put a name to the age-old offenses "sex discrimination" and "sexual harassment." However, the bill's sponsor, New York congressman Emanuel Celler, "protested . . . designation of women as a 'minority' stating that [situation] certainly wasn't true in his house, where after nearly fifty years of marriage 'I would suggest [the reason] that we have been living in such harmony, such delightful accord for almost half a century is that I usually have the last two words, and those words are "Yes, dear." '"[62] In other words, in his house a woman wielded the sexual power of Jezebel that men so fear.

The inability, even today, of some congressmen and other male politicians to deal with women and women's issues except with the same sort of sniggering and disdain is apparent. Congresswoman Schroeder complains her male colleagues "are so afraid of the reproductive thing," both because of the controversial nature of some of the issues and because they are uncomfortable dealing with the subject matter, that it is difficult to move legislation on issues critical to women's health. "They don't want to fund anything on women, reproduction, pregnancy, fetuses. . . . It's not malfeasance; it's nonfeasance—they really don't get it. In the breast cancer debate I had a couple of men come up to me and just chew me out for not pushing on prostate cancer. I'm like 'I really am concerned about that. Why I'm not mentioning it is because, I assumed, 95 percent of you being male, that you were going to handle it.' "[63]

Former Ohio congresswoman Mary Rose Oakar concurs. "I think it's a combination of many things . . . certainly some of the fellows here have told me that they have a hard time articulating problems . . . that dealt with organs such as our breasts."[64]

Political women no longer shy away from confronting the political ramifications of the fact that they and their sister citizens are complete biological, sexual, economic, and social creatures who just happen to be other than male. In directly confronting the issue, the men, and the elements of the bureaucracy such as the NIH that still put women into a "lesser creature" category, women have overcome much of the prejudice against their gender's participation in the process. They also have begun to speak out against the sexual harassment and sexual violence that was the ultimate threat inherent in those prejudices, and have turned the sexually hostile environment they face into a strategic issue for themselves and other women. In so doing they have made a case for women's issues that recaptures the historically empowering element of altruism, allowing them to openly push for women's issues, and have transcended suspicions that they are asking for unfair special treatment for their sex.

During the 1992 controversy over whether or not to ban silicone-gel breast implants, Tennessee congresswoman Marilyn Lloyd went public with the story of her own mastectomy and asked the National Institutes of Health, on behalf of herself and other breast cancer survivors, to allow women to continue having breast replacement surgery.

Schroeder jokes about spending her August recesses "explaining chlamydia to the Rotary Clubs all over the state of Colorado."[65] In her 1992 race for the Senate, Barbara Boxer tweaked any remaining male discomfort with members of the opposite sex with an item that became her campaign's best-selling fund-raising gimmick—BOXER shorts emblazoned with her last name. Feinstein openly confronted the notion of women as a sexual threat when she referred to herself and Boxer as Thelma and Louise, the sexually victimized movie heroines who took vengeance on their male harassers.

Schroeder, the founding co-chair of the Congressional Caucus on Women's Issues, confronted the issue most directly when she answered another of those probably inevitable, but nonetheless inane, questions with another of her off-quoted lines. The question was how she, a woman, could run for Congress: "I have a brain and a uterus, and I use both."

4

=

Squaring the Personal and the Political

The Liability of Being Ms., Mrs., or Mommy

" **D**earest little Susanna," begins a letter scrawled on stationery
from the Hotel Seneca in Rochester, New York. "Mother is
very tired . . . [and] is going straight to her little bed." There follows an
amateurish drawing of a mommy prostrate on a bed, then one last poignant line: "I wish S. were here to kiss me goodnight. . . . "[1]

There is no date on that letter from Frances Perkins to her daughter,
but the fact that it is written in a tired, loopy cursive suggests it may have
been several years after another mommy-daughter "Dearest Susanna"
missive, dated January 27, 1927, and carefully block-printed on
mommy's official stationery, that of chairman of the New York State Department of Labor. (The modern phrase "chairwoman" had not been
coined in Perkins's groundbreaking days, nor had today's concepts
"working mother," "superwoman," or "dual career couple" been born):

> I was so glad to get your lovely letter last night & particularly glad to have
> that lots & lots & lots & lots & lots & lots—of love!! . . . I am so sorry the
> gas went out. I suppose I had forgotten to pay the bill. Aren't they mean to
> shut it off just for that!! So glad father got it fixed. . . . The ice in N.Y. must

be wonderful. Don't fall & break your nose. [She includes a drawing of a little girl sprawling on an icy sidewalk.] . . . I love you dearly . . . "[2]

Frances Perkins, who became Franklin Roosevelt's secretary of labor (1933–45)—the first woman to hold a cabinet-level position and the first woman in the United States to hold national executive office—was also among that first generation of post-suffragists who tried to reconcile the jobs of political professional with those of wife and mother. There are few role models for such women now; there were none then.

Studies by the Eagleton Institute's Center for the American Woman and Politics at Rutgers University show that women have understood politics was not conducive to their having more, much less having it all. Fewer political women are married, and historically, those women who are and have children have delayed their entry into politics until their motherwork is done.[3] The mother of young children in politics is nearly as much a curiosity today as she was in Perkins's time, witness the press that attended Carol Browner, named in 1993 to head the Environmental Protection Agency (EPA), who was confirmed with a babe on her hip, or one of the first bits of speculation to emerge regarding President Bill Clinton's first, and ultimately failed, choice for attorney general, Zoë Baird. It was not whether, as a woman, she might be tougher on sexual discrimination cases, but that, as the mother of a three-year-old, she might become pregnant with a second child while a cabinet member. After that, the scrutiny of her child-care arrangements was almost predictable.

Some of the personal issues Perkins wrestled with—how to mother long distance (or between governmental crises), the guilt from off-loading domestic responsibilities onto a possibly also forgetful, overburdened spouse (forgetting to pay the gas bill in the middle of a New York winter!)—are the same issues political women have faced (and many still do face) since suffrage began to pry open the doors for female officeholders.

The mere fact that the doors were opening did not mean that the traditions and expectations of their mothers' generation would give up their demands on them. The mere fact that women had established their legal right to become candidates and officeholders did not absolve them from "women's work"—the multitude of family responsibilities that, according to the old truism, "is never done."

Indeed, until very recently, combining politics with a private life simply seemed impossible even to many of the strongest women. One example, Margaret Chase Smith, had many years out of office during which to reflect on her accomplishments when she confided to *The Washington Post's* Paul Hendrickson that she "would have loved to have had children . . . I've regretted [not having them] very much. Maybe the priorities were wrong. I don't know . . . I was only married 10 years [before being widowed]. It seems so long ago." She also candidly acknowledged the persistent Washington, D.C., rumors about her relationship with longtime aide William Lewis, and admitted: "Some people wondered why [we] never married. Well, our relationship wasn't based on that. . . . Of course we had a relationship. Of course we loved each other. But not like that. Looking back, I wish I would have made more time for love."[4]

In a profession—politics—in which self-esteem and energy level are virtual Siamese twins, both constantly in danger of becoming casualties, the burden for the woman politician is as many times greater than the same burden might be for her male colleague as the number of roles she plays in her life. The political woman often must be several persons, yet she is given the same twenty-four-hour day as a man.

All of the nonsense attached to stereotypes about what women are or should be has conspired over the years to dissuade women from running for public office. It has also undermined their support from parents, spouses, and voters when they try. The hard-campaigning wife or mother historically finds herself having to explain—to voters, colleagues, possibly even her own mother, her husband, and herself—why she's not home putting food on the table and otherwise caring for her family.

Just one example of many, Georgia's Virginia Shapard, said the critical issue in her 1978 congressional race against Republican Newt Gingrich was Gingrich's continually harping that office-holding would cause her to neglect her children. She described her decision to run as a "family decision," but a Gingrich campaign piece headlined "This Time You Have a Choice" cast doubt on that in a side-by-side comparison of the candidates' families with this line: "When elected, Newt will keep his family together."[5]

At the Republican National Convention in 1992, the showcasing of vice presidential wife Marilyn Quayle made that same side-by-side sort of comparison to Hillary Clinton. Because it was well known and understood that Mrs. Quayle, like Mrs. Clinton, was both an attorney and a member of the baby-boom generation that has challenged so many of the preexisting norms for what women were expected to be, she was able to cast herself as that old ideal, the "true woman" who welcomed the privileges of coverture. By inference, Hillary Clinton was painted as a sexual aberration, neglectful mother, and a possible too-powerful meddling wife—that is, a Jezebel. That evocation was particularly potent because Mrs. Clinton is a Yale Law School graduate, as is the other unnamed bogeywoman whose presence was felt at the GOP convention, Anita Hill.

With Mrs. Quayle's references to "the essential nature" of women, that which had been merely a subliminal political issue, floating in and out of the public consciousness for many years, became an explicit question that one party suggested the voters could decide: What is it America's women citizens are to be? Because women were naturally altruistic, Quayle claimed, and she offered herself as an example, they therefore could and should be expected to put their lives at the service of their families. Even though it became clear within weeks that what the press called "Hillary bashing" was not working, Mrs. Quayle had handed the issue of womanly correctness to any Republican, male or female, up against any of the Democratic women running for Congress.

Mrs. Quayle's speech followed Patrick Buchanan's opening-night remarks, which escalated conservative concerns about society's gender-role and ethnic changes to "cultural war." Later in the campaign, former presidential-candidate and televangelist Pat Robertson helped defeat an Iowa state equal rights amendment, as well as several Democratic women, with a fund-raising letter for the Christian Coalition in which he claimed that "feminists" were "a socialist, anti-family political movement that encourages women to leave their husbands, kill their children, practice witchcraft, destroy capitalism, and become lesbians"[6]

Robertson is the religious right wing's foremost champion of family values, and it may be instructive to take a closer look at his own commitment to family. He is another product of Yale's law school and the son of a former senator, but never himself a political officeholder. He married his wife, Dede, ten weeks before their first child was born, then went back to Yale to finish his law degree—without mentioning to his roommates he had married, or later that Dede (Adelia) had borne him a son.[7]

Later when she was bedridden with a miscarriage, Robertson prayed to God that he might not be "forced to stay home and take care of my wife."[8] When Dede was eight months' pregnant with their second child, according to The Washington Post, (September 11, 1987), Robertson went off to Canada to commune with God, despite Dede's frantic pleading that he not leave her alone with a toddler to move into a new house. The point: As difficult as it may be to believe, this man was considered a "significant" enough candidate, according to League of Women Voters criteria, to be included in the league-sponsored presidential primary debates.

Virtually no similar personal fact about a political woman would escape public critical review, even the most basic—her very name. Frances Perkins was criticized for not taking the name of her financial statistician husband, Paul Wilson, when they married. In 1984, Geraldine Ferraro was still treated as an anomaly because she used her "maiden" name out of respect for the widowed mother who sacrificed to raise her and put her through college. However, and more than one newspaper thought it such revealing news that it was trumpeted in headlines, for the eighteen years before she first ran for public office, she had voted as Geraldine Zaccaro, her husband's name. As Zaccaro, or an erstwhile Zaccaro but nonetheless a married woman, she was considered to be the puppet of her husband. As a born-again Ferraro, she was considered to be hypocritical or opportunistic—her cousin was then a well-known political figure in the same Queens district.[9] She was damned when she acceded to tradition and used her married name, and she was damned when she didn't.

The importance the press gave to that fact was never explained in the stories beneath the headlines; perhaps even the headline writers could not have explained their choice of emphasis. Today we no longer think of a woman moving under coverture when she marries—that is, ceasing to exist as a citizen except as cloaked in, or covered by, her husband's authority just as we no longer assume a married woman is "under her husband's thumb"—a linguistic artifact from the common law tradition that held a man legally could beat his wife but with a rod no larger than his thumb, "the rule of thumb." That these relics of an earlier age's attitudes linger in our language suggests that hidden in the psyches of the headline writers (and the society whose prejudices they reflect) was the perhaps not fully conscious notion that a three-term congresswoman and potential vice president of the United States could not be trusted to act on her own because she was a wife.

Perhaps a woman's decision to change or not to change her name at marriage would not seem a political issue, yet the issue has begun to prove troublesome for modern-day male politicians as well. Hillary Clinton belatedly adopted her husband's last name in deference to Arkansas voters,[10] who apparently worried that a governor whose wife would not take his name was less than a man, or under a woman's thumb. Early in the 1992 race, no less an expert than former president Richard Nixon suggested to *The New York Times* that the Clinton campaign would have to be careful about how it used Hillary Clinton, because "If the wife comes through as being too strong and too intelligent, it makes the husband look like a wimp," or somehow unsexed by mere partnership with a powerful, independent woman.[11]

It seems fair to conclude, therefore, that while by any name a rose may smell as sweet, a woman's name may conjure many potent yet elusive things in politics. Both Mrs. Clinton and Mrs. Quayle reinstated their family names following the election, becoming Hillary Rodham Clinton and Marilyn Tucker Quayle, respectively. Senator Carol Moseley-Braun added a hyphen, putting her family name preeminent on both the Senate's rolls and in the history books. Kathleen Brown, the daughter of one former California governor and the sister of yet another, ran for treasurer in 1990 not under the name of either her first or second husband but under the slogan "A Brown of a Different Color." The clever line played on her female identity yet simultaneously embraced her family legacy—in effect, "covering" her with their masculine authority. It made her a legitimate heir to the positive feelings voters might still have for either her father, Edmund G. "Pat" Brown, or her controversial brother, Jerry Brown (Edmund G. Brown, Jr.), while subtly enabling voters to distinguish her from the latter. She won, and is considered Democratic front-runner for the 1994 gubernatorial nomination.

Coverture may become a campaign issue when a political woman decides to remarry. Certainly that seemed true for Indiana congressman Andrew Jacobs, Jr., and Kansas congresswoman Martha Keys (first elected in 1974), who met and married after she came to Washington. Her 1976 opponent took umbrage at the fact that his representative had married an out-of-stater, and unsuccessfully tried to make "pillow talk" a campaign issue. Keys herself says Kansas voters failed to return her to office again in 1978 because it was a strong Republican year, not because of her domestic arrangements. But neither Jacobs's opponents nor his constituents raised similar concerns, for the norm that had been challenged was that of "the wife's place."

The lingering residues of coverture are a problem for any woman in this society who is attempting to transcend the traditional place of women, but they are a particular problem for women who would be political leaders. Women are born lacking one attribute men appear to acquire by accident of gender: authority.

In the last century, the authority of women was without doubt. It came from their bastion, the home, and from their role as the mothers and shapers of future citizens. Mothers felt no hesitancy to call upon President Abraham Lincoln to lecture him on the course of the war. In the early twentieth century, homemakers took their brooms and swept down Main Streets proclaiming the need for political reform and clean politics, and their own innate fitness for the role of cleaning lady.

But by the middle of this century, American motherhood had become a suspect and despised thing. Philip Wylie's *A Generation of Vipers* was vicious in its assessment of "moms," a third sex of "middle-aged puffins," "noisy postmenopausal neuters" with "stones for hearts," who were to blame for virtually every problem men endured. No longer did a mother exercise moral influence; on the contrary, the very fact that she exercised her relatively new-won right to vote had brought a "new all-time low in political scurviness," Wylie harped.[12] Yet, as Betty Friedan and others would later point out, a woman's connection to a man, as his wife or his mother, was virtually the only role she was allowed in society, disparaged though it might be.

Even on the eve of John Kennedy's New Frontier, *The American Voter* still echoed St. Paul: "Role beliefs pressure a woman to be a submissive partner. The man is expected to be dominant. . . . She is not, therefore, expected to see herself as an aggressive agent in politics."[13]

In 1989, Madeleine M. Kunin, then governor of Vermont, addressed this core dilemma. She told a group of political women, gathered by the Women's Campaign Research Fund at Harvard University's Institute of Politics, that she had expected questions about gender would simply go away once she and other women achieved high office.

"I used to think so," she added, stressing the past tense. "Hoping there was some safe perch on which I could land, where no more gender questions would be asked."[14] She went on to describe a host of small but symbolic indignities she suffered as governor—a committee chair at a National Governors Association meeting who would look directly at her and address the entire group "Gentlemen," White House Marines who were flummoxed by a situation whereby they had to announce an official couple other than "Governor and Mrs." "The expectation, the centuries of expectations, have been and continue to be that the man is the leader," she said. "You realize your very presence is a defiance of tradition and sometimes you internalize the feeling that this is not normal behavior."

The speech touched a very raw nerve among many of the women present, for Kunin talked not only of political battles but the "inner skirmishes" women fight with their own psyches. And she wondered, quoting playwright Wendy Wasserstein's *The Heidi Chronicles* heroine, "What is it women tell their sons that they don't tell their daughters?"

The question could be expanded: What is it husbands tell their wives? What is it society tells mothers about their duties to their children? What is it voters tell women about their proper place? Whatever it is, it is obviously a version of the same message that one famous political father had for his daughter. Shortly before Caroline Kennedy was born, her father, then Senator John F. Kennedy, the man who later would create so much opportunity and change with his Presidential Commission on the Status of Women, was asked on television: "'If your child is a boy, would you want him to get into politics?' The senator replied: 'If it's a boy, certainly I'd want him to get into politics; and if we have a girl, I'd want her keenly interested in politics.'"[15]

Let us imagine for a moment we have a woman "keenly interested in politics" who wants what her brother has been bequeathed—a right to run for high political office, the right to be a leader, to be a participant not an observer in her own citizenship. She's stuffed envelopes and canvassed voters. She burns with, probably silent, ambition. Yet her most painful "skirmishes" still may be on the horizon. Those are the daily battles she has with who she has been told she is (daughter, wife, mother, woman) and all she is trying to be (power-wielder, candidate, politician, leader, daughter, wife, mother, woman).

A friend of Carol Moseley-Braun speaks with aching empathy of "the burdens on her—trying to be an attentive mother and, at the same time, attentive to her public self." She had left the Illinois legislature and run for local office in order to be with her young son and elderly mother, and despite the demands of a Senate campaign that catapulted her to near rock-star celebrity, she was determined to be at home most nights to have dinner with her child. Meanwhile, her campaign manager underwent triple-bypass surgery and her housekeeper was hospitalized, leaving her no child-care backup. Then campaign staffers planned a major fund-raising event on Mother's Day, a day Moseley-Braun desperately wanted to spend with her invalid mother.

The cumulative result of voters, colleagues, family, and societal expectations about what a political mom or wife should do or be is that she often goes to absurd lengths to try to do it all and it takes its toll. For Moseley-Braun the conflicts had near-fatal results for her campaign.

"She's very smart. She knows her issues. She knows what she thinks. And she was a smart state legislator. But the way a woman's confidence works after all that sort of battering, battering, battering . . . Well, one day she just froze. It was on issues she had down pat. Issues she had answered many, many times."

Unfortunately for her, she did not freeze on the stump in some tiny farm town in the southern part of the state, but during one of the most critical moments of her campaign—her candidate endorsement interview with the state's largest newspaper, the *Chicago Tribune*.

"It was part exhaustion. Part [loss of] confidence. She basically broke down and cried." The *Chicago Tribune* did not report the incident, but it also did not endorse in the Senate race.

While every working woman suffers a "double shift," to use sociologist Arlie Hochschild's insightful phrase, for the political woman it is both a twenty-four-hour-a-day logistical nightmare and a politically symbolic burden. Her womanly-wifely-motherly attributes are a woman's traditional source of authority and the core of her self-esteem, yet these very important parts of her do not seem to have merit in the eyes of others. Ann Richards has written movingly about the void:

> What seems to be of merit or significance about what I've done in life hinges around activity that one ordinarily would see men doing. There I was living this incredibly active life that was bits and pieces stitched together, and those pieces that were female activity don't seem worth telling about.
>
> What little girls read in history books or are assigned papers to write on, is always about men and what men do. . . . The obvious result is that, as we live our lives, we have to make things up as we go along. It's as if each woman has to create her own solutions.[16]

No matter what level of success she experiences in her political life, the political woman may turn to jelly inside trying to reconcile who she knows she is and wants to be with the messages about who she should be. Even the formidable Margaret Chase Smith, at the time a four-term House veteran who had been widowed almost a decade, got a lecture from her mother when she decided to step up and run for the Senate: When was she "going to stop all this nonsense and get married"?[17]

In interviews with contemporary political women, the regularity with which they would spontaneously volunteer early in a conversation some remark made by their mothers underscored how vital a mother's approval must be to a woman politician's confidence level. Usually the comments were along the lines of Barbara Kennelly's "My mother thinks I can do no wrong." Some felt they were getting decidedly mixed messages: When Bella Abzug won her first congressional race her mother said, "'Congratulations. Let's hope next time it will be for President.' The way she said it, she could have been saying, 'Let's hope next time it will be a boy,'" Abzug recalled.[18] Pat Schroeder's mother taught when her children were young. "In one of our campaigns . . . someone said, 'I wouldn't vote for Pat Schroeder, and I think she ought to stay home with her kids.' My mother said, 'Well, I was a working mother and I had two kids.' And the lady said, 'Oh, yeah? Well, what happened to 'em?' And my mother replied, 'Well, one's a lawyer and the other one is Pat Schroeder.'"

Geraldine Ferraro is always lavish with her praise of the support she received from her widowed mother, who she has said virtually went hungry to make sure her daughter had a good education. Ferraro was appalled, however, and personally very hurt, at the profoundly negative reaction of her mother's generation to her 1984 vice presidential candidacy.

"They hated it. Hated it," she says.

The sentiments mirrored a poll taken after Senator Margaret Chase Smith's announcement that she was contemplating a run for the presidency in the early 1960s; it showed "quite a bit of feminine animosity toward women who wished to change women's roles."[19] In other words, it was not just men who felt some sexual threat in the emergence of politically powerful women. Women themselves can feel unsexed by powerful women.

In Ferraro's polling the following year, 1985, when she was contemplating a 1986 Senate campaign, she found that what pollsters called her "negatives" were insurmountable. The problems were almost exclusively with "women who had taken the traditional role of wife and mother . . . and now it was too late for them to do anything else. It was *fascinating* to see. They watched with horror. Not because of me personally. What we found in the focus groups, which I found mind-boggling . . . was that they were concerned about what would happen to them if I had become vice president. How would their husbands view them if 'all they could do'—

and that's in quotes—'was be a wife and mother'? Weren't they lacking something. And wouldn't that somehow make their husbands see them as less than they were. Would it jeopardize their marriages? I mean, the way people thought about this!"

Colorado treasurer Gail Schoettler also ran into that feeling on the campaign trail, but says she understands it because of her own mother. There's "a real anger that I'm doing things she never could have done herself. I see it in a lot of women . . . exactly how my mother feels, I'm sure. She knew she was smart, she knew she could have done these things, and now at seventy she can't afford to look back."

Given the departure from the norm that running as a woman continues to be, it is perhaps no wonder that it is only the exceptional woman who dreamed of being in politics as a young girl. Senator Barbara Mikulski says it plainly, "I didn't sit around in my little sandbox in a Baltimore ethnic neighborhood saying, 'Oh, one day I'm going to be a U.S. senator.'"[20]

Claudine Schneider remembers that her own childhood fantasies had included "being an ambassador and working for world peace." In other words, she found a respectable way of being political, in a family that disparaged the field, by camouflaging her ambitions as classic female altruism. The expectations her family had for her were more conventional: "I remember when my parents said they were saving money to send us to college—neither of them went. They were sending my brother in order that he might become a professional. They were sending me in order that I might marry one."

Given expectations that a daughter will achieve through her husband's success, it is not surprising that many of the women who have run for governor or senator or congresswoman came into politics, in Ann Richards's image, dancing backwards. They came in as daughters and municipal housekeepers: Mary Rose Oakar had been a college professor whose political career was triggered by the decay of her old neighborhood, where her mother still lived. They came in as mothers and champions of others' causes: Gail Schoettler ran for school board when her children were young because it was "almost a family tradition." Even Bella Abzug, though a lawyer, came to electoral politics indirectly because of her concern as a mother about nuclear war—and she founded Women Strike for Peace. They came in through the sort of nurturing careers parents felt were appropriately ladylike for their daughters: Congresswomen Marge Roukema of New Jersey and Ilena Ros-Lehtinen of

Florida were schoolteachers, as were Colorado's Josie Heath and Geraldine Ferraro. (Ferraro went to law school later.)

They answered all manner of altruistic calls: South Carolina's Liz
Patterson was a Peace Corps and VISTA volunteer.

They came in, as women had since the mid-nineteenth century, via
their pens: Senator Barbara Boxer, Congresswoman Helen Bentley of
Maryland and Kansas's 1992 Senate candidate Gloria O'Dell were newspaper reporters, as was Harriett Woods, former lieutenant governor of
Missouri and current president of the National Women's Political Caucus (NWPC). Even Nancy Kassebaum of Kansas dreamed of newspaper-
ing as the conduit for her keen political interests—she and an elementary
school friend published a neighborhood paper using Kassebaum's toy
typewriter. "The kind where you have to turn the type ball for every letter. I was the political columnist," she recalled with a laugh.

And they came in, if one would believe their self-effacing recollec-
tions, almost by accident: Madeleine Kunin admitted over a quiet lunch
near the Dartmouth campus where she was teaching, "I didn't ever think
of politics for myself [when I was young]. My first political inclination or
yearnings were fantasies of marrying a politician. I thought that might be
fun. . . . " Almost as an afterthought, she added, "My older brother was
thought to be the person with political potential. I must have just sort of
absorbed it. . . . "

All of the above came into politics under the still-lingering banner of
selfless womanhood, acting in behalf of others or with deference to others, as Kunin's modest afterthought infers. Even Ann Richards's transformation into a professional political operative came only after years as a
volunteer—read "wife"—on the sidelines of the Texas Democratic party,
which she recalls being dominated by the men. She played bridge with
the law school wives. Played hostess. And in 1961, packed children and
household goods and followed her husband, attorney David Richards, to
Washington, D.C., where he spent a year in the Kennedy administration.
She was therefore astonished, in 1972, when she was asked to actually
run a campaign, that of a young "very attractive, twenty-five-year-old,
with lots of curly blond hair, who was all business,"[21] Sarah Weddington,
the attorney who had argued *Roe* v. *Wade* before the Supreme Court.
"This was also the first action I'd taken in my adult life that I'd done on
my own."[22]

The significance of this feminine "dancing backwards" cannot be over-stressed, particularly in contrast to the Iwo Jima–like assault on male power that began with the congresswomen's march on the Senate during the Battle of Anita Hill. While many early women members of Congress gained office through the deaths of their husbands and not by actively seeking political power, that means of entry still is responsible for a number of contemporary representatives, among them Congresswoman Olympia Snowe, who was first elected to the Maine state legislature in 1973 to fill the seat vacated by the death of her first husband, Peter Snowe.

Even the number of current or recent officeholders who came into politics via a political spouse or at the impetus of husbands is a surprise. Pat Schroeder, for example, may be a product of Harvard Law School, where she met her husband, James, but it was he who first ran for public office in Denver—and lost. He was the one who persuaded her to run for Congress in 1972 in what "was supposed to be a hopeless but honorable race." Barbara Boxer's labor lawyer husband, Stewart, in a rare interview during California's 1992 state Democratic convention, explained how it was she not he who became the candidate in the family: "We [Marin County, California, Democrats] needed someone to run for supervisor, and I looked like every other candidate. Barbara was different."[23]

Claudine Schneider's husband pushed her first race in 1978. At the time she was head of the Conservation Law Foundation of Rhode Island, which she had founded. He was a better-known environmentalist, and it was he who was first approached in 1978 to run for governor.

"I said terrific," she recalled in early 1991, in a series of lengthy conversations at Harvard University's Kennedy School of Politics. "I'll be your right-hand woman. . . . I was still operating under the mind-set I had received from my parents. . . . At the last minute, my husband decided he's not going to run. Too big of a risk. Then he turns to me and he says, 'You should run.'

"The Republicans were excited when they had this Dr. Schneider to run. He was a somebody. He could be a credible candidate. But then, when it was his wife who would be running, that didn't quite have the impact." She filed for Congress instead.

Schneider did not realize it at the time—the phrase had not yet been coined—but she had just bumped up against the "glass ceiling" politics erects against women. It wasn't until 1974, with Ella Grasso of Connecticut, that a woman had ever been *elected* governor in her own right—that

is, not acting as a surrogate for a dead husband, a husband who was pre-
vented from serving consecutive terms, or, in at least one case—Texas's
infamous "Ma" and "Pa" Ferguson in the 1930s—a husband who was in
jail and could not serve. Until 1990, when ten women ran—and three
(Texas's Richards, Oregon's Barbara Roberts, and Kansas's Joan Finney)
won—there had been only five women (Grasso, Washington's Dixie Lee
Ray, Kentucky's Martha Layne Collins, Vermont's Kunin, and
Nebraska's Kay Orr) who had been "elected in their own right," political
shorthand that indicates a woman won without the usual male family
member to first pave the way. (Imagine it said of a man that he was
"elected in his own right.")

Schneider lost, but so did the man the party had fielded for governor.
In 1980, she ran again and won, and began to bump up against yet another of the invisible barriers politics and society puts in women's
paths—the subtle and not-so-subtle burdens a political career inflicts
upon a marriage.

Perhaps the most difficult of the inner skirmishes that can undermine
a woman's political ambitions is the question: Will it destroy her marriage? Even Ann Richards, when she ran for Travis County commissioner because her husband, David, had encouraged her, "hesitated,
afraid that office-holding might destroy her marriage."[24]

The pain a woman's success theoretically inflicts upon her husband
has been an article of faith during much of this century. No American
woman alive could have escaped the message. Margaret Mead noted that
men are unsexed by failure, women are unsexed by success.[25] In the
1950s, *Life* magazine quoted psychiatrists who blamed husbands' emotional upsets, as well as sons' homosexuality, on the ambition of their
wives and mothers.[26] In 1964, the same year Margaret Chase Smith was
running for president and yet right on the heels of Betty Friedan's 1963
best-seller, *The Feminine Mystique,* Alvin Toffler warned "working
wives" in the *Ladies' Home Journal* that they were a threat "on many
levels, challenging a man's comfort, his social life, his children's welfare,
his sexuality, and his self-esteem."[27]

Is there any connection between political success and marital failure
for women? Probably not. Yet nearly twice as many women politicians
are unmarried—29 percent as opposed to 15 percent of elected men,
according to a study released in November 1991 by the Center for the
American Woman and Politics. The CAWP study did not analyze how

many of those unmarried officeholders were divorced or why they were unmarried, but from the fact that roughly equal numbers had children— 84 percent of the men and 85 percent of the women—it would seem that divorce may figure in the discrepancy.

To understand the inner skirmishes a married woman who would be a politician must endure, let us step back in time to the Ferraro focus group and look very carefully at the women who voiced fears of what it might mean to the men in their lives if a woman were elected vice president of the United States. Is a Claudine Schneider, an Ann Richards, or any other middle-aged political woman all that different from those women, who were so horrified at Ferraro's candidacy that they thought it threatened their own marriages?

And what would we hear if we were to put together a focus group of similarly aged men? What would we hear if we let these men talk—about their feelings and fears of what might happen to their marriages, their standing in the eyes of other men, their ability to feel manly if one of their wives were to suddenly add Senator, or Congresswoman, or Governor to her name. Would we have a kind of mirror-image of the Ferraro focus group women? More to the point, would we hear anything that women politicians do not already suspect and have uneasy dreams about?

Claudine Schneider is not unique among politicians, male or female, in tying the demise of her marriage to an expanding political career. In 1984, after just two terms in office, she and her husband were divorced.

"The divorce was very difficult on me. I spent a lot of time looking at the situation. . . . I was on an upward incline; his career was not . . . I felt I was married more to a campaign manager than to a man, than to a lover. . . . At home I wanted to run in the garden, put on music, dance when I cooked. . . . It seems that all of our conversations focused on 'Why aren't you saving the starving children in Ethiopia?'"

In her memoir, *Straight from the Heart,* Ann Richards suggests much the same sort of change in her marriage after she was elected in 1976 to the Travis County *Commissioners Court.*

> All of a sudden *I was being me,* and I was having a hard time handling it . . . my old political friends . . . would discuss events and would come to totally erroneous conclusions. . . . What a threat to our little circle . . . [and on] my relationship with David. . . .

We had traveled the same road for twenty-some-odd years and then suddenly my life just went straight up like a skyrocket. . . . It was hard on him and a terror on me. . . . My most valued relationship was beginning to spin out of my control. [emphasis added][28]

A younger generation of women politicians, those who always planned careers whether political or not, may have been able to avoid some of the personal conflict experienced by women whose lives were more constricted by older role expectations. Congresswoman Rosa DeLauro of Connecticut did not marry until she was in her thirties, and then married another political operative, pollster Hank Greenberg. Joan Kelly Horn's and Gail Schoettler's second marriages were undertaken after each had set her political course. The problems for these new dual-career political couples may be similar to those of other two-career couples—just the managing of the two careers. However, politics is never an easy or straightforward career track, and the prejudices of voters put extra burdens on the nonpolitician partner, as political spouses from Paul Wilson, who was Frances Perkins's husband, to Hillary Rodham Clinton have discovered. But that cozy ideal—a politician with a helpmate keeping the home fires going—has never been what was happening for women politicians.

Between the two extremes, women who have come to public service through traditional marriages and women who never doubted they would run for office, is a transitional "generation" to which most contemporary political women seem to belong. These women, though their ages span several decades, have tried to juggle both the traditional marital and family expectations they were raised with, and the post-women's movement ideals and politics they have helped make real. Two interesting examples are Colorado politicians and very good friends, Gail Schoettler and Josie Heath.

In 1986, a congressional seat came open when Timothy Wirth, a fellow Boulder liberal, decided to move up to the Senate. Democrats in that district appear unanimous that the opportunity virtually had Josie Heath's name on it. As county commissioner, a former member of the Carter administration, a woman who had sat on the Tenth U.S. Court Judicial Nominating Committee, the head of former governor Richard Lamm's Status of Women Commission, Heath was very visible, very well liked, and a politician who had paid her dues in party service. She did not run; she still had a child in junior high and a husband who was adamantly opposed to the idea of a wife and mother who commuted to Washington, D.C.

The psychological cost of the family crisis created by this deferred opportunity is something Heath almost cannot discuss without tears welling in her eyes, nor can her executive husband, Rollie.

"I just basically told her that we just . . . well, I just couldn't do it," Rollie Heath admits. "It was probably the toughest time [in their attempts to juggle two careers and one marriage] . . . I said I don't think we can retain the marriage and [you] do it . . . I have second guessed it a lot . . . I was a top candidate for president of a Fortune 200 company . . . and I said I'm just not going to give it up."

When Rollie drew the line and said, "Don't run," Josie acquiesced. Now, he said, even she realizes it was important for their family that she defer her dream; she may, but in early 1991, discussing her husband's ultimatum—"He said he would leave me"—and her decision not to run, all she spontaneously recalled was the pain.

Schoettler's tale is more succinct. She participated in the founding of two women's banks in Colorado, concurrent with serving on her local school board, then served in Governor Lamm's administration, and in 1984 ran for state treasurer. She says her husband gave her an ultimatum midway through her first term as state treasurer that if she ran again, he would divorce her.

"I said, 'fine.'"

It was not a case of putting politics ahead of everything else; she said her marriage was already in trouble, something she blames on the difficulty some modern men still have accepting nontraditional wives, or the difficulty some modern women have being traditional wives.

"I think it's why so many women of our generation are divorced. And I don't know how much easier it's going to be for younger men, because I don't know how much they have been able to pull themselves out of the traditional male mold. . . . Oh sure, he thought I should run for school board—somebody needed to have some responsibility for the kids' education. But he really resented my being out at night" after she won.

Schoettler surprised herself when asked when she began to stop thinking of herself as a banker-businesswoman on temporary duty as a public servant and began thinking of herself as a career politician. "Oh, gosh, I've never even thought of that. I guess about two years ago." In other words, about the time of her divorce.

The tension between political ambition, something that would never be suspect in a man, and the priority of family life, a priority that women, because of their special history and status, still are not allowed to put anywhere but first, is something each political woman has to work out.

Even today, a Claudine Schneider, a divorced woman, no longer responsible for the care and feeding of a male ego, cannot totally own her political ambition. She talks in terms of "public service." Although she has been formidable in congressional hearings, staring down bears on more than one occasion, she still euphemizes. In effect, she speaks of "doing good" not "having the power to do good." Josie Heath has no such qualms—now. Clearly she has passed through the maelstrom with marriage intact, children now in college or grown, spouse now totally committed to her career—indeed, in 1990, when Josie ran for the Senate, Rollie quit his corporate job and campaigned full-time for her—and a growing confidence in her right to seek public office. Gail Schoettler, happily remarried, is still in office, and openly talking about running for governor of Colorado.

Ann Richards is already governor of Texas. But even on the eve of her election in 1990, her friend and political catalyst Jane Hickey worried where Richards's heart was. "I've always thought that if David came back on October 31, 1990, and said, 'I've made a big mistake. Can't we go off to the Peace Corps and work in Nigeria?' she'd be gone."[29]

Given the prevalence of divorce in society today it may seem that to raise the issue in respect to a Claudine Schneider or an Ann Richards, indeed any political women, is irrelevant. It may also appear to echo the right wing's family values fears or Pat Robertson's damning claim that political women's hidden agenda is baby-killing, witchcraft, and the destruction of marriage. It may even seem sexist, suggesting that a woman tough enough for politics cannot get or keep a man. But while there have been many celebrated divorces among political men, in our society the care and maintenance of marriage, and somewhat by extension, a husband's ego, are still conferred, however fairly or unfairly, upon the wife.

The "inner skirmishes" society inflicts upon the married woman politician are exacerbated by how the culture often treats them: as a joke—but as with many jokes, one that thinly veils hostility and a sense of some perceived threat to the natural order of things. The 1964 comedy *Kisses for My President,* when Margaret Chase Smith was an announced candidate, was Hollywood's version of "the plight" of a man married to the first woman president. He ran the home while she ran the country.[30] "As a husband he minds, but as a citizen he is too patriotic to protest,"[31] *Time* magazine's reviewer said. Humorist Roy Blount's 1990 novel *First Hubby* may have been triggered when Pat Schroeder contemplated a presidential race in 1987.

Ruth Mandel, director of the Eagleton Institute's Center for the American Woman and Politics (CAWP) at Rutgers University, recalled the old, 1970s television series "Maude" in her 1981 book *In the Running*. Even though Maude, played by feminist Bea Arthur, was the sitcom apotheosis of the newly liberated woman, she could not bring herself to directly tell her husband, Walter, she was thinking of becoming a political candidate. She could not admit her own ambitions. She danced backwards into a discussion of running by saying, "I've just had the most incredible honor bestowed on me." She went on to praise him—"You're the most sympathetic, compassionate, supportive, woman-oriented . . ."—to which Walter had but one response: "When you're in Albany, who's going to take care of me?"[32]

> The struggle over Maude's candidacy entertained evening television audiences for five weeks. It was a high point in the series, drawing twenty million viewers. Walter took up life as a separated husband. Maude followed her candidacy. The result? The script took the easy way out—Walter came home and Maude lost the election. . . .
>
> Maude's flirtation with politics was based on real life, inspired by Sabrina Shiller's candidacy for the California state senate. The candidate's husband, Robert Shiller, was a writer for the "Maude" series. . . .
>
> Sabrina Shiller, like Maude, eventually lost by a narrow margin [but] the similarities went deeper. "There was a line of Walter's that was Bob's," says Shiller. "I have an uncommon need not to be alone."[33]

Maintaining a marriage and a political career may be another proof of Ferraro's Law: It's easier for the guys. Elaine Baxter, Iowa's secretary of state, has a ready solution to the problem and the very personal questions a woman candidate must answer. "The secret is," she tells audiences, "you marry a man whose mother was in politics because he doesn't know that a woman isn't supposed to do these things."[34]

Although married women increasingly may feel they are entitled to some form of equity, in other family relationships earlier norms may prevail. Because women traditionally have had to defer their political ambitions, the stage of life at which they find themselves stepping onto the ladder may keep them from reaching the top. A congresswoman cannot tell a crying toddler she has a roll call in two minutes. A woman candidate may have trouble explaining to a teacher that her primary is in three weeks and no matter what the other mommies are doing, her cookies will have to wait. A dying parent or spouse or a troubled teenager requires attention immediately, not during a legislative break.

Dianne Feinstein had twice run for mayor of San Francisco and lost, when her second husband, Bert, became ill with cancer. She was managing to juggle her county supervisor's job and still nurse him through what would be a painful, lingering death. When one supervisor threw a chair at another during a particularly heated meeting, she snapped, "You can all go to hell. My husband is dying and I'm going home."[35] A year later, in November 1978, still exhausted by her husband's death, she was within hours of a press conference at which she planned to announce her retirement when the assassination of Mayor George Moscone made her mayor.

One of Hawaii's state legislators grieves that because she had delayed entry into elective politics for so long, because of small children, because of a divorce, because of all the things that life can put in the path of a dream, that now, at age fifty-six and with a newly retired, second husband in his early seventies, it may be too late for her to run for Congress. "I don't know how much time we have left together."

In the early stages of her gubernatorial campaign, another female problem hit Feinstein. Hemorrhaging and other complications of menopause required surgery. "It was not elective or certainly not minor in any way," according to her campaign manager Bill Carrick, yet the campaign's then chief strategist Clint Reilly pushed her to keep campaigning. When she didn't, he faxed his resignation to newspapers all around the state. "The *San Jose Mercury News* . . . used a headline font that hadn't been used since the Hindenburg went down," said Carrick. "That was the worst day of the campaign . . . [it] was on the ropes . . . [but] she weathered a press conference." And when one reporter asked skeptically, "Do you have the fire in the belly for the race?" She fired back, "I thought I had that removed."

Many women interviewed for this book talked movingly of the emotional conflicts and logistical crises having elderly parents presented for them. Bella Abzug, commuting to Washington while setting up her congressional office in 1971, agonized that she was unable to visit her eighty-two-year-old mother. "My poor sister Helene has had to take the whole burden. . . ."[36] Evelyn Murphy, who has been the subject of attacks during each of her campaigns, but suffered particularly during the 1990 campaign because of rumors alleging she is lesbian, has decided she will not run again for office during her elderly father's lifetime. "He went through an enormous amount of upheaval and I can't do it to him again. He's eighty-eight . . . I'm the last family he has. . . . Every single bit of criticism . . . was very hard on him. . . . I owe him."

For some pro-choice Catholic women, there is a delicate balancing act they must do that goes beyond how they present the issue to voters. "If I were ever excommunicated it would kill my mother," one congress-woman confided.

Traditionally, in our society, the nurturers—the shepherds of others' self-esteem, the nurses at the mother's deathbed, the providers of hugs, and the bakers of cookies—have been the women. That has not changed because women now run for public office. For the male politician, the tradition is the precise opposite: One of the women in his family will no doubt take care of the nurturing. Maybe this will change now that the world knows it is okay for the nurse at Chelsea Clinton's school to "Call my dad, my mom's too busy," for permission to give a child an aspirin, and that Senator Patty Murray's husband, Rob, "did the grocery shop-ping, took care of the kids and made sure they had a parent with them every night during the campaign," according to Beth Sullivan. She added that he "just smiled and nodded graciously" when, at a reception for new senators, Lynda Johnson Robb welcomed him to the Senate Wives Club and then, blushing, stammered, "Oh, I guess we'll have to change the name now." In early February 1992, none other than George Bush re-portedly asked his son Jeb, who was considering a gubernatorial race in Florida, "Are you sure you want to do this to your family?"

Usually, however, there is an almost inevitable Mommy Track for mothers in politics. In a CAWP study released in 1991, only 15 percent of women officeholders were forty or younger, compared to 28 percent of the men. CAWP's study also suggests, and anecdotal evidence con-firms, that mothers of very young children rarely run for office. While the median age for men's children was twenty and the median age for women's twenty-three, not so great a difference, the more revealing find-ing is that the men were twice as likely to have preteens. The only woman ever to have had a baby during her congressional career, Yvonne Brathwaite Burke, "kept duplicate baby equipment on both coasts, from cribs to strollers and sandboxes."[37] In 1978, when her daughter Dawn was four and nearing kindergarten age, Burke unsuccessfully risked her con-gressional seat to run for California attorney general.

Based on her own experience, Congresswoman Nancy Johnson of

Connecticut encourages young mothers not to be discouraged. "At the state level, politics is not usually year-round . . . you juggle the three- to five-month sessions and you are out for summer vacations." Johnson also argues that "politics isn't something you should do until midlife anyway. . . . It's better to have elected officials who have some real life experience under their belts," a message 1992's women candidates took to the voters.

Certainly none of the modern-day senators, congresswomen, and other women politicians who are juggling all the parts of a woman's life make it look easy. But they make it look doable, and they make it clear they believe that the many challenges of being public women and private persons have made them better representatives. For example, it was Barbara Boxer, fresh from juggling a household and a local political career, and not one of the men of Congress, who first pointed out the absurdity of the Pentagon spending $7,622 on coffeepots. It also has been the women of Congress who have taken the lead on child care, family leave, and sex equity issues—or have continued to push those issues when male legislators found other priorities.

"The women of America should basically be on their knees to the women in Congress of both political parties," declared ABC-Television and National Public Radio political analyst Cokie Roberts, in a commencement address to the 1990 graduating class at Bryn Mawr College. Roberts, the daughter of former congresswoman Corinne "Lindy" Boggs and her late husband, Congressman Hale Boggs, both of Louisiana, added that it is the women of Congress who

> carry the burden of the importance of issues to women and children day in and day out. They use it like Chinese water torture on their colleagues. They constantly bring those bills back to the top of the pile: child support enforcement, day care, pension reform, equal credit, domestic violence, all of these things are being brought to the floor by these women. . . . They found themselves the water carriers on women's issues because they quickly discovered that if they didn't do it, nobody else would.

Pat Schroeder was the first mother of small children elected to Congress. Her daughter Jamie was just two when Schroeder won her upset victory for the House in 1972, and a photographer for one of the Denver papers caught the impish toddler "when I was chasing [her] up the stairs for the eighty-fifth time election night," Schroeder recalls. The caption on the photo still makes her laugh: "When a Congresswoman tells you to go to bed, you go!" No one in her family, least of all Jamie, was impressed by her new-won authority. In fact, Schroeder's first few days in office were spent dealing with nearly universal skepticism that the juggling act she'd just undertaken was doable. There were literally hundreds of press and constituent queries about how she was going to do "it."

"My favorite phone call was from Bella Abzug. I hadn't met her yet. She said, 'Congratulations.' I said, 'Thanks.' She said, 'I hear you have young children.' I said, 'I do.' She said, 'You aren't going to be able to do it. It's impossible.'"

Until the influx of new congresswomen with the 1992 elections and the arrival of former journalist Marjorie Margolies Mezvinsky of Pennsylvania, who is the mother, stepmother, or legal guardian of eleven children, ages ten to twenty-eight, Congresswoman Connie Morella of Maryland arguably had the most impossible double life—she and her husband are parents to nine children, three of their own, the rest her late sister's children. She admitted the logistics of running a nine-child household plus a congressional district have been "stunning. . . absolutely," but notes her husband learned to cook and has taken over a lot of the traditional "women's work."

"He never did laundry though. I remember one Sunday he came back from shopping while I was out campaigning and he had like ten towels. He said, 'They were on sale.' I said, 'But, honey, we have towels . . .' And he said, 'Yes, but none of them is clean.'"

Morella says that since then she has taught each child to do laundry, but "sometimes in the middle of the night you hear a 'clunk, clunk, clunk.' It's sneakers going round and round in the dryer. It's a small price to pay."

She was chuckling over that story with visitors to her office, when she suddenly recalled the party slating meeting in 1976 when she first ran. "One of the men who hoped he would get the nomination . . . asked, 'Well, Mrs. Morella, in light of your extended family do you think you'll really have time to run for Congress, much less serve?'

"I knew right then he didn't have the votes," she said with a laugh. "And I said, 'Well, if you want to get a job done ask a busy *man*. . . . My point being, of course, they never ask men those sorts of questions."

5

Crossing the Credibility Threshold

Credentials, Confidence, and Credibility

"There was never any question that I wanted a political career," said Rosa DeLauro, just after her first election to Congress in 1990. Both of DeLauro's parents had been active in local politics. "My mother is the senior member of the Board of Aldermen of New Haven [Connecticut]," she says proudly.[1] Her father, no longer living, had also been a New Haven alderman. DeLauro's earliest political memories, beginning in grade school, are of ward politics. By high school, she had learned how to do an old-fashioned vote pull, identify her father's supporters on 3×5 cards and get them to the polls.

By the time DeLauro ran for Congress at age 47, she had been a city hall official during the War on Poverty, a U.S. Senate aide and campaign manager, a political fund-raiser, and a campaign operative for two presidential campaigns. Despite her father's caution that "she could not learn politics from books," she studied political science in graduate school and attended the London School of Economics.

DeLauro was able to cross the threshold into electoral politics with relative ease, confident of her goals and equipped with political experience and credentials relevant to the office. She is unusual, however, even for the generation of women currently entering politics. Few women have grown up with the conviction that politics was a desirable career, or found so direct a route to fulfilling their political ambitions. "You keep your eyes focused on what you want to do and you make the necessary adjustments on what you have to do to move along toward a goal."

As a first-time congressional candidate, DeLauro had another quality: credibility, an elusive but all-important prerequisite for electoral success. The primary way women candidates have achieved credibility is by entering politics at the local level, running for a city council seat or a school board, and then working their way up the political ladder. Historically, women's office-holding experience has been more convincing to voters than credentials earned in another arena. DeLauro was credible without having been elected before.

DeLauro gained her experience on a trajectory that would seem commonplace if we were talking about a young man's rise to electoral success. Such a direct route, however, has only recently become open to young women. She was the *first* executive assistant to the New Haven mayor, and she was the *first* woman in the state to manage a statewide campaign. When she became the executive assistant to her successful candidate, Senator Chris Dodd, in 1980, she remembers, "There were maybe ten women who held those jobs."

For women born before DeLauro, the steps to electoral politics were harder, the thresholds higher and more difficult to cross. Some barriers were intensely personal. Women needed the right level of confidence in themselves and a belief that it was legitimate to run for office. Some were determined more by social and political factors than personal ones. The women might have been supremely confident of their skills and ability but still have found their paths blocked by party elites. If women were successfully elected to one office, they found other thresholds needed to be crossed for new or higher offices. Their every action was scrutinized. Potential backers could decide a woman was a great candidate for a local school board but not viable for more prestigious offices. With every step a woman took into the political arena, she faced this constant "testing, testing, testing," as Dianne Feinstein describes it.

In the absence of female politicians as role models, women previously had to imagine themselves as politicians, the most male of roles. They had to visualize raising money, speaking in public, taking positions on controversial issues, shaking hands with voters, distributing leaflets, and soliciting votes. This required a mental leap that, even as late as 1974, few were able to make. Such women as Helen Gahagan Douglas and Shirley Chisholm came to their decisions to run individually and privately, unsustained by a public movement.

A 1974 study of women who were deeply involved in local party politics, a likely source of prospective candidates, found most of them could not see themselves in office. Two thirds of those surveyed thought running would not be "proper." Women also believed that "most men would prefer women to contribute to politics in ways other than running for office."[2] With reluctance to run so widespread, and the risk of male disapproval so high, the question of whether or not women were qualified to run in their own right was secondary, if it arose at all.

During the transitional period of the 1970s, when running for office was still a "novelty," women who entered politics usually remember the exact moment, as Bella Abzug does, when they were able to envision themselves as candidates. Abzug had worked for and helped to elect a number of men over the years. In 1969 she was badgering New York City mayor John Lindsay, one of the men she had helped elect, with some of her agenda items. An exasperated Lindsay finally said to her, "You're always so critical of politicians and government . . . why don't you try it yourself, and you'll find out how hard it is."[3]

"Then and there," said Abzug, "I decided to run for Congress. It was like a light switch being turned on in my brain. . . . I realized that if I had strong beliefs and ideals about how our country should be run, I could best work for them right up front, out in the open, in my own way." As she thought seriously about the men she had helped elect over the years, she decided they "weren't any more qualified or able than I, and in some cases they were less so."[4]

Once in office, however, women faced the absence of other women as colleagues or mentors. "I made a real effort to meet Margaret Thatcher, Indira Gandhi, Corazon Aquino—just to touch, just to sense, just to have a feeling of them," says Dianne Feinstein of her long political odyssey.

If DeLauro's path, and her relative ease with political life, are not yet typical of women candidates, at least four readily identifiable shifts can be documented over the last twenty years that have allowed women to imagine themselves as politicians, to overcome the sense that running for office was improper, and to pursue their political goals, like Bella Abzug, "out in the open."

First, as more women have run, prospective candidates have had less and less trouble imagining what a female politician might look like. Over the years, voters have a chosen a variety of women, freeing candidates from having to fit into any one mold. Second, as women have acquired office-holding experience, they have become more competitive candidates, better able to climb the electoral ladder. In turn, as these "first" women broke through traditional barriers and won their elections, subsequent women found it easier to run. Third, a handful of breakthrough candidates has given way to a pool of veteran women politicians with experience in office fully comparable with male candidates. Today, the opportunities for women to run for open seats not held by incumbent politicians have increased along with their success rates. Finally, with greater voter acceptance, women have been able to extend the range of what voters consider appropriate qualifications for office, freeing women candidates to come from backgrounds or to offer voters credentials that are different from men's. In short, in the last twenty years, women have lowered the height of the threshold that kept women from running and voters from considering their candidacies favorably.

These changes are not uniform across the country or to all political offices, but some simple benchmarks will illustrate the magnitude of these shifts. A useful study was conducted in Pennsylvania by Raisa B. Deber, who studied 2,476 candidates for Congress between 1920 and 1974, of whom 88 were women. Three women, all widows, won. The widows conformed to the "Mother Mary" model of women in politics; they were women who displayed a "mature, grandmother image." Deber's work confirmed other studies: Only 5 percent of the female candidates had professional occupations and few had any office-holding experience. Deber concluded that a woman with superior qualifications could probably be elected, but none of the women in this study had them.[5]

In every level of government studied, most female elected officials in the early 1970s were serving their very first term. In a study of congressional winners between 1964 and 1983, women with some prior office-holding experience rose to 67 percent, comparable to that of men.[6] By the 1986 election cycle, the average woman candidate for congressional office had fifteen years of office-holding experience, which compared favorably with the average male candidate.

Before reaching this threshold of comparability, women's limited electoral experience made it hard to compete successfully against male candidates, especially for prestigious offices. Women candidates faced a catch-22 situation. Surveys showed voters would seriously consider a woman's candidacy once she had captured her party's nomination.[7] However, few women were considered good enough candidates to win important party nominations. Even when women offered credentials that resembled men's, they were stunned to find voters believed their male opponents were better qualified.

The net result was that most women brave enough to cross the initial threshold into politics ran in races they had little chance of winning. Most women candidates ran as challengers against longtime incumbents, or they ran in districts where the opposing party usually won. The more prestigious the political office, the more this pattern was likely to occur.

By the mid-1980s, this pattern of running in impossible races had reversed itself. Women candidates had acquired enough office-holding experience as a group to put them on roughly the same footing with men in seeking higher office. More important, more women were taking the risk to run for unoccupied seats.[8] Between 1986 and 1992, success rates for women candidates soared. In the 1992 election cycle, women candidates ran for 39 open congressional seats and won 22 of them. When women challenged incumbents, they did so because they thought they could win, not because they were sacrificial lambs able to capture the party nomination because no one else wanted it.

Increased electoral success was not limited to congressional candidates. The success rates for *all* women candidates who ran for state-level offices in 1990 was 78 percent. In 1992, CAWP data show the success rate for women seeking state legislative offices was over 50 percent in most states. Success rates over 65 percent were not uncommon.[9] Many local jurisdictions have equal, or nearly equal, numbers of men and women on their city councils.[10] Some even have a majority of women.[11]

A less quantifiable measure of change may be found in the composition of the pool of women candidates. It is not an exaggeration to say that the sheer variety of today's female politicians was unimaginable twenty years ago. Openly lesbian candidates have won local office in San Francisco and Seattle, and have been elected to legislatures in Maine, New York, and New Mexico. Young women have been elected. Women with young children have won. Women have won and then have had babies while in office. Asian, African-American, and Hispanic women have won.

Women's success in the political arena has been reinforced by women's entry into other equally male bastions of the business and professional world. As the first generation of women has risen within predominantly male occupations, they have faced the twin problems so familiar to female politicians: They have painstakingly had to establish themselves as authoritative, and they have had to present credentials that men perceive as credible and accept as comparable. Female politicians had an easier time running for office in places where there are women decision-makers in a variety of nontraditional occupations. No better evidence of these changes can be found than the pool from which the newly appointed female members of the Clinton administration were drawn. Female cabinet officials and advisers, as well as others on various "short lists," were drawn not just from politics but from academia and corporate America.

This pool of female politicians, whether elected or appointed, is absolutely new in American history, and its existence is overturning most of the old generalizations about women and electoral politics. These women are creating a tradition of political leadership that is altering fundamentally the dynamics between voters and female candidates. The question today is rarely Can *women* be good candidates? The question, historically unprecedented, is whether a *particular* woman—Mary Smith or Sara Jones—is a credible candidate.

For individual female candidates, personal confidence and the acquisition of credentials are still two of the most critical elements they need to possess in order to establish credibility with voters. Finding the confidence to run is a problem for any candidate, but for women this has been historically difficult, often exacerbated by their dislike of the political process itself. Women need to feel comfortable or at ease with political life, including campaigning, if they are going to build a long-term career in politics.

Jane Danowitz, director of the Women's Campaign Fund (WCF), thinks there are certain aspects of politics that have a decided chilling effect on prospective women candidates, including the prospect of dealing with the media. "Whenever this comes up in our training," she says, "you can see the women physically cringe."[12]

"It is not the lack of polling data or campaign contributions which keeps many political women from ascending high on the political ladder . . . it is fear and loathing of the political system itself," argues former governor Madeleine Kunin. She believes women are deterred from entering politics or thinking about it as a career simply because the political world is still so alien to them.[13]

And even DeLauro cautions that women need to be realistic about "how brutal and how personal" campaigns can be. "People don't like you.

People will say terrible things about you. It's never easy . . . it's the first time somebody says, 'you're a lousy s.o.b.' or that you got your job by sleeping with other people, or with this person or that, or whatever it is that they come up with."[14]

Political scientists have long documented how entry into politics is facilitated by an "intimate exposure to politics."[15] Marion K. Saunders, a defeated congressional candidate in 1954, and author of *The Lady and the Vote,* put it rather more succinctly: "Those who take to politics like ducks to water have generally grown up in the pond." Distinctly new to the pond, Saunders declined to take a second plunge in 1956.

Among those who readily acquire this intimate exposure are the sons and daughters of political parents. Analysts have documented how men born into political families have benefited, but few have examined the boost that daughters, like Rosa DeLauro, have gained.

The life histories of many successful women officials in politics today reveal that they were born in the pond of politics. Nancy Pelosi of California, Barbara Kennelly of Connecticut, Susan Molinari of New York, and just defeated congresswoman Elizabeth Patterson of South Carolina all have fathers who were in politics. Congressional newcomers include Lucille Roybal-Allard, whose congressman father just retired in 1992. The pattern continues at the state and local level. Mary Landrieu, the state treasurer of Louisiana, is the daughter of former New Orleans mayor Moon Landrieu. State treasurer Kathleen Brown of California is the daughter and sister of former governors Pat Brown and Jerry Brown, respectively.

A firsthand glimpse of politics, especially what it is like to campaign for office, seems to help daughters enter politics, regardless of whether their fathers support their ambition—and frequently they do not. The very first political daughter to run for Congress was Ruth Bryan Owen, the daughter of three-time presidential seeker William Jennings Bryan. Bryan's attitude? "He was emphatically opposed," remembers Owen's daughter Rudd Brown.[16] Owen had been deeply involved in her father's 1908 campaign, serving as his secretary. A professor and member of the Board of Regents at the University of Miami (Florida), she had followed in Bryan's footsteps, acquiring familiarity with public speaking on the Chautauqua lecture circuit. Despite her father's lack of support for her candidacy, in 1928 she defeated a seven-term incumbent for a seat in the House of Representatives, and won one more term in 1930, before her support for Prohibition doomed a longer career.

Nearly fifty years later, Kansas senator Nancy Kassebaum, daughter of former presidential candidate Alf Landon, found she, too, had to run without his blessing. "Sheer incomprehension" is how Senator Kassebaum describes her father's reaction, smiling at the memory. "[He] urged me not to run." At first she thought he just didn't want her to experience a loss; however, later she concluded her father's attitude reflected a generational difference toward women in politics. "Like Ronald Reagan . . . he just doesn't get it."[17]

Growing up before the women's movement, Kassebaum never imagined that she would one day pursue a political career even though she loved politics, especially campaigning. She liked riding in parades, and listening to all "the machinations of the national campaigns."

When the idea of running for office did occur to her, she realized her childhood experience was important to her confidence to run. "I think it was growing up in a political family and at the dinner table, whether I was a participant or just listening, and in our house I listened more than I was a participant." A great boon to Kassebaum's courage to run came from a surprise source—her mother, who had not shared her daughter's love of Alf Landon's political career.

After his daughter was elected, Landon continued to find her new career a puzzlement. Before he died, Kassebaum and members of her staff would visit him in Kansas. Landon would often turn to Kassebaum's male aides for the latest political gossip. Once, when a discussion was interrupted so the senator could take a phone call from her press secretary, Landon seemed mystified. He queried her aides: "Nancy? Nancy has a press secretary?" She remained in his mind a daughter, not a U.S. senator who had a staff.

Contemporary political daughters, whether they are supported by their fathers or not, exhibit considerable ease with politics as a result of their early familiarity with political life. Not only are the nuts and bolts of politics—campaigning, parades, leafleting—more familiar to them, they seem more at ease in the pursuit and exercise of power. Political daughters readily claim the label "politician" for themselves, a label many women who are elected to office find distasteful.

Political daughters seem more likely, once elected, to take the risks necessary to move their political careers along. Barbara Kennelly and Nancy Pelosi are two congresswomen who embody this ease. They are both daughters of powerful, old-fashioned machine bosses. Barbara Kennelly of Connecticut is the daughter of John Bailey, "The Legend" of

Connecticut politics and former chairman of the Democratic National Committee. Pelosi is the daughter of former congressman and mayor Thomas D'Alesandro of Baltimore, Maryland.

John Bailey died before he could witness his daughter's political career. Would he have been supportive? "Not if he thought I was competition," she quipped. In less than two decades, Kennelly has built a political career that includes ten years in the House of Representatives, a coveted slot on the Ways and Means Committee, and a leadership appointment. She plays golf with House Speaker Tom Foley, affording her access to a powerful leader in an informal setting, something few women have achieved. After Foley was criticized for not having any women in the leadership whom he could consult on critical issues, he turned to Kennelly and appointed her to an expanded leadership group.

In July 1991, Kennelly eagerly awaited the outcome of a Democratic Caucus election that would mean a chance for her to move into the House leadership. The candidate she backed lost his bid for a higher post, thus foreclosing the possibility of a vacancy she could seek. Perfectly at home with her own ambition, she was annoyed with a political commentator on television who attributed her "leadership instincts" to her bloodline.[18]

Nancy Pelosi, like other political daughters, says it had never occurred to her to go into electoral politics. Family hopes focused on her brother, who eventually did follow in their father's footsteps to become the mayor of Baltimore. She describes herself as being a very shy child who "didn't like being the center of attention, so I didn't ever really think of myself as being the one to run." But the intensity of family politics created a passionate bond with the Democratic party, and an intense feeling for "issues of economic fairness and justice." And Pelosi, like Nancy Kassebaum, loved campaigning.

As she grew up, she translated her partisan passions into an extensive career in the Democratic party. Even in her college years, she ignored student politics in favor of the Young Democrats. Later, as a married mother of five living in California, she worked her way up from a volunteer in the Democratic party to become elected statewide chair. Nationally, she was appointed finance chair for the Democratic Senate Campaign Committee, and she chaired the Host Committee for the 1984 Democratic National Convention.

She then waged a campaign she called "one of the toughest of my life" to become head of the Democratic party after the Mondale-Ferraro ticket was defeated. She ran against Paul Kirk for national party chair in 1985. She argues she was the one with the lifetime party credentials, while Kirk was a relative newcomer who had become involved with the national party only months before the 1984 election.

"I had really every credential for that job. I had done everything, organized every kind of thing from platform committees, to rules, to delegate selection, or organizing voter registration, or winning elections." Told by colleagues that if you prepared a person from birth "to be national chair, [Pelosi] would be what would happen—in the course of a life you couldn't be better prepared."

She lost in a bitter fight, and feels the defeat of the Mondale-Ferraro ticket influenced the dynamics of her campaign. "They didn't want an Italian-American—this was 1985, right after the Ferraro race, and they had every excuse in the book. . . . " Despite all her qualifications, what did she learn? "In a political fight, well, political friend is an oxymoron."[19]

Pelosi understands well Madeleine Kunin's observations about women's reluctance to get close to an unfamiliar political system, and isn't willing to paint a rosy picture of the political process in order to encourage women to get involved. "The word *campaign* is a war term. So when you go into a campaign you just prepare to go to war. If you think it is an exercise in civic activity . . . then you are going to be surprised."

However tough Pelosi's loss of the national chairmanship was in 1985, or Kennelly's lost opportunity in 1991, both women considered their losses one battle among many, and not the war. Today, Pelosi is in the House of Representatives, reelected in 1992 for her third full term in Congress.[20] Just two years after Kennelly's first hopes were dashed, she was elected Deputy Whip of the House Democratic Caucus.

While these political daughters—Kassebaum, Kennelly, and Pelosi—received the gift of political familiarity, they didn't reap the rewards sons of a political dynasty usually do. The lingering residues of coverture, the custom of taking a husband's name upon marriage, means they did not benefit from the name recognition a popular or powerful political father could bring them. Kassebaum thinks she was advantaged anyway, having remained in sparsely populated Kansas, where she "grew up in the public eye." More and more married daughters are keeping their family names, as Kathleen Brown has done, or hyphenating them as Lucille Roybal-Allard has done. They are benefiting in ways previously reserved for political sons, including name recognition, endorsements, and outright succession.

Yet parents didn't have to be directly involved in politics to raise daughters confident of their ability and capacity to break out of prescribed roles. Many of today's political women credit a parent or parents with their courage to enter a nontraditional field. Recently, two social psychologists set out to study women in elective office, assuming they would spend most of their time discussing the obstacles these women had overcome. Over and over again, the female officials kept asking "What obstacles?" Uniformly, the women responded in personal and psychological terms: "I always knew I could do what I wanted," or "I always knew I could be whatever I wanted to be."

As a result of these protestations, the two researchers, Dorothy Cantor and Toni Bernay, revised their assumptions and interviewed the women more closely, confirming the importance of these supportive early messages. They contrast the attitudes of successful women with a description of "Marjorie Lockwood," a composite character, whose early and conflicting messages about herself and aspirations were crippling rather than confirming.[21]

A strong beginning is only part of the explanation for how or why women found their way into politics specifically. No matter what level of confidence a political woman exhibits, until recently the route to politics has been very indirect, almost accidental. Some women developed leadership skills in another arena, especially in women's colleges, which enabled them to make a transition when an opportunity arose, but most breakthrough women came to electoral life almost unwittingly, through the pursuit of an issue that became important to them.

Mary Rose Oakar, defeated in 1992 after serving sixteen years in Congress, started her political career by running for the Cleveland City Council. She credits her confidence to run directly to her experience in student government at Ursuline College, a small Catholic women's college in Ohio. Ursuline's small size, and the absence of male competitors, gave her the opportunity to become student body president. "If I had gone to Ohio State, can you imagine? I mean, there I would be lost in the crowd." Being student body president gave her an opportunity to travel, to attend national association meetings, and generally gave her an expanded glimpse of the world. When she moved back to her old neighborhood and saw its deterioration, she was more easily persuaded to run, having had this taste of political life.[22]

Oakar is not alone in believing this experience prepared her to take advantage of new opportunities when they arose. Women at all levels of government were ten times more likely than the norm to have attended women's colleges, according to a recent study.[23] Other studies have confirmed that the experience—and confidence—gained in women's colleges enabled women to assume leadership positions in a variety of nontraditional fields, not just politics. For instance, women who have reached the upper echelon of corporate life were more likely to have this background as well. Reportedly, half of currently serving congresswomen attended all-women high schools or colleges, and sometimes both.[24]

Many of the most senior politicians today made a transition to politics similar to Oakar's, carried forward by the momentum of a family, neighborhood, or community issue about which they felt passionately. The current governor of Oregon, Barbara Roberts, is typical. She was drawn into politics by the needs of her autistic child. Senator Barbara Mikulski was a social worker who got involved in civil rights, and was prompted to run for the Baltimore City Council in 1969 as a result of an effort to stop a major highway from destroying a Baltimore neighborhood.

These particular factors—being born into a political family, being encouraged by parents, acquiring experience in college or at the community level—may have aided women's desire to enter politics, but until the women's movement challenged the general limitations on women's roles, opportunities for a political career were extremely limited.

Elizabeth Dole, former secretary of both the departments of Transportation and Labor, speaks for many women who found opportunities unexpectedly opening up for them. "There has been in my view a revolution in this country, what I call a quiet revolution. I experienced it myself, which makes it very real to me, because at the time I entered law school back in 1962 [as one of 25 women in a class of 550], I was on the cutting edge of a social revolution and didn't realize it."[25]

By the early 1970s, this quiet revolution had been translated into slogans that specifically encouraged women to think about politics. "Make policy, not coffee," touched the chords of confinement many activist women felt over organizational roles that diminished their contributions. Bella Abzug's campaign slogan "A Woman's Place Is in the House—the House of Representatives" became a national slogan. Some expanded Abzug's original slogan and proclaimed "A Woman's Place Is in the House and Senate," while others expanded it to "A Woman's Place Is Everywhere." In asserting the legitimacy of public roles, these slogans became the epigram of an age.

During a period of brief euphoria, when Abzug and other women were catapulted into Congress, and the National Women's Political Caucus (NWPC) was founded, it looked as if the barriers to women's political careers would fall almost of their own volition.

"Nineteen seventy-two is the year for women . . . things will never be the same," proclaimed Abzug at the founding of the NWPC the year after her election. In a similar vein, Betty Friedan talked about electing a hundred women to Congress, "or tens of hundreds to city and county offices and party committees . . . hundreds of thousands, even millions of us will experience the political passion in trying to elect them . . . " She predicted that a woman would run for president by 1976 and, by then, the "second American Revolution" could be declared achieved.[26]

NWPC encouraged states to form their own caucuses, and many did. U.S. Senate candidate (1990 and 1992) Josie Heath of Colorado remembers how nervous she was when she went to her first precinct caucus in 1972, the year McGovern ran for president. She carried in her pocket the instructions she'd memorized from the brand new Colorado Women's Political Caucus on how to ask for equal representation in selecting delegates to the state convention. Hesitantly, she raised the question. "You're right," said the chair, "there should be more women. Take my place." The victories of other congresswomen, Elizabeth Holtzman in New York, or Patricia Schroeder in Colorado, in addition to Abzug, seemed to confirm a new era.

Within a few years, however, it was clear that women weren't going to break into politics, at least at the national level, overnight. At the same time, some of the traditional routes into politics for young men were opening up for young women as well.

A California study showed that fully two thirds of successfully elected minority politicians, both male and female, had been aides to politicians before seeking either local or state office on their own. In fact, regardless of race or ethnicity, half of all candidates who were successfully elected had done a stint as a legislative aide.[27]

Currently a Los Angeles County Supervisor, Gloria Molina, perhaps the most powerful Hispanic female politician in the country, got her start as an aide to California assembly member Art Torres. When her ambitions came to include seeking office for herself she was told by East Los Angeles assemblyman Richard Alatorre that "it wasn't her time." Molina, like Shirley Chisholm before her, refused to be discouraged by the existence of male competition. She ran for the assembly seat anyway, pitting herself against Alatorre's candidate.

Molina won her race, and credits two African-American women in particular with helping her. Maxine Waters, then a state assembly-woman, and Yvonne Brathwaite Burke, who had represented a Los Angeles district in Congress, helped connect Molina with key people throughout the state. "They helped me establish that credibility. Without them I could never have been out there."[28] To this day, however, Alatorre has supported Molina's opponents as she has run, in succession, for the Los Angeles City Council and now the Board of Supervisors.

Anita Perez Ferguson from Santa Barbara, California, who lost her congressional races against incumbents in both 1990 and 1992, found her first opportunity to run when her boss, California's State Senator Gary Hart, decided not to. Initially, it looked as if Ferguson, unlike Molina, would have the backing of her former boss. Ferguson remembers the exact moment she approached him about declaring her candidacy.

They'd been jogging on the Santa Barbara beach at the end of a day in the district office. Dripping wet, she said to Hart: "Sit down. I've been thinking about something. If you are not going to do this [race], I'm going to do it. I know it's a long shot but somebody's got to talk about his record." Ferguson remembers Hart being "quite taken aback," but ultimately he responded to her with a spirited, "okay, Congresswoman, go for it."[29] Hart's original enthusiasm cooled when it looked as if she would defeat the incumbent congressman, Robert Lagomarsino, whom he had failed to oust two years earlier. Ferguson came within four points of defeating incumbent Lagomarsino, nearly as close as Senator Hart. There was one major difference between them: He spent nearly four times as much as Ferguson had. Whether more money would have boosted Ferguson over the top remains unanswerable.

Both Molina and Ferguson gained their early experience in campaigns and by working at the state level. A major alternative to an apprentice-ship route has been to run for office at the local level and work up to running for the state or federal level. The opportunities to embark on this path vary greatly, depending on the regional or even local factors. Geographically, where the electorate has become accustomed to female officeholders, voters are more comfortable with women candidates and are less likely to stereotype them negatively. "There is a ten- to twenty-point difference, systematically," in voter receptivity in areas where women have been elected before," says Democratic consultant Celinda Lake. Republican consultant Linda DiVall describes it as a "snowball effect," helping both women and minorities. "When you have more and more blacks and women running for office and winning, the 'experience factor' becomes less and less of a prejudice in the minds of the voters."[30]

As of 1993, no woman has been elected in her own right to Congress from many states including Alaska, Mississippi (which has never ratified the Nineteenth Amendment, granting suffrage to women), Delaware, Iowa, Vermont, New Hampshire, and Wyoming.[31] States such as Massachusetts and Pennsylvania, where female representation in the state legislature hovers around 7 percent, and where ethnic and machine politics once dominated, are among the least hospitable climates for women candidates. Lynn Yeakel's primary Senate victory was more significant seen in this light, for she ran in a state that had never elected a woman to Congress who wasn't a widow of a congressman.

These are not just statistical patterns known to scholars and consultants. Women candidates feel the difference. When Evelyn Murphy ran for the office of lieutenant governor in 1982, she was the first woman to run for a statewide office in Massachusetts. As a candidate, she benefited from the spill-over effects from neighboring Connecticut, where Ella Grasso had been elected the first female governor in the country on her own.

"I didn't have a base out there," said Murphy, "but because of Ella Grasso's staying power . . . people would listen." Murphy felt that since voters were accustomed to a female face in a position of political authority, she could move beyond her novelty as a female candidate to talking about her political position on issues.[32]

"I know I benefited from Norma Paulus's run for governor in 1986," said Oregon Governor Barbara Roberts after her victory in 1990, even though Paulus was defeated. The Roberts family has helped credential each other in Oregon. Governor Roberts's stepdaughter, Labor Commissioner Mary Wendy Roberts, ran for secretary of state in 1991. When Mary Wendy is confused with her stepmother, the governor, she "just smiles and says thank you." Mary Wendy Roberts's father was also an elected official. He, his daughter, and his future wife had all served in the legislature. (His ex-wife, Betty Roberts, had been a legislator as well as an Oregon Supreme Court justice.) How do the voters respond to all the Robertses in office? "As long as we get there on our own hook, the voters don't seem to mind," says Governor Barbara Roberts.[33]

The effect of a "breakthrough" candidate on future races is so strong that it can affect the same candidate running a second time for the same position. New York comptroller and former congresswoman Elizabeth Holtzman remembers how much change there was between her first and second race for district attorney: "When I first ran [in 1981] for district attorney, voters had a hard time imagining a female D.A. When I ran the second time, it was not a question."[34]

But the WCF's Jane Danowitz cautions that whether or not a state's climate is hospitable for women candidates depends upon more than political breakthroughs. "You look at the South, there's a lack of women in power . . . [a]nd there's not much of a history to build on," says Danowitz. "I think you have to draw parallels between how many women are running corporations down there or how many women are running newspapers and how many women are running for office." Danowitz, speaking just before the 1992 elections, pointed to the fact that the Mississippi legislature has a total of three women members. "We are talking about states which don't even have elected women statewide."[35]

In general, the more women campaign for all elective offices, enabling voters to become accustomed to the idea of female politicians, and the more they break through to top offices, they reduce the "strategic burden" for all women candidates to make their political positions known.

A further complication to establishing credibility is that voters have different standards for different offices. Consultant Tanya Melich says, "It is as if different offices have different personalities." Executive positions are especially hard to win. When a woman runs for mayor or governor, instead of a legislative office, voters want even more assurance that she has the requisite fiscal and managerial skills. At the state level, as in Congress, the "lower" house of the state legislature is less prestigious than either the state senate or statewide executive positions, such as governor, state treasurer, or attorney general.

Traditionally, the threshold has been lower for women to win the secretary of state's position than the attorney general, or state's top cop, position. In 1989 there were only two female attorneys general in the country, and one of them was appointed, not elected. By 1993, women increased their numbers to nine, eight of whom were elected—Colorado, Indiana, Iowa, Nevada, North Dakota, Utah, Virginia, and West Virginia elected women attorneys general; Oklahoma appointed one.[36]

Next to governor and attorney general, the most male-dominated position at the state level has been that of state treasurer. With major victories in the 1990 and 1992 election cycles, women are now the elected state treasurers in sixteen states. Two additional women, Lucille Maurer of Maryland and Georgie Thomas of New Hampshire, were elected treasurer by their respective state legislatures.

The offices of state treasurer and attorney general are two major stepping stones to running for governor. Hence, to increase the pool of women in either of these two positions is to increase the pool of future female gubernatorial candidates. Governor Ann Richards used this office to build her statewide base in Texas, serving eight years prior to running for governor. Republican Kay Bailey Hutchison, who succeeded Richards as Texas state treasurer, positioned herself for higher office by challenging Robert Kruger for the U.S. Senate seat vacated by Lloyd Bentsen when Bentsen became President Clinton's choice for U.S. Secretary of the Treasury.

"It's a key statewide position from which you can move up," says Jane Danowitz. "It's also a very good position from which to raise money. When moguls on Wall Street and moguls in New York in fact have to reach out to these folks, that is extremely important." Danowitz points to California's state treasurer Kathleen Brown as "one of the most powerful political people in the country, if the amount of money managed by her is any criterion."

Brown herself refers frequently to the size of the state's financial portfolio that she manages. One morning she told a radio audience she had invested $463 million before 10:00 A.M. that day. "If those aren't credentials, I don't know what is," she told a gathering of high-powered women on another occasion.

Ohio's state treasurer Mary Ellen Withrow, who is head of the National Association of State Treasurers, notes with irony that just because voters think women are qualified for these posts doesn't mean their defeated opponents think they are qualified. Virtually every man who was defeated in his bid for election or reelection to the position of state treasurer called Withrow after his defeat in 1990 to complain that the women who won were not qualified. The men apparently found Withrow's gender irrelevant, and assumed she would provide a sympathetic ear.

Iowa's first female attorney general, Bonnie Campbell, has not been coy about building a base from which to run for governor—and her critics have made it an issue. Her aggressiveness in prosecuting consumer fraud scams targeted to senior citizens, and her extensive travel around the state to explain her programs and actions—forty-four counties out of ninety-nine in her first year of office—had her potential rivals sputtering about the inappropriate use of office. Her behavior, however, is a tried-and-true approach to climbing the political ladder and building a political career.

How important is establishing this credibility? Both Celinda Lake and Republican campaign consultant John Deardourff believe that a woman's campaign message—her stands on particular issues—cannot even be heard by voters until they are convinced she is qualified for the office sought. "Men are perceived to be competent until proven otherwise, whereas women have to prove that they are competent," says Deardourff. "[B]eing perceived as a credible candidate remains the Gordian Knot of women's campaigns," argues Lake.

"Since competence tends to be the threshold question about all questions . . . issue positions, and everything else, I have always felt that women's campaigns have to have a fast, early start in which the purpose is to demonstrate that you have the competence and the experience to do the job that you want," adds Deardourff.[37]

When Deardourff, DiVall, or Lake use the term *credibility*, they are using a word that captures one of the most important—and elusive—requirements in politics. Establishing credibility is the most critical threshold test in politics, extending far beyond good credentials or paper qualifications. And in most cases, it must be established long before voters actually cast their ballots in a general election.

The more unfamiliar the voters are with a woman candidate, the harder she must work to demonstrate her competence. In areas where few women have run or held office, women candidates will be viewed through a perceptual screen of general female stereotypes. Archetypical images evoked by the terms *female* or *feminine* challenge women candidates on several fronts simultaneously. As discussed earlier, even images that evoke positive feelings and respect in the domestic realm, such as those of the nurturing mother, have lacked authority when projected into the public realm. When voters see women candidates more as mothers than experienced politicians, they are unsure how a mother's compassion and empathy will play in the governor's chair.

Evoking a candidate's image as mother is so powerful that it can "drown out her political experience." Lake described one Midwestern candidate's television ad: She was shown with her children while her office-holding experience was described in a voice-over. Despite her excellent political credentials, "she was perceived as just starting out."

Political accomplishments, Lake says, are diminished by "the least visual image to the contrary . . . "[38] By contrast, a male politician can count on a picture of him with his family sending a positive message to voters.

Opponents play to this vulnerability in women's campaigns regardless of how much experience women candidates have had or how comparable to men their credentials might be. Democratic consultant Michael Berman is blunt about what strategies he would use to run against a woman.

He would identify "the community's perception of the role of women, and where it is on the spectrum of advancement about the roles of women." And once he knew that? "Then I would play to that in a way that was not particularly harsh, because the harsh always backfires."[39]

When Barbara Roberts ran for governor of Oregon, she had acquired political experience that spanned more than two decades and encompassed every level of state government. Since the days she had been spurred into local activism by the special needs of her autistic son, she had moved from a lobbyist, to elected school board official, to state legislator before winning a statewide race for secretary of state in 1985.

President George Bush, in Oregon to campaign for her rival, Republican attorney general Dave Frohmayer, warned voters that if they voted for Barbara Roberts, they would have to put up with "on-the-job training."[40]

President Bush's remark may appear thoughtless, but he was making a strategic hit, aimed directly at the vulnerability of women's campaigns. He was deliberately playing to the enduring skepticism voters have about the qualifications of women candidates, especially for executive positions. Are they really capable of running a state? Experienced enough to put down a prison riot? Tough enough to call out the national guard?

Voters had the same question in 1990 about Dianne Feinstein's bid for governor, despite her two decades of experience in the volatile politics of San Francisco, many as its mayor. In 1969, when she was elected to the San Francisco Board of Supervisors, she was the top vote-getter, entitling her to become president of the board. She served two terms, running once unsuccessfully for mayor, before the assassination of Mayor George Moscone thrust her, as the board's president, into the mayoralty in 1978. Reelected mayor in 1979, she survived one recall effort and won yet another term as mayor in 1983. She governed San Francisco until 1987. Yet, according to California pollster Mervin Field, the key question in voters' minds was whether Feinstein was competent enough to handle the governorship.

Feinstein's opponent in the primary race for governor, Attorney General John Van de Kamp, exploited this vulnerability in his television ads: "If she couldn't manage San Francisco, how could she manage a state?" The ads maintained that Feinstein left her successor with a budget deficit, which Feinstein vigorously disputed. Whether the deficit existed or not, the issue allowed Van de Kamp to adapt a very old strategy against which comparable credentials were no guarantee.

Feinstein lost her race for governor in 1990; Roberts won hers.

If women candidates whose credentials were as equivalent as possible to male candidates (as "like-male" as possible) have had trouble winning voters' confidence, women whose leadership experiences have been in community or volunteer organizations have had a more difficult time establishing their qualifications. If they have never held office, they face the challenge of convincing party officials and voters that their credentials are simply different, not inferior, to those acquired through legal and business experience, more typical of male candidates who also lack office-holding experience.

In this respect, Lynn Yeakel's victory in the 1992 Pennsylvania primary for the U.S. Senate may be seen as a landmark. She was able to establish herself as a credible candidate for high office without prior electoral experience. Her background as a fund-raiser for charitable institutions was almost prototypically female. The difficulty of parlaying a nonpolitical career into a top office, however, may have caught up with her during the general election. Her vulnerability as a candidate stemmed from voter perceptions that she was a one-issue candidate, running against Arlen Specter on the basis of his treatment of Anita Hill but without strong policy stances on other issues.

Minority women must establish their credentials through two perceptual screens: one female and the other racial or ethnic. Congressional candidate Anita Perez Ferguson assessed how ethnicity and gender affected her candidacy in a district where primary images of Latinos were likely to be as "janitors, maids, or gardeners." "The general public image of Latinas is not one of competency or leadership . . . [it] is a greater leap from housekeeper to a leader than from [an image as] a professional woman."[41]

Irene Natividad, former head of the National Women's Political Caucus, agrees with Ferguson's observations and adds, "[b]ecause the experience that brings a woman of color to decide to run for office may not always be known to a larger group beyond her immediate community, there is always a perception that she somehow brings less credentials as a candidate."[42]

The surest way to establish oneself as a credible candidate—one who is competent *and* can win—is to raise the most amount of money early and discourage other contenders. Money is often so controlling a factor in establishing credibility that the entire next chapter is devoted to it. Yet money is unlikely to flow into a campaign unless credentials are in place, along with a record of voter confidence expressed through successful elections. This catch-22 has been particularly maddening to women candidates: You need money to be credible, but you have to be credible to obtain money. Estimates of a candidate's credibility are frequently based on the likelihood of winning, an assessment that is difficult to quantify. Money is quantifiable—a full treasury conveys key support.

The fact that political parties no longer do as much recruiting or grooming of candidates for office as they once did has been a mixed blessing for women. While it may open up opportunities in parts of the country where party officials are not receptive to women candidates, it vastly increases the focus on individual initiative. This is especially true for the top offices, and generally requires that women own some of the ambition they need to make such a decision, even though they are still likely to put it in terms of serving others.

The formal process of obtaining a party's nomination will vary from state to state. Some nomination contests are fought out among voters in a primary election. In others, candidates are nominated by caucuses or by statewide conventions. And still other states combine all three modes—caucus, convention, and primary—before awarding a nomination. While these formal procedures dictate which specific steps a woman must take to win the nomination, many of the important decisions involved in running are made informally, including the decision to come forward and solicit support from key officials.

Barbara Mikulski says of her eventual decision to run for the U.S. Senate, "There is no one moment where you wake up one day and decide." She thinks her overriding goal "has always been to help everybody who is middle class stay there or get better, and everyone who is not middle class . . . "[43] Running for higher office where she could make more of a difference became logical.

Mikulski conforms to a pattern that analysts have found holds for politicians generally. Office-holding generates its own ambition. While political scientists have spent considerable time studying the subject of ambition and politics, few studies have focused specifically on ambition in women or compared men and women. One study that did compare male and female local officials concluded there were no differences in aspirations between the two sexes. The differences arose when aspirations were translated into action. Both sexes were willing to run when they felt they had a good chance of winning, but when women weren't sure of electoral success, they tended not to run. "Insecure men ran anyway," according to the researchers.[44]

Senator Mikulski's counsel is often sought by officeholders thinking about moving up; she says she has noted a difference between how men and women think about making the decision. Men ask "Is it worth it?" Then they want to talk "strategy, tactics, organizing, who's a good pollster . . ." The women all want to talk about their issues: "It's almost like they are prepping for their SATs or their doctoral orals. They think they have to have answers to every question they are going to get, everything from the water quality of the Chesapeake Bay to solving the savings and loan crisis."[45]

In the absence of a vigorous party effort to recruit candidates for office, obtaining support from key individuals or organizations becomes critically important. Organizations or key individuals can give or withhold support from individual candidates, encourage or discourage them from running. Over the last twenty years the Women's Campaign Fund and the National Women's Political Caucus are credited by women candidates with providing critical moral and psychic support, and lots of concrete help through their training sessions.

Congresswoman Jolene Unsoeld says it was the WCF, and Celinda Lake in particular, that urged her to think about making the move from the Washington state legislature to Congress.

"We grew up with these women," says Danowitz. The Women's Campaign Fund has not only supported women for the top offices, they have identified potential candidates through their training sessions, and supported them as they have climbed the ladder from local to state office.

One of the marked changes in these sessions over the years has been the subtle shift from male to female experts who conduct the training sessions. Whether the topic addresses the nuts and bolts of politics, such as managing a media consultant, or a public policy issue, such as public finance, the experts are women who have broken into these previously male domains. They help to create a warm and comfortable atmosphere where women feel thoroughly at ease in asking questions they might feel otherwise to be naive or unsophisticated.

Clint Reilly, Feinstein's first campaign consultant when she ran for governor, paid this new network of women's organizations a backhanded compliment. After months of ambivalence about running, Reilly says Feinstein became particularly motivated to run after returning from Washington, D.C., where she received "the succor of the sisterhood."

These new networks are particularly good at providing support at the beginning of a woman's candidacy; however, as Danowitz says, eventually "she has to go to the male establishment." One of the important commodities this establishment possesses is the capacity to endorse or withhold support from a candidate.

With a record of office-holding experience, a woman candidate is more likely to obtain endorsements from people whose own power and prestige can enhance her own standing and impress the voters. Until very recently, of course, most of these figures have been men. Used strategically, they could reassure voters on key elements of a woman's competence or credentials.

Now, some women have become heads of networks or sought-after figures who can give other up-and-coming politicians, male or female, a boost. Los Angeles supervisor Gloria Molina, whose political career began as an aide to Assemblyman Art Torres, now heads her own network. Powerful women do not always credential other women, even from the same political party. Two years before Barbara Boxer and Dianne Feinstein went on the road as Thelma and Louise, Boxer had endorsed Attorney General John Van de Kamp in the Democratic primary for governor. "The best feminist in the race," she called him, an endorsement deliberately designed to exploit Feinstein's rocky relationships with some women's organizations.

In 1990, Claudine Schneider was outraged when Geraldine Ferraro came to Rhode Island to campaign for her opponent and fellow Democrat, Claiborne Pell. Most politicos would say it's expecting a lot to think women should cross party lines to support other women. Others argue that women should simply stay out of the state in such cases.

Comparable credentials, money, endorsements, and hard work, however, do not mean that any political step will be easy. Women with years of office-holding experience have been surprised to find themselves described as "overnight sensations," or "coming from nowhere," when they announced their candidacies for higher office.

"I'm a twenty-two-year overnight sensation," quipped Barbara Mikulski when she won her U.S. Senate seat after twelve years on the Baltimore City Council. Josie Heath, with twenty years of political experience in Colorado, won the nomination for the U.S. Senate race in 1990 after a grueling campaign that required winning in turn local caucuses, a statewide party convention, and a primary. She was continually described as "coming from nowhere."

In fact, Heath was the only one of the three candidates who had *any* office-holding experience. Her sense of humor intact, she thought about changing the sign at the entrance to Boulder, Colorado, to read: "Welcome to Virtual Obscurity," the phrase used most often by the press to describe each level of her victories.

What galls many women candidates is that the lack of office-holding experience is not a deterrent to male candidates. Heath, for instance, had been chair of the Governor's Commission on Women, administered the regional office of a federal agency during the Carter administration, and had been twice elected to the Boulder County Commission. Despite this local, state, and federal experience, she was frequently accused of "aiming too high."

Wendy Sherman, who managed Barbara Mikulski's campaign in 1986 and is now a media consultant, cautions that women have a very hard time skipping any step in the political ladder. "There are no short-cuts to the U.S. Senate," she argues.

It was this reality that lay behind Governor Ann Richards's comment to Robert Schaefer at CBS during the 1992 Democratic National Convention that women were probably not ready to run for president. Viable presidential contenders are generally drawn from two pools of politicians: U.S. senators and state governors. The more seniority and experience acquired in each arena, the more likely candidates are to be considered presidential timber. Without credentials that are comparable—and perceived as comparable—to the most qualified men, women are unlikely to be considered viable candidates for the U.S. presidency.

Ironically, just how much change there has been in women's campaigns over the last twenty years is revealed by an examination of men's campaigns. Men are turning to powerful women to give them *credibility* with women voters.

Arlen Specter turned to Teresa Heinz, the widow of a recently deceased senator from Pennsylvania, to offset his Anita Hill problem in the campaign against Lynn Yeakel. Heinz was featured in a television ad praising his record on women's issues and giving him her hearty endorsement.

Mel Levine tried to establish his credibility against Barbara Boxer in the primary by running ads that featured endorsements by incumbent female politicians and from Sally Ride, the first female astronaut.

The reason for these changes are not ephemeral. They are firmly rooted in the need to win women's votes. Like the emergence of strong and experienced female candidates, the increased clout of women's votes has altered the dynamics of modern campaigns, and will be explored in a later chapter. What is important in this context is that men, for the first time in history, are routinely turning to female authority figures for help in establishing their credentials with voters.

The cumulative effect of the changes analyzed in this chapter and the following two—on financing campaigns and winning women's votes—is a mutually reinforcing dynamic. As women have acquired political experience, they have been more able to raise money to finance their campaigns, a feat that in turn enhances their credibility—even if they are challenging entrenched incumbents.

As more voters give women candidates their votes, and increase their success rates, the more competitive women candidates become, in part, because they are breaking through one of the last barriers to their candidacies: the perception that however qualified they are, they can't win. The final and greatest equalizer, however, is incumbency.

"Incumbency, male or female, it doesn't matter . . . it is gender free . . . " says Jane Danowitz of the Women's Campaign Fund. Studies confirm her observations. At a gathering of political women at the University of Texas in Austin, Max Sherman, dean of the Lyndon Baines Johnson School of Public Policy at the University of Texas, discussed the effects of new female officeholders and incumbency in his state.

"People know about big city mayors, like former Houston mayor Kathy Whitmire," said Sherman. "But they don't realize how many medium-size cities in Texas are governed by women." Now that Ann Richards is governor, Sherman believes her presence will reinforce a positive climate for women simply by her being at the helm. More important, for the long run, one can expect her to use her considerable appointment power to advance women even further. The real story on women and politics in Texas, says Sherman, "is what happens ten years from now."[46]

Women feel this debt to the women who have come before them, even if they don't fully comprehend the dynamic. As Governor Barbara Roberts put it, "We stand on the shoulders of the women who came before us."

And veteran officeholders, such as Senator Barbara Mikulski or Governors Ann Richards and Barbara Roberts, exhibit the same passion for their work and confidence in their skills as do political daughters.

"The genre in which I choose to live my life is the best place in the world ... absolutely," claimed Senator Mikulski. Then, she paused: "Though Ann Richards told me last Monday that governor was where it's at."[47]

Richards, Roberts, Mikulski, Kassebaum, Kunin, Schroeder, Feinstein, Boxer, and others are among the handful of women who are leading a growing parade of women, slowly but inexorably, toward the presidency—the last threshold women must cross.

6

==

Raising the Ante

Campaign Finance and New Women's Networks

hree thousand people, a majority women, filed out of San
Francisco's Davies Symphony Hall on the evening of October 19,
1992. They had each paid $100 to support Dianne Feinstein and Barbara
Boxer in their bids to represent California in the U.S. Senate. It had been
an evening of gospel and folk music, poetry, and laughter, a combination
of unrestrained partisan bashing, feminist celebration, and spiritual revival.

The ability of women candidates to raise $300,000 in one evening did
not exist twenty, ten, or even six years ago. The sheer amount of money
raised, however, is only one change in fund-raising for women candidates. All the elements of this women's event, from the gamble to try and
fill a venue as large as Davies Symphony Hall at a $100 a throw to its
corporate sponsorship, featured speakers, and mostly female audience,
reflect significant changes in the financial independence of women and
therefore the funding of women's campaigns.

The first fund-raising event to yield big money for a woman candi-
date—$400,000 in one evening—occurred just two years earlier, during
Ann Richards's race for governor of Texas. Billed as "Another Man for
Ann," it had featured Senator Sam Nunn of Georgia. Now, Ann Richards

was the star attraction, regaling the audience with political jokes and ringing endorsements of Boxer and Feinstein, her voice hoarse after twenty-four hours of campaigning for Lynn Yeakel in Pennsylvania and Carol Moseley-Braun in Illinois.

Listening to Ann Richards were women who had not only opened their checkbooks for this event, but who had written thousands of dollars to support women candidates across the country. Also in the audience were women whose incomes were much more modest but who nevertheless wrote small monthly checks to women candidates, or regularly had contributions deducted from their bank accounts.

Many of the women in Davies Hall that evening supported women candidates they had never personally met, thanks to the existence of a new national organization designed specifically to support Democratic women. EMILY's List, which is an acronym For Early Money Is Like Yeast (it makes the dough rise), founded in 1985, provided candidate information to its members, each of whom joined the list for $200 and a commitment to write at least two other checks of $100 each to recommended candidates.

In 1992, EMILY's List claimed to be the largest single political action committee (PAC) in the country, raising $6 million for women candidates, exceeding the $4.3 million raised and spent by the powerful Realtors PAC. In recognition of its new and powerful role, founder Ellen Malcolm had been invited to rally the audience at Davies Hall.

Even the major corporate sponsor of the event, Esprit, was owned by a woman, Susie Tompkins. Most corporations try to remain publicly nonpartisan, but Tompkins chose to put her corporate stamp on this event even at the risk of losing customers whose partisan sentiments were different. Only one tiny moment of embarrassment had marred the evening; that was when speakers exhorted women to make additional contributions by foregoing an Armani dress or a pair of Ferragamos, since these items cost considerably more than those in the Esprit line.

Why was this event so historic? Some elements, such as the amount of money raised—$300,000—are obvious; others must be set in context.

Twenty years ago most married women did not have bank accounts in their own name, even if they were employed. If their husbands disapproved of women in politics, the women were unlikely to use their joint accounts to make campaign contributions. If the women did have access to resources, and no one to consult about their use, they were no more inclined than men to support women candidates.

Twenty years ago it was hard to find women candidates with the political experience and stature of Boxer and Feinstein. Not only had these women amassed years of office-holding experience, each of them had survived hotly contested primary elections against highly ambitious and politically experienced men. Even support from co-sponsor of the Davies Hall event, the Democratic Senate Campaign Committee (DSCC), had been elusive for women candidates, since the DSCC support is targeted primarily to incumbent officeholders.

Just as women candidates such as Boxer and Feinstein have unlocked the catch-22 that kept women from being competitive candidates, they have also unlocked the money needed to run for office. As they have developed a tradition of political leadership, gained experience, and increased their stature, both new and old sources of political money have opened up to them.

Yet for all this new success in raising the money necessary to be competitive, the candidacies of Feinstein and Boxer illustrate a negative side of politics: Together, their Senate races cost over $17 million. The imperative to raise such large sums is perhaps the most potent force shaping politics today. It pushes the campaigns of both men and women in a similar direction, and undercuts the argument that women will campaign, legislate, or govern differently.

The dollars candidates have to raise escalate with virtually every election cycle. The average cost (1990–92) of a Senate race is $3 to $4 million, while the average cost of a seat in the House of Representatives is roughly $400,000, although an individual congressional race often costs $1 million or more.[1] These figures vary across states and districts.

The extraordinary growth in campaign spending in the last several decades has been driven primarily by the need to hire a battery of consultants and the cost of television advertising aimed at potential voters. In all but very local elections, it is impossible to convey a candidate's credentials or message by knocking on doors. That means money is needed for television and radio ads, direct mail solicitations, brochures or bumper stickers, and other media that can reach large numbers of voters. As a profession, political consultants barely existed twenty years ago. Today, while candidates might like to do without them, most would agree it is perilous not to hire professional pollsters, media consultants, or campaign managers.

"Before you give your first speech you have committed yourself to anywhere from $500,000 to $1 million in infrastructure," says Maryland senator Barbara Mikulski, recalling the beginning of her successful 1986 Senate race.

Such large sums scare off potential candidates. Both men and women have been discouraged from running, with the effect of reducing competition for most offices and increasing incumbency return rates.[2]

"Convinced that they did not have access to large amounts of political money, over the last decade many women attracted to politics decided not to run for office, especially not to bid for higher offices than the ones they held on local councils or in legislatures," such was the conclusion reached by Ruth Mandel, director of the Eagleton Institute's Center for the Study of the American Woman and Politics at Rutgers University.[3] Mandel reached her conclusions through extensive interviews with political women, although how many women decide *not* to do something is impossible to measure.

The theme of money as a deterrent to moving up was prevalent during interviews for this book. Months before Los Angeles mayor Tom Bradley announced he would not seek reelection in 1992, Gloria Molina, supervisor on the Los Angeles County Board, was forthright about her interest in the mayor's race. Did she ever think about running for mayor? "Over and over and over again." She then sighed. "But, I could never raise that kind of money." By January 1993, Molina had removed herself from speculation about her candidacy.

There is no evidence that money alone determines the outcome of political races, although it is widely perceived as doing so. The best evidence that money isn't definitive is that Republican spending for Congress has far exceeded Democrats'; however, Democrats have won most of the races.

The strategic use of money in a campaign is what makes it so critical, even when it cannot guarantee winning. Money raised early in a campaign can buy a candidate much needed name recognition and can discourage competitors from entering a party primary. Many individuals and organizations insist on polling data or other concrete evidence of electibility, such as key endorsements, before coughing up any cash. For cash-poor candidates, this requirement may seem another insurmountable catch-22, since polls cost money—usually thousands of dollars. Before money can be raised, it must be spent.

The sheer amount of money amassed early in a campaign can be a determinant of credibility itself.[4] Any doubt about a woman's political credentials or her competence often translates directly into the lack of campaign contributions. Former Vermont governor Madeleine Kunin puts it bluntly: "I think your strength as a candidate depends on how well you can raise money. . . . If you don't raise it, you are in trouble."[5]

Just as the dwindling strength of political parties has made it imperative for prospective candidates to be aggressive in seeking party nominations, raising the all-important early money requires similar initiative. And unless the candidate is an incumbent, these early financial tests must be met without party assistance.

The first money candidates ante up is often personal, raising some complicated feelings for women who must commit family resources. If her husband has been the wage earner, will she feel entitled to commit these resources? Will financing the campaign mean she must jeopardize the children's college education money or long-dreamed-of retirement plans? Widowed, divorced, or single women candidates without personal wealth have had to mortgage their homes, take out terrifyingly large loans, and otherwise gamble their savings on winning their races.

Male candidates must take (and have taken) these risks as well. For most women, however, such financial risk-taking is a new experience, requiring a departure from a deeply imbedded tradition that puts the needs of others before personal ambition.

Even if husbands are fully supportive of their wives' political ambitions, the decision to commit family resources means "tough conversations to have," says Josie Heath, who ran for the U.S. Senate in both 1990 and 1992. During her first race in 1990, Heath described going to the bank to assume sole responsibility for a $200,000 line of credit, secured by the couple's joint assets, as one of the most sobering moments in the campaign.

"Even though I was very comfortable with the fact that I had contributed [to our family income]—my husband was making probably twenty times what I was making in one year—I really had a hard time . . . " With three children in or headed for college, Heath kept asking herself if she was mortgaging their future. "Somehow [women] have been really comfortable giving our time, giving our talents, but we've never felt like we could mortgage the farm. I took that loan knowing that I would be completely responsible for it if I couldn't raise it."

Heath lost, and after raising about $25,000 in funds from small donors, she had to assume the remainder of the debt. No novice to politics, Heath knew she couldn't expect any post-election assistance from the Democrats, but she also knew that sometimes wealthy individuals will assist a candidate with a debt. Despite a record of extensive political and financial support for others, Heath says, "Not one big Democratic party person called and said, 'What can I do, can I help?'"[6]

Although most candidates carefully budget how much of their personal assets they will commit, holding to the original plan can be difficult in the heat of a campaign. The pressure to commit more funds can be terrific if the election looks close. Geraldine Ferraro committed $25,000 in personal resources at the beginning of her first congressional campaign in 1978, believing, falsely as it turned out, that personal loans could be paid back by the campaign. By the time it was over, she had spent nearly $43,000 in family money, nearly one third of the campaign total of more than $130,000. "Once you're determined and you spend, you can't just walk away from it."[7]

Married women may be hit with a double whammy if they do summon the courage to commit family resources. The commitment of joint resources is the main vehicle that thrusts husbands into the political limelight. Voters want full disclosure of the sources of joint income and contributions, as Geraldine Ferraro found out so brutally and painfully in the wake of her historic nomination as vice president.

While male candidates also commit family or joint resources, few of their wives have received similar scrutiny, even if they are known to be the source of the family's wealth. At least one consultant has suggested that any man's first rule of thumb when faced with a woman candidate should be to "investigate the damn spouse."

Next to Ferraro's husband, Richard Blum may be the most investigated spouse in American politics. Married to Dianne Feinstein, he loaned her 1990 gubernatorial campaign $3 million, making the full range of his business dealings the subject of media investigation.

The controversy over the loan was not so much that it was large—that is not unusual if a candidate has considerable resources—but that it thrust the composition of Blum's financial holdings into the campaign. Feinstein had attacked her opponent, Pete Wilson, for receiving more contributions from the savings and loan industry than any other senator. Her attack was undercut by the fact that Blum bought a small interest in a savings and loan bank that had received federal bailout money. The amount was less than one percent of the savings and loan, and no part of the transaction was conducted in her name. An angry Feinstein had to repeatedly defend Blum's investments.

"Technically, no woman married to an investment banker, then, could ever be in public life," argued a furious Feinstein. "This is all his business. I have nothing to do with it. It's his—and it was before we were married. A woman marries a man as she finds him."[8]

Wilson also repeatedly demanded to see Blum's corporate returns and his client list, a demand that Blum initially refused. Not wanting to hurt Feinstein's campaign, he finally acceded to the request. Ironically, Wilson's own wealth came mostly from his second marriage. Before that event, he counted himself among the modestly endowed senators. A close friend runs his blind trust. Yet there was never a hint that his family resources, or the investments of the trust, should be subjected to public scrutiny.

In the aftermath of the Feinstein-Wilson campaign, California congresswoman Nancy Pelosi observed that, even if opponents can't find anything wrong with financial transactions, "they try to make it into class warfare," citing Dianne Feinstein's case. "They tried to say she has all this money, she wouldn't understand our problems. They play it a few different ways. I think the only way you can confront that is just to confront it."

Whatever the level of family income or how much of it is committed to the campaign, women candidates are learning that the couple's financial affairs must be impeccable. If they are not, wifely ignorance is not an effective defense. When Eleanor Holmes Norton was running to become the voting delegate to Congress from the District of Columbia, *The Washington Post* reported that she and her husband had not paid city taxes for the very district she wanted to represent. While she survived the last-minute revelations, claiming her husband was responsible for paying the tax bills, her support dropped and her reputation as a feminist was tarnished.

If the sources of joint income are earned in any way that conflicts with a woman's political or policy position, her credibility can be undermined. In 1982, Roxanne Conlin tried to move up to the governor's chair in Iowa, the first woman in the state's history to seek a major-party nomination for governor. A progressive Democrat who advocated closing various tax loopholes to raise state tax revenues, her campaign plummeted when it was disclosed that the family's income included investments that took advantage of those very same loopholes. "On July 1 it was revealed that she and her husband, whose combined net worth exceeds $2 million, paid no state income taxes in 1981 and only $3,000 in federal income taxes."[9]

The most poignant tale of financial risk came from Congresswoman Jolene Unsoeld of Washington. A mountain climbing accident had claimed her well-known husband, Willy Unsoeld, and she was widowed when she decided to run for Congress. Her only asset was her mortgaged home. The campaign ran up what Unsoeld believed was a small debt, but she then discovered the debt was $78,000—substantially larger than she thought. To add to the tension, her election had been so close that the outcome was unclear. A re-count dragged on for weeks after the November election, leaving Unsoeld in agony well into December.

"I had to face the possibility I would not only lose the election, but I might also lose my home."[10] Fortunately for Unsoeld, she won, but just 618 votes separated her from a bleak financial future.[11]

Joan Kelly Horn from Missouri ran her first race for Congress in 1990. Her dilemmas, like Unsoeld's, are different from those that wealth can bring to a campaign. Horn had little personal money, and she was taking on an incumbent. She estimated that her total assets, including a house she owned, came to under $60,000. She gave up her campaign management business before the campaign in order to avoid any conflicts of interest, and put $9,000, or one sixth of her total worth, into the campaign kitty. Like Unsoeld, Horn had to wait weeks for a re-count before learning whether or not she had won a narrow upset. She had—by only forty-eight votes. Winning enabled her to recover her initial investment of $9,000. But she had to use it for living expenses between the November election and January, when she could draw a congressional salary.[12]

Sooner or later, regardless of personal resources, candidates must hit the fund-raising trail. They must seek donations from individuals and organizations who have the resources.

Candidates, newcomers and veterans alike, express their feelings with a mantralike chant. "I hate it, I hate it, I hate it." "I would have to gear myself up until I could eat ground glass," is the way Governor Ann Richards described her feelings about fund-raising.[13]

Ironically, women have long been pioneers in the field of fund-raising, and as individuals they are often experienced fund-raisers. Yet most of the money they raise is on behalf of others, whether people or causes, and not for themselves. Thus, the need to raise funds to support their own ambition sets into motion another "inner skirmish," requiring not only a set of skills but a level of self-promotion that does not come easily to many women. They must say to friends and strangers alike: "Support me, I'll be an excellent candidate."

"Women must usually surmount inner obstacles before asking for other people's support to further their own personal ambitions," Ruth Mandel wrote after interviewing women candidates from the 1970s. Despite the greater success women have had raising money in the 1980s, Celinda Lake observes that "[w]omen are often apologetic in asking for money."[14] While male candidates often hate fund-raising, their hatred doesn't seem to be based on a struggle to put themselves forward.

"Women are not comfortable with 'I'm good, invest in me,'" says Congresswoman Nancy Johnson of Connecticut as she remembers her first difficult race. "Boy, my first campaign . . . if I hadn't been able to have as my finance chairman one of the most respected businessmen in Connecticut, I probably could not have raised the money." But, she added, "It's a matter of professional development . . . you get to know the business better and you respect the contributions of an able elected official." Then it's easier to ask people for backing. She is forthright in her pitch, "You know how I do this job. If you can do a better job, run, and I'll back you."[15]

Congresswoman Nancy Pelosi is not only a veteran fund-raiser but someone who is known for her fund-raising proficiency. For instance, as past finance chair of the Democratic Senate Campaign Committee, she raised huge sums of money for Democrats running for the U.S. Senate. But for herself? That's harder: "I can bake the pie or I can sell the pie, but don't ask me to sell my own pie. It's embarrassing."

Campaign consultant Clint Reilly, who has worked for many women candidates, including Pelosi, singles out her willingness to do fund-raising and her skills at it—despite her own ambivalence—as exemplary and exceptional.

"Women don't know how to fund-raise. Pelosi puts it all together. Knows how to raise money. With the others, every day is a psychodrama." As if to temper what might be an impolitic remark, he adds, "Most women make better governors . . . if you can get through the campaign."

Reilly points to a lack of knowledge or skills as an explanation for why women have difficulty fund-raising. More likely, the explanation lies in women's absence from the financial networks to which they must gain access. After women have gained incumbent status, they find, along with

Congresswoman Johnson, fund-raising becomes easier since their status as an incumbent solidifies ties to financial networks.

For incumbent and nonincumbent candidates alike, after personal money, there are three basic sources of political money to tap: individuals, political action committees (PACs), and political parties.

Campaign reform laws of the mid-1970s, passed in the wake of the Watergate scandal, limit the amount of money both individuals and PACs can give to an individual candidate. In federal elections (state laws may vary), individuals may give $1,000, while political action committees may give up to $5,000.

These reforms, however, have actually increased the clout of wealthy individuals, because the need to raise large sums of money was not eliminated. If wealthy individuals could no longer bankroll an entire campaign because of contribution limits, they were needed to broker political money by creating "networks of well-heeled associates" who could be called upon to support specific candidates.[16]

"[T]he majority of fund-raisers are in business involving extensive financial dealings with wealthy people: investment banking, movie production, real estate development, insurance, prestigious law firms, stocks and bonds, venture capital and lobbying," argues Tom Edsall of *The Washington Post*, who has studied extensively the relationship between money and politics.[17] These are the groups of individuals who receive invitations for $500- or $1,000-a-plate dinners and fund-raisers.

These businesses are precisely the ones from which women have been most excluded. Hence, whatever access women candidates gained from these traditional sources was determined by men. Similarly, the absence of female decision-makers in those business, labor, or professional associations making up the bulk of political action committees reflects their absence from these professions.

Access to all three sources is primarily tied to incumbency status. Women candidates have complained that, even when they have gained access, they receive smaller contributions than male candidates. Yet most women have run as challengers, and challengers generally raise much less money than incumbents. One study found that even when the seat was open, women tended to run in districts where the opposing party generally won the seat.

In 1980, for instance, out of eighty-four congressional candidates running for open seats, six were women. All but one was running in a district where the opposition party had held the position. As the researchers put it, "women were running in greater numbers for the most impossible races."[18] When two factors were taken into account—the nature of the race and the district's partisan character—the differences in monetary support between men and women dwindled. In fact, "donors behaved like bookmakers—what mattered was which horse would cross the finish line first, not whether it was a filly or a colt."[19] The fact that most women did not run as incumbents helped to solidify the belief that women, as women, could not raise political money.

Between the power of incumbency and lack of access to financial networks, it was not surprising that women candidates have found fund-raising so frustrating over the years.

Not until 1978 did a woman candidate raise over $100,000 in a congressional race.[20] Republican Marge Roukema of New Jersey won both a primary contest, which cost $18,000, and the general election, which cost another $125,000. This milestone, however, took place in an election cycle in which it was not unusual for House seats to cost a quarter of a million dollars.

As women became more competitive, their fund-raising capacity expanded. By 1986, women candidates raised 25 percent more than they were able to in 1980, reflecting their increased ability to capture party nominations.[21] As women started to solve the circular equation that had kept them from being competitive candidates, their access to traditional sources of political money began to increase.

However, the single most important change in funding women's campaigns is the creation of a new base of financial support among women. To some extent this new base reflects women's rise in business and professional circles. Even if their resources are inherited or earned by husbands, this increased support for women candidates is illustrative of a new independence among female givers. A number of women's organizations, many of them brand new, are helping both to create this donor base and to direct its resources to women candidates.

Two bipartisan organizations have labored in the fund-raising vineyard for most of the past twenty years, and their history chronicles these changes. The Women's Campaign Fund (WCF) was founded in 1974 specifically to raise money and to support women candidates. The National Women's Political Caucus (NWPC), formed in 1971, while a more multifaceted organization than the WCF, provided the first mechanism for women to financially support women's candidacies through state or local chapters. Subsequently it created a political action committee similar to the Women's Campaign Fund. Until the formation of the first partisan organization specifically for women candidates, EMILY's List, these two organizations have provided the bulk of financial support to women candidates.

In 1974, the WCF diagnosed two fund-raising problems for women's campaigns. First, its founders realized that since most women candidates were challengers not incumbents, they were unlikely to receive PAC funds.[22] Second, they believed that there were PACs potentially sympathetic to challengers, but that female newcomers seldom knew who they were or how to solicit their support.

Actual monetary support over the years from the WCF has been modest, until the Thomas/Hill hearings precipitated a general explosion in funds for women candidates. The pool of donors who could be counted upon to fund the WCF's bipartisan agenda of electing more women, whether they were Republicans or Democrats, was very small. Rarely was WCF able to give candidates the full $5,000 it was entitled to under federal election rules. Candidates were more likely to receive $250 or $500 than they were a $1,000 contribution.

As recently as the mid-1980s, the estimated total giving of all women's PACs was $50,000. By the 1990 election cycle, Jane Danowitz, director of WCF, estimated cash contributions from the Women's Campaign Fund alone had risen to $240,000, a figure inclusive of state and local races.[23] This money had supported 149 candidates. If "in-kind" or noncash contributions were taken into account, Danowitz estimated the figure was closer to half a million.

Yet for many women candidates, particularly first-time candidates, the WCF was a godsend. Not only did the WCF provide critical moral and psychic support, it helped guide candidates through the labyrinth of Washington power brokers and conventional PACs. The WCF could identify labor unions or professional associations, such as the American Nurses Association or the American Federation of Teachers, that might be sympathetic to women candidates. Introductions could also be provided to issue-oriented PACs, such as the National Abortion Rights Action League (NARAL) or Voters for Choice.

The possibility of increasing women's political giving was foreshadowed by Geraldine Ferraro's fund-raising efforts during the Mondale presidential campaign of 1984. From her own experience, she knew that women didn't hold many "high donor" dinners of $1,000.

"Fritz's fund-raisers at a thousand dollars a head pinpointed the traditional Democratic donors. My low-ticket fund-raisers, often held over great opposition from the Mondale campaign fund-raisers, because there had been no history of major fund-raising at low-ticket events, raised money from many people who had never made a political contribution before. Whole families—mothers, fathers, and daughters—came."[24]

Female politicians who wanted to hold fund-raisers to help Ferraro were often nixed by the Democratic National Committee (DNC) as "unproven." Ferraro went ahead with one such event, sponsored by California State Senator Diane Watson and Gloria Molina, who was at that time a state assemblywoman.

"They won't deliver, the DNC warned us; don't do it." Molina and Watson had promised to raise $50,000 at a breakfast. They exceeded their goal, says Ferraro, "the breakfast brought in $82,130 at $35 per ticket from over twenty-three hundred women."[25] Most touching to Ferraro were the checks that came from women who pleaded "[p]lease don't acknowledge this contribution . . . [m]y husband doesn't know about it."

The advent of EMILY's List significantly increased "organized" money for women candidates. It was Ellen Malcolm's personal experience with Harriett Woods's first campaign for U.S. Senate in Missouri in 1982 that led to the formation of EMILY's List. The memories both Malcolm and Woods have of that race give a more detailed look at the dynamics of funding women's campaigns.

Harriett Woods found her way into politics in 1962, like many women prior to the women's movement, through a neighborhood issue—traffic noise. It disrupted children's nap times. By 1982, Woods had logged twenty years in politics as an elected official—on the city council and in the state senate. She decided to run for the U.S. Senate against John Danforth.

Party officials told her the same thing they had when she decided to move to the state senate in 1976, "We have to have a man for the job." But, noted Woods, "No congressman had any interest in running for senate, no mayor, no one . . . " She decided to pursue the nomination. "I stepped forward and they panicked and got a bank lobbyist, who'd been a national committeeman but never held office, to run."

Woods stayed in the race, but raising money was tough "without the support of the party." There were no statewide organized funding networks for women. "Some women for the first time wrote checks," she remembers, but adds ruefully, "those were the days when women didn't control the checkbook." Nevertheless, Woods won the primary. She had been assured that if she captured the nomination, she would receive money from the national party.

Late in the campaign, she received $18,000 from the national Democratic party and assumed that, although it was tardy, it represented an amount most candidates could expect to receive. She learned from Senator Howard Metzenbaum, however, that it was a token contribution, or, as he put it, a "minimum guarantee."

"I was absolutely shocked," says Woods. Mobilized by anger, she got on the phone and contacted several women in Washington whom she thought might be of help, including philanthropist Ellen Malcolm.[26] Malcolm shared Woods's outrage and began making phone calls. Pulling out all the stops, she finally put together a meager $50,000. Woefully short of money, Woods and Malcolm both watched helplessly as Woods was pummeled by powerful negative ads during the closing days of the campaign—with no money to launch a counterattack. Woods lost—by less than one percent of the popular vote. Money had been a key element in Malcolm's eye, and it was "too little, too late."

In the aftermath, Malcolm founded EMILY's List. Malcolm's analysis of Woods's and other women's campaigns convinced her that women suffered the most when it came to raising the early money that could make them truly competitive candidates.

Malcolm put together a list of women who could be solicited for $100 contributions for Democratic women candidates, sight unseen, based on the strength of Malcolm's analysis and profile of the candidate. Members of EMILY's List join the organization for a $200 membership fee, and then send checks made out to the candidate they wish to support via EMILY's List.

The fledgling organization faced a crucial test in 1986 and passed with flying colors. Congresswoman Barbara Mikulski of Maryland decided to take on a popular congressman and incumbent governor for the vacant U.S. Senate seat. Mikulski knew she would have to demonstrate that she was the superior candidate, and the best way was through polling data.

"That's why EMILY is so important to me . . . that early money enabled me to have the first poll with Harrison Hickman." Mikulski's poll showed that, contrary to prevailing assumptions, she was the most popular candidate of the three.

"Even when I had substantial quantitative analysis from a pollster who had not only polled for me but for Senator Sarbanes [the incumbent Democrat] and for the governor [one of her prospective opponents], there was disbelief that it was there for me."[27]

Mikulski's two opponents remained unconvinced until she beat them both on primary day. Malcolm is as proud as Mikulski is grateful. EMILY's List raised $250,000 for Mikulski in the primary, nearly a fifth of her primary funds, the most money ever raised by a women's network for a single candidate to that date.

In 1990, EMILY's List gave $1.5 million to 14 candidates. This was the same year the WCF was able to give just $240,000—to 149 candidates. The $6 million in contributions that EMILY's List gave to Democratic women candidates in 1992 made it among the largest political action committees in the country.

EMILY's List is being flattered through imitation. Republican women formed their own EMILY's List called WISH (Women in the Senate and House)—with the help and advice of the Democrat Malcolm. WISH will require the women it supports to be pro-choice, placing the new organization at odds with the Republican platform. While WISH was formed too late to play a major role in the 1992 election cycle, this tension was made explicit when Marilyn Quayle, and other wives whose husbands served in the Bush administration, tried to counter WISH with an organization called the Republican Women's Leadership Network (WLN). At a fund-raising party, for instance, Quayle reportedly urged the group not to let "the pro-choice thing" get in the way of support for Republican women candidates.[28]

New financial support for women is being organized at the state level, drawing upon preexisting networks of women's organizations. In Minnesota, Democratic women are looking ahead to 1994 when a U.S. Senate seat will be open. In anticipation, they have formed Minnesota $$ Million (M$$M), so that a woman candidate will know there is a pool of money available for her even before she announces. Organized by State Senator Carol Flynn in the summer of 1991, prior to the Thomas/Hill hearings, the group wants prospective candidates to be undeterred by the huge sums that have to be raised. Co-chair Nina Rothchild said that when women became "mad as hell," they were quickly able to harness the anger to get M$$M off the ground.

A hundred women came to the first meeting, and each pledged to give or raise $1,000. As of January 1993, 250 pledges had been received, and the organization has a goal of 1,000 pledges by the summer of 1993. Likely beneficiaries are four current officeholders: Joan Growe, secretary of state; Ann Wynia, majority leader of the Minnesota house; Dee Long, speaker of the Minnesota house; and Marlene Johnson, lieutenant governor.[29]

In Washington state, the affiliate of the NWPC formed May's List in 1992. To avoid duplication with national groups, May's List assists candidates for state and local races, gathering checks for specific candidates in the same fashion as EMILY's List. Candidates may be from either party, but must be endorsed by the state women's caucus to receive support. In the first election cycle of November 1992, approximately one thousand people made contributions, and four of the six candidates supported by May's List won their races, including the two statewide positions of attorney general and lands commissioner.[30]

Funding for women candidates has not been limited to organizations that specialize in supporting them. The entry of more women into the economy has influenced the flow of dollars to women candidates from business and professional associations. Most active have been PACs organized in occupations that are female-dominated.

In 1992 the American Nurses Association (ANA) gave $330,000 to 260 candidates, 69 of whom were women. However, women candidates received roughly half of all the money. The largest contribution a PAC can give is $5,000, and according to officer Debbie Campbell, "Just about everyone that we supported with a full contribution was a woman." In 1986, a few election cycles earlier, the ANA had only approximately $70,000 to give to candidates. It has since developed a reputation for encouraging good challengers to seek its support. In 1992, for instance, 37 percent of the candidates supported by the ANA were not incumbents. Its criteria, in addition to the usual elements of "winnability, fundraising ability, campaign skills, desire to win, and to do what it takes," include a willingness to listen to nurses from the congressional district.[31]

The American Teachers Association gave nearly $1 million in 1992, and most of the women Senate candidates received its support, with the exception of Lynn Yeakel in Philadelphia. Yeakel received the support of her local American Federation of Teachers (AFT) chapter, but the statewide group stayed neutral. Washington's Senate candidate Patty Murray was a member of the AFT, so the organization was particularly active in her race.[32]

Ironically, one political action committee whose members are among the wealthier women in the country, the Hollywood Women's Political Action Committee (HWPAC), did not make funding women candidates a priority until the 1992 cycle.

HWPAC's formation was sparked by the anger of one woman: Songwriter Marilyn Bergman became annoyed with Ronald Reagan's claims to the Hollywood community and decided to challenge those claims by forming a committee of liberal celebrities. While this committee was "of women" it was not exclusively "for women," and its considerable clout was demonstrated when it raised $300,000 for the Mondale/Ferraro ticket at one dinner. Then, in 1986, a Barbra Streisand dinner produced a staggering $1.5 million to assist Democrats in their efforts to regain a majority in the U.S. Senate.

While HWPAC is most well known for its famous actresses, from Jane Fonda to Meryl Streep to Barbra Streisand, it includes over 200 women from all segments of Hollywood life—scriptwriters, producers, and directors. HWPAC is unabashedly liberal, setting forth a multiple issues test that candidates must meet in order to receive funding. No Republican candidate, male or female, has ever received its support.

The shift toward women candidates came slowly, and partly as a result of HWPAC's increased activism in the abortion rights battle. Just prior to the Supreme Court's handing down the *Webster* decision in July 1989, which restricted abortion rights, HWPAC organized a large contingent of celebrities to join the mass march in Washington, D.C., in April 1989. The following year, however, it refused to support pro-choice Democrat Dianne Feinstein in the California governor's race. She didn't meet all the progressive criteria. Her Republican opponent, of course, didn't either, with the net result that HWPAC simply didn't invest in the governor's race.

HWPAC's reaction to the Thomas/Hill hearings was swift and decisive: It decided to make women candidates a priority. On July 1, 1992, seven women running for the U.S. Senate, irrespective of whether they had yet captured the nomination, got the same treatment as the Senate candidates in 1986. They were featured at a Hollywood event with celebrities such as Goldie Hawn and Barbra Streisand.

HWPAC even changed its mind about Feinstein, claiming she had changed hers. Director Margery Tabankin explained the decision to support her in 1992: "This time she was carrying a message. We were stunned by her passion."

HWPAC has significance for candidates far beyond its capacity to sponsor single events. Access to this network can mean contributions in addition to those received from an organized event, yielding the equivalent of many months of pancake breakfasts.

When the Thomas/Hill hearings touched off an explosion of anger among American women, these organizations were in a position to receive and channel the increased flow of money to women's campaigns. While EMILY's List was the biggest beneficiary, money also began pouring in to all the other organizations, much of it unsolicited. Jane Danowitz said women whom the Women's Campaign Fund had pursued for years to no avail suddenly sent in checks. In 1992, the Women's Campaign Fund gave a record $1.5 million to 242 candidates.[33]

In 1992, NARAL supported pro-choice women candidates with $900,000, up from 25 women and $55,000 in 1986, although staff stressed that NARAL tries "not to make distinctions based on gender." The year 1992 was a banner one for NARAL's coffers and support for pro-choice candidates; it gave over $2.5 million. Senate incumbent Arlen Specter, who met all of NARAL's criteria and who had long received NARAL's endorsement and financial support, lost its endorsement in 1992 as a direct result of his support for Judge Thomas and his role in the Thomas/Hill hearings.[34]

What was new about 1992 was not just the amount of money that poured in, but that many women were first-time donors, and some had never been politically active before. While there is no way of knowing precisely how many first-time donors became involved, the anecdotal evidence suggests that as many as one third of all donors were new. EMILY's List is a potential gold mine of information on support for women's campaigns. For the moment, it has not been analyzed. Just before the election cycle ended, Malcolm was asked if she were tracking the new donors. It was all she could do, she said, "to just get the checks to the bank."

EMILY's List, however, set up a Majority Council of donors who gave at least $1,000 to candidates. One would anticipate that these larger givers were the more seasoned political donors. What caused repeated comment, however, was how many were new to the process.

Minnesota $$ Million's Nina Rothchild estimated that *most* women who attended the first organizing meeting had never been political contributors, and about one fourth *had never* been active in politics.

Ten years after Harriett Woods observed that women don't support women candidates, eight years after Ferraro tried to convince the DNC to seek support from women even though their contributions were smaller, and a mere seven years after the formation of EMILY's List, most women candidates can get their campaigns off the ground without depending on men or traditional sources of political money.

As women's contributions have grown, and as organized women's PACs have acquired more clout, some women express disappointment that the threshold tests are becoming as stringent as the traditional sources of support. Women, no less than men, are having to prove their candidacies are viable—that they can win. For instance, the only Democratic woman to successfully take on an incumbent in 1990, Joan Kelly Horn of Missouri, said she received no funding from any of the women's groups, even during the general election.

"No poll, no dough," says Ellen Malcolm, who, like many donors, considers polls the best measure of whether or not a candidate is viable. Malcolm argues that "[t]here's a lot of risk for us to take on a campaign. If you really get down and look at those [poll] numbers you get a much better sense, if you are running against an incumbent, exactly how vulnerable the incumbent is and what kinds of issues you can attack him on. . . ."

A supporter of New Hampshire's gubernatorial woman hopeful Arne Arneson confronted Malcolm at a conference on prospective candidates. She was upset about the tough requirements of EMILY's List, which her candidate had not met. "Who's defining the issues?" she asked. Her candidate, Arneson, claimed to have been told "she wouldn't win if she ran on taxes."

"If you can't answer our questions, you are not going to succeed," said Malcolm in defending her requirements, which include the submission of both polling data and campaign plans. "Pull together facts that support the contention you can win," said Malcolm.

A woman from the audience yelled out, "$14,000 for a benchmark poll!" referring once again to a candidate's dilemma of having to spend money not yet raised in order to raise money. Malcolm held fast, describing her position as "tough love."[35]

Anita Perez Ferguson from Santa Barbara, California, experienced Malcolm's tough love stance in 1990. She approached EMILY's List after she decided to challenge incumbent congressman Robert Lagomarsino. "[State Senator] Hart raised $1.5 million and couldn't do it, so how could you?" Ferguson was told.[36] EMILY's List officials were technically correct: She didn't win. But she came very close—within four percentage points—roughly the same margin as her better-funded boss.

Spending more money might not have put her over the top, but many women candidates expect women's PACs to be better gamblers on their behalf.

When EMILY's List does support a woman candidate, it confers instant credibility on her candidacy. Other PACs, faced with a Democratic woman seeking support, want to know whether she has the support of EMILY's List. If she does, she almost automatically wins points. If she doesn't, she may find other committees reluctant to take the first risk.

Unlike EMILY's List, the bipartisan Women's Campaign Fund has a much less stringent test for receiving financial support. The organization seldom requires polls or other evidence of electoral viability. Its current director, Jane Danowitz, describes its strength as the ability to "give early seed money." Danowitz says WCF tends to "grow up" with the women candidates, often funding and assisting them from the time of their first state legislative or even local race. By the time they run for higher office the relationship has been well established, and both the candidate and the district are well known. WCF requires candidates to be pro-choice and to support the Equal Rights Amendment (ERA).

Yet its support decisions have also angered women candidates. If more than one candidate for the same office meets the criteria, how does the board decide which one to support? Pam Fleischaker, a former staff member, says these battles were fought out on a case-by-case basis, but in two significant cases incumbent men won out over women.[37]

In 1980, for instance, the Women's Campaign Fund chose to support Democratic Senator Gary Hart of Colorado in his U.S. Senate reelection bid over Secretary of State Mary Estil Buchanan, the Republican nominee, who was also pro-choice and pro-ERA. The rationale? The WCF board members believed that Hart had been a friend, and "you don't abandon your friends."[38] More recently, and for similar reasons, WCF supported pro-choice Senator Paul Simon of Illinois in his reelection bid when he was challenged by Republican Congresswoman Lynn Martin, also pro-choice. "We didn't support Lynn Martin—Simon was too close to many of our donors," Danowitz says candidly, although "in retrospect . . . her record on choice, frankly, was better than his."[39]

These are the traditional reasons PACs usually support incumbents. Since both these women were challengers, and therefore unlikely to win, disrupting the established relationship with two powerful Senate incumbents could have damaged WCF's capacity to raise the very money it distributes.

NATIONAL AMERICAN WOMAN SUFFRAGE ASS'N

Lacking the vote and prohibited from public speaking, early political women such as famed anti-lynching crusader Ida Wells-Barnett (below with her children) wielded their pens. New York's Belle Moskowitz worked behind the scenes with Governor Al Smith yet consorted with consummate operatives like Boss Hague of Jersey City (below center). The first congresswoman, Montana's Jeannette Rankin (shown with Carrie Chapman Catt), was cheered in 1917, but her first vote—against America's entry into World War I—confounded suffrage supporters. The first woman senator, Georgia's Rebecca Latimer Felton (below right), served one day in 1922.

National Women's Hall of Fame

Courtesy Elizabeth I. Perry

Library of Congress

Asked in 1928 was she "running as a woman," Ruth Hanna McCormick (above) snapped that she was running as the wife of *Chicago Tribune* publisher Medill McCormick and the daughter of Ohio boss Mark Hanna. For women, the most available route to power was via a man, as 1929's congresswomen demonstrate (left). (*Left to right, back row*) Ruth Bryan Owen was William Jennings Bryan's daughter, Mary Norton a product of Boss Hague's New Jersey machine. Florence Kahn and (*front row*) Pearl Oldfield and Edith Nourse Rogers were congressmen's widows. Eliza Pratt had been an aide to her late predecessor; McCormick was, as she declared, a widow and a daughter. By 1956 (below left) an increasing number held office "in their own right," but widows (*starred*) still abounded and one husband helped defeat his wife's re-election bid. (*Left to right, back row*) Mary Farrington,° Ruth Thompson, (*second row*) Leonor Sullivan,° Iris Blitch, Gracie Pfost, Martha Griffiths, Marguerite Church,° (*third row*) Edna Kelly (*standing*), Edith Green, Coya Knutson (whose husband's "Coya, Come Home" letter helped defeat her in 1958), Senator Margaret Chase Smith,° Maude Kee,° (*front row*) Cecil Hardin, Rogers° again, Katherine St. George, Frances Bolton.°

First Lady Eleanor Roosevelt championed and recruited women, such as actress Helen Gahagan Douglas (in 1947), who helped create a new tradition—the independent woman politician who could be an advocate for women. ER herself (with John F. Kennedy in 1963) later chaired JFK's President's Commission on the Status of Women. Critical of special privileges for women, Congresswoman Margaret Chase Smith (in 1944 with women marines) nonetheless fought for equal treatment for military women who "shouldered equal responsibility."

Noting "compelling reasons against" it, Senator Margaret Chase Smith announced in 1964 to a delighted National Women's Press Club that she would run for president. Her race disturbed men—one told pollsters, "Men are not ready to surrender to a woman"—but inspired a new generation of women. Yet politics was still so male a place that only with the founding of the National Women's Political Caucus in 1971 were women urged to run. (Early NWPC leaders in 1983, from left, Harriett Woods, Bella Abzug, Kathy Wilson, Eleanor Holmes Norton, Alice Travis, Maxine Waters, Gloria Molina, and Patsy Mink).

Margaret Chase Smith Library

National Women's Political Cauc

Courtesy Senator Nancy Kassebaum

The Marin Independent Journal

Courtesy Luisa DeLauro

The gender gap, identified in 1980, persuaded Democrats to risk a woman, Geraldine Ferraro, on their 1984 national ticket. But despite political women's progress, old prejudices remained and politics was easier for women born into it, such as Senator Nancy Kassebaum (opposite, being supported by her father Kansas Governor Alf Landon). Of many modern-day political daughters, few can boast pioneering political mothers, as can Congresswoman Rosa DeLauro, with her mother Luisa, a 60-year veteran of Connecticut ward politics. The first mother of young children elected to Congress, Colorado's Pat Schroeder helped break the mommy barrier in 1972—a fact that didn't impress daughter Jamie (being sent to bed on election night).

Denver Post photo

Women's campaigns face two perilous hurdles: How to win women's votes while not offending men; and how to project authority while crafting an appropriate womanly image. Gracie Pfost sought Frank Church's endorsement when she tried and failed to move up to the Senate in 1962. Michigan's Martha Griffiths proved in 1952 that a woman could be in the driver's seat. Barbara Boxer posed in her kitchen in 1974, sharing her recipe for peach cobbler with voters.

Detroit News photo copyright © 1952

Politics leaves little time for fancy cuisine

BARBARA BOXER whips up peach cobbler, in between conversations

The Marin Independent Journal

In 1992 Barbara Boxer was still demonstrating the lengths to which a successful politician must go for name recognition. Dianne Feinstein's 1990 "Forged in Tragedy" TV ad—with its stark images of her taking charge of San Francisco after Mayor George Moscone's assassination—was designed to show she was "tough" enough to be governor. By 1992, women no longer had to be so tough; indeed, male politicians were counseled to show a caring side. In her Senate campaign's closing days, Feinstein posed with her infant granddaughter in an ad that demonstrated the new freedom to "run as a woman."

Courtesy Senator Dianne Feinstein

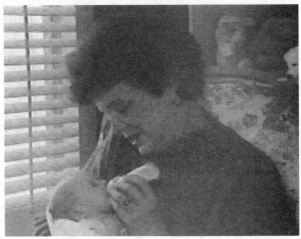

Courtesy Senator Dianne Feinstein

California's Barbara Boxer and Dianne Feinstein joined forces in 1992 to remind voters in their giant, ethnically diverse state of the all-white, all-male Senate Judiciary Committee's treatment of Anita Hill. Ethnicity and gender already were winning issues in 1982 for Los Angeles' Gloria Molina (*see arrow*), shown celebrating with Latina supporters. There was a new comfort level and sense of legitimacy among women politicians in the late 1980s and early 1990s. No longer "aping men," they honored their gender's life experiences and talents. Texas's Ann Richards posed in 1990 with her hairdresser, who quipped, "We defy gravity," of the soon-to-be governor's mile-high coiffure.

With more women candidates running, organizations are now faced with a dilemma when two or more women run in the same race. In 1992 the race that challenged decision-making was the Senate race in New York where two veteran women, Elizabeth Holtzman and Geraldine Ferraro, were running against each other. Different organizations made different decisions—each of which set off a separate furor.

EMILY's List decided to endorse Ferraro, acknowledging that there were "two wonderful women in this race, but in every measure we can find Gerry is the strongest candidate." The heads of the New York State and New York City chapters of the National Organization for Women, acting as individuals rather than official representatives, endorsed Holtzman in a mass mailing. The NWPC and the WCF supported both women. Manhattan borough president Ruth W. Messinger summed up the feeling of many when she said, "There are a lot of women who are just tortured about this . . . it is making people crazy." Ann F. Lewis, former political director of the Democratic National Committee, went so far as to suggest that individual women split their donations between the two candidates, prompting a response from Holtzman: "That is not how Solomon solved the problem. You can't give Gerry half a vote and me the rest. The voting booth is about choices, and in the end you only get one."[40] After all the decisions were made, WCF head Jane Danowitz characterized women's PACs as organizations "going through adolescence" and observed that "women versus women races are something we are going to have to live with."[41]

As women's PACs grow in power and clout, there is less and less to distinguish their behavior from that of other PACs, except of course for the fact that most of the money goes to women candidates.

In fact, as more women are considered viable candidates, or become incumbents, the differences generally between women's and men's campaigns recede. The biggest difference in fund-raising appears to be that the average size of an individual donation to most women candidates continues to be smaller. The strongest evidence of this comes from primary data. No large-scale or systematic study on the difference in funding men's and women's campaigns has been done in the last few years.

This contrast between men's access to high-dollar donors and women's need to find two or three times as many donors is vividly conveyed in a comparison of how Barbara Boxer, Mel Levine, and Leo McCarthy raised money for the 1992 Democratic Senate primary in California. Mel Levine spent most of his fund-raising time on the telephone asking big donors for donations. Barbara Boxer relied heavily on direct mail and fund-raising events. Leo McCarthy's strategy resembled Levine's more than it did Boxer's.

According to Levine, he devoted over eight hours a day to fund-raising. His network is extensive, stemming from his twenty years in California as a state legislator and as a U.S. congressman representing relatively affluent West Los Angeles. His telephone bill for seventeen months was "$61,229." It paid off. Press reports on his campaign contributions indicate that "nearly 80% of his total receipts [were] from large contributors while small donors (less than $200) accounted for only 6%."[42] "'It is an overwhelming person-to-person task. . . . The difficulty of what I am doing is that it requires so much of my own personal time,' lamented Levine."[43]

By stark contrast, while Boxer's contributions averaged a stunningly low $28 and came from over 52,000 donors, she managed to raise a total that matched Levine's. Both Levine and Boxer raised approximately $4.5 million for the primary race. She spent less time on the telephone, and much more money on direct mail. Nearly 60 percent of her donors contributed less than $200; 6 percent of Levine's did so. While Boxer had amassed 7,000 donors before the Thomas/Hill hearings, afterward not only did her donor base expand but its composition changed. Before the hearings, men gave her 60 percent of her total funds; after the hearings, the figure reversed and women gave her two thirds of her contributions.

Lieutenant Governor Leo McCarthy raised less money, $2.5 million, but his approach was similar to Levine's. He called 150 friends before he announced and asked them for financial support. "What I was doing was phoning people who had been loyal to me and good at fund-raising. . . . Mostly this is done on a personal friendship basis. Over the years you just develop close friends."[44] McCarthy had 17,500 contributors, recruited mostly through events in people's homes. For instance, one dinner at the home of Los Angeles Kings' owner Bruce McNall raised $100,000.

Certain offices generate "close friends" more readily than others. Massachusetts lieutenant governor Evelyn Murphy ran for governor in 1990. While money wasn't as big a problem as was her identification with Governor Michael Dukakis, Murphy describes the difference between her fund-raising base and that of her opponents, Attorney General Francis Belotti and Boston University president John Silber.

"Belotti," said Murphy, has "thirty years of IOUs and some really hard muscle in forcing contributions in ways a woman can't." Murphy's close friend and Democratic party activist Ann Lewis elaborates on Belotti's fund-raising base. "What do attorney generals do? They hire young law-yers and they go on into private practice and make great campaign con-tributors."

John Silber "controlled an institution that hired a lot of people and let out a lot of contracts," says Lewis. "Each had an ability to raise money that Evelyn didn't have." While Murphy had a base among developers, which was diminished due to the recession, Lewis says Murphy's ability "to raise money was personal."[45]

Jane Danowitz sums up the difference between men's and women's campaigns for top offices: "Women [donors] will give you your start, but in the end if you are running for the United States Senate you've got to go to the male establishment. Like it or not."

In these networks, "viability," whether or not a candidate can win, be-comes the critical distinction, not whether a candidate is male or female. Consider, for instance, the fund-raising for the 1990 governor's race in California between Senator Pete Wilson and former San Francisco mayor Dianne Feinstein. The *San Francisco Chronicle* analyzed their fund-raising for a period of approximately six weeks, from May 20 to June 30, 1990. Each candidate had raised slightly more than $1.2 million. More important, Feinstein and Wilson *shared four out of five donor cat-egories as their top contributors.*[46] Their major contributions were from lawyers, doctors, developers, and real estate interests, with lawyers, the "Daddy Warbucks" of the race, giving the most money overall.[47] Only the fifth source of funds for these two candidates differed—because of their partisan differences. As a Democrat, Feinstein received more contribu-tions from labor, while Wilson, a Republican, received more support from Central Valley agricultural business interests.

Consider Rosa DeLauro's first race for Congress discussed in the last chapter. Without office-holding experience or personal wealth, she raised $1.1 million for her first race in 1990. "I don't have trouble asking for money," she says, perhaps stating the obvious. Without personal wealth, her earliest money came from friends who could afford a $1,000 contribution.

DeLauro's success in raising early money achieved several of her po-litical goals. By raising $100,000 in the first month, she scared off other competitors. Many of her potential competitors were state legislators whom she knew would be more credible, since they had the office- hold-ing experience she lacked. Money in hand, DeLauro got to the delegates first.

"It was March . . . when these other guys went out to look at delegate support. I had already talked to people three and four times, I had mailed them two or three times, and met with them. I talked to thirteen hundred people, and this was before [other potential candidates] got started or were willing to put themselves on the line to get the money."

She had built a base among people in her district beginning with her job in New Haven's office of the mayor. She honed her fund-raising skills as campaign manager for Chris Dodd's successful U.S. Senate campaign. DeLauro, an ardent Democrat with strong labor support, had no trouble asking for—and receiving—contributions from the business community.

"Not my natural base," she says, and describes her success as a function of her familiarity with politics. "You [speaking of herself] had been in this system. You had been in this process. You know how to get things done." She adds that the business community values precisely those attributes, "tough, aggressive, able to get things done," not often associated with women. "We worked damn hard," she says, now comfortably ensconced in her congressional office. In 1992, DeLauro successfully won reelection and raised another $1 million; however, this time she beat her opponent, Tom Scott, by a comfortable margin.[48]

One indication that the benefits of incumbency are gender free can be seen in Barbara Mikulski's reelection campaign for the Senate in 1992. She had no competition from her own party. She did not have to rely on women's contributions. Two thirds of her donations were from men, as reported in July 1992, four months before the general election.

The next time, 1992's new women senators—Moseley–Braun, Boxer, Feinstein, and Murray—run, they will do so as incumbents. There is every reason to expect that they, like Mikulski, will not have primary challenges, and will not have to rely on women donors to boost their initial campaign.

While incumbency equalizes the funding between men's and women's campaigns, not all incumbents are equal. For instance, just how much money an incumbent can raise, generally speaking, is linked to an incumbent's position inside a legislative body. The biggest congressional fund-raisers are in the leadership or chair the most powerful committees. In the Senate, some of those powerful committees are Budget, Appropriations, and Foreign Affairs. The Ways and Means Committee, Appropriations, and Armed Services are the most powerful in the House. As of this writing, no woman heads a major committee in either House.

One can speculate, however, that Feinstein's success in being appointed to the Senate Appropriations Committee will help her raise funds for her next Senate race, which she must face within two years, rather than the normal six. (She was elected to Wilson's unexpired term.) It is not speculation, however, to say that since Feinstein is now a senator from a state critical to the Democrats' future, the Senate Democratic leadership has given her a boost for her 1994 campaign. Their interest is in keeping the seat in the Democratic column, not engaging in acts of generosity to new female senators.

As one looks ahead to 1994, continued success in fund-raising for credible—and viable—women candidates can be expected, although fewer congressional seats will be open. The opportunities for electoral victories for women must necessarily diminish; however, there is every indication that their rate of success will continue. Incumbents serving their first term are the most vulnerable if their races were close the first time. Women who run as challengers can expect to find new levels of interest and support for their campaigns, provided they meet the threshold tests outlined in the last chapter and can demonstrate the possibility of success. The likelihood is that the base of support for women candidates will increase. Hidden in the statistics for 1992 was evidence that women are beginning to develop their own high-dollar donor networks.

In Colorado, two women, a philanthropist and a corporate oil and gas owner, motivated by abortion rights, Anita Hill, and the fear of another conservative Supreme Court Justice, each wrote checks totaling $250,000 to various Clinton committees in 1992. Swanee Hunt, president of the Hunt Alternatives Fund in Denver, said she had supported local candidates before but never presidential ones. Merle Chambers, owner of Axem Resources and chair of the executive committee of Clipper Exxpress, was the other donor. However, these donations turned out to be just a beginning of their new political involvement.

Hunt and Chambers put together a fund-raising event called Serious Women, Serious Issues, Serious Money, and charged $1,000 a head. They chose to feature Hillary Clinton and Tipper Gore, not the candidates. Using their personal Rolodexes, they called friends. According to Hunt, "There was a lot of sympathy for the cause, and a gasp at the level we were asking." They set an overall goal of $1 million, and they asked each friend specifically for a donation ten times as large as they had ever given.[49]

Investment management counselor Judi Wagner gave $10,000 instead of $1,000; Jane Ragle, owner of a music store and restaurant, gave $10,000. Two women gave $25,000. According to Hunt, the money fell into three categories: women who inherited their money, women who earned it themselves, and women who married rich husbands.

Hunt and Chambers also invited 300 women who couldn't afford large contributions. "I knew when we were doing it, we were breaking a mold," Hunt said. "They told us we couldn't mix big money women with women who couldn't pay as much, that we were going to have to serve caviar and champagne. I told them this wasn't about eating, or socializing, it was about ideas." Both women insist their agendas are identical to Clinton's and Gore's, and neither is seeking jobs in the administration. "I'm not angling for a job," said Hunt. Similarly, Chambers remarked, "I didn't do this for a reward. . . ."

A Denver activist, Marjorie Seawell, who helped the two women organize the event, acknowledges the two women have won access, the traditional goal of most large contributors, "but this access will be used on behalf of the homeless, children, mental health—no one has ever given big money for that purpose before. Usually that level of money is given for self-interest."

Whether the motivations of high-dollar donors are altruistic or self-interested, Congresswoman Patricia Schroeder underscores the significance of the change. "With money the only thing the big boys really understand, Chambers and Hunt have made sure women will now be at the table—to do more than set it."

These new trends—the growth of a women's donor base and women's increased political involvement—should not obscure the fact that women candidates are now raising the same sizable amounts that men do. In California, State Treasurer Kathleen Brown has not yet stated she will run for governor in 1994, although she is widely expected to do so.

On one evening in December 1992, two years before the election, Brown held a fund-raiser in San Francisco. Her proceeds for that one event were $850,000. Irrespective of which race Brown chooses in 1994, whether she runs for reelection as state treasurer or declares for governor, donors were willing to support her. By March 1993, a still-unannounced Brown had amassed a $2 million campaign chest, previously unheard of for a female candidate.[50] No one can assess what effect having Feinstein and Boxer as the state's two senators will have on Brown's campaign if she chooses to run for governor and captures the party nomination. If voters choose to put three women in the top offices in one of the largest, most significant states in the country, the glass ceiling for women and politics can surely be called shattered.

Yet there is another side to the convergence between men's and women's campaigns. Gone forever are the days when a candidate could eschew campaign contributions, as Margaret Chase Smith did throughout her legislative career (1949–73), which included five U.S. Senate campaigns and a presidential bid. Smith not only refused to accept any campaign contributions, she returned unsolicited ones. Nor can sufficient campaign funds be raised with one annual fund-raising event, the custom of Congresswoman Martha Griffiths (1954–75). The Michigan congresswoman used to host an annual pancake breakfast, charging $15 a ticket, which provided her with most of her campaign funds.

Even women candidates who had no trouble asking for money felt the amounts had troubling future implications. While costs have risen most at the national level, the costs of local campaigns for city councils, special districts, or county supervisors have shown a similar escalation.

High campaign costs often bring with them a campaign debt. In 1992, a newly elected congresswoman who had labeled her opponent "Mr. Special Interest," sent 100 letters to political action committees asking for assistance in retiring her campaign debt of $50,000. The letter was dated December 11, 1992, less than six weeks after she was elected, and contained the following appeal: "With your help I will be able to begin serving on the House Committee on Public Works and Transportation without worrying about how much money I owe." In using this approach to retire her debt, she was following a practice common to successfully elected politicians.[51]

If candidates, or incumbents, are candid, most will agree with Geraldine Ferraro's statement on money and politics: "It's a corrupting influence on the system," said Ferraro. "And don't let anyone tell you different."[52]

Ferraro was referring to more than the overall costs of a campaign. The need to raise large sums of money ties women, as well as men, firmly to a structure of economic interests.

Ellen Miller, executive director of the Center for Responsive Politics, an organization that studies the relationship between campaign contributions and politics, notes the contradiction that most women candidates face: Women candidates usually run on a platform of change but play into the "same political system that requires that they raise millions of dollars, spend all of their time doing it, and succumb to the same pressures."[53]

7

Mobilizing Women's Votes

The Elusive Specter of the Gender Gap

Nothing has so tantalized women activists, made male politicians more nervous, or raised the hopes of individual candidates higher than the possibility of women banding together to create a unified voting bloc. What sustains its imaginative force today is that women are a majority of the electorate (53 percent), and have been voting in numbers equal to or greater than men since 1968.[1] As a purely mathematical proposition, women *are* in a position to determine electoral outcomes. But do they?

In 1992, women's votes helped George Bush win his primaries.[2] In the general election, however, women preferred Bill Clinton to either Bush or Ross Perot. Women's votes helped Pennsylvanian Lynn Yeakel trounce all four men in her primary race, but they weren't enough to beat Arlen Specter in the November election. Many commentators initially announced that Feinstein and Boxer won their primary victories in California because of women's votes; in fact, they would have won if all the women voters in the state had stayed home. Feinstein received a majority of men's votes, 53 percent, over her opponent, Gray Davis, who received 36 percent. In her three-way race, Boxer gained a plurality of men's votes, winning 39 percent, while her two male opponents received 35 percent and 23 percent.[3] In the general election, a majority of men and women supported Feinstein, but women gave Boxer her winning margin. Feinstein won 66 percent of the women's vote and 52 percent of the men's. Boxer won 59 percent of the women's vote and 45 percent of the men's. While Boxer was advantaged by women's votes, other women candidates lost their congressional races when women voters failed to help them attain the magic "50 percent plus one" number needed to win a two-way race.

The ever-present possibility that women voters might give candidates their winning margins, along with their frequent failure to do so, has a kind of peekaboo quality about it. Now you see it; now you don't. Women's votes seem to tilt the scales in some races but not others. Women's votes seem to favor some woman candidates but not others. In the 1990 election cycle, for instance, Dianne Feinstein lost her race for governor of California when many of the potential Republican crossover women "went home" to Republican candidate Pete Wilson. By contrast, Democrat Ann Richards won her governorship of Texas by adding Republican and independent women voters to her Democratic votes. But earlier in Richards's campaign, the polls showed voters favored her opponent, Clayton Williams, by a whopping twenty points.[4]

For all its mercurial qualities, we can say that there is now a women's vote. It emerged in the last decade. All candidates, male and female, must court it in a way they have never done before. If the major presidential and congressional elections that occurred in the last decade are considered together, some tentative conclusions about the elusive nature of the women's vote can be reached.

First, there is no automatic relationship between women's *voices,* as registered in public opinion polls, and their *votes* for a particular candidate. In order for opinions to become votes on election day, candidates must seek and persuade specific groups of voters, including women, to vote for them. Many candidates, both male and female, have failed to grasp this important distinction and have been devastated by the failure of favorable opinion polls to translate into votes. Second, there is no evidence that the women's votes will necessarily be cast in favor of women candidates, although in 1992 women candidates did benefit from women's votes more than ever before. Third, there is some evidence that the Democratic party is the current beneficiary of a women's vote, despite the fact that nationally Reagan (twice) and Bush (once) won the majority of women's votes in presidential elections. Fourth, while an increasing number of analysts can describe women's votes, there is no agreement or explanation as to why certain patterns have emerged. Stumping some activists is the additional fact that women's votes do not appear to be based on feminism or women's rights ideology.

Between 1920 and 1968, when women voted less often than men, there were few incentives to target or mobilize women voters, and women candidates were cautioned against targeting women. While Senator Margaret Chase Smith is well known for her vigorous denials of feminism, which she viewed as special pleading for women, she displayed a keen recognition that women voters didn't contain the key to victory.

"I never was a woman candidate," said Smith in 1990, as she reflected on her historic congressional career of more than thirty years. "Had I been a woman candidate I wouldn't have been elected." Comparing women to other groups whose members do not make up a numerical majority, such as Blacks or labor, she said bluntly, "No minority could be elected."[5]

In other words, the prohibition against mobilizing women voters in the past could be considered a politically astute one, since it was not a strategy that could deliver a victory. Exacerbating the danger of wooing this minority of women voters was the prospect that male voters would defect from any candidate who singled women out.

In 1968, when women began to vote in presidential elections in numbers equal to men, their minority status ended. In fact, the pre-1968 patterns have been reversed, and today more women than men are registering to vote, turning out, and going to the polls. The fear of alienating a majority of male voters has given way to the need to court the new majority of women voters.

Before women became a majority of the voters, neither candidates nor scholars were especially interested in how they voted. The few studies of their voting behavior suggested that when women did vote, they did not vote differently from men. Married women were assumed to vote the same as their husbands, either because they shared the same beliefs or because wives took their political cues from their husbands. The occasional sex differences that showed up in opinion polls were regarded as a natural by-product of women's social and familial roles. For instance, the results of polls in the 1960s, which showed more women than men favored a nuclear test ban or favored George McGovern's anti-Vietnam position were seen as the natural reluctance of mothers to send sons off to war.[6]

Few candidates or analysts gave these occasional expressions of sex differences much thought. The few who did concluded that it was logical for women to be more conservative. The slight preference of women voters for Nixon over Kennedy in 1960, for instance, was viewed squarely in this tradition, as was their earlier support for Eisenhower over Stevenson.

Apart from a brief historical moment after women obtained the vote in 1920, when men feared that hordes of women would "upset the established order" and rushed to pass legislation advocated by women's organizations, the specter of a unified women's vote was not raised again until the women's movement of the late 1960s and early 1970s.

When women's suffrage was finally adopted in 1920, male legislators suddenly realized they were about to face 24 million new voters whose actual predilections were unknown. Some men's responses to the newly enfranchised women were vitriolic. For instance, when the newly formed League of Women Voters tried in 1922 to unseat Congressman James Wadsworth of New York, his ally, Governor Nathan Miller, called the women "a menace to our free institutions and to representative government." Particularly upset about the possibility of a voting bloc, Governor Miller continued to blast the League, arguing there was no place for a "league of women voters," just as there was no place for a "league of men voters."[7] Just in case this public rebuke didn't strike home, Governor Miller invoked the "Red Scare" and accused the women of introducing "sex-antagonism" into the electorate, a "socialist" ploy allegedly used by the Bolsheviks in the Russian revolution of 1917.[8]

Other responses to the newly granted suffrage were more politic. In anticipation of a massive women's vote, a nervous male Congress passed many of the items supported by the Women's Joint Congressional Committee, a coalition of most organized women's groups that claimed a membership of 10 million. When several election cycles passed and the anticipated women's vote didn't materialize, Congress not only slowed its pace but actually reversed (by letting it expire) the Sheppard-Towner Act, one of the major pieces of legislation, creating a system of publicly funded clinics for maternal and infant health care.[9]

As soon as it became clear women were not voting in consequential numbers, politicians stopped worrying about this new influx of voters. Candidates saw no reason to seek out women's concerns or to curry their favor through specific campaign promises. The sentiments of one post-suffrage party official in the 1920s might have been uttered in any one of the decades prior to the more recent women's movement: "I know of no woman who has a following of other women. I know of no politician who is afraid of the woman vote on any question under the sun."[10]

When the women's liberation movement emerged in the late 1960s, women activists proclaimed a new era. Women, now active voters, would exercise the vote for their own ends, and those ends would be distinctly different from men's. Activists hoped to create a common consciousness among women that would result in "preferential voting for female candidates, unified support for government policies benefiting women, and support for political candidates based on the degree of their support for women's issues."[11] The rousing speeches made at the founding of the National Women's Political Caucus (NWPC) in 1971 capture the flavor of these early political hopes.

"What unites women as a majority is the refusal to be manipulated any longer [by white male minority with power]. What unites women across the lines of race, class, generation and man-made party politics is the demand for participation ourselves: our own voice in the big decisions affecting our lives," cried out co-founder Betty Friedan. A powerful new consciousness would transcend partisan divisions, creating a new majority of "women who are Democrats and Republicans, women disgusted with both parties and young women turned on to neither."[12] This new movement of women would "upset all the old political rules and traditions in 1972, with a new human politics that bosses won't be able to contain nor polls predict."[13] In other words Friedan was prophesying what men earlier had feared.

Whether or not women will ever constitute a unified or reliable voting bloc is the subject of much confusion. Scholars of voting behavior argue that, strictly speaking, three elements must be present to turn a demographic group of voters into a voting bloc. Members of a group must perceive that "a disparity of power or other resources exists between this group and others," that this disparity "is illegitimate and based on systemic factors," and that "the group should engage in some form of collective action to rectify the situation."[14] When these beliefs are shared, members will vote alike, share support for specific policies, and prefer candidates who are members of the same group. These beliefs are precisely those articulated by the National Women's Political Caucus speakers in 1971.

There have been such voting blocs in American politics. The most stable and persistent one has been among African-American voters. Since the time of Franklin Roosevelt, African-Americans have consistently given most of their votes (80–90 percent) to Democratic candidates nationally.[15] The basis of African-American solidarity stems from the common history of slavery and racial segregation, resulting in a long-standing belief in collective action as a means of improving life for all members of the group. As a result of this tradition, the collective clout and ability of Blacks to influence elections is substantial, particularly in the South and in urban areas where their numerical strength is concentrated geographically. Presidential elections may even depend on the percentages in which African-Americans turn out and vote. Both Democratic and African-American candidates assume that Black voters, if they go to the polls, will support them. It is accurate to speak of this vote as a bloc vote—its expression can be analyzed historically and the success or failure of candidates who seek to mobilize it can be documented.

Scholars, who study how voting blocs develop, argue that it requires more than an awareness of a common characteristic, such as reproductive capacity or biological similarity, to develop. Creating political solidarity among demographic groups is difficult, given an American culture in which "[G]roup-based politics tends to be regarded with suspicion as special-interest politics."[16]

Historian Nancy Cott, who has studied women's political evolution, agrees that, to date, there is no basis on which to characterize women's voting patterns as analogous to those of African-American voters. Assertion of a women's voting bloc in this strict sense is an "interpretive fiction."[17] Women's allegiances have been determined historically much more by race, ethnicity, religion, or social class than they have been by their gender. Cott also argues that the existing two-party system is "profoundly at cross-purposes to such a proposition [of a voting bloc]."[18]

Historically, women voters have not exhibited a preference for women candidates; indeed, until recently, they have been significantly more reluctant to support women candidates than have male voters.[19] When this gap closed in 1972, as measured by polling data, it was not due to "a decrease in support among men but rather by a substantial increase in support by women."[20]

In the decade following the rousing rhetoric of the National Women's Political Caucus, no women's voting bloc materialized. Nor did a women's vote emerge as significant in individual races. No evidence sug-

gested that women candidates received an advantage from women voters. The hopes of the early women's movement for a dramatic show of
women's political power dwindled in the face of intense division and po-
larization among women voters, especially over the issues of abortion and
the Equal Rights Amendment (ERA).

Activists claimed majority support on both issues and pointed to opinion polls to support their claims, but the presence of well-organized
women mobilized against ERA and abortion rights—and winning key
legislative votes—frustrated and shattered these claims for popular support. Forces opposed to feminism gained enough strength in the Republican party by 1980 to overturn its forty-year-old support for ERA and
adopt a platform plank against abortion rights.

That year, Joanne Howes remembers searching for evidence of a
women's vote during the presidential primaries. She was working for
Senator Ted Kennedy, who was opposing the sitting president in his own
party, Jimmy Carter. Howes could not find enough evidence to make a
convincing case. Neither Kennedy nor Carter sought out women voters
during the primary, and neither the Democrats nor the Republicans targeted women specifically during the general election the following November. Activist women's organizations, such as the National Organization for Women (NOW) and the National Women's Political Caucus
(NWPC), did little to mobilize their members, even though many believed Reagan's policies were antithetical to women's interests.

Paradoxically, the election of Ronald Reagan as president in 1980 renewed the debate over a women's vote. Most election analysts looked
only at exit poll results, which showed that women seemed to have divided their votes almost equally between Carter (47 percent) and Reagan
(46 percent). However, Eleanor Smeal, then director of NOW and a
trained political scientist, focused instead on the nearly 8 percent difference between men's and women's level of support for Carter. Looking at
the Carter vote alone, Smeal determined that more women than men
had voted for him, by approximately eight points. Carter received a little
over 37 percent of the male vote, while Reagan captured 54 percent.[21]
This difference in the votes cast by men and women became identified as
a "gender gap."

Smeal reasoned that if women were voting differently from men,
there might be a voting bloc among women voters after all, and showing
its existence could be key to NOW's strategy in the ERA ratification
fights. Evidence of a potential women's vote just might scare legislators

into positive action in three more states before the ratification deadline passed on June 30, 1982. If there really was a women's vote, it could be used to defeat legislators who voted against the ERA or to elect sympathetic replacements. One of Smeal's primary concerns was that if the ERA was defeated, after twelve years of concerted effort, headlines must be avoided that equated its defeat with the failure of the women's movement.

To supplement the analysis of the 1980 election, NOW staff members began assembling polling data that showed evidence of male/female differences in other areas, including party identification, President Reagan's approval ratings, and attitudes toward specific government policies and issues. NOW's strategy—to focus media attention on the possibility of a women's vote, and in turn to gain the attention of the two major political parties—was extraordinarily successful. Monthly "gender gap updates" were sent to media outlets, and NOW kept the spotlight on the 1982 races, where women's votes appeared to make the difference between a candidate's success or defeat. Three governors' races were featured: those of Mario Cuomo in New York, Mark White in Texas, and James Blanchard in Michigan. *Washington Post* columnist Judy Mann was the first to use the term *gender gap* in the popular press.

By 1983, its use was widespread. Whatever complexity scholars might find in the statistics analyzed by Smeal, and whatever cautions they might make about the failure of opinion polls to translate reliably into votes, were lost in the pithiness of the phrase and the possibilities it seemed to imply.[22]

The gender gap took on a life of its own as pollsters and consultants joined the search for differences in voting behavior and policy preferences between the sexes. An especially important Harris poll, taken in early 1983, fueled activist arguments for the existence of a women's vote, showing that women voters were the significant element in the congressional elections of 1982, when Democrats had gained twenty-six seats in the House of Representatives. The Harris poll also showed general movement of support away from President Reagan and toward the Democratic candidates, with women defecting in greater numbers. Women now said they preferred the Democrats by a whopping 17 percent over the Republican Reagan. By contrast, men were sticking with Reagan.[23] The data seemed solid enough, and intriguing enough, to keep the image of an emerging women's bloc before the public's eyes in the years leading up to the next presidential election.

By the spring of 1984, Smeal was convinced that women's votes existed and could play a powerful role in the 1984 elections. "Reagan can be defeated on the women's vote alone," read a press release announcing Smeal's new organization, The Woman's Trust. Completely immersed in the possibilities for Reagan's overthrow, Smeal devised two projects to heighten the excitement over a women's vote. "The Gender Gap Action Campaign" would "create high visibility for gender gap issues in order to energize and motivate especially concerned women to register and to vote."[24] All issues on which persistent sex differences had been found in public opinion polls were defined as gender gap issues, including "equal rights and reproductive choice, economic issues of unemployment and inflation as well as our nation's budget priorities, and issues of peace/war and the nuclear arms race. . . . "

A second project would provide support for women candidates since "both public opinion polls and experience indicate that women on the ticket who have positions supporting women's concerns strengthen the entire [Democratic] ticket."[25] The phrase "women's concerns" was the new way to refer to any issue on which sex differences could be found and on which women held different attitudes or opinions from those of men. Specifically, it encompassed an array of issues far beyond women's rights, and was compatible with the emerging notion that women spoke with "a different voice."

Smeal laid out the math. Opinion polls showed that a majority of men, 55 percent, thought Reagan was doing a good job, but only 38 percent of the women thought so, a gap of seventeen points. She then calculated that a 10 percent difference between men and women voters was all that was needed to defeat Reagan. A Democratic candidate could afford to lose some men's votes, so long as each percentage point lost could be made up by an increase in women's votes. Smeal's figures, which were meant to sound simple and straightforward, suggested that the most sensible strategy to defeat Reagan was to mobilize women.

The two political parties would respond to the growing evidence—and increasing hype—of a women's vote in vastly different ways. For Democrats, the promotion of gender gap data promptly turned into a bid to put a woman on the 1984 presidential ticket. The Republicans, by contrast, analyzed past voting behavior, then targeted and appealed to the groups of women they identified as sympathetic or potentially sympathetic to Reagan.

The story has been told of how five, and ultimately seven, activist women used the gender gap data to create a widespread demand to place a woman on the 1984 Democratic ticket. Working behind the scenes, the women, who came to be known as the A team, included Ranny Cooper of the Kennedy Political Action Committee Fund for a Democratic Majority, who had previously run the Women's Campaign Fund; Nanette Falkenberg from the National Abortion Rights Action League (NARAL); Eleanor Lewis, administrative aide to Geraldine Ferraro; Joanne Howes, a former Kennedy and Mikulski aide who was working full time on a Women's Vote Project; and labor and feminist activist Millie Jeffrey. Their strategy was to first publicize the potential power of women's votes and the general idea of a woman on the Democratic ticket before floating specific names.

Judy Mann of *The Washington Post* wrote several "Gender Clout" columns, advancing the idea of a female vice president and spelling out the mathematical possibilities if women, the majority of the population, registered and voted. "This is the decade women can be expected to take their problems and their priorities into the political arena, as candidates, campaign staffers and as significant campaign contributors," wrote Mann, who previously had publicized NOW's findings on the gender gap.[26]

The A team drew up a list of potential candidates from which they selected Congresswoman Geraldine Ferraro of New York. The women invited an unsuspecting Ferraro to a Chinese dinner, with fortune cookies filled with specially designed portents, such as "You will win big in '84," and "You will meet a man in San Francisco [site of the Democratic Convention] and travel with him."

"I was both flabbergasted and flattered . . . the actuality of getting the vice presidential nomination continued to seem very farfetched to me and out of reach," remembers Ferraro. Prior to this evening, both Democratic party chair Charles Manatt and Ferraro were on record as saying they believed neither a Black nor a woman would be on the 1984 ticket. A dramatic event of this nature probably would not occur until the end of the century.

By the time the A Team finished promoting the idea, however, both Manatt and Ferraro had begun to change their tune. When Manatt offered Ferraro the chair of the Platform Committee, a position whose visibility at the Democratic National Convention would bolster her chances for the nomination, he added that Ferraro's presence on the ticket would "further invite the gender-gap vote."[27] As the time drew closer for

Democratic presidential nominee Walter Mondale to announce his running mate, Lane Kirkland, head of the AFL-CIO, a crucial constituency of the Democratic party, went on record as saying a woman would help, not hurt, the ticket. But as Ferraro flew to Mondale's home in Minnesota for the interview, she had doubts about the entire strategy. "I kept hearing my own voice at the National Women's Political Caucus the year before," she said, "advising my disgruntled colleagues that no male candidate would choose a woman as a running mate unless he were fifteen points behind. And on the morning I flew to my vice presidential interview, that's just what the spread was: fifteen points."[28]

In the euphoria of the moment, few noticed the fallacy of the Democrats' assumption that the mere presence of a woman on the presidential ticket would induce women to vote for it. Believing their mission had been accomplished, some of the women's organizations even stopped tracking the gender gap.

The Republicans, by contrast, and after a slow start, took pains to analyze women's voting behavior in depth and developed an understanding of what would motivate women to vote for Reagan. While White House officials tried to dismiss press coverage during the first several years of the new administration on "Reagan's Woman Problem" as "cute," by 1983 the situation had changed. Reagan's loss of support among women voters was apparent in the public opinion polls. And Reagan had had problems with several individual women, all of which had attracted considerable media attention. Kathy Wilson, the Republican chair of the bipartisan NWPC, called Reagan a "dangerous man," and suggested he resign from the presidency. In a more damaging episode, Barbara Honegger, a Justice Department official assigned to work on a project to eliminate sex discrimination in existing laws and regulations, quit and called the project a sham. White House officials exacerbated the situation by ridiculing her publicly and describing her charges as those of a lower level "munchkin." Reagan also created headlines with his maladroit quip before the Business and Professional Women when he said, "I happen to be one man who believes if it wasn't for women, us men would still be walking around in skin suits, carrying clubs."[29]

Key Republican operatives Lee Atwater and Ed Rollins began to perceive women's lower approval ratings of the president as a potential threat to Reagan's reelection. Pollsters Bob Teeter and Linda DiVall, working for the National Republican Congressional Campaign Committee, had already begun to conduct surveys on the gender gap for Republican House members nervous about their own reelection prospects in 1984. A special unit headed by presidential aide Michael Deaver was set up in the White House to coordinate strategy.[30]

Elizabeth Dole, secretary of transportation, who chaired a coordinating council on women, and who was charged with publicizing Reagan's record on women's issues to the public, argued the Reagan administration had a good record on these issues but had failed to communicate it to American women. In particular, Dole believed that economic equity was "where the real needs are; if those problems are properly handled, I believe the gender gap can be closed."[31] "This was the first time we'd had a lot of assistants to the President working on women's issues—child care, dependent care, issues like enforcement of child-support laws," observed Dole.

The single most important directive, however, was to the president's pollster, Richard Wirthlin, who was asked to take a hard look at the evidence of a women's vote. Wirthlin dissected the gender gap with the anatomical skill of a surgeon, slicing the single category of women into sixty-four separate segments. He looked at the demographic characteristics of women—their ages, educational levels, incomes, marital status—and examined the differences *among* women on various issues.

By the time Mondale and Reagan were toe-to-toe in the 1984 campaign, the Republicans were armed with a sophisticated quantitative analysis of women voters that allowed them to target *particular* segments of women, putting the Republicans far ahead of the Democrats, who had confused a woman's presence on the ticket with a strategy for mobilizing women voters. The Republicans appealed to women on the basis of their economic interests, quite apart from their identities as women.[32] The Republicans made television ads emphasizing economic issues targeted to three groups of women in particular: single working women, married working women, and elderly or widowed women.

"Their basic strategy was to sell the Republican economic program as a success . . . [b]y stressing that the economy had turned around and was providing increased opportunities for all—and by committing themselves to preserving Social Security. . . ."[33]

The campaign theme was "Vote Republican for a Better Future," and Republican campaign operatives expended considerable energy briefing other Republican candidates on the changing demographics of American voters and American families. New data, for instance, showed the traditional two-parent/two-child family was no longer the dominant model, and that election messages must be targeted to more diverse groups of women.

The Democrats never developed any targeting strategy involving women voters during the 1984 Mondale-Ferraro campaign. The Mondale staff did not even want Ferraro to discuss women's issues on the campaign trail. Ferraro's staff felt that women voters should be addressed specifically, and they argued for a "women's media spot." Mondale's staff stalled, finally promised to make one ad, and then stalled again, infuriating Ferraro's staff. By the time the spot was made, the campaign was virtually over. It aired just a few times, largely as a news item rather than as a campaign ad. In a 1991 interview, Ferraro claimed not to remember much about these intraticket arguments, and felt any lack of specific attention to women's issues was compensated for by her presence on the ticket. "The candidacy was a statement in and of itself."[34]

Regardless of the original logic of Ferraro's nomination, the inconsistency between Ferraro's presence on the Democratic ticket as an intended magnet for women voters and the Mondale campaign's reluctance to emphasize women's issues has never been fully explained. Democratic pollster Dotty Lynch has said the campaign was focused on "issues of deficits and a strong defense in order to garner support among white male ethnics."[35] The late Paul Tully, who worked for Ferraro during the 1984 campaign, described the disputes over the women's spot and other issues as a "culture clash with the Minnesotans." Using today's parlance, Tully said, "They just didn't get it."[36]

The Republican strategies were effective, and Reagan was reelected in a landslide with a majority of male and female votes. The specter of a unified women's vote strong enough to defeat an incumbent president evaporated. When the gender gap failed to work in the Democrats' favor, the political fallout was immediate. Democrats who didn't see the Ferraro candidacy in historic terms, as a significant breakthrough for women regardless of election results, thought it had been a disaster. Suddenly "women" were not seen as a bloc of voters in the electorate who might help the Democrats or win the presidency, but as just another special interest group, along with labor, Blacks, and environmentalists, whose selfish and liberal leaders had led the Democrats down the primrose path to defeat.[37]

Women voters had not rallied to Ferraro simply because she was a woman. In fact, as Ferraro learned subsequently, many older women voters had been downright hostile to her candidacy. One member of

Mondale's staff explained that Ferraro's presence was often downplayed (she was frequently sent to less important states) because the campaign's daily tracking polls showed she was hurting the ticket. Exit polls, which indicated that she neither helped nor hurt the ticket, did not affect the widespread belief that she had been a deficit.[38]

The Democrats made two fundamental errors: one was the belief that specific mobilization strategies were unnecessary, that Ferraro's presence alone would provide the motivation for women to vote Democratic, and second, the belief that the women's vote was feminist, a reaction to Republican positions on ERA and abortion rights. The Republicans' careful analysis had revealed a new diversity in women's relationships in both the family and the work force, and had therefore disclosed a new relationship between women and policy issues. The Republicans did not presume that the issue of women's rights was driving the gender gap; they tested to see which issues stimulated which distinct groups of women to support President Reagan.

Ethel Klein was one of the first political scientists to examine the gender gap in the aftermath of 1984. Her conclusions resemble those of the Republican analysts. She says the gap technically exists "when either men and women prefer different candidates, or when men and women vote for the same candidate but for different reasons." Klein stresses that it is based on serious issues, largely economic, and not on superficial qualities.

"It is an issue vote and can be triggered only by policy discussions that incorporate women's perspectives," emphasizes Klein, who adds that women are now "markedly more willing to express policy preferences" than they were before the women's movement.[39]

Klein's conclusions point to the link between women's increased political involvement and the women's movement, but do not confuse the two. Her work highlights the multiplicity of interests women have developed, not what women might have in common.

In retrospect, it is easy to see why Smeal and others believed the gender gap of 1980 to be feminist. The correlation between feminism and Reagan's low standing with women seemed intuitively correct especially after Republicans repudiated their forty-year support for the ERA, and because Reagan so vigorously opposed abortion. Scholarly analysis, conducted long after the results of the 1980 and 1984 campaigns, however, has shown little connection between feminist issues and women's weaker support for Reagan. While scholars differ in the weight they assign particular issues, most insist that the composition of the gender gap was based on economic and foreign policy issues, not on women's rights.[40]

Jane Mansbridge, one of those scholars who has reexamined the 1980 data, argues that Smeal's focus on the 8 percent gap between men and women ignored the fact that their support for women's rights was similar, particularly their mutual support for the Equal Rights Amendment. Mansbridge, who was also an ERA activist, believes that Smeal's emphasis on the difference between men's and women's votes rather than "feminist" votes was driven in part by NOW's organizational needs. A focus on *support for women's rights by both men and women* implied a coalitional strategy. Smeal preferred a strategy based exclusively on the numerical strength of women's votes, not their issue preferences. Whether or not there was a large enough constituency of men and women who might have shifted their votes from Reagan to Mondale on the basis of these issues cannot be answered in the abstract. Campaigns are rarely won or lost on one issue, but then again a few percentage points can make the difference in who wins and who loses.

The confusion between the gender gap (statistical differences between the sexes) and feminism (an ideology and a platform) is substantial. Because the gap was identified during a period of heightened consciousness of sex discrimination and gender inequality, and because feminist groups in particular have given it enormous play, an implicit connection between the two has been established. To date, however, where support for women's rights exists among voters, there is little evidence of a gender gap. Men and women of similar socioeconomic status tend to register similar beliefs on specific issues.

Along with the presumption that the gender gap is feminist and therefore might become a voting bloc is the presumption that it must work in favor of women candidates. While a gender advantage can develop for particular female candidates, as it did in 1990 and 1992, there is no guarantee that it will.

A race that provides a good glimpse of how a gender gap can materialize and then recede is the 1990 California governor's race between former San Francisco mayor Dianne Feinstein and Senator Pete Wilson. Before Feinstein faced Wilson in the general election, she had to run against a candidate in her party primary whose record on women's issues was superb. Attorney General John Van de Kamp was strongly prochoice and had championed other women's issues. Feinstein herself had vetoed several items considered important to the feminist community, including a reproductive rights commemorative "day," and comparable worth legislation. Then Congresswoman Barbara Boxer coined the phrase designed to win women's votes for Van de Kamp. She called him "the best feminist in the race."

Early polls showed Feinstein with a wide gender gap—favorably advantaged by women who said they were going to vote for her. At the close of the primary, however, the gender gap disappeared. While Feinstein ultimately won a majority of women's votes (54 percent) in the primary, she also won 53 percent of men's votes. Van de Kamp divided men's and women's votes almost equally (41 percent men to 40 percent women). In short, neither candidate had an edge or advantage with women voters.

Indeed, CBS exit polls showed that among voters who decided upon their candidate early in the campaign and those who decided in the last few days of the campaign, there was a "reverse" gender gap: "It was created by men who decided to vote for the *woman,* and women who decided to vote for the *man.*"[41] Nearly two thirds of the late-deciding voters were women, and when they decided on their candidate, a majority picked John Van de Kamp. Men who decided at the last minute chose Feinstein. According to Mervin Field, who conducts the California poll, Van de Kamp held the edge among women on the "harder" issues of crime and the economy, while Feinstein had an edge on the "softer" issues of education and the environment. None of these issues were "feminist" in the sense of pertaining to women's rights.

When Feinstein moved on to the general election against Pete Wilson, another pro-choice candidate, she kept emphasizing that she was more trustworthy on abortion rights: "The best person to safeguard a woman's right to choose is another woman." Wilson's staff privately complained of a "double standard." Publicly Wilson would say, "The idea that you must be a woman to be pro-choice doesn't hold water. . . . I don't think I'm entitled to the vote of men because I'm a man. I think I'm entitled to the vote of both men and women because I'm the best candidate."[42]

Wilson also countered with spirited claims that all issues were women's issues and made strategic use of women in his campaign ads, many of which emphasized crime. Throughout the campaign the gender gap ebbed and flowed, showing Republican women were considering voting for Democrat Feinstein. In the end, however, Republican women went back to their party to vote for Wilson, and they did so over an unexpected issue: Feinstein's advocacy of the appointment of women and minorities to public positions in rough proportion to their numbers in the population. Wilson quickly depicted Feinstein as advocating quotas.

A Wilson ad questioned, "Can we afford a governor who puts quotas over qualifications and promises before performance? . . . It is unfair, it's extreme and it's wrong." Then, in a twist designed to criticize her previous record on appointments, the ad concluded by saying, "especially when you consider that in nine years as mayor of San Francisco, the number of women appointed by Feinstein increased by only one percent." That ad "stopped Republican women cold."[43] Mervin Field thinks this strong effect on Republican women made it "easier to drift back into the fold."[44] Thus, an issue that could be considered feminist—parity between men and women in public appointments—was used to win women's votes for a male candidate. In November, Feinstein lost to Wilson by four percentage points.

Many women candidates have been disappointed to learn that women voters do not automatically rally around their candidacies. In an off-the-record debriefing of female Democratic candidates and their campaign managers from the top-level races of 1990, the disappointment of those who thought they could count on women voters was palpable. Many spouses could identify with Rollie Heath's lament after women voters failed to rally to his wife Josie's 1990 U.S. Senate campaign. "I'm disappointed in your sex," he told this co-author.

Republican Linda DiVall is among those political consultants who argue that the gender gap of the last decade isn't advantageous to women candidates because it is largely a partisan phenomenon, favoring the Democratic party. She is critical of the media for not scrutinizing its partisan nature: "[W]hat they have missed, particularly since Reagan became President, is that women have become more Democratic over the years and men increasingly more Republican." DiVall's convictions are based on personal experience as well as polling data. She worked with many Republican women candidates in 1990, including U.S. Senate candidates Claudine Schneider in Rhode Island and Lynn Martin in Illinois: "[W]hat we found, and exit polling data proves this, is that women are still more inclined to vote for Democrats, even male Democratic incumbents, over female Republican challengers."[45]

"[T]he great myth, I think, in 1990, was that if we recruited Republican women to run we would be singularly successful in overturning the gender gap." DiVall does not note the irony that this was the same myth the Democrats succumbed to in 1984. Conversely, DiVall continued, "if one looks at male voters, the picture is precisely the opposite." She calls the movement of young, white male voters, particularly in Southern states, to the Republican party "simply stunning." She points out that in the last ten years, their allegiances have shifted "from something like a 25 percent Democratic registration advantage to almost the same on the Republican side."[46]

What, then, is the significance of women's votes if they are not a reliable voting bloc, not feminist in orientation, and do not translate into a guaranteed preference for women candidates? Majority status ensures the significance of women's votes and distinguishes women's voting behavior from other demographic groups, such as ethnic or racial minorities.

This sheer numerical power means that both female and male candidates must compete for women's votes. Therein lies one of the central paradoxes of women and political life: The significance of women's votes has increased markedly because of this competition. What makes this competition necessary is that women are not a predictable voting bloc, despite their slight preference for Democrats over Republicans.

Consider the 1988 presidential election. Republicans once again found themselves defending against waning support from women. In May 1988, polls showed women favoring Democratic governor Michael Dukakis over vice president Bush by sixteen to eighteen points. Once again, however, Republicans were able to win back women's support by the end of the campaign, and elect George Bush.

Linda DiVall helped Bush turn around his low standing with women. Thoroughly familiar with gender gap polling since her initial work in 1982, she analyzed Bush's initial lower standing with women: "When Dukakis wasn't very well known, women were in his camp. George Bush was better known, but not well liked." Women's preferences and support for the two presidential candidates were totally reversed by September, just four months later.

How did such a reversal occur? DiVall's analysis showed women disliked George Bush because they didn't see him as a family man who could relate to their problems. Rather, they saw him as indecisive, weak, and "somewhat removed from what they were going through on a day-to-day basis." Armed with this knowledge, Bush's campaign strategists used the Republican National Convention and his acceptance speech to "showcase his family." This corrective action was successful, according to DiVall, since "the numbers that moved the most after that speech were with women." Not only did May's deficit among women voters disappear by September, but Bush ultimately won 51 percent of the women's votes—a majority—as Reagan had before him.[47]

Political scientists Barbara G. Farah and Ethel Klein examined this reversal after the campaign. Their analysis is not significantly different from DiVall's. Women voters were concerned about the state of the economy and needed to feel that Bush could identify with their everyday concerns. Farah and Klein argue that a key issue for women in the 1988 campaign was their sense of economic vulnerability, both for themselves and for their children.

Bush addressed these feelings through the announcement of specific programs, targeted media advertising, and strategic campaign visits. He chose sites where women workers were prominent, such as hospitals, child-care centers, and so on. He aimed speeches at women that developed the theme of economic empowerment, and argued that the path to economic security was through private-sector job creation. Bush also focused on crime and personal security, issues that also directly affected women. Campaign polls showed that women thought initially that Dukakis was the tougher of the two men on crime, but as the campaign evolved, they became convinced that Bush was tougher. Farah and Klein note that the Dukakis campaign failed to develop economic themes to counter Bush's until the last few weeks before the election, when it was too late to win them back.

The fact that George Bush had to shape campaign strategies and target issues that would bring women back into his camp illustrates how women's voting strength is influencing campaigns. The Bush campaign singled out young women, single working women, middle-aged married working women, and elderly or widowed women—women expected to be most receptive to his campaign messages. Polling data had suggested these groups of women were among those voters who could be persuaded by strong appeals from Bush. President Bush felt no need to articulate "feminist" issues to win women's votes, and remained strongly against abortion throughout the campaign.[48]

The specific groups of women targeted by the Republican party are an indication that the divisions among women are more complicated than those between homemakers and working women, although homemakers do tend to vote Republican. Women's new relationship to the economy, especially their vulnerability to its vicissitudes, whether married, divorced, or single, seems to form the basis for segmentation.

The National Women's Political Caucus commissioned a survey in

1987 to learn more about voters, and especially their attitudes toward women candidates. Those voters who are most supportive of hypothetical women candidates were "younger voters, minorities, voters never married, Catholics, urban residents, and higher educated, white-collar workers—and especially women in these groups." Those voters who said they were least inclined to vote for women candidates were "over 60, those who live in small towns and rural areas, those with lower levels of formal education, voters in lower-white-collar and blue-collar jobs, homemakers and the retired, and voters in the South. . . ."[49] The findings of this survey were consistent with other surveys conducted throughout the decade, according to the report's authors. The toughest sell for women candidates remains older women and homemakers.

Democratic campaign strategist Niki Heidepriem, who managed Barbara Mikulski's winning Senate campaign in 1986 and is a veteran of several presidential campaigns, agrees that the key to understanding the gender gap is in the examination of subcategories of women. For instance, competition between parties is especially sharp for young women, ages eighteen to twenty-nine. Examining their voting behavior over several presidential elections, Heidepriem argued that the Democrats' problem with young women can be put simply: "They are not for us [Democrats]; they're voting Republican."[50]

Analysts from both parties also agree that abortion rights has been an increasingly important issue for young women voters, even though abortion rights rarely determines the outcome of a political campaign. Since the Supreme Court began to restrict abortion rights, young women have become aware that they may lose rights they have always taken for granted. Some Democratic strategists talk about abortion rights as a "wedge" issue, one that "slices" a segment (wedge) of voters and brings them into one political party or the other; in this case, pro-choice young women would be targeted to support the Democrats. Democratic strategist Frank Greer, who has handled a number of races where the issue of abortion rights has been critical, says, "Young voters are the strongest voting bloc in the Republican party," and after the Supreme Court's decision in *Webster*, there was a "political sea-change" in the significance they attributed to abortion rights.[51] In 1992, a majority of young women voted for all four new female senators. As Table 7–1 demonstrates, young women were far more supportive of these candidates than young men of the same age.

At the other end of the age spectrum is support from older women

TABLE 7–1

Young Women's (18–29) Votes for Women Candidates in 1992 (%)

State	% Total Vote	Democrat	Republican
Pennsylvania (Yeakel/Specter)[a]	19	54 (44)[b]	46 (56)
California (Boxer/Herschensohn)	20	60 (42)	40 (60)
California (Feinstein/Seymour)	21	64 (47)	36 (53)
Illinois (Moseley-Braun/Williamson)	20	64 (54)	36 (46)
Washington (Murray/Chandler)	23	56 (51)	44 (49)

[a]All women candidates listed in this table were Democrats.
[b]Young mens votes (%) in parentheses.
Source: Voter Research & Surveys exit polls, taken on Election Day, 1992. VRS is an association of ABC News, CNN, CBS News, and NBC News.

voters, traditionally a tough group for women candidates of both parties to reach. In 1992, all the newly elected women senators— Moseley-Braun, Feinstein, Boxer, and Murray—all Democrats, won a majority of votes from older women. Lynn Yeakel, who lost her race against Arlen Specter, also lost older women voters, both in the primary and in the general election. (Women over sixty preferred Specter 52 percent to 48 percent.) These few races show that women candidates can overcome the skepticism of older women voters in particular cases. Since older women voters often comprise one fifth or more of all women voters, winning their support can be very significant for the outcome of an election (Table 7–2).

The two incumbent senators, one Republican and one Democrat, have had good support from older women. Senators Nancy Kassebaum of Kansas and Barbara Mikulski of Maryland have both been reelected to second terms. Kassebaum speculates that older women support her because they've "watched me grow up." As the daughter of Republican

TABLE 7–2

Older Women's (60+) Votes for Women Candidates in 1992 (%)

State	% Total Vote	Democrat	Republican
Pennsylvania (Yeakel/Specter)[a]	23	48	52
California (Boxer/Herschensohn)	17	57	43
California (Feinstein/Seymour)	16	66	34
Illinois (Moseley-Braun/Williamson)	20	52	48
Washington (Murray/Chandler)	20	61	39

[a]All women candidates listed in this table were Democrats.
Source: Voter Research & Surveys exit polls, taken on Election Day, 1992. VRS is an association of ABC News, CNN, CBS News, and NBC News.

presidential candidate Alf Landon, Kassebaum had been in the public eye for many years before she ran for office. "It's my own age group I have trouble with," she laments. Yet in her first reelection bid for the Senate, she did extremely well with women in all age groups.[52]

Senator Barbara Mikulski also has solid support among older voters. Mikulski's advisers think this is due to her policy positions on issues of concern to them. For instance, Mikulski has a record of support for "displaced homemakers," those women whose lives were devoted to marriage until divorce left them both financially destitute and without useable employment skills. Mikulski has fought for changes in the social security laws to recognize the contributions of homemakers.

Among women voters, homemakers were the group most reluctant to support the new women senators. However, Patty Murray of Washington, the youngest of all the women candidates, gained the highest level of support among homemakers of any of the new senators. Homemakers divided their votes evenly between Patty Murray and Rod Chandler, fifty-fifty. Whether Murray's slogan, "Just a Mom in Tennis Shoes," won her this support among homemakers is impossible to determine. Boxer had the least support (35 percent), while Feinstein gained 45 percent of their vote (see Table 7–3).

Even though African-American voters are such strong allies of the Democratic party, exit polls show a significant difference in how African-American men and women distributed their votes to the winning women senators. African-American women gave virtually all their votes to the newly elected women senators. African-American men, however, gave the same kind of support only to Carol Moseley-Braun, an African-American candidate. African-American men gave 22 percent of their votes to Republican Bruce Herschensohn, one of the most conservative candidates running on a Republican ticket anywhere in the country. Similarly, 18 percent of African-American men who voted in the other California Senate race preferred moderate Republican John Seymour to Dianne Feinstein (see Table 7–4).

In some races, women's issues put male candidates on the defensive for the first time. Male candidates scrambled to defend their records on

TABLE 7–3

Homemakers' Votes for Women Candidates in 1992 (%)

State	% Total Vote	Democrat	Republican
Pennsylvania (Yeakel/Specter)[a]	15	45	55
California (Boxer/Herschensohn)	13	35	65
California (Feinstein/Seymour)	14	45	55
Illinois (Moseley-Braun/Williamson)	18	44	56
Washington (Murray/Chandler)	13	50	50

[a]All women candidates listed in this table were Democrats.
Source: Voter Research & Surveys exit polls, taken on Election Day, 1992. VRS is an association of ABC News, CNN, CBS News, and NBC News.

TABLE 7–4

African-American Votes for Three Women Candidates in 1992 (%)

Sex of Voter	Boxer	Feinstein	Moseley-Braun[a]
Women	93	92	96
Men	78	82	94

[a]Sample too small to produce data for Murray or Yeakel.
Source: Voter Research & Surveys exit polls, taken on Election Day, 1992. VRS is an association of ABC News, CNN, CBS News, and NBC News.

women's issues, and prove their "feminist" credentials, especially if they were running against a female opponent.

Attorney General Robert Abrams of New York faced both Elizabeth Holtzman and Geraldine Ferraro in his Democratic primary. "Mr. Abrams," said his adviser Ethan Geto, is "'a feminist man' with an unrivaled record on behalf of abortion rights." Geto went on to argue that other issues would be more important in the long run. "We understand the impression that women candidates are more outsiders. . . . We think that when this campaign gets close to the end there'll be questions in the voters' minds about Bob's principal opponent on other issues."[53]

The two Senate primary campaigns in California were filled with examples of the strategies used by both male and female candidates to reach women voters. In general, male candidates intensified their use of female surrogates on the stump and in television ads. Men's ads also featured issues they felt would be of concern to women. One of Boxer's two opponents, Lieutenant Governor Leo McCarthy, held forums throughout the state on breast cancer and backed a legislative resolution declaring breast cancer a state emergency. Her other opponent, Congressman Mel Levine, ran television ads that featured endorsements of his candidacy from notable women, including elected female officials and former astronaut Sally Ride.

Any male candidate down ten to twenty points with women, as both Ronald Reagan and George Bush had been in their elections, had to take corrective action in 1992 or his chance of being elected evaporated. And many male candidates were conceding a ten-point advantage to their female opponents from the outset. That meant they needed to be "up" with male voters by at least ten points to offset the loss.

"I literally had one male colleague in the House say to me that this was the first time in his life he wished he were a woman," said a surprised Patricia Schroeder. "It was very funny and it was said very sincerely."[54]

While the 1992 women's campaigns, especially those for the U.S. Senate, were highly visible and dramatic, giving the impression that women candidates finally had won the advantage of "bonus miles" among voters, the central point remained intact: Both men and women candidates had to compete for women's votes. They did not go automatically to the female candidate, as losing candidates Josie Heath (Colorado), Gloria O'Dell (Kansas), or Claire Sargent (Arizona) will attest. As a result of this competition for women's votes, the historic proscription against raising issues of particular importance to women has been overturned. Precisely where the boundaries are, just how vigorously or aggressively women's votes may be sought without losing men's, continues to be tested in specific campaigns.

Each particular race must be seen in the context of the factors described in the last two chapters. No woman won a seat in the U.S. Senate by challenging an incumbent candidate in the general election; the other successful female candidates all won in open-seat races. (Feinstein, and in June 1993, Kay Bailey Hutchinson of Texas, could be considered exceptions, but both ran against men appointed to hold seats until the next election.)

A few commentators tried to point out that, while the Year of the Woman in 1992 was working for Democratic candidates, there was no equivalent wave on the Republican side. Senate Minority Leader and Republican Robert Dole protested to the press that such talk was "a piece of liberal media hype." Buried deep in some of the news stories was journalistic caution that the ultimate outcomes in November would be more of a test between Republicans and Democrats than for women in general.

New York Times reporter R. W. Apple, Jr., for instance, reported that a California poll conducted for the *Los Angeles Times*, "found that 6 out of 10 California Democrats agreed with the proposition that 'it is important to send a woman to the Senate,' but only 4 out of 10 Republicans did so."

In Yeakel's losing race, while she received support from three out of every four women voters who thought Thomas should not have been confirmed, nearly half (42 percent) of the men said "no" on Thomas yet still voted for Arlen Specter. Similarly, 58 percent of the men who thought electing a woman to the U.S. Senate was "somewhat important" voted for Specter as well. Women who thought it was "somewhat important" gave Yeakel 42 percent of their vote. Those who thought it was "very important" gave Yeakel three out of four votes. None of these issues was of overriding importance in any of the campaigns. Most voters checked "economy/jobs" to the question of what really guided their vote.

Ethel Klein has been arguing for at least a decade that women's greater allegiance to the Democratic party was "staving off a Republican realignment." She argues they shortened the coattails of both Reagan and Bush and have helped keep Congress Democratic. Democratic strategist Ann Lewis concurs, and claims that, at the congressional level in 1990, women's votes were responsible for keeping the House of Representatives Democratic. "According to exit polls taken during the 1990 elections, it is only because of the gender gap that Democrats control the United States Congress."[55] In House races, women voted Democratic 54 to 46 percent, and for Democratic senators, 53 to 45 percent.[56]

Bill Carrick, a strategist for Dianne Feinstein's Senate race, remembers the moment in 1992 that he realized the new relationship between women and the Democratic party. "I remember sitting in a coordinating campaign meeting with the Clinton folks looking at tracking numbers and the usual get-out-the-vote stuff. . . . Our polling data was showing we had 70 percent working women [for Feinstein]. Clinton and Boxer's numbers were a little less but in the same neighborhood. And I said, 'Let me tell you something, guys. We ought to start thinking about working women as a Democratic party base constituency group.'"[57]

Indeed, all newly elected female senators won tremendous support from working women, ranging from a low of 58 percent for Murray to a high of 67 percent for Feinstein. Moseley-Braun and Boxer also received roughly two out of every three working women's votes.

The pattern of Republican presidential victories, winning a majority of women's votes, was interrupted in 1992 by Democrat Bill Clinton's victory. However, how women will vote in 1994 should be regarded as an open question. President Clinton won in a three-way race, and while more women preferred Clinton to Bush or Perot, a two-way race could be more competitive.

Before the Democrats' victory occurred in 1992, Linda DiVall had cautioned Democrats against any euphoria over the women's vote: "Nationally, the Democrats will have to seek even more women's votes if they expect to win, since they cannot do so with only 49 percent of the women's vote," referring to the percent of women who voted for Democrat Dukakis in 1988.[58] The danger in increasing the margin of victory with women's votes is, of course, whether such a strategy would drive men out of the Democratic party.

The unanswered question is why women prefer the Democratic party over the Republicans in these races. Answers remain partial and full of speculation. As Ethel Klein says of the gender gap, "Both parties understand that it exists; few people, whether candidates, pollsters, or academics, however, would claim to understand it."[59]

This new Democratic partisan allegiance reinforces the search for a distinctive women's perspective on policies and issues. Pamela Conover, a political scientist, has speculated that the women's movement activated women to assert fundamental values, which register in polls as "more positive feelings than men['s] . . . toward the disadvantaged in society."[60] Yet Conover also found that "men and women do not generally differ in their political values: "As a group, women are no more or no less egalitarian, individualistic, racist, or liberal than men."[61] Hence, sex differences in opinion polls on questions of this nature are not a reliable guide to partisan differences or actual votes. But the fact that women are currently favoring the Democrats continues to fuel the search for a distinctive female perspective on politics.

Since women voters, along with men, now are listing the economy and jobs as their number one concern, some analysts are speculating that women, who are more likely to be in lower-paying or sex-segregated occupations, are becoming more conscious of these inequities in employment and their economic consequences. Both Democratic and Republican strategists noted this aspect of women's economic concerns in 1992. Bush campaign operative Mary Matalin says, "The men don't get this. It is insulting to be paid less for the same job, but more importantly, it's harder to make ends meet." Democratic strategist Celinda Lake, who worked for Bill Clinton, said, "I've been stunned [at the polling data]. [Women] feel very marginal. They feel they don't get paid the same amount of money for the same work. You could have a revolution in this country on pay for women because they've really become aware of it."[62]

Whether women will continue to favor the Democratic party or whether women's policy preferences are or will be different from men's, women voters have gained the attention of analysts, strategists, and candidates alike. Analysts will try and understand them more deeply. Strategists will try to analyze what motivates women voters. Candidates will raise more and more issues of concern to women, ranging from the economy to child support to the incidence of breast cancer.

Therein lies the new power of women's votes.

8

Decoding the Press

Finessing the Gender Trap

She was a "feisty and feminine fifty-year-old with the unmistakable Dorothy Hamill wedge of gray hair . . . a congressman's daughter [with] a wardrobe befitting a First Lady . . . an unlikely standard-bearer . . . a former full-time mother . . . "gushed *The Washington Post* (August 26, 1992). That Lynn Yeakel also happened to be the woman who won a hard-fought primary to become Pennsylvania's Democratic Senate candidate was mentioned, but it was not until halfway through the *Post*'s lengthy profile that any of the credentials she brought to the race were noted. The *Post*'s next-day profile of incumbent Republican senator Arlen Specter, however, led with the facts that he had been "a crime-busting district attorney and a mayoral hopeful."[1]

The New York Times gave the world much the same view of Illinois's 1992 Senate candidates Carol Moseley-Braun and Richard Williamson: "She is commanding and ebullient, a den mother with a cheerleader's smile; he, by comparison, is all business, like the corporate lawyer he is. . . . " Not until the twenty-second paragraph did the *Times* note that Moseley-Braun was also a lawyer and a former federal prosecutor and veteran state senator, as well.[2]

Was this merely the result of media enthusiasm over the Year of the Woman in Politics? Maybe, but during the 1990 U.S. Senate races, a reporter in Rhode Island hounded Congresswoman Claudine Schneider for a look inside the refrigerator of her single-woman's bachelor apartment. Similarly, a television reporter in Colorado pestered Josie Heath for a chance to film her at home fixing breakfast for her family. Then, when Heath's sleeve accidentally caught on the egg compartment, flinging eggs across the kitchen floor, the reporter opened her film piece with a vignette of Heath on her knees wiping up broken eggs.

Why is it that such attributes—women's hairstyles and family relationships, their femininity or cheerleader smiles, their kitchens or whether they can scrub egg yolk off vinyl—are grist for the media mill, while similar attributes of comparable men are not?

One might ask, as well, why the media seemed obsessed in the summer of 1992 with the Great Cookie War between the two women "running" for First Lady of the land.

The answer is at once simple and complex: To discuss political women in intimate, almost Playboy-like detail is an expression of confusion, not about any individual woman and her politics or public record, necessarily, but at the very concept that women should be out in the public world and running for office. To fixate on their physical appearance is as tacit a suggestion of a sexually hostile environment as a pinup of a naked woman might be in the office of, say, the U.S. Navy–affiliated Tailhook Association. To ask political candidates to help create a "photo op" or "TV visual" by invading their homes—or to ask the wives of male candidates for their cookie recipes—symbolically forces all women back into their kitchens, or back in time to a place where gender roles were rigidly defined, where husbands were the public persons and wives "covered" things at home, and the mythologies about men and women's sexual natures could go unchallenged. To put it another way, the press coverage of women in politics is an artifact of this country's age-old but unresolved debate over women citizens' proper roles versus "proper women's" place.

However, it is also something more and that something further complicates the situation. It is still news when women are running for office and taking charge of big cities, governors' mansions, and congressional districts in the same way it is still news when infants' mothers are called up and shipped off to war, and other women are flying helicopters into battle and coming home in body bags. In short: It is still news whenever women tackle any job American society traditionally has seen as male.

What constitutes "news" is partly whatever editors or news directors decide and partly a hundred years of a tradition that has defined women and their issues as "soft" news, while politics is "hard" news and a man's domain. Ergo, the national headlines when tiny Pacifica, California, elected an all-woman city council in June 1992. An all-male council would not have been newsworthy. All-male-is-normal was the paradigm—until Anita Hill started the beginnings of serious questioning in the press about that paradigm, from the Senate Judiciary Committee on down. The result: The media-defined but still astonishing Year of the Woman in Politics.

"Calling it the Year of the Woman makes it sound like the Year of the Caribou or the Year of Asparagus. We're neither a fad nor a fancy nor a year," fumed Senator Barbara Mikulski of Maryland whenever reporters brought up the subject during her 1992 reelection bid.

Mikulski was wrong. In 1992 that was precisely what women candidates were in the imperfect mirror that is the media. If the television broadcasts of the Clarence Thomas Supreme Court Confirmation Hearings starring Anita Hill could beat the baseball playoffs in the ratings—on a Saturday and Sunday when men, and not just women, were at home—then the women who successfully began invoking Anita Hill in their campaigns were precisely that: the hottest new fad. The totally unexpected. A curiosity. News. But there was little new about the way they were covered.

Not that women never complained before. In 1989, after the *Boston Herald* photographed Massachusetts's lieutenant governor and gubernatorial candidate Evelyn Murphy jogging in shorts—a front-page photo so "large and unflattering"[3] that another Boston paper commented on it—and inside the paper, a female columnist lectured that candidate about cellulite, Murphy cried foul: "I don't mind if a newspaper holds us all to the same standards and goes and tracks everybody else down on their vacation and takes similar photos," Murphy told the *Boston Phoenix* after the *Herald*'s unflattering front-page photo. "Just some kind of parity among us, that's all I'm asking."

Murphy's words echo those of one exasperated woman writer who suggested: "I think that I will report this convention the way the men did the women at [the Republican convention]. I will describe the clothes of these men from all over America, the strange cuts of their coats, the unaesthetic figures, their shiny hair, their lack of 'it.'"

That year was 1924, and although much has changed, women are, well, perhaps Pat Schroeder says it best, "still treated like a novelty act" by the press.

Indeed, from the first day the first elected woman set foot in Congress—Montana suffragist Jeannette Rankin—the media have been the bane of the political woman's existence. Rankin's sixteen-word vote against World War I, and the manner in which it was covered, brought scorn upon an entire gender's would-be politicians, divided feminists, erected or reinforced still existing barriers to women's full participation in the affairs of state, and set a pattern for coverage of women politicians that has evolved little in seventy-five years.

The New York Times's headline announcing the war included this subhead: "One Hundred Speeches Were Made—Miss Rankin, Sobbing, Votes No."[4]

Press coverage of the two looming cataclysms—the advent of the nation's first congresswoman and an apparently inevitable war—had made the nation nearly as eager for news about Jeannette Rankin as it was about the Kaiser. When Montana became the first state to elect a woman to Congress, a full two years in advance of the Nineteenth Amendment and national suffrage, the *Kentucky Courier-Journal* responded: "Breathes there a man with heart so brave that he would want to become one of a deliberate body made up of 434 women and himself?"[5]

That the singular woman in question was dainty and feminine,[6] not a hard-faced Amazon from cattle country "who packed a .44-caliber six shooter and trimmed her skirts with chaps fur," went against reporters' preconceptions about what a woman politician might be. "Her physical appearance was emphasized so extensively that America could have concluded Jeannette was a painted young hussy of the Calamity Jane variety."[7] One writer in the *Evening Mail* wrote he was "glad, glad, glad even to pollyannaism that Jeannette is not 'freakish' or 'mannish' or 'standoffish' or 'shrewish' or of any type likely to antagonize the company of gentlemen whose realm had hitherto been invaded by petticoats."

Rankin was understandably distressed by her press. She had campaigned seriously on issues, blasting the male-dominated Congress for spending $300,000 one year on hog research when they appropriated only $30,000 to study children's needs—"If the hogs of a nation are 10 times more important than the children, it is high time that women should make their influence felt."

Rankin's biographer, native Montana newspaperman Kevin Giles, writes that she "suffered great shock in being exposed to such publicity, and could not comprehend she would be in the public eye from that moment."[8] He added in a 1992 interview that "some of the questions really made her mad. Questions about what she wore. Interviews that painted her as a lady about to faint . . . Nothing that got to the heart of what she was hoping to do." Rankin's inability to deal with the press, or her distaste, was compounded by the reluctance of Montana Republicans to tout her successes for her, and her own feminine reluctance to do so.

Rankin also was painfully aware that as the only woman she was expected to represent all women. In a symbolic thank-you, National Woman's Party leader Alice Paul and Carrie Chapman Catt, who later founded the League of Women Voters, brought all factions of the suffrage movement together for a breakfast honoring Rankin on the morning of Wilson's scheduled war message. Catt, who was insisting that Rankin vote for the war lest a no vote imply women were incapable of tough decisions, welcomed the group with optimistic words: "The day of our deliverance is at hand . . . at the hand of a woman. . . . "[9] White arm bands "flashing like beacons in the night," Giles wrote, "signalled open and heated discontent between pacifist Alice Paul and war advocate Carrie Chapman Catt, although a truce had been called to recognize this unprecedented and strategic advance for womanhood. Ironically, Paul set [sic] at Jeannette's left and Catt to Jeannette's right, and each envisioned an opposite role the new Congresswoman must play in legitimizing the political realities of their sex."[10]

When the war resolution came to a vote at 3:00 A.M. Good Friday, April 6, Rankin broke with 140 years of House precedent and explained her action before she cast her vote: "I want to stand by my country, but I cannot vote for war. I vote no." Her biographer writes that "Tears wandered down her cheeks" as she spoke.[11] But *The New York Times* reported her tears differently: "It is possible no more dramatic scene has ever been staged in the House of Representatives," adding that following her vote, she "nodded in a tired sort of way and sank back to her seat. Then she pressed her hands to her eyes, threw her head back and sobbed."[12]

In addition to the lead story's subhead announcing her vote, the *Times*'s second-day coverage included two other stories devoted to Rankin, one headlined "Seek to Explain Miss Rankin's 'No,'" and the other under the headline "Suffrage Leaders Pardon Miss Rankin." The latter included suffragist Harriet Laidlaw's attempt to set the record straight, "Please don't forget to say that Miss Rankin did not weep or faint."[13]

The average American might have been forgiven, reading press accounts of that momentous vote, if he or she came away firmly believing that Congresswoman Rankin was the only member of Congress to oppose the war. That was not so—fifty-five men voted against it as well. Rankin was so disgusted by the unfairness that later, when an Associated Press reporter appeared at her office, she yelled through a partition, "Tell him to go to hell."[14]

Jane Q. Citizen might also have thought Rankin was the only congressperson to shed tears. Not so. Many congressmen wept openly during the vote, no matter how they had voted. Fiorello LaGuardia, then a congressman, even rose to Rankin's defense. Asked if he had seen her weeping, he replied, "I could not see because of the tears in my own eyes."[15]

A look back at the coverage of Jeannette Rankin's first vote reveals a virtual template for all aspects of modern-day press coverage that modern-day women politicians have come to loathe: a focus on what she looked like and wore, not what she stood for or had accomplished; an interest only in her presumably aberrant vote and actions, although many of her male colleagues had voted and acted precisely the same way; an inference that Rankin's act was that of Everywoman, in the very face of the fact that women were bitterly divided over her vote; and constant spoofing, which barely veiled hostility, at the notion a woman had either the right or the authority to be a politician. The coverage could not have been better designed, even by conspiracy, to dissuade women's organizations of the fruitlessness of partisanship or of supporting women candidates. Nor could it have been better designed to carve into stone the already existing stereotypes of women.

To fully understand why today, some two decades after the rebirth of the women's movement and seventy-five plus years after Jeannette Rankin first took her seat, there is still a gender gap in coverage of male and female politicians, we must track the careers of some early women journalists and trace how modern-day coverage of women evolved. Until the twentieth century, a woman who would be active in politics had little alternative to her pen.

One important fact stands out: Throughout the last century and more, not only has there been a largely parallel career course for women in politics and women in journalism, but many women have done both. That tradition continues today—Senator Barbara Boxer, National Women's Political Caucus (NWPC) president Harriett Woods, 1992 Senate candidate Gloria O'Dell of Kansas, former Vermont governor Madeleine Kunin, and many others were journalists at one point in their careers—but it was especially true earlier in our history.

Pioneering political and journalistic women were called to their respective industries by many of the same issues—initially slavery, temperance, community morality, female education, and suffrage, and later the plight of the big city's tenement dwellers and the health of mothers and children.

One unusual early example is not remembered as a reporter—although she did write for *Godey's Ladies Book,* or as a politician—yet President Abraham Lincoln is reported to have said when he met her, "So this is the little woman who made this big war."[16] Harriet Beecher Stowe is better known as a novelist. It is what she did in *Uncle Tom's Cabin*—conveying the human trauma and tolls of a social ill, slavery, and presenting women's life experience as integral to the political debate— that ties her work to that of twentieth-century women politicians and writers. Stowe was able to look beyond the abstractions of the political debate regarding slavery to its effects on women's lives. By doing so, she appealed to the altruism that gave her sisters permission to protest.

Much of the success and influence of *Uncle Tom's Cabin* came from Stowe's ability to induce reader empathy with her fictional fugitive slave mother, Eliza Harris. Eliza flees the slave master who was planning to sell her child. Stowe, who had herself buried a beloved child just a year before passage of the Fugitive Slave Act, explained: "I wrote what I did because as a woman, as a mother, I was oppressed and broken hearted with the sorrows and injustice I saw."[17]

The fact that Stowe looked across class and racial barriers at the impact of the political acts of men on the lives of women was an important contribution to the value given women's lives and concerns, which she detailed with great realism. It was, in fact, an overt example of a phrase that would not be coined for another century: The personal is political.

Despite the limitations, which glorified their role as homemakers and mothers while reinforcing the formidable prohibitions to their public participation beyond those roles, women writers continually pushed at the boundaries that held them back. But "[a]s soon as there was a sizable number of women Washington correspondents, they were barred from the Capitol press galleries. In 1879 [when the ban was enacted] the Congressional Directory listed 20 women correspondents entitled to gallery privileges, about 12 percent of the total of 166 correspondents. Within two years . . . women correspondents began increasingly to be relegated to society gossip instead of covering politics."[18]

Banning women from the press galleries had profound repercussions. It effectively banned the vast majority of women from mainstream political reporting—and what became known, suggestively, as "hard news"— for most of the next century. And it quite literally put women in their place, both as journalists and as subject matter, in "soft news" sections and "society."

There were, however, some singular exceptions. One star was Ida Wells, later known as Ida Wells-Barnett, the Mississippi-born daughter of former slaves. At twenty-two, she brought a test case to fight segregated train cars. As a schoolteacher in Memphis, she fought the low standard of education for African-Americans. As a journalist, she attracted national attention in 1892 with "outraged articles [in revenge for which] . . . local racists ransacked and destroyed her newspaper office."[19] Wells escaped to continue her crusade, and later ran, unsuccessfully, for public office—one of the first woman journalists to make that leap.

For most women attempting to support themselves as front-page journalists, there were just two job descriptions. "For years, if there was a woman on a newspaper who didn't write on fashion and food, she was the paper's 'Stunt Girl,'"[20] a tradition that began in 1889 with the legendary Nelly Bly, who bested the fictional record Jules Verne had created in *Around the World in 80 Days.* That remarkable feat—Bly beat Verne's eighty days by a week and some eighteen hours—obscures the other side of her career, and the only other path open to issue-inclined women journalists, that of the "Sob Sister."

According to Ishbel Ross, in her landmark history, *Ladies of the Press,* the Sob Sister's job "was to watch for the tear-filled eye, the widow's veil, the quivering lip, the lump in the throat, the trembling hand. They did it very well."[21] They also did it in a manner that often raised political awareness and had the power to alter public policy. Bly, "a reformer who wanted to go out among the poor, into the tenements and factories, first hand, talking with people, especially immigrants,"[22] once feigned insanity to get herself committed to a public asylum. She called it a "human rat trap" in front-page exposés. Another turn-of-the-century Sob Sister, the *San Francisco Examiner*'s Annie Laurie, exposed the treatment of poor women by the city's hospitals—by posing as one—and is credited with a major public policy change, that city's implementation of ambulance service.[23]

In each of these cases, the drama of a proper woman who put herself at risk outside the safe haven of her home, beyond the protective cover of husband or father, made titillating reading. It was an era in which few women could make news any other way; indeed, few "proper women" could have their names in the newspapers other than the day they were born, the day they married, and the day they died. Nelly Bly, whose real name was Elizabeth Cochran, and Annie Laurie, the byline of Winnifred Black, could not even write under their own names; it would have been deemed improper.

Despite the limits on them, the pseudonymous Stunt Girls established new freedoms for other public women. Jeannette Rankin borrowed from their bag of tricks and went undercover during her first term in office to expose official malfeasance in the Federal Bureau of Printing and Engraving—busy, in 1917, with Liberty Bonds. She found women being forced to work fourteen-hour days with no overtime, and being threatened with what today probably would be called sexual harassment if they complained.[24] The nation's third congresswoman, Winnifred Sprague Mason Huck, continued the tradition after her brief stint in Congress and, in 1925, went undercover—in jail—to investigate the criminal justice system. "Her articles . . . created a sensation."[25]

The plight of the big cities' downtrodden, which drew many of their contemporary sisters into the settlement houses, was the perfect material for the Stunt Girls' dramatic exposés and the Sob Sisters' tear-jerking prose, and their coverage began to propel women such as Margaret Sanger into the headlines. Often, again because anything other than breaking news about women was left to women to report, the Sob Sister was able to turn the tide of public opinion in favor of political women whom the establishment persecuted. In 1893, for example, after *The New York Times* editorialized in a headline "The Danger Is in Leaving Persons of the Emma Goldman Type at Large"[26] and precipitated the radical's arrest, Nelly Bly came to her defense with a flattering profile that called her "a little Joan of Arc."[27]

These pioneering, politically aware women journalists were carving out a very special niche in American journalism, one that continues to some extent today. For better or worse, they nudged the old stereotypes of women as having special sensibilities and greater morality into a new form and, eventually, a new century. When Jane Addams was lobbying not so subtly for women to be able to vote, arguing in a 1910 *Ladies' Home Journal* that women's domestic skills were needed for "municipal housekeeping," the Sob Sisters had already begun laying out the dirty linen, describing the human costs, and validating the unique authority women were thought able to bring to the political system.

What we know today as feature writing has deep roots in that segregation of women writers and the special treatment given women's issues. The platform created for women in the late nineteenth century—the "social page," the "soft sections," or "back of book" in newspapers and magazines—has evolved into the talk shows of daytime television. The "special sensibilities" that women reporters were assigned, as a "beat" as much as a gender trait, gave them experiences that helped evolve the women's movement. When Gloria Steinem donned the elaborate and scanty pushup bra and gear of a Playboy Bunny for an "undercover" exposé in the early days of the women's movement, she was dipping into a grand tradition established by her journalistic foremothers. When Betty Friedan was fired from her reporting job because she was pregnant, she took her experiences home to suburbia with her and wrote *The Feminine Mystique*.

Even the fact that we look today to the personal character of our political candidates and Supreme Court nominees is arguably the result of the slant women's supposed extra sensitivity brought to the news. The Sob Sisters' ability to suggest some deeper sociological meaning by reporting the small details of daily life, the particular twist of a defendant's grin, or the fancy brand of shoes that might or might not contradict a person's professed populism, set a style that is still expected of women journalists, hard and soft, to this day—sometimes to their detriment, almost always to the dismay of the political women they cover.

The women's movement eventually began to break down the old segregations, but it was another woman from the reform movements of earlier days of the twentieth century who first began to undo the sexual apartheid that to this day colors political coverage of women:

Eleanor Roosevelt insisted that only women cover her news conferences. Since she made news herself, newspaper and wire services were forced to hire at least one woman to cover her activities or to keep on female staffers, whose jobs were otherwise at risk during the Depression. At newspapers all over the country there was a woman here, a woman there—women covering trials, investigating mental hospitals, advising the lovelorn. . . . They had experience, but little opportunity.[28]

If there was a negative to Eleanor Roosevelt's meddling in newsroom demographics and work assignments (a feat that is unlikely to be pulled off today by any politician or politician's spouse without screams about press manipulation) it was that any evolution that might have been occurring in front-page coverage of the still astonishingly new phenomenon—women politicians—essentially stopped. Instead, interest in political women at first focused primarily on the newest phenomenon: the newsmaking First Lady, her social life, her good deeds, as well as the threat that she might become too powerful. And most First Lady stories, whether stories on the wives of presidents and governors or those of local mayors, were relegated to the "back of the book"—with all the limitations on the nature of stories there. Even if the stories ran on the front pages or in the upfront news sections, they were done by the few women reporters who had made it there, and that coverage carried with it the particular slant that made Stunt Girl–Sob Sister coverage so colorful—the attention to gesture, tone of voice, style of dress and manner that to this day often separates the coverage of men and women politicians.

The First Lady tradition created one additional problem for women politicians. Women are not blessed with wives to redecorate the governors' mansions, or to tour the high-risk nurseries of local hospitals, or join the Senate wives in their bandage rolling, or make the speech in Tulsa that the mayor or congresswoman or governor (or, someday, president) is just too busy to make. The First Lady tradition is so strong that politicians are now virtually expected to be "two-fers," a phrase Bill Clinton used to describe himself and his attorney wife, Hillary, during his 1992 presidential campaign, adding, "You buy one, you get one free." While the phrase initially backfired for Clinton—raising such fears of a too-powerful Jezebel meddling in the affairs of state that *SPY* magazine spoofed them with a cover picture of Hillary's face superimposed on the body of a leather-clad dominatrix[29]—it underscores how institutionalized the role has become. Because society still suspects men whose wives are more powerful, husbands of women politicians have shied from playing the surrogate role, and in a contest with a "two-fer," a woman candidate may be disadvantaged by the First Lady tradition.

The nature of First Lady coverage also reinforced the separate sphere to which political women were relegated. It further segregated "hard" and "soft" news and issues, and meant that even a logical "hard news" subject, be it the woman running for office or the issues she was attempting to voice, might be given the same soft news focus that was the manner in fashion or society.

But while the front pages dealt with politics and the business sections with the economy, over the years the women's sections became more reflective, more connected to how the news or economic numbers were affecting the home and society. The revolution in the coverage of birth control and abortion is the best example of how the political and personal collided in the women's pages. By the late 1960s, coverage of abortion in any given city could switch, often within a matter of months, from titillating front-page exposés of abortion rings written by male police reporters, to sympathetic in-depth series generated by women's page staffers. The latter detailed the emotional and societal cost of crisis pregnancies and the ways existing laws victimized women and their families.

The important continuum in the new abortion stories, echoing the Sob Sister exposés a half century earlier and *Uncle Tom's Cabin* a full century before, were the claims being staked out in the public arena by women. Women activists were declaring, and women journalists were reporting, that women's lives and experiences mattered and should be considered in the making of public policy.

Women journalists mounted pressure to adopt "gender neutral" language, and ban such descriptions as "blonde divorcee," for example. And an important battle, fought newsroom by newsroom until *The New York Times* was the last of the self-styled papers of record to surrender, began over whether to drop the use of "Mrs." and "Miss" and substitute the newly coined antonym for "Mr." that became the name of a new magazine: "Ms." The argument put forth by Betty Friedan and others that married women were persons in their own right, not mere appendages of their husbands, and that marital status was no longer the critical factor to any woman's identity, finally prevailed in the style manuals deferred to by editors, if not in the news decisions they made.

Three 1990 studies indicate what women politicians have long suspected: A person-in-her-own-right still has a harder time becoming front-page news.[30] One study reviewed the front pages of eighteen major newspapers and found the percentage of women included in photos was slightly less than one quarter, and "Unlike males, females usually were in group shots, generally with spouses and/or children." Women were only 11 percent of the front-page newsmakers. A second study, showing only 6 percent of top media bosses were women, was summed up in a headline by a trade journal: "Men Manage the Message Machines." A third study of nightly network newscasts showed even fewer female-reported stories, and echoed earlier studies that found a predominance of white male newsmakers and a notable lack of female and minority representatives on politically influential shows such as ABC's "Nightline."[31]

"Do you see me on MacNeil-Lehrer?" asks Senator Nancy Kassebaum of Kansas, who is a ranking member of the Senate Foreign Relations Committee. "I'm not really asked all that often, though I tend to go when asked. Maybe I'm just not as good presenting the facts, but I think [the reason is] most men tend to feel men present foreign policy a little more forcefully."

The first study was funded by Betty Friedan's University of Southern California Media Watch with the American Society of Newspaper Editors, and the team that did it merely counted faces, names, and bylines. Then they sent letters citing the results and requesting comments to the editors of the eighteen papers reviewed, including two of the most important male journalists in America, Max Frankel and Ben Bradlee, executive editors of *The New York Times* and *The Washington Post*, respectively.

"I'm damned if I can see what conclusions should be drawn," Bradlee wrote, adding words that echo St. Paul: "The wisdom of the ages appears to cry out for silence."

Frankel's reaction was as imperious, but it was his language that was so revealing: "As soon as Mr. Gorbachev lets Mrs. Gorbachev do his deciding, or even speaking, we will be quoting or photographing more women on Page One. Or even Chancellor Kohl, or President Bush and their wives. . . ."

Frankel expanded on his letter to *The Washington Post*: "I mean if you are covering local teas you've got more women [on the front page] than if you're *The Wall Street Journal*."[32]

In other words, as late as 1989, according to the editor in chief of *The New York Times*, the all-male-is-normal paradigm—except at tea parties, of course—was the *Times*'s editorial philosophy, and the only women who might be news would be those wives who inappropriately exercised their husbands' authority. This may explain why Hillary Clinton's statement—"I'm not just a little woman who can stay at home and bake cookies and have teas"—so startled the nation's news editors it virtually ended weeks of front-page explorations into her husband's alleged extramarital affairs.

Hillary Rodham Clinton inadvertently had played into one of the conceptual frames by which news of women is defined: She confirmed male fears of the too-powerful woman who doesn't mind her proper place. (The front page of the New York *Daily News* later that summer perhaps summed up male editors' views of Hillary: an unflattering full-page, mouth-agape head shot with an enormous headline that said "Well, Shut My Mouth!") Similarly, Jeannette Rankin's tears had confirmed women's legendary emotional frailty and added weight to the presumption that being able to openly express emotions indicates a lack of serious intellect and judgment. Both are integral parts of the framing of news about the entire gender's politicians. (*USA Today* headlined a 1992 story about women candidates this way: "Women's Emotional Pleas Aren't Conventional Rhetoric." And the female writer of the story went on to note that women candidates, presumably because of their altruistic natures, "avoided ugly partisan rhetoric.")[33]

While we all carry conceptual frames in our heads—they enable us to sort and make sense out of any type of new information—framing can be an insidious, even when inadvertent, barrier to new ideas, as well as a potent drumbeater for both stereotypes and the status quo. Because we expect X, we see X.

Journalists learn early on that they are supposed to rethink every concept they have been taught and approach each new story with fresh eyes—"If your mother says she loves you, check it out," goes an epigram editors use to drill this into the heads of new reporters. Unfortunately, breaking through a conceptual barrier as profound as mother love, or possibly any other traditional view concerning women, is much more easily prescribed by editors than done by reporters, or even by editors themselves, much less any other person along the news processing chain. It is much easier to be witty and original in restating the old paradigm than to thoughtfully address the new.

Virtually all news of women is checked, consciously and unconsciously, against existing frames. If an individual news story fits too neatly—the dog-bites-man test—it probably isn't news. The degree to which a news item or subject challenges the accepted notion of who is what and does what in society—the man-bites-dog test—the more news-worthy the item becomes. The First Lady who won't do teas or the con-gress*man* who cries are as jarring as man-bites-dog.

Even if a woman politician's demeanor is beyond reproach, she is still treated as if Samuel Johnson's two-hundred-year-old simile likening a woman who preaches to a dog that walks on its hind legs—"It is not done well, but you are surprised to find it done at all"—were the rule by which news of political women is judged. Great copy. Good visuals. And if the walking dog/preaching woman is, in addition, undeniably newsworthy because of the nature of the event (a presidential campaign, say) or the title of the subject (member of Congress, for example), the ways in which the press processes the information about her will very likely still express some newsperson's surprise "to find it done at all." In other words, news about women politicians still must be made to fit the frame—that is, "make sense" or otherwise conform to a Ben Bradlee's idea of "the wis-dom of the ages."

Barbara Roberts is philosophical about it now that she is governor of Oregon, but several years ago, when a major political writer for *The Or-egonian*, the state's largest daily newspaper, wrote a series entitled "The Empty Saddle," decrying the lack of real leadership in the state, she was appalled that "out of more than two dozen people mentioned in that se-ries of articles none were women," she told a Women and Politics Break-fast sponsored by the Women's Campaign Research Fund in San Fran-cisco in 1991. "The Empty Saddle" had defined a leader as one who had "skills, guts, vision, charisma, leadership"—the all-male-is-normal para-digm.

"Was it possible that no Oregon woman had those attributes? Not hardly. In fact, when the article was published, a woman was on the Or-egon State Supreme Court bench, a woman was secretary of state, which in our state is also lieutenant governor and state auditor; a woman was the elected state labor commissioner. Twenty women were members of the legislature, fifty-four women were mayors. I was the majority leader of the Oregon House. . . .

"Could it be that the writer found the saddle empty because his per-ception of leadership was male?" she asked.

At times, the conflict between the frame and the reality is so great that a story will be reported in ways that contradict one another. An Ohio State University study of the news coverage of a 1987 opinion poll on whether Americans were ready to elect a woman president brought such widely varying headlines one would be hard pressed to know what the real story was. The poll, commissioned by the National Women's Political Caucus in response to Schroeder's short-lived presidential candidacy, indicated that 70 percent of the American public not only were fully willing to vote for a woman president, but a substantial majority thought a woman could do "as well" or "better" than a man.[34] The press conference to announce the results was covered by more than twenty news agencies that together served virtually every daily newspaper and broadcast outlet in the nation.

"But were the writers of these stories at the same press conference?" asked Dru Riley Evarts of Ohio State University. "One would not think so from reading the headlines," Evarts concluded from her survey of 1,340 newspapers. The big news in NWPC's survey was voters' positive opinions about a possible woman president. Judging by headline writers, however, the results were precisely the opposite. Some 58 percent gave a negative spin to the story. Only 31 percent presented a possible woman president's 70 percent approval rating in a positive light. Just 11 percent were neutral. Yet in the NWPC study, 49 percent thought a female would do "as well" as a male president and 8 percent said "better"—a total 57 percent positive rating. Only 31 percent felt a woman could not do as good a job and 12 percent were undecided.

"Some headline writers seemed too eager to work in a familiar slogan or cuteness that they seemed not to want to be inconvenienced by the fact," Evarts told a 1990 convention of journalism educators. "The *Columbia Missourian* said, 'Anything he can do, she can do better.' The head was 'cute,' but was no more what the story said than were the terribly negative heads."[35] Some of the headlines Evarts's students reviewed were actually incorrect. The headlines make it clear how difficult it is for headline writers to conceptualize something outside the usual, which, in their frame of reference means a president who is a man, and a woman who may be a Ms., Mrs., Madame, lady, or baby but whose place is still the home:

"Ms. President? Many Voters Still Say No"—*San Jose* (California) *Mercury News*

"Mrs. President? Study Finds Most Voters Say 'Not Yet'"—*New Albany* (Indiana) *Tribune*

"Madame President? One-Third of Voters Think Woman Would Not Do as Good a Job"—*Pittsburgh Post-Gazette*

"No Ladies Please"—*Savannah Morning News*

"American Voters Not Ready for Lady at Top"—*Madison Press* (London, Ohio)

"Not Quite Ready for Madame President?"—*Greenville* (Ohio) *Daily Advocate*

"Have You Come a Long Way Baby? Maybe Not"—*Denton* (Texas) *Record Chronicle*

"President Man's Job, Claim 33% of Voters"—*Terre Haute* (Indiana) *Tribune-Star*

"Woman's Place in House But Not White House."—*Breckenridge* (Minnesota) *Daily News*

The true nature of the study of American attitudes concerning women candidates was accurately reflected only in a handful of papers, among them the *Cheyenne* (Wyoming) *State Tribune*, whose simple headline indicates how easy it should have been to merely get the story right: "America May Be Ready for a Woman President."

As the variety of these headlines indicates, the tone of a story about women politicians (whether it is treated seriously or inconsequentially), the spin put on it (whether it is accepted as a matter of fact or fluffed up with unnecessary "explanation" or awkward attempts to force it into a context the newsperson is comfortable with), even a story's adjectives and verbs (some of which, like "shrill" or "bubbly," appear to be exclusively used to describe women) all become ways of making sense of the walking dog/preaching woman, for example:

What does it suggest about women's roles when a paper runs a feature on five persons who will benefit from the 1984 Democratic National Convention being in town and the three women included are a notably young, female newsanchor, Congresswoman Nancy Pelosi (chair of the 1984 San Francisco host committee), and a prostitute?[36] Or, as a *Rocky Mountain News* editorial did in 1990, calls a senatorial candidate—Colorado's Josie Heath—"Madam Mud?"

What mixture of *Playboy* fantasy and talking dog/preaching woman amazement is evident in the *Washington Post* headline noting the election of Senator Kay Bailey Hutchinson of Texas: "Former University of Texas Longhorn Cheerleader . . ."? Or *The Philadelphia Inquirer*'s "Justice and the Baton Twirler" regarding President Clinton's U.S. Supreme Court nominee Ruth Bader Ginsburg? Or the following 1990 *Seattle Times* cartoon portraying Congresswoman Jolene Unsoeld as a girl who apparently just couldn't say no?

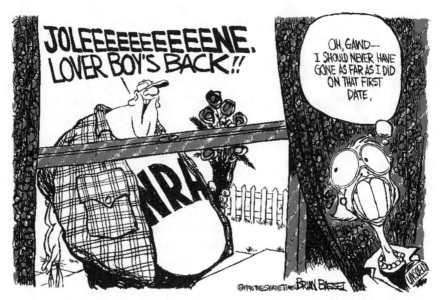

© 1990 Brian Basset in the Seattle Times

Why is it necessary for a political columnist, in this case male, to note that 1992 Senate candidate Barbara Boxer is "a youthful and vibrant 51?"[37] (At what age would a reporter feel compelled to remark that a man running for office was "still youthful and virile"—Sixty-five? Seventy? Seventy-five? Older?)

Why would the Associated Press inquire what a three-term congressional representative's living arrangements might be should that person be elected vice president? "John Zaccaro said Wednesday that he will stay in New York . . . if his wife, Rep. Geraldine Ferraro, is elected vice president. 'I still have to pay the bills,' he explained."[38]

Implicit in all the questions raised here is basically the same answer: Because the residues of coverture mandate a double standard. Because stereotypes about the female sex and women's role in society are explicit in the framing of stories about women politicians. And because among the assumptions journalists have is that what "ordinary" Americans want to know "requires" them to dig up the following sort of "news," which was reported well into Ferraro's 1992 Senate race: As a congresswoman "Ferraro spent two nights a week in Washington, juggling family events with her three children and husband, John Zaccaro."[39]

In many ways, Ferraro has been as much the press's first post-women's movement guinea pig as she was political trailblazer in her historic 1984 vice presidential race. Because hers was "an historic candidacy," she says, there naturally would have been more than usual interest in it, but she admits, echoing a number of other women candidates, "I don't think if Jesse Jackson were the nominee they would have gone after him the way they did me." Racism is no longer acceptable; sexism apparently is.

Ferraro diplomatically refuses to blame sexism for the intensive scrutiny the media put her husband through regarding the second-generation Zaccaro family real estate business and their marital finances.

"Why was the press interested? You knock off the star candidate—Pulitzer Prize time. Cynical? Yes. True? Yes. I sell papers . . . So it's more than gender. It was much more than Gerry Ferraro, that's all I'm saying. And yet . . . "

And yet, in an interview early in 1991, as she reviewed some of the women's races of 1990, Ferraro conceded that the husbands of a number of other women candidates had, fairly or unfairly, become campaign issues primarily because of sexism:

In Colorado, Josie Heath was hit by a primary opponent's charges that her husband somehow was personally responsible for destruction of the rain forest in Brazil. Manville Corporation, for which he had been general counsel (he resigned during her Senate race in order to devote full time to her campaign) did own timberland in Brazil, but "nowhere near the rain forest," Rollie Heath pointed out.

In California, Richard Blum, Dianne Feinstein's husband, came under the same sort of scrutiny as John Zaccaro had. Old rumors surfaced that Feinstein had not made the final cut for vice president in 1984 because of Mondale staff worries about his real estate business, and the Wilson campaign questioned Blum's participation in a group that had bought a failed Oregon savings and loan.

In Oregon, pundits worried that if Barbara Roberts were elected governor the fact that her husband was the state's senate majority leader would mean too much political power under one roof.

In Connecticut, Rosa DeLauro was met at campaign stops by hecklers carrying signs that said "Mrs. Greenbucks" as well as other things in reference to her husband Stan Greenberg, partner of Celinda Lake in the Democratic polling firm Greenberg-Lake. She felt the attack was as anti-Semitic as sexist. One paper "kept wanting to refer to me as Mrs. Greenberg, or they would put 'Rosa DeLauro as Mrs. Greenberg likes to be called.' I was never anyone else. It's not Rosa DeLauro Greenberg."

"This has become an increasing pattern in the campaigns of the 1990s.

The actions of the spouse can become the mistakes of the [woman] candidate . . . much more than for men,"[40] pollster Lake warned. Even when the husband wasn't attacked, his mere existence served to remind voters that the woman's loyalties might be divided.

The historical context here, again, is coverture. Asked if a spouse problem, previous to Hillary Clinton, had ever damaged male candidates, the historian of the House of Representatives, Raymond Smock, and other experts, came up with the same short list: Andrew Jackson's previously married wife, Rachel, was a scandal; Abraham Lincoln's wife, Mary, was thought to be crazy; and the 1928 Democratic presidential nominee Al Smith's wife, Katie, a Catholic and anti-Prohibition like her husband, "simply would not do in the White House," it was said.[41] There were other wives who became controversial after their husbands were in office, but few—and none to the extent of a John Zaccaro or Richard Blum.

Ferraro concedes that it is "legitimate" to look into the joint holdings of a couple should one of them run for public office.[42] Dick Blum acknowledges that it was fair in 1990 for the press to look into his and Feinstein's community property, but says that the Wilson attacks related to his business dealings were "sexist . . . but his campaign was old-boy sexist from the start." Blum threatened to file a libel action but did not go through with it because "the damage had been done."[43]

Feinstein's 1990 general election campaign manager Bill Carrick even admitted (although Feinstein later declined to confirm it) that the campaign "tried [and failed] to get the press interested" in the origins of Wilson's wealth. But reporters were not even curious about the sources of Wilson's marital money and relegated the "bubbly and blond" Mrs. Wilson to the features section—while remaining focused on Blum, Blum's business deals, Blum's clients, and Mrs. Blum's possible conflicts of interest because of them when she was mayor of San Francisco—and if she became governor.

Fair treatment or sexism? A campaign consultant who has worked for Feinstein, and clearly kept open his options to do so again by making his comments off-the-record, said harshly: "Dick Blum gets millions of dollars in commissions for the deals he puts together. He in turn loans his wife three million [in 1990]. Who knows whether those millions were legitimate pay for his work effort, or just a sneaky way to donate money to his wife's campaign? And for what?"

Although the press, in its role as mirror to the society it serves, probably, for the near future, will remain more interested in and unsettled by the advent of truly powerful women politicians whose husbands also are successful (as well as the successful professional wives of political men), it is not difficult to assess where the line that separates fair inquiry and sexism might lie. Often, however, the line depends on which side the observer is on.

The Heath campaign was infuriated by what they saw as a primary opponent's attempt, via the press, to link Josie Heath to her husband's company's actions, but Richard Waddams, 1990 campaign manager for now Senator Hank Brown, thought "the press made it very clear early in the campaign they did not buy into any kind of Rollie Heath handle to this campaign." The middle ground, an important point to understand about how the press-society seesaw works, appears to be that the press aired Heath's opponent's charges and when the stories did not pan out, much less reveal a motherlode of further stories, it dropped them. However, because the press dropped the Rollie Heath stories, Waddams thought it was "vicious and, very unfair" when *The Denver Post*'s Mark Obmascik questioned whether Brown had improperly benefited by voting for an omnibus farm bill that funded the Conservation Reserve Program. Brown's wife and children own a family farm in the southern part of the state and received federal money for taking the acreage out of production.

The differences between the two? Hank Brown was an elected official voting on something that conceivably benefited his family and himself; Rollie Heath was a lawyer whose client was the company he worked for. That he was also part of the management of a publicly traded company meant he shared in fiduciary responsibility to stockholders. Both are public trusts, but neither is one to which "Mr. Josie Heath" had been elected. But the most important difference in politics? Brown won; Heath lost.

Clearly, it is fair to question potential or real conflicts of interest that may arise out of the relationship of any politician to her or his spouse. It is fair to question the sources of a politician's funding. It is fair to question elected officials about decisions they make or votes they cast while representing the public.

It is also fair to question personal acts that the press and society view as revealing of character traits that may be relevant to public service, which, of course, makes fair game of the fact that Eleanor Holmes Norton in Washington, D.C., and Clayton Williams in Texas neglected to be certain their tax records were in order before their 1990 campaigns, or that Clinton's rejected candidate for attorney general, Zoë Baird, illegally had employed undocumented persons as domestics. Arguably, however, the charges against an Eleanor Holmes Norton or Zoë Baird disturbed voters in ways that resonated at far deeper psychological levels then similar charges about a man, because individual voters may still have unresolved feelings about the roles of women.

It seems reasonable to assume, especially given the scrutiny that Hillary Clinton underwent during the 1992 campaign, that as the world becomes a more equal place for women and men, and women begin breaking through glass ceilings to wield power in all fields, the wives of political candidates will be scrutinized for more than their cookie-baking, good looks, and appropriate wifely demeanor. And as more married women and mothers are elected to high office the confusion over who they are and what roles they should play will diminish.

The sexual parity that Evelyn Murphy asked for from the Boston press, after her public lecture on cellulite, already appears to exist only in lower-level contests—the school board and municipal elections where women first broke the barriers, and in higher state-level offices where having a woman candidate is no longer "a novelty act." Still, women candidates express nearly universal fear of the reporters, something Jane Danowitz of the Women's Campaign Fund has grown less sympathetic with, though she admits it's a phenomenon that shows up each time WCF does candidate training.

"My suspicion is . . . that women don't humor the press enough. . . . I think women still need a lot of work learning to deal with the press. . . . Women are fearful of reporters . . . and my sense is that discomfort is like being around a horse and being scared and the horse senses it. The press senses it. I think that's where it breaks down. . . . There are a lot of women like this"—she grimaces in mock horror—"uptight, not comfortable with giving out information."

Some women try and still fail. Murphy, for example, had attempted to meet the press on its own turf. In early 1988 she began a series of off-the-record backgrounders with individual political reporters, hoping to find what one staffer called "some common ground," but "just got sick of it" before she had worked her way through the state house press.[44]

Despite her efforts there were some days in the last weeks before her late summer primary on which one could pick up a Boston paper and get the impression there were only two Democrats, both men, in the race. The man to beat, it seemed, was a consummate machine-politics insider,

Francis X. Belotti, who claimed to be pro-choice but who, as attorney general, had defended a regressive anti-abortion parental consent law. The other candidate, Boston University president (on leave) John Silber, had made headlines just that June when BU lost, in the U.S. Supreme Court, a sex discrimination suit brought by a woman professor denied tenure after Silber called her six-woman, eighteen-man department a "damn matriarchy." He labeled abortion "murder" but claimed he nonetheless was pro-choice—as long as voters were.

How did Murphy get lost in the press coverage? The Belotti-Silber face-off became a series of battlefield skirmishes between two colorful male egos and wonderfully quotable mouths. They were the stuff of great headlines. Murphy's softer voice, and her attempt, in the face of serious funding problems, to be the clearest candidate on the issues and define herself as the only pro-choice candidate without an asterisk, simply got lost, even though she cleverly attempted to recast the battle of titans as the political equivalent of the mutually destructive "gingham dog and the calico cat."

Increasingly, women politicians have learned to take the press as it is—at least until their numbers are such that they can change the stereotypes to which they are held. Jeannette Rankin may not have been the last female politician to tell a reporter to go to hell, but the women who followed in her footsteps learned very quickly that they had to find some way of working within journalism's limitations if they were ever to get their messages across to the voters. The very next woman elected to Congress, Oklahoma's Alice Mary Robertson, took things directly into her own hands when local newspapers ignored her 1920 campaign. A colorful one-termer—she opposed suffrage and likened it to "bartering the birthright for a mess of pottage"—she bought space in the classified advertising sections. "Soon, she had newspaper readers turning first to the want-ads to read her vivid prose."[45] (She later returned to Congress as a reporter.)

Two decades after the Rankin fiasco, Clare Boothe Luce was drawn into Wendell L. Willkie's 1940 campaign when her friend, columnist Dorothy Thompson, a forceful critic of Franklin Roosevelt's, suddenly defected. The outraged Luce attacked her erstwhile friend. "The newspapers loved it. They called it a catfight and cheered the girls on to greater efforts. . . . Thompson responded with a personal attack . . . 'Miss Boothe is a "Body by Fisher" in this campaign' . . ."[46]

Biographer Stephen Shedagg says Luce later told him that the Willkie campaign taught her "one great truth: Men can disagree violently and the press will acknowledge the possibility of a reasonable difference of opinion. If women disagree it immediately becomes a catfight."[47]

When Helen Gahagan Douglas arrived in Washington in 1944, the press appeared eager to have a rerun of the famous Luce-Thompson face-off between her and Luce, two beautiful, former actresses from opposing parties. In her 1982 autobiography, A Full Life, Douglas recounted the next chapter in the Capitol catfights.

> Immediately after my election, newspapers took up the theme that had been created in Chicago and spoke of the coming "battle of the glamour queens." . . . We were two of the nine women in the House of Representatives . . . and there were none in the Senate. . . . For reporters short of real news, it was a simple day's work to speculate that we would claw one another. The implication was that we were frivolous, vacuous women rather than serious, committed politicians.[48]

What happened next depends on which biography one reads. Luce maintained she "told Mrs. Douglas that if she said it was a nice day and I happened to observe it looked like rain, the press would blow it up into a great big dispute. I wanted to make an agreement with her . . . we would never discuss the same subject on the same day, and we wouldn't under any consideration comment on what the other had said."[49] Douglas recalled that it was she who had suggested the truce, at a party for the new congresswomen arranged by the women of the Washington press corps.[50]

While the coverage of Douglas's revolutionary market basket speech vividly indicates the sexual-not-serious frame into which news of political women occasionally still is forced, it also indicates how clearly Douglas understood the trade-offs she faced. Note that in her preparation for the speech, she did not first go shopping; in fact, one wonders if this wealthy, very recognizable woman even did her own marketing. Instead, she savvily had her staff alert photographers she would be going shopping. The Washington Star, in its coverage, did cast her in the category of yammering woman: "Representative Keefe, Republican, of Wisconsin tried unsuccessfully to debate [her]. . . . His role consisted mostly of attempts to break in on the former actress' rush of words."[51] And Time magazine's coverage attempted to paint her as frivolous and vacuous—they noted "Congressmen were treated to a floor show."[52] But Time ran the picture of the "decorative Democrat" and the serious, committed politician got her message across to a national audience. That was her goal.

Possibly the most hoary cliché in press relations is this: "There is no bad publicity." But when Pat Schroeder announced her own decision to withdraw from presidential contention, then shed tears, the reaction of the press—making Schroeder's brief show of emotion the mother of all sobfests—certainly called that cliché into question. The press had a field day. Her tears were evidence to support previous depictions of women, a new way to play upon the prevailing stereotypes, a reinforcement of the template into which all news under the heading "women," subheading "political," can be forced. The *New York Post* said Schroeder was "precisely what her supporters had sought to overcome—the stereotype of women as weepy wimps who don't belong in the business of serious affairs."[53] *The Christian Science Monitor* quoted a woman who said, "The men of this country are not going to vote for a woman who looks like she might break down and sob when she can't get an arms control agreement with Gorbachev."[54]

"Anytime I go to any city to talk, that's the first piece of film the TV stations pull out," Schroeder said. "They've just decided that's the only thing I've ever done that counted."

But a peculiar thing began to happen: "Every time any man anywhere cried, the press would somehow mention her," explains Dan Buck, Schroeder's administrative assistant.

Seeing an opportunity in what others might have considered merely "deep boo hoo," to borrow *Ms.* magazine's description (April 1989) of her problem, Schroeder began a newspaper clipping file on men who cry and used it to demonstrate "she still has a sense of humor about it," opined *The Washington Post* (January 9, 1989). Her ever-expanding list, Schroeder wrote in a thank-you letter to a friend who had added a clipping describing a tearful John F. Kennedy, includes "[hockey player] Wayne Gretzky, . . . Robert Dole [senator from Kansas], . . . George Washington, . . . Ronald Reagan (on multiple occasions—his farewell to Washington was one sob after another), and George Bush." The *Post* story noted that when "incoming White House chief of staff John H. Sununu shed a tear delivering his recent farewell address as governor of New Hampshire . . . [Schroeder] sent him a complimentary letter. 'Speaking from experience, anybody who is afraid to shed a tear doesn't belong in politics.'" Somehow that letter got leaked to the press.

In reviewing the press coverage of political women, it becomes obvious that some have learned they can benefit from some of the old "soft news" tradition regarding women. It can help them connect with voters in a way that is not equally available to their male counterparts, and would not yet seem appropriate in coverage about a man. As the following story may indicate, however, it has been a case of when life hands you a lemon (or ripe peaches), make lemonade (or peach cobbler).

> A Julia Child she's not, but an inventive short-cut cook she most certainly is. . . . "My family and my job mean the most to me. I do not make a fuss about eating." . . . Does she ever miss the East? A frown and a wrinkled nose are answers enough to that silly question. . . .
>
> "I think all women are involved in women's liberation," she said. . . . "I think that every woman who is doing what she wants to do, whether it's being a housewife, or nurse, or being in politics is contributing to that movement. . . . "
>
> She said her husband is interested in politics and supports her political activity. "Our ambition is to see the best people run and get elected."
>
> As a working wife and mother Barbara's simple philosophy on meals is to cook one thing that's a little special "so it's not a super bore." Following is a favorite dessert of the Boxer family, Peach Cobbler."[55]

It was August 1974, and all over America women were rattling their cages, trying to break loose from what they considered limiting stereotypes—wife, mother, cook—and inadvertently creating a new stereotype: superwoman. The double message of the times, also the dilemma for the women who lived those times, was captured perfectly in the *Marin Independent Journal*'s headline, "Politics Leaves Little Time for Fancy Cuisine." The pictures accompanying the story in the paper's "Cook's Corner" were just a reinforcement: Young wife in kitchen with child. Young wife in kitchen with phone. Young wife in kitchen sprinkling streusel on five pounds of ripe peaches in a Pyrex baking dish. "Barbara Boxer whips up peach cobbler between conversations," read the cutline.

Barbara Boxer, then a congressional assistant for newly elected congressman John L. Burton, was one of those brave new superwomen. She had worked as a stockbroker while putting her husband, Stewart, through law school. She had joined the peace movement in 1968 when she "began to realize that people could make changes." She had been a charter member of the Marin County Women's Political Caucus and had run for county supervisor. When she lost, she put her new found political knowledge to work as a reporter and in 1973 won a San Francisco Press Club award.

In short, you might think she, a former reporter who was already a feminist, would have known better than to be caught in her kitchen making peach cobbler, praising her supportive husband, submerging her ambition in the plural "our," reinforcing the very stereotypes she was attempting to overcome.

Perhaps she did know better, but it is illustrative to remember that Boxer went on to become a five-term U.S. congresswoman, and in 1992 made history with Dianne Feinstein, when California elected both to the U.S. Senate. Whatever it is Barbara Boxer knew, other women may want to discover, but one thing is certain: Getting your name known to the electorate is what counts.

Boxer has been so successful at it that she has developed a not-so-attractive reputation for "publicity stunts"—a phrase that often shows up even in positive stories about her.

"Boxer's a great team player until the TV lights go on, then she's the first one in the spot, and the only who's done anything," a disgruntled member of the environmental community complained during the 1992 campaign.

But was that person voting for Boxer in 1992?

The answer was a sheepish nod.

Political consultant Ed Zuckerman, who worked on national newcomer Patty Murray's Senate campaign as well as old-timer Boxer's, makes the point that "Barbara knows what reporters are looking for, when to be careful and when not to be careful. She basically knows that what a reporter is to the candidate is a conduit to the people.

"Patty's still learning it's kind of like that old line: 'Make 'em an offer they can't refuse.' Give them something they can't help but put on because it's good stuff—or keep your mouth shut. Because ultimately the most important thing is that the reporter has to do the job, get something in print or on the air, by deadline."

Playing that game of chicken is harder for women, Zuckerman admits. Women have more trouble not being nice, not answering the questions reporters ask—"All the women candidates I've worked for have had this problem." Boxer, he adds, is the one real exception "because after ten or fifteen years of public life and before that being a reporter herself she's more savvy."

Other women candidates have learned that "television likes women," in Celinda Lake's words. At the very least, television can be used to advantage because of all the things that make women different from the usual all-male-is-normal talking heads—their brighter colors, their more-animated and engaging ways of speaking, in short the very fact they are still a novelty act. Evelyn Murphy now believes that women have an actual advantage on television, especially in candidate debates. "Your face is the same size. Your voice has the same modulation—you don't have to shout down a union hall. And on television you have your chance to make your case directly to the people."

"Most consultants and managers feel that press coverage of women candidates has grown more favorable over time, even if it still has a long way to go," reported pollster Lake. "At one time they had 'not taken women that seriously,' but now they seem more interested."[56]

Bella Abzug, who once complained that news coverage of her made it seem as if "I just came out of my kitchen," now suggests the ideal news story may be one that blends old and new, accepts women as women (who are, if they are at all like her, daughters, wives, mothers, and serious persons who sometimes are interested in fashion, too). Decked out in the color purple with a matching purple and teal hat at the twentieth anniversary convention of the National Women's Political Caucus in 1991, the veteran feminist and former congresswoman mused on the perfect lead for the perfect political story of the future:

"Resplendent in her purple gown, the new president of the United States of America took the oath of office today and welcomed the women of her cabinet. . . . "

9

Delivering the Message

Strategies for Surviving Stereotype

B arely more than two weeks before the March 17, 1992, Illinois primary, Carol Moseley-Braun stood twelve points down in the polls,
had barely $300 in her coffers, and only five phones and five staffers to
run a statewide campaign. When she's gone to Washington, D.C., to
"drum up support for her ragtag campaign . . . [s]he was treated like a
poor relation," reported the *Chicago Sun-Times,* adding "perhaps a
dozen people thought she had a chance to be a U.S. senator."[1]

"Talk about your underdogs," recalled Washington political consultant
Tony Podesta. "I couldn't even find a professional fund-raiser who she
could pay to work for her."[2]

Pundits said the race was between powerful three-term Senator Alan
J. Dixon, a sixty-four-year-old Democrat whose vote for the Clarence
Thomas Supreme Court nomination had triggered Moseley-Braun's
challenge, and his other opponent, Al Hofield, a fifty-five-year-old personal injury attorney who poured $4.5 million of his own money into the
campaign. Every carved-in-stone notion of what goes wrong with
women's campaigns was reported to be wrong with Moseley-Braun's—
rumors had it a disorganized, revolving door, not-ready-for-prime-time

effort. "It was seen as a 'disaster campaign' that didn't have any resources because no one gave it a chance," said political activist Heather Booth, who later became the field director for the general election campaign.

In addition to a substantial African-American base, EMILY's List came through with $5,000. Illinois members of the National Organization for Women (NOW) volunteered in every county—often acting as one-woman county committees. Gloria Steinem made two campaign appearances, lending national credibility and energizing a loosely organized network of liberal, urban, and suburban women.

When Moseley-Braun won the primary with 38 percent of the vote to Dixon's 35 percent, it did not take the political pros long to see there was more to her victory than mere media hype about another "Year of the Woman in Politics."

"Look at the numbers and you realize it's not a slogan anymore," said longtime Chicago alderman Edward Burke. "This thing is really happening and you don't have to look at the top of the ticket. Look at the bottom . . . where the women judges won, and you realize women came out to vote. That's the reality of it."[3]

A month later, when political newcomer Lynn Yeakel won the Pennsylvania Democratic Senate primary against the state's well-known, well-liked lieutenant governor, Washington political consultant Joel Bradshaw exclaimed to a staffer, "If I were a white male running against a woman in a U.S. Senate race I'd be in the bathroom this morning throwing up." One of Bradshaw's clients was a little-known Washington State freshman state senator, Patty Murray. Within days, the two male Democrats who had been thought to have the inside track on Washington's U.S. Senate nomination, former congressman Don Bonker and Governor Booth Gardner, dropped out of the race.

The forces that propelled Moseley-Braun and three other new women into the U.S. Senate and forty-seven others to the House went beyond the voter anger that the instant, post-election analyses proclaimed. It was not just a case of John and Jane Q. Citizen deciding "Women can't do any worse than those bozos have," as one voter told a campaign focus group.

Overlooked in the post-election euphoria was a profound change that had taken place so slowly in America that the press and political pros had missed it: Women had no longer been dismissed as incapable lesser beings by their fellow citizens. Women no longer relied on the authority of their male relatives to provide the status necessary for them to exercise one of the central rights of citizenship—running for and serving in public office. Moreover, there were certain areas of public policy that voters, male and female alike, appeared to believe women were simply better able to address—because of life experience, not just biology. And finally, it was because a new image of what their government was had been seared into the nation's consciousness—by congresswomen who stormed the male cloister of the Senate during the Thomas confirmation hearings, by hour after hour of television pictures of, by turns, solemn and arrogant faces, all-male and all-white, at the Judiciary Committee table. Those pictures had said what decades of words had failed to convey, and women now understood that their democracy was not representative of them.

True, a woman had not yet run for and been elected president, and certainly there were barricades remaining to be scaled, but the accomplishments of 1992 could not be denied.

Old political truisms—that women will not open their checkbooks for women candidates, or mobilize for women's causes—were toppled. Old partisan labels like "tax and spend liberal" did not stick to the group thought most liberal and most likely to be spendthrifts on social issues: women. Old prejudices—that women were too soft to be hard on crime, too emotional to be trusted with the nation's checkbook or defense, too disorganized to be effective because of their family responsibilities or mysterious biology, and too idealistic to play the hardball insider game of realpolitik—were played on in hundreds of hardly subtle sound bites and buzz words, by thousands of cleverly crafted television ads and direct mail pieces, and at a cost of millions in campaign expertise, but in 1992 the voters were not buying.

Three married women—including two from a single state, California—won Senate seats: Barbara Boxer, Dianne Feinstein, and Patty Murray. Only one married woman before them had ever been elected to the Senate—Florida's Paula Hawkins in 1986. And only two of the seventeen women senators who preceded them had no male relative who paved the way for them in politics, the two most recently elected—Maryland's Barbara Mikulski, who was reelected in 1992, and Hawkins, who served just one term. That Murray and the divorced, single Moseley-Braun also were mothers with children still at home was another astonishment: America had never before sent mothers of still-nesting babes to the U.S. Senate. Among the new congresswomen elected in 1992 there was even a former welfare mother, California's Lynn Woolsey.

The successes should not obscure an important fact. Clarence Thomas and Anita Hill notwithstanding, none of these women won by accident—or even by accident of history, being the right sex at the right time. The fact that a candidate was female may have been a potential advantage—for the first time ever. However, veterans like Congresswoman Nancy Pelosi skeptically phrased it differently: "The notion that voters won't vote for a woman is practically not at issue anymore."

Texas Governor Ann Richards had made the same point to a Women's Campaign Fund (WCF) gathering of women politicians and would-be politicians a few weeks prior to Anita Hill's abrupt arrival on the national scene. No one, not even other women, will vote for a woman just because she's a woman: "They are not stupid. They vote for the candidate they think is going to give them the best government."

Whether it was Thomas/Hill and the all-white, all-male makeup of the Senate Judiciary Committee, or some other issue that aroused the voters in her district, it was not the candidate's gender but how the individual candidate made an issue a part of her message that made the difference. However she chose to phrase it, whatever her carefully plotted strategy, wherever the campaign plan allocated resources and her time for getting it across, her message had to be that she was the person who could do what the voter wanted done. And in Ann Richards's pithy manner of speaking, in 1992 the voters were ready to believe "Roosters crow; hens deliver."

The American people "are desperate to hear the words of someone who is ready to fight for them," Richards admonished her audience. "Even if they disagree with you on an issue they will vote for you if they think you are a fighter, because they figure if you are not for them on one issue, that you might be for them on another, and that's what they expect government to be."

That much stayed the same in 1992, as did this: Every race was specific to the candidate presented, the community being polled, and the job at stake. Those who ran good campaigns won; those who didn't—or those whose campaigns "peaked" too soon, too late, or not at all, or who were simply out-campaigned by their opponent—lost.

Dianne Feinstein, for example, lost her 1990 governor's race to a very similar candidate—a moderate, pro-choice, former mayor of a large California city, freshman Senator Pete Wilson. Governor is a manager's job; the word *manager* still translates to some voters as "man." In 1971, when Feinstein first ran, and lost, for mayor of San Francisco, another "manager" job, the incumbent's slogan was "'It's a tough job and [Joseph]

Alioto's doing it,'" explained San Francisco political consultant Clint Reilly. "Dianne's problem then was to make clear she wasn't just another Pacific Heights matron who couldn't make decisions. . . . The basic issue, then and in 1990, was is a woman decisive enough to be a leader?"

Feinstein broke through much of that in 1990, but it was her first statewide race. In 1992, her name was known to voters in every county, and her credibility had been established by her near win over Wilson and Wilson's own troubled first year as governor. She crushed Wilson's appointed successor in her race for the Senate. It was a different job, different year, different race.

Likewise, former Missouri congresswoman Joan Kelly Horn ran a brilliant 1990 campaign—carefully targeting pro-choice voters among Republican and Catholic women in the conservative suburbs of St. Louis—and won the "safe Republican seat" by a mere fifty-four votes. In 1992 the Republicans made getting that seat back a priority, and they did.

Another important example is Lynn Yeakel. In her primary race, she virtually ignored the other Democrats and ran brilliantly against the Republican incumbent, Senator Arlen Specter, her paid advertising constantly reminding the voters of the prosecutorial role Specter played in the inquisition of Anita Hill. She won the nomination, even though, only weeks before, she had been so unknown to Pennsylvania that she did not even register a one percent in voter preference polls. She had the right message at the right time. Yet in the general election, the incumbent Specter was returned to the Senate. Why?

"All candidates have things other than gender that they are about," explains veteran political consultant Joel Bradshaw. "Here's a guy who had every reason to be as scared as anybody. He ran the best campaign he could think of. And he won."

Specter apologized, targeted the audience that was most vocal about their dissatisfaction with him—women—and showcased a new humbler self in unlikely interviews, such as one on National Public Radio's "Fresh Air."

He also played some gender cards of his own, each of them targeted to core Democratic constituencies. When Yeakel was linked to anti–civil rights votes her elderly father had cast as a congressman, African-Americans were the target. References to her husband's restricted country club membership, like Feinstein's "Pacific Heights matron" tag, were meant to distance the blue-collar worker and ethnics. Broadcasting her Methodist minister's negative remarks about Israel was meant to bother

Jewish voters. The Lynn Yeakel these campaign tactics presented was not a person in her own right, but an unthinking dependent: dutiful daughter, probably submissive wife, and too easily influenced church lady. These tactics hit her political inexperience and placed her back among women "covered" by male authority. In other words, the Specter campaign was able to wrap Yeakel in all the negative stereotypes inherent in coverture.

Although Yeakel was able to clarify for the voters precisely what Specter was doing, it distracted her from her own message, put her on the defensive, and in the long run, "She didn't run a particularly good campaign and she didn't win," Bradshaw said.

It becomes clear in reviewing the races of 1992, that despite the unprecedented advances made by women, the most critical remaining problem for any woman candidate still is tacking the fine line of ambiguities and stereotypes that voters and tradition superimpose on her. She must craft a message and a public persona that persuades party, pundits, and public—and not necessarily in that formerly preordained order— that she can be as clear and independent a decision maker as any man, but more caring and trustworthy.

Meanwhile, like every woman venturing into male territory, the woman candidate has to maintain some level of the traditional altruistic and apolitical above-it-all demeanor expected of a lady, all the while beating her opponents in what sometimes seems the closest thing to a blood sport that is still legal.

"Don't think of this as some League of Women Voters type of thing to do," Pelosi cautions women. "It's brutal. It's tough. You are going for power. It's never been just given away. It's highly competitive trying to take power, and as long as you understand that and are ready to take a punch square in the face, then you'll love it."

Beth Sullivan, Bradshaw's partner in the Washington, D.C.–based Campaign Design Group, added this lament: "Women are not taught to play as many competitive sports as men, and they are taught to be nicer," a situation that sets up a peculiar catch-22: "You can't afford as a woman candidate not to be nice, you'll immediately be branded as a bitch. But the men won't play by tea party rules." Or as another political analyst told *Time* magazine, "it takes more for a man to be perceived as a bully than it takes for a woman to be perceived as a bitch."[4]

Until recently, so few women had run and won that the lessons from successful national-level campaigns were few and so far between as to be virtually meaningless. The thirty-one women in the 102nd Congress (January 1991–January 1993) represented nearly a quarter of the mere 134 women ever sent to Congress prior to the 1992 elections.[5] Only two of those congressional women were ever considered serious potential presidential candidates, Maine's Margaret Chase Smith in 1964 and Colorado's Patricia Schroeder in 1987. In both cases merely being female was their Sisyphus stone. Only one has ever been a major party's vice presidential candidate, Geraldine Ferraro, and again it was the reaction to her being a woman that tarnished her race.

The postmortem on what was widely considered the Ferraro Failure in 1984, and Ferraro's own revealing, strongly negative polling in 1985 when she was first considering running for the Senate, perhaps more than any earlier series of events, helped women candidates begin to understand the double-binds they are all in and how those might be finessed.

With male voters, the female candidate's problem is not just men's stubborn reluctance to accept her as Senator or Governor. Some men just can't *see* her in the role. The more traditional the man, the more he may be unable to visualize a woman handling the tough decisions a senator or governor has to make. At a post-election debriefing for EMILY's List in 1990,[6] one woman politician said wistfully, "Voters see a man in a blue suit and they think Senator, Governor, Congressman."[7] Women had been fighting that image dissonance from as early as 1976 when Bella Abzug tried, and failed, to challenge the stereotype straight-on with the slogan "I'm not what a Senator looks like, I'm what a Senator should look like."[8]

While Abzug's might have been a clever strategy to try to win the votes of traditional men, women learned post-Ferraro that it often sends the wrong message to the traditional woman. Women candidates quite literally can frighten the traditional woman. Ferraro discovered that her candidacy seemed, to the traditional stay-at-home woman, to devalue every choice that woman had made in her life.

Ferraro's unique position as the first "wife" to run for vice president— the intense scrutiny her husband and his family's real estate business came under, and the aspects of coverture that scrutiny revealed—has been discussed earlier. But another widely reported incident helps crystallize the ambiguous situations in which women politicians sometimes find themselves.

At one campaign stop, a Southern state's agricultural commissioner, Mississippi's Jim Buck Ross, asked Ferraro if she could make a blueberry muffin, an incident she recounts vividly in her memoir of the campaign.

"'You grow blueberries?' Ross grinned. 'Can you bake a blueberry muffin?'

"'Sure can,' I finally managed to respond. 'Can you?'

"'Down here in Mississippi, the men don't cook,' he replied."[9]

Although the exchange was considered the height of sexism, instead of the incident playing to Ferraro's benefit—after all, she had gracefully and with good humor deflected a foolish stereotyping question—it served to remind worried Mondale staffers that their vice presidential candidate was indeed female. To the male-dominated presidential campaign, appropriate questions to the person who would be a heartbeat away from the presidency were about missile throw-weights not muffins.

Later in the vice presidential debate against George Bush, a reporter cited Ferraro's "little or no experience in military matters" and asked, "How can you convince the American people . . . that you would know what to do to protect this nation's security, and do you think . . . the Soviets might be tempted to take advantage of you simply because you are a woman?"

Again she handled it well. Indeed, she had anticipated the question and posed one of her own in reply. Would she have had to fight in a war in order to love peace?[10]

But again the Mondale campaign—and the Democratic party it represented—was so flummoxed by what it perceived as its inability to make the voters feel Ferraro could be "man enough" to push the nuclear button that it adamantly nixed every attempt she made to reach out to the legions of women voters who were overjoyed that a woman finally had made it onto the ballot.

Mondale insiders criticized her as "strident," a word that seems to attach only to women, and liberal feminist women at that. They complained, and complain to this day, that her tracking polls, the voter preference checks done on virtually a daily basis in the heat of a major campaign, were "terrible. A disaster." She countered with the numbers of new donors she brought to Democratic party rolls—40,000, she says—and maintained that exit polls showed her to have brought the ticket a small extra vote, second only to Lyndon Johnson's contribution to the 1960 Democratic victory. Whichever analysis is correct, the Mondale campaign scheduled her in secondary media markets, a tactic that kept her away from large cities, where, presumably, there were greater numbers of working and professional women who would have been likely to turn out to hear her. There may have been good reason for that: In politics, a candidate doesn't need to preach to the choir but must seek votes among the unconverted. However, the decision arguably cost Ferraro, and the Mondale campaign, exposure in big cities' larger, more influential papers and wider-reaching television stations.

She defends the strategy: "My candidacy was a statement in and of itself. My physically being there meant we would be concerned with women's issues . . . but there was a concern . . . what did I know about weapons, missiles, other things. . . . It was not only a presidency for women."

But the reality is that both the Mondale campaign and the Democrats as a whole were selling Geraldine Ferraro the way they had traditionally sold any male candidate—as a person tough on the hard issues of war and taxes—not the person she was: a tough former prosecutor, a respected member of the House of Representatives, and a woman who could both bake blueberry muffins and handle an awkward good old boy's attempt at affability. Despite indications of the gender gap waiting to be harvested, Democratic men saw Ferraro as a "Queens housewife"—as the press and the opposition often alluded to her—whose political experience had to be enhanced with male-like attributes in order to succeed. They could not make the leap to seeing her as a multifaceted politician whose female life experience could be a part of the message about the Mondale-Ferraro ticket. And when Geraldine Ferraro "failed," it was not just one campaign's failure, but further proof to the men of the party that a woman could not run for high office and win.

Women, however, blame the still predominantly male party structure—and men's blindness to credentials other than their own—for many of women's apparent "failures." The parties, they say, have been slower to accept women than have the voters and, as a result, have often set them up to fail. In 1974, when Barbara Mikulski first ran, unsuccessfully, for the U.S. Senate, she told a television audience that Maryland's Democratic party appeared "very happy to support a woman against someone who they thought couldn't be beat. . . . [It was] 'Okay, good old Barb . . . Let her take the nosedive for the party.'" When the race was winnable, "like most women candidates I was not considered a good investment."[11]

That same year, when former Missouri lieutenant governor and

National Women's Political Caucus (NWPC) president Harriett Woods first ran for the Missouri state senate, she ran headlong into that mindset. "I had been in the city council eight years, a television producer for ten years, two years on the state highway commission. . . . Well, it was the shock of my life when the party said, 'We have to have a man for the job.'" She ran anyway, and won.

"The same thing happened in 1982" when, now a veteran state legislator, she ran for the U.S. Senate. "They called me 'a suburban housewife' and then ran a bank lobbyist [who had never before held political office] against me" in the primary. Again, she flouted party protocol and ran. "The perception was that women were inadequate candidates." She beat the bank lobbyist in the primary, but lost the general election to Republican John Danforth.

Even in the 1990 U.S. Senate races, the party was a barrier, although more so for Democratic women than Republican women. Neither Lynn Martin nor Claudine Schneider faced anything but token opposition from the party. On the other end of the spectrum however, Josie Heath had to fight every step of the way. After years in Democratic politics, including years as a county official and a stint in the Carter administration, she was completely overlooked by the Democrats seeking a Senate candidate. Their anointed nominee was a millionaire developer and former state chair who had never held elective office. When she told him she was considering running against him in the primary, "He said, 'I can understand you think this might be *nice* to do, but . . . '" she recalled.

Even after she had won the primary and the nomination, party regulars not only fought her campaign, but, she said, Colorado's governor, Roy Roemer, pointedly refused to let her join a group of candidates invited to barnstorm the state with him just days before the election. She chartered her own plane to make the trip, but when it was grounded at one small mountain airport because it lacked the instruments to take off in a blizzard, she again asked the governor to join his plane. He refused, leaving her stranded. "He said, 'You know how it is.' I sure did."

Another high-ranking Colorado Democrat conceded in 1991 that "the party treated Josie shabbily," but when Senator Tim Wirth's sudden decision to retire from the Senate opened another seat in 1992, that man not only stepped forward to run against her but, Heath maintained, was behind a barrage of phone calls from party insiders warning her, "This is the end of your political future. . . . Back off, step aside, be a nice girl, get out of the way."[12] Heath later remembered something Celinda Lake had told her: "In politics, women really can be on the inside of the power—until they want power of their own."

Dianne Feinstein faced similar disdain from party regulars in 1990. Despite the fact that as leader of one of the nation's most notable and troubled cities she had been named the nation's most effective mayor, and had been on Walter Mondale's short list for vice president in 1984, her own party did not take seriously her commitment to politics or her decision to run for governor.

Barbara Johnson, manager for the odds-on Democratic front runner for the nomination for governor (California Attorney General John Van de Kamp) poohpoohed the idea Feinstein would even deign to make the 1990 race. "We didn't believe she had the heart for the race. We thought she was insular, local, and had never spent a single night in southern California. . . . She was unwilling to travel and, from everything we heard, would be unwilling to go through even the moderate rigors of a statewide campaign."[13]

Despite the condescension to, or outright dismissal of, women by the political pros, which never fails to percolate down to voters via the "insiders" quoted by the press, by 1990 things were changing. A number of social and historical events had begun to alter society's perception of women's abilities, as well as to give women candidates a new sense of both their own legitimate place in government and the validity of their role as champion of other women.

In early April 1989, one of the largest protest demonstrations ever to assemble in Washington, D.C.—estimates ranged from 300,000 to 600,000—joined in the "March for Women's Rights, Women's Lives," to send the White House the message that middle America, as well as vast numbers of women, were for abortion rights.

The strength of that showing started male politicians flip-flopping all over the place on all issues, but especially abortion, that seemed to promise a "bump" at the polls with women voters. In the U.S. House, forty-one representatives moved themselves to the pro-choice column, and a majority, for the first time, voted to fund abortions for poverty-stricken victims of rape and incest. President Bush vetoed that bill, saying it would be too easy for a woman to lie about rape or incest, and refused even to meet with Congresswoman Olympia Snowe of Maine and seven other Republican women House members who wanted him to hear a differing view. Another Republican, Congresswoman Nancy Johnson of

Connecticut, labeled Bush's actions "deeply, profoundly inhumane and unjust."

That fall, the Republicans lost two gubernatorial races to pro-choice candidates, New Jersey's James Florio and Virginia's Douglas Wilder, who had a simple explanation of his position on abortion: "I trust the women of Virginia."

Then, in late 1989, the invasion of Panama and the stunning news that 770 American women troops had participated in Operation Just Cause and that three had been nominated for combat medals, despite regulations that supposedly banned them from combat situations, catapulted back into the headlines the old debate about the role of women in the military and society.

At the same time that the economy was in decline and jobs were becoming scarcer, even the affirmative action laws, those federal policies that are supposed to provide equal employment opportunity for women and minorities, came under attack, both by the Bush White House and the increasingly conservative Reagan-appointed U.S. Supreme Court. Ordinary women, who no longer had the economic option of being stay-at-home wives and mothers, felt the threat and could echo Justice Sandra Day O'Connor's gentle reproach to Justice Antonin Scalia in a closed-door meeting as reported by *The New York Times*. Scalia had been fulminating against affirmative action, especially for women, when O'Connor stopped him cold with, "But Nino, how do you think I got my job?"

Yet ultimately, it was the winding down of the Cold War, and the promise of an end to more than a half century of war mentality, that provided the light at the end of the tunnel for political women. Finally, in 1990, some seventy years after winning the vote and two full decades after politically minded feminists had banded together to recruit and support women candidates, it seemed that women politicians and women's issues—those policy areas women have championed throughout the nation's history (often, Pat Schroeder has said, because no one else did)—would be welcomed like war orphans come in from the cold.

All of these changes, taken together, meant that 1990 had given women as a group the freedom, almost a mandate, not just to run but to embrace issues such as child care, family leave, sex discrimination, breast cancer, and other particularly female concerns once labeled "special interests"—in other words, to run as women.

"We really thought that this particular year being a woman was a plus," said Bobby McCallum, press secretary in the 1990 Heath campaign.

"The Cold War had ended, the Persian Gulf War hadn't started, and people were focusing on domestic problems—the area where people tend to trust women most."

The media picked up on this newfound optimism among women candidates. The buzz words *peace dividend* seemed to hold out hope for an era in which women's age-old altruistic politics would be welcome, the "kinder and gentler America" that George Bush had promised in his inauguration speech. That gender-gap savvy phrase had been put into Bush's mouth by a woman speech writer, Peggy Noonan, more proof that the establishment was taking women and their voting power seriously. Republican strategist Lee Atwater suggested even pro-choicers would be welcome under the party's "Big Tent," and Republican women wistfully grabbed onto a rumor, reportedly floated by the White House, that Barbara Bush and the Bush daughters were for abortion rights.

It George Bush was softening his own rhetoric, the language women used to campaign for office was changing as well. There had been almost a mantra for political women in the past, a defensive "It doesn't matter that I am a woman." Suddenly, in 1990, this rote self-denial was no longer a key element in the stump speech or press interview. Instead, there was a new boldness, as woman after woman said "Women's voices should be heard" and "Women's concerns should be a part of the national agenda." Josie Heath emblazoned on bright red T-shirts the blatantly feminist message "A Woman's Place Is in the House and Senate." The elegant, convent-educated Dianne Feinstein dropped her ladylike demeanor in the final rousing weeks of her California gubernatorial campaign, and used language more often found in military barracks—"We need more skirts and fewer suits!"—and seemed to longtime staffers to be genuinely moved by the uproarious cheers those words produced.

The 1990 vibes were so positive that, even before she finally announced she would run for governor, Dianne Feinstein had both voters and political insiders seeing her as a winner. Johnson's early opinion that Feinstein wouldn't run seemed like wishful thinking after Johnson confessed to a post-election audience that Van de Kamp's own early polls showed the veteran state attorney general would win easily only if the field were exclusively male. But add even "a one-dimensional Dianne Feinstein . . . [and] we would have to count on luck and the gods smiling on us."[14]

Even without knowledge of those early polls, Darry Sragow, who had just come off Democrat Leo McCarthy's unsuccessful 1988 Senate race against Wilson, had a gut sense: "You couldn't run another middle-aged white guy against Pete Wilson and win."[15] He signed on to manage Feinstein's primary campaign.

Then there was the notion of "making history"—a powerful emotional draw for women to vote for a sister, acknowledges Bill Carrick, who ran Feinstein's 1990 post-primary campaign and did her political ads and strategy in the 1992 Senate race. Immediately following her 1990 primary victory, a *Los Angeles Times* poll showed 58 percent of all Democrats who voted felt "It's time we had a woman governor." More significantly, a third of the Republican women in the state agreed.

The same phenomenon was occurring across the nation. Among Republicans, Congresswoman Claudine Schneider's Rhode Island race against Senator Claiborne Pell and Illinois Congresswoman Lynn Martin's against Senator Paul Simon looked eminently "doable." Among Democrats, the money was on Feinstein, Josie Heath's Colorado race against now-Senator Hank Brown, and Ann Richards's gubernatorial race in Texas against oil millionaire and rancher Clayton "I am Bubba" Williams.

Then voters got cold feet. Saddam Hussein invaded Kuwait. Suddenly change looked scary. Both Heath and Schneider said they sensed a change in the electorate immediately. For Schneider and Martin, the problem of establishing comparable credentials was exacerbated when the war thrust their two opponents onto the nightly network news shows—both Pell and Simon were members of the Senate Foreign Relations Committee. Pell, the chairman, essentially ceased campaigning in Rhode Island and popped up at American troop facilities in Saudi Arabia—with TV cameras in close pursuit. Schneider and Martin's polling numbers finally crashed when their party's leader, George Bush, broke his "No new taxes" promise.

In California, Feinstein consultant Carrick could pinpoint the first moment he realized his candidate was in trouble: "We were two weeks out from the election. In a San Bernardino focus group a woman, a 35-year-old single nurse, went into this long discussion about how much she liked Dianne, what an incredible role model Dianne was, how proud she was to have voted for Dianne in the primary . . . then, embarrassed, she said, 'I'm worried how we are going to pay for all this,' and I knew we were in trouble," he recalled in a 1991 interview.

"The economy was beginning to slide and not taking a risk meant the old blue-shirted white male 'felt' better," Carrick explained.

Even Ann Richards, a seasoned politician who as treasurer of Texas had made the state millions of dollars with shrewd investments and modernizations, looked like a lost cause; with less than three weeks to go *Newsweek* (October 15, 1990) gave "Claytie" 4–1 odds, even though Williams had never before run for office, and noted "Claytie managed to offend *everyone* and is still winning." Then, on election-eve weekend, a freshman wire service reporter discovered that Williams had failed one year to file his income taxes. Texas voters went with Ann.

Duane Garrett, Feinstein's campaign chair, said later, "I think what happened is that the electorate, which was voting its hopes in June, was voting its fears in September."[16]

In retrospect, 1990 could not have provided a more perfect look at the remaining voter prejudices against women's campaigns if it had been designed as a laboratory experiment. It was a clear battle between the so-called hard and soft issues, between issues on which voters trust a man— war and the economy—the same issues they worry a woman is not tough enough to handle, and the issues on which they trust a woman—social welfare and health care, children and education, the environment . . . all the classic "municipal housekeeping" issues.

After 1990, which also had been given the optimistic label "Year of the Woman in Politics" because of the unprecedented number of women in high stakes national races, a group of Democratic women candidates and their staffs were brought together for a debriefing by EMILY's List to assess why so few of the eight women running for the Senate and ten running for governor had won their races.

What the weekend-long confab determined is that entering the 1990s, despite twenty years of women's movement trailblazing, women candidates were stuck "squarely on the horns of a dilemma," said the report, which pollster Celinda Lake had compiled.

"Voters want change and new faces, which women candidates clearly represent. At the same time, voters firmly believe that the business of politics is still conducted in the back room" by the good old boys. In other words, voters were ready for women to get in and clean up politics, though still a bit worried that women might not fight dirty if need be. But Washington, D.C., mayor Sharon Pratt Kelly successfully had demonstrated it could be done, with her 1990 slogan "I will clean house—not with a broom, but with a shovel." Her battle cry cleverly echoed the historic "ladylike" rationales women have used to enter the political fray, while not so subtly suggesting the extreme level of municipal mess created by the city's then mayor, the jail-bound Marion Barry, and, the guilt-by-gender inference suggested, her male opponents. Shovels are used to clean out livestock stalls.

The "central challenge," however, remained: "Women find that, in successfully establishing themselves as credible, they risk losing their natural edge as outsiders."

Established women politicians had already intuited much of this. Heath talked about "Politics as it ought to be." Dianne Feinstein positioned herself as a Washington outsider and, significantly, it was she, not one of her hired guns, who crafted her 1990 political slogan "Tough but Caring." In those three little words, she instinctively had gathered to her bosom all the positives her gender afforded her, yet strategically made the masculine "tough" message preeminent. It was so well done that even the late Otto Bos, Wilson's campaign director and political best friend, confessed to Feinstein's campaign staff after the election, "You owned the caring part to begin with."[17]

Feinstein had gotten out front on the crime issue, too. She was, as her primary ads trumpeted, "the only Democrat for the death penalty," the truth, but also words that attacked the double presumption that Democrats, and particularly Democratic women, are soft on crime. But Wilson played the crime issue as a sometimes gender thing, by changing his tune for different voter groups. He promised in rural areas to build more prisons—translation "jobs." He curried urbanites' favor with rousing promises to beef up the war on drugs—every voter's concern. To suburban audiences he declared that "no woman should be afraid in her own home"—a line that had potent, though subtle, racial connotations, and could not have been better targeted at the suburban white women who, the early polls had shown, were already defecting or thinking of defecting to Feinstein's camp.

Feinstein's campaign was so well done, and the phenomenon of running against an equally qualified woman seemed so new and untried, that Republican insiders worried that "Wilson was going to have to 'go to school' to learn how to run against her."[18] Otto Bos admitted, "We were concerned how we would be perceived, vis-à-vis roughing up Feinstein,"[19] especially after the Wilson campaign realized that whenever they attacked her, it was male voters who reacted negatively. "They became very protective," pollster Dick Dresner reported. Women, on the other hand, started off "much more positively oriented to her [but] became more critical."[20] (The latter phenomenon is one Celinda Lake has since identified in other women's races, and one that concerns her. "We still hold women to higher ethical standards, so if they are knocked off the pedestal they fall farther faster.")

Wilson complained he was the victim of reverse sexism, and he most certainly was, especially when Feinstein brushed away his claims to being pro-choice with a message that essentially boiled down to "Trust me on this one. I'm a woman. He's not."

Feinstein did stumble on some specific issues. She was unable to keep control of one powerful issue, and let her promises to make gender- and race-balanced appointments be repackaged by Wilson's campaign as "quotas," one of the Republican's hottest issues in 1990. Campaign manager Bos actually admitted that the Wilson campaign was "less concerned about the quota issue itself" than getting "Feinstein to engage us on our terms. Underneath the gloss of new and novel and exciting and outsider," all factors that bode well for women, "our [polling] data indicated she was a traditional liberal,"[21] which can be a negative. She was also a career politician, and Wilson's campaign was determined to portray her as such, with all the negatives they could pile on.

One "defining moment,"[22] Bos claimed, was when Feinstein allowed the Wilson campaign to goad her into responding to his charges about her husband's involvement in the bail-out of a failed savings and loan. It was a no-win situation for Feinstein. She couldn't let the charges stand— indeed, she did a television ad that called Wilson a liar—but any response put her into the category of wife, and worse, one of those politicians who sling mud. It was a strategic strike at her gender positives.

"We had to draw Feinstein into some sort of an attack," Dresner explained. "If we could have her seen as attacking us first ... then it became simply a battle between basically two normal kinds of politicians. ..."[23]

"As it went on we paid a lot less attention to gender *as an issue* and focused much more on 'Can we just simply make this a race between two politicians?'" Wilson's polling numbers turned the corner after what Wilsonites called the "S&L shoot-out" and "started to drift up."[24]

Carrick has maintained that he was never able to see that this tactic hurt Feinstein's polling numbers. But he did admit it hurt the campaign because, simply, "it was distracting as hell."

The bottom line, according to most analysts, was that Pete Wilson became governor of California because Saddam Hussein invaded Kuwait and more and more Americans were out of work. The final vote count was 3,791,904 to 3,525,197 and during the last week Feinstein had begun to bring the worried San Bernardino nurses back into the fold. Her own tracking polls, done the Saturday before the election, "showed the campaigns in a dead heat. A dead heat," Carrick claims. "If we'd had one more week. . . . "

As that play-by-play of Feinstein's 1990 campaign indicates, it was a race between "two giants going toe to toe," as even Wilson's campaign conceded. Even so, as the EMILY's List report makes clear, "Women and men candidates face many common obstacles . . . but the gender difference for women reduces their strategic options, drains extra resources, adds visibility to their mistakes, and filters their messages [and] may ultimately be the marginal difference between winning and losing."

Women candidates bring both advantages and disadvantages to the table, the report added, listing themes that were then played out in 1992: "They are . . . presumed to be honest, not owned or captive. . . . They are presumed to be populist—able to understand the struggles of ordinary people . . . [but] women candidates are seen as shaky on taxes and fiscal issues, as too liberal and too inexperienced. They are seen as weaker and soft-hearted on issues of personal security—war and crime."

In fact, the prejudices that still exist against women were so clearly understood by the political pros that, coming out of the 1990 races, *Campaigns and Elections Magazine* listed them in an article "How to Run Against a Woman or a Black."

One bit of advice: "Emphasize macho middle-class issues." Pull out the military records, ride a horse, be photographed playing touch football with your children. A second suggestion: "Rope-a-dope"—try to goad a woman into attacking or fighting back so she looks shrill and unladylike. If all else fails "say something soothingly paternalistic." During one debate in 1990, Congressman Hank Brown accused "Mrs. Heath" of "being cute," which painted her as a puppet of her husband as well as a frilly sex object. The latter tactic, being dismissively patronizing, is so commonly mounted against women that Republican consultant Linda DiVall has warned her candidates not to respond to it, because "A lot of voters are ready to believe a woman is overly emotional . . . [but] crying foul too much could unleash a backlash."

Campaign and Elections' number one rule, however, was listed as "Steal the rainbow." Beat your opponent to her strongest issue. For example, define yourself as pro-choice before she has a chance to explain that your voting record shows you've missed some critical abortion rights votes or that you've waffled on the issue in the past. Or steal the pro-choice rainbow, turn her pro-choice stance into a negative, by portraying her as overly radical on the subject, as the 1990 opponent of Congresswoman Jolene Unsoeld of Washington did in what has become almost a predictable script in races between a liberal woman and a conservative man. "I do not plan to make an issue of her extreme position on abortion," Republican Bob Williams told the *Seattle Post-Intelligencer* (March 28, 1990) in announcing his candidacy, then went on to do exactly that, claiming, falsely, that Unsoeld supported "abortion for abortion's sake" even in the third trimester and for selection of the child's gender.

After Feinstein's 1990 primary election rival tried and failed to steal a different rainbow, the woman issue, by claiming he was "the best feminist in the race," it was odd that in 1992 State Treasurer Gray Davis trotted out the same argument and even some of the same endorsements for himself. It seldom works, primarily because a woman gets a presumption from voters on women's and feminist issues, Celinda Lake explains.

But by 1992, Feinstein's answer to this charge—as one put it, "When she was mayor of San Francisco, women's groups found fault with her"—cleverly and movingly made use of one of the key things the EMILY's List debriefers discovered after the 1990 races. The "toughness" a woman candidate needs to prove that she has need not be a military record, it can be any story of any personal adversity overcome. Ann Richards talked convincingly about her decade-ago struggle with alcoholism. Governor Barbara Roberts of Oregon told of coping with the cancer that has crippled her husband. Lynn Woolsey, the successful businesswoman who won the congressional seat Barbara Boxer vacated, made a strategic decision to reveal that she had once supported her three children on welfare. It was a story, she admitted, her now-grown children didn't even know.

Feinstein's toughness had been burned into voters' minds in 1990 by a stunning, much-talked-about "grabber" ad. It began with the words *Forged in tragedy* over stark black-and-white news film of her calming San Francisco in the aftermath of the double assassination that thrust her into the mayor's office in 1978. In 1992, she used that story to put a new spin on her toughness, making it the explanation of her slow evolution as a feminist.

"The job I did [being mayor] affected me greatly. I had to deal with warring department heads. I was mayor directly following 'Prop. 13' [a state voter initiative that slashed property taxes and impoverished local governments]. I had to deal with the nitty-gritty, potholes in the streets, graffiti on the buses, flowers in the parks, books in the schools, and I was the first mayor to deal with AIDS. In those roles it was management, not advocacy, that was needed," she argued. "My predecessor had been assassinated and the year before I had lost my husband. I was in extraordinarily deep grief. I was just a different person then."

But by the elections of 1992, the electorate did not need quite so much persuasion as before to vote for a woman. The electorate was different, as well.

At the same moment Saddam Hussein's invasion of Kuwait was dashing women's electoral chances, all across America families awoke August 26, 1990, to front-page pictures of U.S. Army Spec. 4 Hollie Vallance, twenty-one, wearing combat gear and a helmet, kissing her seven-week-old baby daughter goodbye. Medic Vallance was only one of several new mothers in one unit—some of whom hurriedly had to wean their nursing infants—called up for the looming Gulf War. A quarter million American women on active duty and tens of thousands in National Guard units were prepared to follow.

CBS's "60 Minutes" reran a series of interviews with female military officers and enlisted women, in which one answered the question that was suddenly on every political commentator's lips: Was the U.S. public ready for its womenfolk to come back in body bags? Maybe not, she told Mike Wallace, but the military women themselves already had accepted the possibility. So, apparently, had their families. Vallance's husband, Anthony Kirk, did what many a soldier's spouse has done in wars past— he and baby Cheyenne moved back in with his family. Vallance's mother, a bit tentatively but proudly, told the *Detroit News*, "Women have finally made it, I guess." By spring, the awful reality of women coming home in body bags had happened, and two had been taken prisoner by Iraqis. And still the women's families voiced only pride.

That fall, the Clarence Thomas nomination went to the Senate for confirmation.

Congresswoman Patsy Mink of Hawaii, one of the six female House members who made the front-page frontal assault on the Senate during that tumultuous week, said that Hill's "almost criminal status" during her interrogation "very dramatically" changed the nation.

"The electorate, wholly apart from how they felt about Anita Hill, couldn't sit there with no women on the Judiciary Committee. That's what really hit everyone. Looking at all those faces. Not seeing a single woman. The huge disadvantage. Not only in that world but throughout

America in business, corporations, in other courtrooms," the Anita Hill debacle made a reality of the claim that women were being left out of the major decisions about their own lives.

The president again vetoed the Civil Rights and Family Leave bills. The economy's slide worsened, raising fears that women, often the "last hired, first fired," were taking much of the brunt of the recession, and exacerbating the already critical health care dilemma as family after family lost medical insurance along with jobs.

"Anita Hill had opened the door for a national conversation not just about sexual harassment but also on the role of men and women in this society," explained Carrick. Polls taken immediately after Anita Hill's testimony indicated the majority of Americans believed Clarence Thomas, not her; a year later, 44 percent of registered voters said they now believed her. Moreover, 47 percent told *The Wall Street Journal*/NBC News pollsters they thought the Senate had not treated her "properly and respectfully."[25]

What had happened, Carrick said, is the mothers told sons, wives told husbands, daughters told fathers that "sexual harassment was a real thing that touched a lot of people's lives. . . . It had been a sort of a weird Uncle Harold thing, something people hadn't talked about, then the Tailhook Association thing reinforced this deep dark family secret on the table for discussion."

The Tailhook scandal—a young woman naval lieutenant's charges that she and other military and civilian women had been forced to run a gauntlet of drunken navy pilots who stripped, groped, and otherwise sexually molested them during a convention of the U.S. Navy–affiliated pilots organization—had been ignored by military brass until a San Diego reporter got wind of it. It hit the news nearly simultaneously in early 1992 with America's realization that during the Gulf War women troops had been raped and molested at the hands of their own fellow soldiers.

By summer 1992, George Bush's Operation Desert Storm was no longer seen as the national victory it had been celebrated as the previous year.

"Now," Mink said that summer, "when you talk about Desert Storm, what comes up in people's minds is how badly women were treated over there. Even if we get into another military mess, that issue will become even more intense . . . equity for the women. The whole environment has been very profoundly changed."

Suddenly, issues that women politicians had been fine-tuning since

Helen Gahagan Douglas took her market basket into the House of Representatives were on the table. There were echoes of Martha Griffiths on economic fair play for women, and exasperated charges posed by Republican and Democratic congresswomen on the House Armed Services Committee that were reminiscent of Margaret Chase Smith's battles for equal treatment and equal opportunity for World War II's women who nursed, flew, drove, became prisoners of war, and saw enemy fire.

"I had always believed if women want equal rights, they have to shoulder equal responsibilities. These women were doing just that," the ninety-two-year-old senator recalled in 1990. Throughout society women were shouldering equally all manner of responsibilities once thought exclusively male, and it finally had become starkly evident they were not being treated as equal citizens.

Moreover, these pioneering women legislators had shown that going against the male bastion that Senator Smith once derisively labeled "the Galahads," going directly to the American people with an appeal to their sense of fair play and common sense, was a strategy that could move women forward. Putting all the elements together—the right issues, right race, right year—had been the stumbling block. In her first Senate campaign way back in 1974, Barbara Mikulski had talked about the daily problems of ordinary people trying to make ends meet to no avail. Democratic strategist Ann Lewis, who worked on that campaign, recalled: "I was sure that Barbara's very differences from traditional candidates were an asset. She looked and thought and talked like people; she knew what it meant to try and keep a family grocery store going when credit soared out of reach."[26]

But by 1992 voters were ready to consider trusting their lives and livelihoods to a new kind of politician, one who "looked and thought and talked like people." Women candidates were ready, and women voters were especially ready.

Patsy Mink said that summer, "Women now feel we have the chance as majority voters to make a difference, and it's time to do it. I think that's what's far more revolutionary."

An election that was the harbinger of 1992's acceptance of women candidates was the November 1991 Seattle municipal election. Veteran campaign manager Cathy Allen, who literally wrote the book on winning for women candidates (*Political Campaigning: A New Decade*) for the NWPC, was working dawn to midnight running city council races for four female candidates. The night before the election, she rushed home to change for some frantic last-minute, get-out-the-vote efforts and was broadsided by that Monday evening's episode of the television comedy "Designing Women," in which Julia Sugarbaker gives the Senate Judiciary Committee a piece of her ripe Southern mind. Allen's first reaction was a teary realization that she was not working herself to death campaigning "just for me. I'm doing this for history. For Anita . . ." Then she says a second thought overwhelmed her: "My God, they're all going to win tomorrow."

Three of her four candidates did indeed win the next day. Three other women won as well, bringing the total of women on the nine-person council to six. Moreover, Allen's campaigns all emphasized her candidates' female attributes first. Margaret Pageler's campaign brochure showed a well-worn pair of pumps with the line "Walk a Mile in Her Shoes . . . " and touted her as a "Mother, lawyer, community leader" who would "Walk a Mile for Us." It was a line that captured the essence of traditional female authority, maternal love, the extra length to which a mother would go, and situated Pageler in roles that have traditions of public service.

Pageler's campaign was absolutely the counter of virtually all previous advice to women. As recently as Josie Heath's 1990 race, Chicago political consultant David Axelrod admits that he was telling her and other women candidates, "A lot of what is going to accrue to you by dint of being a woman you are going to get. You don't need to remind people." The underlying concern, almost a First Commandment for women who would run, was: "Don't offend men voters." To offend male voters also meant risking offending more traditional, stay-at-home women whose economic well-being was tied to their menfolk. But "Don't offend men voters" also meant muddying whatever the candidate's message might be by remaking her to fit, as closely as possible, the all-male-is-normal paradigm. It was, in effect, a gag order that made it impossible for her to link her classic strengths—women's altruistic tradition—with the issues that were distinctly hers.

Cathy Allen's breakthrough was to find messages for her candidates that established female authority in nonthreatening terms and let them be who they were. One of Pageler's mail pieces showed a neatly tended, white-shingled bungalow and the words *"How you see your house. . . . "* Inside was a house made of stacks of $20, $50, and $100 bills and the words ". . . *how* they *see your house.*" The message, a version of the same message that Pageler was using on every issue, whether it was abortion, the homeless, the health care crisis, or the threat of crime: *"Margaret Pageler sees your house the way you do."*

Allen produced her most radical campaign literature and candidate in black, lesbian Sherry Harris, whose most striking direct-mail piece was a folder emblazoned with a close-up of an American eagle motif on a red-and-white Colonial-style woven coverlet. The one word on the front page was *"Values."* Were it not that the messenger was a large, African- American woman engineer with a memorable white-streaked Afro, whose acknowledged domestic partner is a grandmother, one could easily have imagined Barry Goldwater using the same message in his 1964 presidential campaign. The nuances, and the new appeal to fairness and common sense, were inside:

> Values define a person's soul.
>
> They are the basis for what you believe, what you feel and what you do. Values are also what unite us. When differences divide, values are what keep us together . . . building the trust needed to get things done.
>
> Seattle is a diverse and proud community . . . our values make us greater collectively than we are individually. Community leaders need to reflect the values of the people they represent; when those values change and opinions grow more enlightened, so must their leaders.[27]

Harris's campaign was so compelling that the *Seattle Post-Intelligencer* editorialized "For better or worse, Seattle voters have a clear choice. . . . One is the candidate of yesterday. The other [Harris] is the candidate of tomorrow."

While Allen and Harris were changing the gender makeup of Seattle's city council, Ann Richards in Texas was counseling a WCF audience on what she had learned in years "at this business of politics and government."

Her key message was listen to the voters—in focus groups if the campaign can afford it—but, wherever, really listen, not just to what voters might be concerned about, not just the issues, but the ways in which they voice their concerns about the issues:

> I said for years if my mama in Waco, Texas, cannot understand it you have wasted your time. My mama is not stupid . . . she knows it when she hears

the truth . . . This does not mean I am only going to go out and campaign on what I think my mama wants to hear about. It means, when I campaign on an issue, I am going to put it in words my mama understands . . . language that is theirs [voters] not mine. . . .

Most women [candidates] . . . want to tell me what they are for . . . and I am glad that there are issues of importance to you, but they are not going to win a political race. . . . Unless you . . . hear what the people actually think about the issues, you have completely and totally wasted your time. . . .

If the electorate in 1992 was primed for more women candidates like Ann Richards, the phenomenon nonetheless took much of the political establishment by surprise, especially more conservative Republicans. Republican women were already sharply divided on the abortion issue, but after Patrick Buchanan's call to cultural war on opening night of the national convention, some very high-profile, formerly staunch party activists and major donors, among them Harriet Wieder, a veteran Orange County, California, supervisor, threw their support to Democrat Bill Clinton.

Democrat Carrick, though clearly partisan, watched the Republican party's convention with near disbelief: "I think they really thought they could make a case that Wade and June Cleaver were the perfect model for American society, as well as the natural order of things. The Democrats were proposing radical changes, and the Republicans were opposing the changes that had already happened. They wanted to put everyone back into their little boxes, starting with women."

Sharon Rodine, the former president of the NWPC, noted that "Democrats were showing women who were seeking power on their own. Republicans, by putting Barbara [Bush] and Marilyn [Quayle] out front meant to showcase non-offensive, appropriate women, women who were affiliated to men who had power."

By the national party conventions, however, it had become clear that the most perturbing question of the 1992 electoral cycle was what the future role of American women would be. It was a central theme in the presidential contest, and it played out in every contest in which a woman was running, although it presented a different strategic problem in each. Would Washington voters accept as senator a woman who was proclaimed as "a mom in tennis shoes"? Could Californians accept two women who not only no longer seemed worried about offending male voters, but, in claiming their affinity with the movies' murderous heroines Thelma and Louise, were openly on the offensive against the male-dominated system? In Illinois, the Land of Lincoln, would voters looking for outsiders be able to overcome both gender and racial prejudices and elect to the U.S. Senate a black, divorced, single mother who opponents claimed was tainted by years of fealty to Chicago's infamous Democratic machine?

Patty Murray's race in Washington State was probably the most groundbreaking, and could be the textbook case of the 1992 elections: She decided to run because of Anita Hill. Few gave her a chance. Early on she won over likely constituencies—women's groups, educators, labor. She was able to link her candidacy to national issues because of local events, most notably the sexual misconduct scandal that caused the incumbent, Senator Brock Adams, to abruptly drop out of the race. She had more than one "hardship" story that both provided any needed "toughness" and established her as a fighter for ordinary people. Most recently it had been nursing her elderly parents through health problems; earlier it had been the incident that launched her political career and gave her the nickname "just a mom in tennis shoes."

"In 1980, Patty had two small children at home and was part of a parent-run coop nursery school at the local college," recounts campaign manager Theresa Purcell. "One day the legislature cut out the funding, and Patty just loaded her kids into the car and went down to Olympia to see what she could do. She was told by some legislator 'You can't do anything. You're just a mom in tennis shoes.'" Murray went home, organized 12,000 Washingtonians, and got the situation changed.

"People who work to make a living and raise kids and take care of elderly parents feel they don't have a voice in government. Patty knew, from talking to them, there was a real frustration with government. She wasn't talking political language. . . . Our message was very clear. We didn't have to monkey around with it much. Patty Murray had shown she's one of them," explained Purcell.

The message was so simple, essentially it was Murray herself, that Beth Sullivan recalls having to fight with other political professionals not to try to bury the "just a mom in tennis shoes" label. "Most of the people in the campaign were adamant against using it in any way, shape, or form. They said, 'She'll be accused of being insubstantial. . . . It reinforces the negatives. . . . It says she's not experienced, not ready,'" which was precisely the tack taken by her general election opponent.

Sullivan argued back that she wasn't going to use the line in the campaign literature. "I wasn't even going to push it a whole lot . . . but we did use it in the first getting-to-know-you ad. . . . And in her speeches Patty would say, 'A lot of people are saying I can't win, but I'm used to tough fights' and then tell the story. 'I might not fit the standard people expect a U.S. senator to be, but I'm used to fighting the odds.'"

The proof was in the polling. "In the first polls, Patty had a 1 percent name ID, but the margin of error was plus or minus 5 percent. Nobody seemed to know her but Theresa, me, her next-door neighbor, her family, and her kids. But by July, the 'mom in tennis shoes' had a 28 to 30 percent name ID. No one still knew who Patty Murray was," but by the primary, voters had put label to name and she was the highest vote-getter.

Ed Zuckerman, who worked on both Barbara Boxer's and Murray's campaign, said, "It was a combination of who Patty was, what she said, and how she said it which did an end run around all the men. And that's how her campaign won out over [party] insiders, and ultimately won. It was a race like this state has never seen before.

"As strategists our biggest concern was . . . the word *average*. Average is just like you and me, but the downside is do we want our United States senator to be 'average'? Don't we want 'excellent'? What we really wanted to emphasize was that Patty was middle class, not one of those millionaire country-club types who go to the Senate, and she had some very extraordinary qualities, so that when someone voted for her they could feel they were voting for someone very very unique."

Boxer's race, on the other hand, presented two very complicated and totally different strategic problems, Zuckerman explained.

"While both were riding the same wave, the way they implemented their campaigns was totally different. They were two totally different people, with totally different backgrounds. . . . If we had generically run women as women it wasn't going to work. . . . In Barbara's situation, we had to deal with the change issue in a very different manner. She'd been in Congress ten years. . . . "

Boxer had also been caught up in the House banking scandal and was one of 355 representatives revealed to have written checks on insufficient funds, a situation her primary opponent, Congressman Mel Levine, tried to capitalize on by pointing out he had bounced zero. Boxer had bounced 148, but her handlers hoped she would benefit by facing the issue squarely and strategized that voters' presumption that women are more honest and less corruptible would hold for her. Ironically, it did not work as either candidate had hoped. Boxer felt the full brunt of the negative, especially in the general election, but Levine, by making so much of the issue, confused at least some of the voters—polls showed 3 percent thought he was a check bouncer, too. Boxer was later cleared of any illegality.

In the primary, Boxer clearly benefited from the outsider status tendered her simply because of gender. "Her opponents were two middle-aged white men," and, as consultant Bradshaw explained, "her natural style made it possible for voters to believe she was the agent of change. In the general election, we weren't the outsiders anymore."

In fact, Boxer's opponent was a political newcomer, the extreme right-wing television commentator Bruce Herschensohn.

"We had to do something extremely difficult in politics. Between the primary and the general, we had to totally shift the focus of the contrast that had gotten us where we were. Our polling showed us that as soon as voters realized Barbara was an 'incumbent,' with all the problems and the checks and all, our support would erode quickly."

Indeed, it did. But the campaign had anticipated that "the dynamic of the race was to come out of the primary with a big lead. Sooner or later we would see the race tighten up and the reporters would be writing 'Boxer's in trouble.'" The campaign then would have to grin and bear it and save its ammunition—money for the big television ad buys—until they could, in effect, see the whites of the voters' eyes, the last three weeks before the election. "Even knowing ahead of time that it's going to spin, it's hard to hold a steady course," Bradshaw admitted.

The turning point in mid-September was aided by serendipity. Some two dozen Herschensohn supporters, mostly college-age men according to press reports, harangued a group of women "Republicans for Boxer" at a Newport Beach campaign stop. The Herschensohn gang was so rowdy and the possibility the event might turn nasty so evident that Boxer watched from her car a few minutes, then decided to cancel her appearance. "They were calling supporters sluts, lesbians and femi-Nazis," Boxer aide Julie Buckner told the *San Francisco Chronicle* (September 17, 1992). "Barbara's a tough guy; we didn't cancel it for her, but for our people." Television cameras captured it all, and wavering Republican moderates, who had begun to feel more comfortable with the toned-down Herschensohn of campaign ads, began to turn again to Boxer.

Those last three weeks, Boxer hit Herschensohn with ads that showed his own television commentaries in which he had opposed not only abortion rights but social security, and had declared the only governmental budget he would not cut was defense.

"We knew all we had to do was convince voters Herschensohn was out of step with California."

And the most important positive the campaign had going for it was "Barbara's style. Her feistiness. She makes people believe 'This woman is going to go to Washington and fight for me.' It was a case where the style of the messenger and the substance of the message was merged."

Whereas the word *feisty* had always been considered a putdown by women candidates—"You talk about a feisty little dog," sniffed one—Boxer now capitalized on it as a *feminine* way to be a fighter, and played with her fighter image by selling bright yellow "BOXER" shorts. Celinda Lake explained, "Voters like feisty," and they were no longer so certain that they liked the idea of "tough"—that is, like-male, like-old politics—in women candidates.

"Barbara's hot and Dianne is cool," Lake added. "In both cases they had to make voters comfortable with their personal styles. Too far either way and the voters would balk. Barbara's 'hot' became 'feisty'; Dianne's cool became 'senatorial.' And [when Feinstein ended her campaign with an ad showing her nuzzling her newborn grandchild] that grandchild ad showed her warmth. Voters respond to women candidates' personalities. Women are much more vivid to them because they are in a nontraditional role."

Not only was Dianne Feinstein no longer trumpeting her toughness, but she appeared to be making up for a lifetime of being too-male identified with explicit acts of sisterhood. When, on the eve of the primary at a pro-choice rally in Los Angeles, she joined Boxer on the dais and the two held their hands high, Boxer's male opponents "were furious" that she had appeared to endorse Boxer and link their candidacies. When someone confronted her and asked if she was endorsing Boxer, she smiled and said, "I came very close, didn't I?"

The question on everyone's mind was whether even a state so trendsetting as California would elect two women to the Senate. Even *Ms.* magazine had headlined the notion that two women could be elected from the same state the same year "California Dreamin'?" Women Democratic loyalists were worried that "a lot of people will say one woman is enough. Like it's a kind of personal affirmative action—one women, one man." Mervin Field, of the California Poll, admitted he had no hard numbers for his gut feeling that "they could be locked in a silent subtle battle for the same supporters and the same dollars." Ironically, Feinstein's opponent, the Republican appointed to fill Pete Wilson's Senate seat, John Seymour, was counting on the same thing. But his spin on it, according to his staff, was that even Republicans wouldn't be able to vote for the right-wing Herschensohn, so would throw that vote to Boxer. Seymour then would benefit from even Democrats' guilt at voting for such a left-wing woman.

In fact, Bill Carrick said, from the beginning the two women's campaigns knew the political pundits were out of touch with the voters. "Basically, no matter how we posed the question [in polls]—'Would you rather vote for two Democratic women, or are you more inclined to vote for one Republican man and one Democratic woman?'—we got better than 50 percent for two women. We did it all kinds of ways. 'Is it time to have a woman in the U.S. Senate?' Again an overwhelming majority said yes. 'Would it make you feel better if California was to have this historic opportunity to send two women . . . ?' Again, overwhelming majorities."

Boxer's consultant Bradshaw said, "When we phrased the question: 'Is it about time to send two women to the Senate?' sixty-two percent said yes. And those were general election voters, not just Democrats."

Carol Moseley-Braun's numbers were equally supportive, but there was one disturbing hint that portended a strategic nightmare. In early focus groups, Celinda Lake had posed a rather routine question about Operation Head Start.

"Normally, voters just love the Head Start Program. They think of it as helping everyone. But with Carol they were suddenly interpreting it far more narrowly. 'Yeah, it's help [for] her own people. . . . Welfare . . . etc.' That response tipped us to the fact that everything about her was being viewed through a racial prism."

When the first three ads from Republican candidate Richard Williamson's camp linked Moseley-Braun to Jesse Jackson, Harold Washington, and then Gus Savage (a notoriously anti-white, anti-Semitic former congressman from Chicago), "It was clear that the Republicans were saying, 'This is a black woman. Watch out,'" says Heather Booth. Because Moseley-Braun had been close to Harold Washington, and had worked with the Daley organization, Williamson tried to negate her "outsider" advantage by calling her a "machine Democrat." A whisper campaign linked her, falsely, to Nation of Islam leader Louis Farrakhan. And once the racial framework was established, even the messages "It's time to make history" or "It's time for a change" fell on troubled white ears: "Not all white people were sure they were part of that history . . . part of that change," Booth added.

The campaign countered all of this by putting the candidate on camera, full-face, "with that incredible smile of hers" talking about who she was—a policeman's daughter who had worked her way through the University of Chicago Law School, a woman whose upbringing and values were as middle class and comforting to the voters as their next-door neighbor's.

"None of this increased his numbers or decreased hers" until Moseley-Braun was accused of benefiting from a $20,000-plus windfall profit on some land that her elderly, nursing-home-bound mother should have declared to Medicaid authorities. "Then, the entire language around that—'welfare fraud,' 'laundering money'—was so racist that if Williamson had had more positives he might have won," Booth declared.

"In the end, the campaign was between racial fears and women's hopes. Women's hopes won."

Women won a great deal in the 1992 elections. They proved themselves to themselves as much as to the voters. "Enough women ran and ran well that questions of viability won't be raised again, and white men will now have to work on the assumption that, in the Democratic primary at least, a woman may have the advantage," Lake said.

There are problems remaining, however. Carrick believes women "still have to establish their credentials and record. [It's] still more important for a woman to communicate [that] to voters than it is for a man, but now," he says, political consultants are faced with a new problem: "Find the ways in which you can tell men to be like women. Absolutely. The Alan Alda New-Age Guy is sort of a joke, but it's now more important for a man to establish his sensitive, caring, empathic side than for a woman to establish her tough, hard-nosed edge."

As this discussion about the nitty-gritty of political campaigns was taking place in January 1993, American troops—men and women—were waging peace and trying to feed the multitudes in Somalia. The last of the old Cold Warriors, George Bush, was boasting of "going into the grandchildren business" now that his term as president was over, and the irony was that the "kinder and gentler" America he had promised four years earlier seemed to be becoming real. A New-Age Guy, peace-loving and possibly even draft-dodging, was settling in as president and commander-in-chief at the White House, with a First Lady who not only had demonstrated cookie baking skill but also had vast reservoirs of political savvy. On one emotional day in what was a very emotional month, Barbara Boxer, after the swearing in of the new United States Senate, was asked by a reporter whether she would tone down her legendary feistiness now that she was a senator?

"Nope," she said, grinning through tears. "I'm just going to be me."

10

Losing

Risk as a Rite of Passage

As the races of 1992 were beginning to take shape, and day one of an election cycle is the day after the results have confirmed who has won and who has lost the previous race, a peculiar phenomenon was occurring. There were smiles, confident smiles, on a lot of losers' faces. One of those was Dianne Feinstein, who lost little time in announcing she would run in 1992 for the U.S. Senate. Another was a striking, dark-haired, dark-eyed Santa Clara County supervisor named Anna Eshoo, who had run unsuccessfully for Congress in 1988 against California Congressman Tom Campbell.

Eshoo's had been a grueling but innovative race. Campbell, a pro-choice liberal Republican with strong ties to the Silicon Valley business community, had appeared to be an unbeatable candidate: He was young, attractive, a Stanford professor on leave from the law school; and, the district was thought to be a "safe" seat for Republicans. Also, one of the campaign gimmicks Democrat Eshoo had tried had some political operatives almost laughing. They said she'd wasted her money on a videotape that she distributed to targeted on-the-fence voters instead of putting the money where campaign pros always want money put: last-minute television and radio buys. At a Women's Campaign Fund (WCF) function that fall, she tried to explain it to skeptics: The videotape meant busy people could listen and think about what she had to say when they had the time and the motivation to turn their attention to the election. Her message wouldn't get lost in some thirty-second break between the evening news and a dog food commercial.

Campbell won. Eshoo lost and ran again for supervisor in 1990. Then it became clear there would be dual Senate races in California in 1992. Campbell saw an opportunity to move up, and Anna Eshoo suddenly had Campbell's open seat to run for in 1992. Lo and behold, some of the key voters she would be targeting in that race still had her videotape on the shelf.

Losing the 1988 election had merely slowed, not stopped, Anna Eshoo. In late 1991, at a small WCF fund-raiser for another candidate, Eshoo brandished a 1984 *Time* magazine she said her sixteen-year-old daughter kept framed on her bedroom wall like a rock star poster, and then recounted what the woman on the cover had meant to her. Geraldine Ferraro had flown cross-country to campaign for her, boosted her spirits when she was down, and, most important, taught her how to go on when she lost.

"Gerry, you were there for me."

Election night 1984, Geraldine Ferraro had done her motherly-wifely-womanly best to keep her own family's spirits up, too. "It was ridiculous," she admitted. "We couldn't just sit there like corpses watching the Democratic ticket being slaughtered on television. Impulsively I sat on Johnny's lap to cheer him up. Then Laura got on my lap and Donna on hers. *Life* magazine snapped a photo of this family pile. . . . The picture looks like we had all just come home happily exhausted from a family wedding . . . [except] it was more like a wake."[1]

She would boast, later, near midnight that night, that her candidacy meant "American women will never be second-class citizens again," but her words would have the hollow sound of concession, not victory. All the hopes, the dreams, the surge in the polls that so enthusiastically hailed her nomination, had fizzled like a campfire on a rainy night. She'd known it would be Reagan-Bush for days. Even while she was delivering some of the most powerful and personal rah-rah speeches of the campaign, she had gently prepared her own disbelieving mother for the defeat.

That final day she worked on the concession speech that, for her supporters' sake, she wanted upbeat, cheery, and congratulatory. She could say to herself, and she believed it, that the voters hadn't really rejected her—"No incumbent President has ever been turned out of office in a year of economic growth."[2] She could blame a sluggish voter turn out, and console herself that the pundits were saying "the American public hadn't voted in a President. They had voted in a king."

She could say, and later did in her memoir of the campaign, that the fact she had not even carried her own Queens district was "irrelevant . . . my constituents were voting as they always had, for the Republican presidential candidate, not against the Democratic vice presidential candidate."[3]

Even though one of her secret service detachment, who would disappear the following day along with all the other trappings of power, assured her "You're a winner,"[4] she had lost the most important race an American woman had ever participated in, and she knew it.

As she made her last public appearance as the first woman vice presidential candidate, she couldn't look at her own family for fear of crying. The bottom line was this: 36 million voters had said yes to the Mondale-Ferraro ticket, 42 million had said no. Geraldine Ferraro was not only out of a job—a job she'd excelled at and loved—but her family was deeply in debt because she had stood in for all the women of America and run for vice president, plus Mondale staffers bitterly blamed her and her much-discussed "negatives" for sinking the Democratic ship.

Those negatives would haunt her over the next few months as her name was bandied about as a potential senatorial candidate for the 1986 race. Women, at least traditional wives and mothers, the very voters her nomination had been designed to reach, hated her candidacy. Polls in early 1985 showed their fear of her had not abated. She declined to run. To some observers, it appeared Gerry Ferraro's political career was over.

Then one day the phone rang, she recalled in an interview in January 1991. It was her attorney, with a rather unusual offer, one that would add another controversy to her already controversial image.

The Pepsi-Cola Company was planning a television ad campaign using nationally known "leaders" talking about choices they had made in their lives, implicitly suggesting viewers choose Diet Pepsi over Diet Coke. Would she consider it? Chrysler Corporation chairman Lee Iacocca had already filmed one of the commercials, and Pepsi was said to be negotiating with Russian defector and ballet star Mikhail Baryshnikov.

"When my lawyer first called me up and said, 'Gerry, Pepsi wants you to do a commercial,' I said, 'Oh, give me a break!' But he said, 'Gerry, it's a lot of money.' I said, 'How do I do a Pepsi commercial? I mean, am I gonna start singing and dancing around?' He said, 'No, it's a campaign about choices and you can write your own script.'"

That, Ferraro maintains, was the reason she could accept doing the ad.

"We had just had this poll. And I said, 'Okay, can we do it talking about Choices in Life?' And they said, 'Yes,' so we wrote our own script. . . .

"Now the exact wording I don't know . . . It's like thirty seconds . . . My elder daughter walks in and I'm sitting cozily . . . reading. And, I looked pretty good in my little Anne Klein outfit . . . Typical housewife!

"We sit . . . I'm reading the *Times* and Donna walks in and says, 'Looking for a job?'

"And I go, 'Very funny.'

"With that my younger daughter walks in supposedly from out on the beach or wherever . . . and she says, 'Well, I am.'

"Donna turns around and says, 'Well, what is it this week? Astronaut?' Because Laura is the type of kid who can never make a decision. . . .

"One of them turns to me and asks, 'What choice was the best choice you ever made, Mom?'

"Laura says, 'Politics?' At which point Laura is sitting next to me and I have my arm around her.

"I go, 'Uhmmm, no, being a mother.'

"And that's how the thing fades out, with Laura in my arms, me being a mother.

"And the reason we did that was to show that as much as I had accomplished, perhaps as much as any person in the country, except for the people who actually get elected to national office . . . there was one accomplishment that far surpassed everything else and that was my family. Motherhood.

"Now I don't know if anybody saw that and realized that's what we were doing. . . . [And] and I would lie to you, I would be less than candid, if I said I did not like the money. I got extremely good money. I have never gotten paid that way in my life. And I will never again I am sure. It was wonderful."

The money was variously reported to be in the range of $500,000 (*The Washington Post*) to $750,000 (*San Jose Mercury News*). Both Pepsi and Ferraro declined to confirm the actual dollar figure, but the amount must have been considerable because, according to the Associated Press's Kim Mills, Ferraro included more than $500,000 1991 income from PepsiCo in federal campaign finance disclosures at the beginning of her Senate campaign.

Ferraro was immediately attacked by the press, as well as by some of the very women who had helped conceive her candidacy for what they saw, and in some cases still see, as a devaluation "of what we had tried to do," said one campaign insider in early 1991. "I believed American women and Mondale and the Democratic party had a great investment in her. . . . Then to see her take what I thought was an investment in her and use it for commercial purposes . . . I mean I was appalled. Completely appalled."

Another woman, one of Ferraro's most stalwart backers, was also still furious in 1991. "I have finally blanked it out of my mind. I don't go to sleep at night thinking 'That——Pepsi ad!' the way I used to," she said. When asked if Democrats had had the same reaction to retired House speaker Tip O'Neill's ads for a luggage firm after he left office, this woman replied sharply: "Tip O'Neill was not ours."

San Jose Mercury columnist Joanne Jacobs was among many journalists who blasted Ferraro for trivializing women and their choices in life after her campaign had said women should be taken seriously.

> Ferraro's commercial takes a symbol—the tough, smart, competent professional who is also a traditional wife and mother and turns it into [something like] . . . Mr. Whipple's ardor for toilet paper.
>
> Even if it was mostly hype, that symbol meant something to a lot of women, even those who didn't vote the Democratic ticket. Now it's been made to look as silly as a comparison between choosing a career and choosing a cold drink.[5]

The Washington Post reported that Ferraro was "neither identified by name nor shown full face" in the commercial and quoted a Ferraro adviser, Frances O'Brien, "'They don't hawk the product. . . . It's a gamble. There's no doubt about it,' said O'Brien. 'Ninety-nine percent of the people in this town will assume that by doing this commercial she's dead politically.'"

Ferraro obviously knew that the press and her supporters would label such an ad a sell-out, and that she might indeed be politically dead as a result. Why did she open herself to such criticism? Clearly it was the decision of a very pragmatic woman, and, judging by the strange new media venues, "Saturday Night Live," "Donahue," and gossip columnist

Larry King's radio and television call-in shows on which 1992's presidential candidates showed up, a precursor of the ways candidates would learn to use whatever opportunities were made available to get their messages across.

The Pepsi ad was "free media." In one fell swoop Ferraro wiped out much, perhaps all, of her financial debt from the 1984 campaign and took a stab at reducing her much-publicized negatives. However, for the risk it posed to her credibility among political feminists and others, it appears unlikely it delivered the sympathy from traditional stay-at-home wives and mothers that Ferraro had hoped. She still polled badly that year and did not run in 1986. The entire Pepsi-Cola "choices" campaign was yanked soon after Ferraro's segment aired in March 1985. Ferraro says she was told it was because anti-abortion activists thought the campaign was a subliminal push for abortion rights.

Clearly, however, Ferraro was already laying the groundwork for whatever her next race would be. And by 1991, when she was ready to run for the U.S. Senate, both of the anonymous women quoted above were back in her camp, citing, among their reasons, their earlier "investment" in her and all that her candidacy had meant to women.

In retrospect, it is only in the magnitude of Ferraro's loss in 1984, and her willingness to gamble her future on a diet drink ad if it would help her career, that Ferraro was any different from any woman who runs for political office and loses. Note: We did not say any man *or* woman who loses, but "any woman."

To lose any election is a painful and potentially devastating thing, whether the candidate is female or male. But it can be argued that losing is still a different experience for women than it is for men, because of many of the same constraints to women's candidacies that we have discussed earlier, plus one more. Women have not been taught how to lose. For the generations of women who grew up before Congresswoman Patsy Mink led the fight to add what she has called "those three little words"—saying opportunities for education cannot be denied "because of sex"—to Title IX of the Education Amendment Act of 1972 (that is, before the days little girls were welcomed in Little League, before schools were required to invest equal funds in boys' and girls' sports and educational programs) women had fewer experiences with losing, especially as part of a team. Women's experiences with losing had almost always come from competition with one another—for parental attention, grades, friends, and especially for men. As a result, they seldom developed a sense of sisterhood or team give-and-take. Further, that meant most of their experiences with losing were limited to very personal and painful events.

Add to this the fact that many women still cannot acknowledge their political ambition and the act of running for office has to become an expression of a role they feel is more acceptable—the female mother-wife-nurturer-altruist. These women declare they are running for office for their children, for the environment, and for future generations. This denial turns running for office into a very personal, almost intimate gesture that, if rebuffed, is experienced as a rejection not of the party or the political issue but of the person herself. When politics is a cause, not merely a career that women can acknowledge they have chosen, losing also becomes a failure to deliver for those who were counting on them and, by extension, a failure to nurture, a failure to adequately care for those for whom they are the mother-doers. The personal psychic risk for women in running for office becomes something very different from the risk experienced by a man.

Madeleine Kunin talked about this limitation in women's lives and political abilities in her 1989 speech at Harvard's Institute of Politics. "Our motivations for entering [politics] are, in fact, personal, a reflection of our values, our desire to see change occur according to some ideal. But the public life necessary to realize that ideal is very different. We are still learning the culture of public life; dealing with the conflict, going into battle, and emerging from battle with the strength to continue the fight."

She went on to describe "an innocent insight" she'd gleaned from a conversation with the mother of a small boy who "described how her son prepared for a hockey game. He put on his shoulder pads, his knee pads, his six layers of clothing, his helmet. He was literally armed for the battle, and he expected to fight. He was prepared to get hurt, and he had built up his protective layers."

Not being prepared for the risks of the political battle has another dimension. The consensus among many political professionals—and a problematic flip side that is a major barrier to women's success—is that women often don't understand it is okay to lose. They have not grasped, or haven't yet completely internalized, the plain fact that losing an election, especially one deemed unwinnable, can be a rite of passage in a political career, a way of paying dues or earning stripes and collecting markers. In other words, it can be a positive, not a negative, event.

Much has been written about Richard Nixon's angry "You won't have

Richard Nixon to kick around anymore," after he lost the California governor's race in 1962, and of both Bill Clinton's and Michael Dukakis's black days after voters in their states showed them the door following their first stints as governor. They seem exceptions to the rule. Whatever their internal grief, outwardly most male politicians appear to deal with a lost election as an unfortunate but often necessary step in a long journey. This doesn't seem to be just a political manifestation of "Big boys don't cry," or the way men are socialized in our society, but a by-product of the way men view political careers.

There is an economic component of this as well. Because women often "find" themselves in politics, as advocates of an issue rather than as a result of a career plan, they seldom have structured their lives around political realities.

Sharon Rodine, the former president of the National Women's Political Caucus (NWPC), thinks that women need to take a lesson from men: The way the good old boys prepare for a career in public office also helps them lose and come back.

"They do a little stint in the National Guard. Maybe Indiana, who knows? A little military stuff . . . Then they go to law school and they have a photogenic wife and a couple of kids and they run for office the first time knowing they are going to lose, but just for the name recognition. . . . They can always come back to the law firm.

"They get on the United Way board [or] a public corporate board. And they are finance chair for somebody else's campaign, [meanwhile] they are always watching for openings, and the second or third time they run—fine. They are in.

"It's all part of the process," she says.

"When women run, they jump out too late, with too little money. They come from a background of issues. The guys are there to advance their careers; the women are there as issue advocates. They care about something. Or they really want to serve the public. . . .

"And so they jump in, and if they lose very few of them over the years have ever come out again. They feel they have let everybody down. They take it personally.

"There's a grieving process [for both men and women]. As men grow up they have a network. They can take a certain number of risks. They expect they may lose. They don't take the loss personally, and there's always a group to help them whether it's a sports team way back in junior high or [the law firm]. . . . You win, you lose, you are part of a team, you go on to the next game.

"I'm not saying men don't take it personally, but what we hear over and over from women is they feel they have let their supporters down. As opposed to men who say, 'Too bad, didn't win this time,' while they are already starting to look for their next option. Women just close up. And fold their tents. . . ."

The exceptions to the pattern Rodine describes have truly been exceptions, especially early on. "I would not have gotten here [Congress] if I had not been more persistent than a hound dog worrying a bone," declared Idaho's Gracie Bowers Pfost.

Pfost, a veteran state and county-level politician, first ran for Congress in 1950 but lost to the incumbent by only 783 votes. She bounced back in two years with a campaign slogan designed to etch her name in the voters' minds: "Tie Your Vote to a Solid Post: Gracie Pfost for Congress." She won by 591 votes and went on to serve five terms.[6]

Looking back, it is clear that the spirit that gave the early women in Congress the will to run brought them back again and again to the political arena despite formidable barriers in their way. In an era in which women were shielded from risk-taking, much more so even than among later generations, their "bravada" is astonishing. For some it may have been the toughness they developed as suffragists, for others it may have been an extension of the pioneer ethos that had brought their immediate ancestors west—Westerners are represented disproportionately among these early congresswomen. Many maintained an astonishing level of denial about the sexism they could see existed elsewhere, but somehow couldn't see applied as fully to them as to their less politically astute sisters.

Those who lost a race and came back to win are such a minuscule sample, a minority within an already tiny minority, that it is hard to draw any conclusion other than they were very determined and unusual women who set high standards for those who have followed. And in doing so, they suffered indignities political women still experience.

When Jeannette Rankin, the nation's first woman in Congress, faced her first reelection campaign for her Montana seat in 1918, she also found herself the first victim of a ploy that has been used on more than one occasion since to oust a woman from office. She was gerrymandered: The lines of her district were changed in a way that gave her opposition an advantage. It is a tactic that has been used to unseat some formidable women, including Bella Abzug, Margaret Heckler, and Millicent Fenwick.

Rankin's first race in 1916 had been for one of two at-large seats, and she campaigned despite and against "just-below-the-surface prejudice against women," her niece Mackey Brown wrote in 1971. In fact, she seems to have campaigned very much as 1992's winners did.

> Jeannette had faith in the women, and in the men who were big enough to know what women were worth. She spoke to them about World War I and whether they wanted their sons to be sent to fight it; she made them believe that what they thought mattered; she talked to the women as if they were people of pride and dignity instead of chattels who should take their pea brains off into the kitchen and pretend they had no minds or opinions. And running in a field of eight candidates [two to be elected] she was elected . . .
>
> But when the 1918 campaign for that seat rolled around, she faced two great obstacles: one was her vote against U.S. entry into World War I . . . the other bigger one was the fact that [politicians and mining interests] . . . apparently alarmed by the fact a woman had actually beaten six male candidates . . . gerrymandered the state into two districts, one heavily Republican and the other, the western district from which Jeannette, a Republican, must run, heavily Democratic. . . . Jeannette decided to run for the Senate instead, and lost. But she learned a lot.[7]

It would be twenty-two years before Jeannette Rankin ran again; she was a peace activist throughout the interim. But she did run—in 1940, again on the issue of "foreign wars are no part of the American way of life."[8] This time she won, in the same heavily Democratic district that had rejected her in 1918. In December 1941 she was the only member of either house of Congress to vote against entering World War II. "She needed protection from the Capitol Police to get back to her offices in the Cannon Building, and after her vote . . . [i]n the heat of patriotic fervor it was said that her second term ended for all practical purposes the day the Japanese bombed Pearl Harbor."[9]

Another remarkable woman, and one of the first to openly acknowledge that defeat is a part of the political process, was Gladys Pyle, South Dakota's first woman U.S. senator.

A high school teacher and the daughter of a suffragist mother and an attorney father who also actively supported suffrage, Pyle worked her way up through the ranks of the Republican party in the 1920s, and was still active in public service well into her nineties. In 1930, however, she was defeated in her bid to be the Republican nominee for governor. She led a field of five at the party convention, but the three top vote-getters behind her, all male, threw their support to the fifth place candidate, another man. She lost on the last ballot. More than a half century later that race was still being recalled as the most bitter in the state's history.[10] Her response, which was repeated in a congressional tribute in 1984, could be engraved on the lintel of any government edifice: "If a person decides to enter politics then they must risk both success and failure—you have to take both with a smile."[11]

Although Gladys Pyle arguably could be called the first woman elected to the U.S. Senate in her own right, she was never sworn in and therefore was never a senator in anything more than title. She won a special election in November 1938—by 43,000 votes—to finish the three months remaining in the term of the late Senator Peter Norbeck. During that time Congress was never in session.

Pyle's accomplishments indicate she was quite aware of the inequalities inflicted on her gender, but oblivious—or perhaps purposely impervious—to those inflicted on her because of gender. She fought throughout her life for children and women, and was instrumental in 1947 in ensuring that South Dakota women would be represented on juries. But she refused to admit that her sex played any part in her own 1930 defeat or the fact that she was never slated for a meaningful national office. In 1984, at the age of ninety-four, she summed up her career for television's "First Monday," a network magazine show: "It just took somebody to break the ice in the harbor so more important ships can come in."

Pyle's metaphor is well taken; for women, politics may indeed be very icy waters. Politics is always a risky business, and women have traditionally been protected from risk rather than urged to embrace it. Culturally, women have been limited to *kinder, kirche, küche;* professionally, their sphere permitted teaching and marginal entrepreneurial endeavors of the butter-and-egg-money sort. Even well into this century, women were "protected" out of the mainstream because they were thought too frail and easily shocked to be exposed to the real world.

In one ironic sense, political women are often protected from risk by being slated for unwinnable offices or by being given only token opportunities as a kind of payment for years of envelope stuffing and precinct walking. To paraphrase Michigan's legendary feminist congresswoman,

Martha Griffiths, one wonders if the protection is of women or of men's jobs.[12] Pyle's three months as a senator when Congress was not in session and could not act was essentially meaningless. Rebecca Latimer Felton's one day in the Senate in 1922, after more than fifty years of public service, was a sop to the fearsome new "women's vote."

This sort of tokenism extends to status offices within the parties as well. "In politics, as in marriage and business, women get pretty much the treatment they are willing to accept," Democratic national committeewoman India Edwards told *Independent Woman* magazine in 1947.[13]

Five years later, the presidential election year 1952, saw a sort of boomlette of interest in political women. Clare Booth Luce and Margaret Chase Smith both were touted as possible vice presidential candidates on the Republican side; Judge Sarah Hughes and Edwards were mentioned on the Democratic side. Acting on her own earlier advice, Edwards already had declined an opportunity that year to become Democratic National Committee chairman, saying, "A moment when party affairs [are] so snarled that no man appeared to be available for the job was not the moment for the first woman to hold it." She did, however, allow her name to be placed in nomination for the ticket.

Perle Mesta, in her autobiography, recounted an incident from the convention that suggests what a token this nomination actually was:

> One naive women from Florida . . . came up to Sam Rayburn, almost sobbing, to ask, "Is it true that India is going to withdraw?" Sam gave her one of those glowering looks that only he can give and replied, "You are damned right she is going to withdraw. If she hadn't agreed to, I wouldn't have let her name come up in the first place."[14]

In the excitement over the flurry of vice presidential rumors about her, Senator Margaret Chase Smith was asked and agreed to address the Republican National Convention, an unusual honor for a woman to this day. "As the time approached, she was informed that instead of the 20 minutes that had been planned . . . there would only be time for a five-minute statement as a representative of a 'minority.' Mrs. Smith called the whole thing off."[15]

In a memorable interview with the then ninety-two-year-old Senator in 1990, she made it absolutely clear she had never allowed herself to be treated as a token. "I was a Senator," she said proudly. "Not a woman Senator. But I always demanded what was due me."

The slating of women for unwinnable races has not entirely abated. In

1992, Democrat Gloria O'Dell took advantage of the tradition in her unsuccessful race against powerful Senator Robert Dole of Kansas by likening the race to the biblical battle between David and Goliath. It was an unwinnable race, but by running, and by using biblical language that marked her as a daughter of the plains, she arguably positioned herself for a more successful future race.

While it is no comfort to women to know that research indicates they have always tended to be slated for the least winnable races, men also enter races that they have no chance of winning. Why? To learn the ropes. To put the party in their debt. To be ready for the next race—the race that is deemed doable.

Until 1992, however, it was the rare woman who understood that male lesson.

Claudine Schneider is one of those who did. She learned virtually by default the night she lost her first race, in 1978, with 48 percent of the vote.

"What was interesting election night was people kept asking me what it felt like to lose—but I hadn't lost. Everybody was cheering. I remember there was a photograph the next day in the *Providence Journal*. There I am with hordes of people jumping up and down and I am smiling and happy. Underneath there was a caption that said 'The Loser.' On the other side of the page was a picture of my opponent, who was in his hotel room, sitting like this [with his head in his hands], all alone, watching the returns, and it said 'The Winner.' Those pictures were worth a thousand words. I beat him next time."

Barbara Boxer lost an election in 1972 and admits, "It was a big ache because it was a difficult year-long campaign . . . a year of my life. . . . But it was an important experience that turned out to be a tremendous growth experience." It showed, she said, "there's a life after politics."[16] And as she showed, by keeping her name before the voters in innovative ways—sharing her peach cobbler recipe with Marin County cooks—there are ways to make the down time work for an out-of-office politician, too.

That sense of snatching some sort of victory from the jaws of defeat is apparent in Josie Heath's reflections in early 1991 when she was a fellow at the Kennedy School's Institute of Politics. "Of course it was an enormous disappointment to lose [her 1990 race for U.S. Senate]. But I knew from the outset that it was a long, uphill struggle, *and this was only a pause in that struggle.* I would have had to do everything right and my opponent would have had to stub his toe a couple of times. We thought we'd catch him on the [savings and loan scandal]. We thought a couple of other things would have to break and they didn't.

"I guess it is easier for me not to personally own the defeat. . . . It was more than a year of my life, every breath I breathed. But I did not see myself as a loser. But [by contrast] in 1976, I was devastated when I lost a state senate race."

When Arliss Sturgulewski was, first, double-crossed by Walter Hickel and other male Republicans in Alaska, and then lost the three-way race for governor in 1990, she shrugged and said simply, "I am a successful politician. I don't think of myself as a loser; I'm just not governor."

She is, however, a survivor. She admits that after losing her first race she "sort of slunk away to a warmer climate and just kicked the sand. But I had not realized there was a tremendous body of supporters who also were grieving for me. . . . The second time I had better sense. I stayed home ten days and went into my senate office and helped others grieve with me."

Then, at the invitation of Harriett Woods, then at the University of Missouri at St. Louis, she went to the Midwest and shared experiences with Midwestern women who had lost races. "I realized that what had happened to me is universal," Sturgulewski said. That trip "was very helpful. There's a certain feeling of pride now in what I've done.

"I believe in mentors. I tell other women, 'Don't be afraid to lose. You may get hurt very badly, but it'll make it easier for somebody else. I'm not going to run for governor again, but it has been fun. I want to move on."

Sturgulewski was at the vanguard of a group that has been playing a remarkable game of catchup football. In a very real sense, the political experiences of and lessons learned by the women who have run for office since suffrage have been compressed, in effect fast-forwarded, in the electoral careers of some of the newer women on the scene. For Heath as with Sturgulewski, the change is apparent in the way she experienced her loss in her first and most recent races—the first, for state senate, as devastation, the other, a much larger race for U.S. Senate, as a "pause in the struggle."

In part, this speed-up in the learning curve of women politicians is to the credit of such groups as the National Women's Political Caucus, Women's Campaign Fund, EMILY's List, and, in a less direct sense, the League of Women Voters—all of which recruit and train women in various aspects of politics. NWPC, WCF, and EMILY's List also do post-election debriefings, which serve as a kind of reunion of soul sisters, winners and losers alike, at which they can be Monday-morning quarterbacks and talk about what went wrong and what went right.

In some part, this new awareness and behavior on the part of women may be an end product of the women's movement's insight that the personal is political—in other words, a new understanding among women as to how their lives are affected by a government in which their voices are seldom heard.

In one important way, this insight has been attained because women have ceased to deny that they are, like their less political sisters, the victims of sexism. They have stopped aping male politicians and begun to compare notes about who *they* are instead. Ending this denial enables them to see the degree to which the men of their parties, the men who are their colleagues and have even, sometimes, been their mentors, are part of the institutional and psychological problems they face as women politicians.

Finally, this change is in large part simply because the last few decades have given women more than just a handful of token role models.

Pat Clagett of Baltimore is an example of the kind of woman in whom the patterns and experiences of political foremothers have coalesced in a very short time. A Planned Parenthood staffer, in 1990 Clagett decided to run for the Maryland House of Delegates essentially because of one issue, abortion. She had not run for office before nor even considered it. She did precisely what Sharon Rodine says women too often have done—she got in too late, with too little money (none) and no organization. She lost, by only ninety-four votes, but she did not fold her tent and disappear. She is already planning her next race in 1994.

"I had an epiphany of sorts," she explains. "Several things sort of came together at one point in time, within a week of each other. I was staff person on site when Operation Rescue hit one of our local clinics, and it took about six hours to disentangle the protesters and get them processed by the police. Then I was doing a public speaking event and I was on the platform with these anti-choice people. A light bulb went off. I had all this anger and frustration and I said 'Damn it . . . I have to stand up for something. I have to take some risks myself.'

"I decided to run. I can't say it was a rational decision. It was late. I didn't have a committee. I didn't have anything."

She came in fourth in a field of eight. The top three vote-getters won spots on the general election ballot.

"My immediate reaction was to become a recluse. . . . It took a lot out of me, financially and emotionally. Like a lot of people in public life, the glad-handing stuff comes hard for me. To me, going out and shaking hands and going door to door was so daunting. I think as women we can be very charming and accessible but inside we think, 'Oh, God! How can I do this?'"

There were other aspects of "the game" that distressed Clagett. The almost predictable: Rumors circulated about her because she was single and because she was affiliated with an abortion services provider. "It didn't come out publicly . . . but it hurt me very deeply. I had to compartmentalize it, but it was at great anguish to me that I guess you have to go through. You can't win without facing it. . . .

"Maybe I'm not a person who sees public office as a career yet. More of a statement. I'm not sure yet if I'd want to have some of the things happen to me that happen to people who are in office a long time or to try to be part of the power structure, but I think we have to have women part of the political process."

Part of her disillusionment is that she was told by the party early on that there would be no endorsements for the three spots on the general election ballot, then at the last moment the two front runners—both male—endorsed another woman.

Clagett had had more than a year to reflect on her loss; she admitted that "party regulars saw me as an upstart, coming out of nowhere, someone who hadn't paid her dues, and they weren't interested in me winning and it was clear the momentum was going my way.

"If I had just had two more weeks of door-to-door, there's no doubt I would have won. I was very effective. All [politics] is is the same stuff women know how to do best: Make each individual know that they count. I'm smart and I know how to talk about the issues without being alienating. . . .

"The loss was a crushing blow. It was just crushing. I am a single woman. I would never run again and do it without a personal support network in place. I had to run my whole life [including managing the death of her father in June before the primary], work full time, and run a campaign. You call on such deep reserves. Reserves you never thought you had. There's a whole psychology of crisis mentality . . .

"But to lose . . . after I had just put out one thousand percent emotionally, mentally, financially . . . I felt righteousness was on my side. I ran a
clean campaign and had dirty tricks done to me I thought couldn't be
rewarded—I was so naive. It just hit me like a ton of bricks. . . . After
getting through Christmas and the holidays I think I did kind of fold my
tent. . . . My hair is real short now. It used to be long. I guess that was my
purging."

In July 1991 she attended the twentieth anniversary convention of the
National Women's Political Caucus "and some of the fire began to come
back. I realized I needed to be around [other political] women like that.
We all have that fire and we are either helping somebody else do it or we
are pushing ourselves. I came away convinced there's no reason why I
shouldn't win—I'm capable, perfectly qualified, and I have a vision. I
don't presume to have a monopoly on vision, but I'm as trustworthy and
principled as anybody out there and if I can't translate that into running
I'm not fulfilling my destiny. We need a woman's point of view in government."

Clagett has already set her goal: to run for the same house of delegates
seat. "It's now held by a Republican. He's vulnerable," she says confidently. And she has taken steps to maintain visibility in her district—
working on an environmental committee, working for other candidates,
being active in the Caucus, letting people know she's still in the running.

Clagett is fortunate, and unusual, in that she did not have to take leave
of her job in order to run, and now that she is between races, her job
gives her visibility on an issue she cares fervently about, as well as providing an identity other than loser—and an income.

One of the major problems for women who have lost an election is that
there often is no such career to fall back on until the next political opportunity presents itself. Or if there is a career, it is usually not one so easily
resumed as going back to a law firm, or a real estate or insurance brokerage, or an accountancy, businesses where those who are in or out as a
result of electoral cycles can be more easily absorbed and the business's
connection to a politician is considered an enhancement. In contrast,
to be a teacher-politician, nurse-politician, or social worker–politician
may be too much of a clash for employers. If a woman has come out of
the school board–League of Women Voters–volunteer mold, it may appear when she loses a race that she has folded her tent and disappeared,
but the fact may be she had no place to go but home.

The law firm model obviously has much to commend it. The money is generally good, and a lawyer can continue bringing in clients for the firm even while running for office and otherwise not producing. It is a place to land safely when leapfrogging up the political ladder. And it offers another thing that women have only recently understood how much they need: a ready-made support group.

"You have to support somebody after they lose," insists Madeleine Kunin. "What's hard [for the out-of-office politician] is if you don't have a shingle to hang out at the law firm. As hard as it is to find the niches that actually are created for men, they do get places as investment bankers or law partners, sort of these rest stops where they can make some money and have visibility. Those niches just don't exist at the same rate for women.

"It's not easy, not pleasant to lose," Kunin also admitted. "It's a very devastating, very public experience." She lost one race for alderman of the city of Burlington, and it hurt, even though she had gone into the race reluctantly. She lost again when she ran for governor of Vermont the first time, after having been the state's lieutenant governor. "I guess the biggest decision when you run again is do you want to take that risk. Losing twice seems worse than losing once."

For her, the emotional support after losing that last race, and the emotional reserves that enabled her to come back and run successfully, came from a stint as a fellow at the Institute of Politics (IOP), at the John F. Kennedy School of Government at Harvard University.

"My time at the Kennedy School sort of getting recharged . . . was a real important time. Time to follow some truly intellectual interests. Just step back. Like I'm doing now [writing and teaching].

"I'm a real believer in a sort of cyclical career. I don't think you should do it straight through forever and ever. Sometimes [the IOP] is confused with a place old politicians go to die. But it certainly helped me."

Institutional opportunities to rest and reflect between stints at public life, themselves an acknowledgment that a failed candidate has been welcomed in for the long haul, are not the only things that have created a more comfortable environment for political women. Women no longer are fighting a society that tells them they should be in the home; indeed they sport T-shirts proclaiming "A Woman's Place Is in the House and Senate."

The growing number of women in the work force, including a majority of mothers of young children, has meant more women in law firms and law schools, and in virtually every profession and professional school that, as recently as two and three decades ago, were thought to be the exclusive domain of men. Martha Griffiths has proposed a monument to her husband Hicks, inscribed: "He always thought women were human." After she married him in college, he was accepted at Harvard Law School but she wasn't even allowed to apply because she was a woman. "Hicks had a fit," she said, and in 1940 they became the first married couple to graduate from the University of Michigan Law School. When Harvard did begin admitting women, one of its early graduates was Pat Schroeder, who never fails to get laughs when she tells audiences about the classmate who chewed her out for "taking a man's place." She notes wryly that it is a rare Harvard event she attends that some man does not come up to her and claim proudly to have been that villain.

The number of women who now have these sorts of professional niches has skyrocketed in recent years, and again it is thanks to the groundbreaking 1972 Title IX legislation that was floor-managed in the House by Congresswoman Patsy Mink of Hawaii, in a fight she recalls was "violent." How profoundly different the world has become as a result. Title IX has been given credit for Olympic Gold medals won by American women and girls, but its impact was probably never so evident as at a 1992 American Bar Association luncheon that honored, among others, Anita Hill, for her testimony regarding Clarence Thomas; Hillary Clinton, for her work, as first chair of the ABA's Commission on the Status of Women, to make legal language gender neutral; and Patsy Mink, for Title IX.

"How many of you entered law school after 1972," asked Lynn Hecht Schafran, director of the NOW Legal Defense Fund's national program to educate judges on issues of gender and equality. Three quarters of the women in the audience raised their hands. "Each of you owes our next honoree . . . Patsy Mink. . . . Without Title IX, most of you would not be here today." Those who had raised their hands included Anita Hill.

Because of changes begun first by the inclusion of "sex" in the 1964 Civil Rights Act and then in Title IX, more women are in the pipeline coming up at all levels of business and government. A look at some of the backgrounds of these women shows a new and different sort of risk- taking career: Barbara Boxer was a stockbroker, Gail Schoettler an entrepreneur involved in the start-up of two banks, Carol Moseley-Braun a federal prosecutor.

Where once little girls daydreamed about the exploits of an Amelia Earhart, who risked and lost her life in her attempt to become the first woman to fly around the world, little girls today can realistically consider careers as fighter pilots or astronauts. Not only are there now role models for them to look to, but the laws that kept them from the flight training their brothers could have "compliments of my Uncle Sam" were over- turned by Congress as a direct result of women's performance in the Gulf War and after decades of prodding by congressional women from Margaret Chase Smith, Frances Bolton, and Martha Griffiths to Patsy Mink and Pat Schroeder.

"Men have been making these same choices for years," Ferraro pointed out in 1991. "Now a girl who's going to school can say 'I'm going to go to law school.' Or 'I'm going to Wall Street,' and all she has to do is keep her grades up and she can do it. In my time, I had good grades in law school but I couldn't get a job. They weren't hiring any women that year, I was told."

Unlike a little girl growing up in the 1940s (Nancy Kassebaum, Bar- bara Mikulski, Geraldine Ferraro, Lynn Martin, Patsy Mink, Jolene Un- soeld, Cardiss Collins, Marge Roukema and others) or the 1950s (Pat Schroeder, Olympia Snowe, Jill Long, Barbara Boxer and Claudine Schneider among them) or perhaps even before 1984 when Ferraro be- came the first woman on a major party ticket to run for vice president, a little girl today will be cheered on, not laughed at, if she says she wants to be president when she grows up.

Martha Griffiths made that point touchingly clear in 1990 when she posed, as Michigan's lieutenant governor, with the newly crowned fifteen-year-old Miss Teenage Michigan; she told her, "Grow up and be president, my dear." This from a woman who, at fifteen herself, saw so many barriers in her way that she confided to her diary on January 28, 1928, the day before she turned sixteen: "One more year of life has gone. What have I accomplished? . . . I must be, I will be successful in some- thing, if it is merely washing dishes."[17]

In her 1989 Harvard speech, Madeleine Kunin talked about what these growing numbers of women in office mean to other women. She spoke from experience, how just having a number of women on her ex- ecutive staff meant that the women, including herself, reinforced one another simply by their "mutual presence, by being able to share the nu- ances, the subtleties of the pressures of political life for women, that are usually not articulated. It makes us feel like insurgents, more like we really belong." And she went on to consider what gender means to women's comfort level in and out of office.

> I think we can conclude it is both a positive and a negative force. It is, at times, a barrier, both practically and emotionally, on levels which, I think, we still cannot fully define even to ourselves. But it also adds excitement to the race. The very fact of breaking down the barriers, being one of the first, fighting the good fight for things in which we deeply believe, provides the adrenaline of politics for many women. It may not be what makes Sally run, but it sure gives her energy for the race.
>
> That is why the spirit of sisterhood, which exists within the political structure and is felt very strongly in circles such as this, is sustaining and, in fact, necessary for survival.[18]

Kunin expanded on this in a thoughtful interview in early 1991. "I don't have all the answer," she said, and then laughed. "And I'm not saying we should train all little girls to become hockey players. That wouldn't solve it. I think the most obvious answers are still the most solid ones—the more role models little girls see, the more likely they are to emulate them."

In this context, Ferraro, even as an out-of-work politician since 1984, has been the role model. In 1990 she became almost a textbook example of what a loser does to keep her career on track. She and Bella Abzug ganged up to bludgeon the New York State Democratic party to slate more women by threatening to withhold their support—and considerable donor lists—if the party was not responsive. Then she traveled thousands of miles, campaigned for innumerable candidates—a few of them men, many of them women running for major seats such as Josie Heath, Dianne Feinstein, and Anna Eshoo and the majority other New York women in podunk towns running for minor jobs that she, as someone who had been there, recognized as the foot in the door.

She was in Cortland and Ithaca in August campaigning for state senate candidate Beverly Livesay, one of fifteen women running for state senate seats. She visited the McCadam Cheese Plant in Chateaugay and dropped in at Mary McKillip's home in Saranac Lake where local Democrats were caucusing.

In Stattsburg she spoke at a fund-raiser for former lieutenant governor Mary Ann Krupsak, then running for state senate. "This is not a payback," she told the gathering of some fifty Democrats and the *Poughkeepsie Journal*. "I'd be helping her even if she hadn't helped me. But it's particularly nice to be here for someone I know and respect . . . [women] bring another dimension to the whole process."

In Plattsburgh she was asked about Kelly Craig, the first-ever female starting pitcher in a Little League World Series, who was in the news that day because she had been yanked from the game for failing to retire opposing players.

"She's the first so people focus on her, but the fact she got in there and tried, hey, I think that's terrific."

She was still at it in October, in Utica, telling the Business and Professional Women and the Chamber of Commerce: "I look back on 1984 with mixed emotions. What's wonderful about it is they can no longer say you cannot participate in government because of your gender."

By the November 1990 election, the now self-described "former Queens housewife" who was running for nothing that year had stumped every corner of the state of New York—Tannersville, Woodstock, Cayuga, Oswego, Poplar Ridge, and more—telling women who were running and women who were listening not to worry if they couldn't do it all: "Know what you are capable of doing and don't try to be Superwoman."

Ferraro even stumped Peggy Santillo's front porch on Rinewalt Street in Williamsville. There she told the crowd of eighty and her hostess, who had run and lost a race for town board in 1990, "If you run and you haven't won, don't stop. Run again."

By January 1991 she was ready to start polling New York voters to see if they were willing to consider her as a U.S. Senate candidate.

In late spring, when she announced she would challenge Republican incumbent Alphonse D'Amato, she did not rent a hotel ballroom and invite the press and the bigwigs. She made her announcement in some of those same women's homes around the state.

She did not win her 1992 Senate primary, considered one of the meanest intraparty primary battles in memory. But barely two weeks later, she flew back to California to campaign for the Democratic party ticket and helped in the final, frantic last-minute money-raising for Dianne Feinstein and Barbara Boxer. Among the sixteen California Democratic women running for the U.S. House of Representatives was Anna Eshoo, now Congresswoman Anna Eshoo.

Throughout 1991 and 1992, as we interviewed women who had won and lost, and watched the successes of 1992 and the races of 1994 shaping up, several things became clear. More women than ever before will run for Congress next time. (At this writing, twenty-three are considering

Senate races, fourteen Democrats and nine Republicans, and the number of women planning 1994 House races grows too rapidly to keep track.) And then the next. And then again and again. More women will risk the safety of offices and districts where they were known and well liked to move up to bigger challenges in Congress or governor's mansions. (Twenty-seven have announced for the thirty-six gubernatorial seats up in 1994, and women are running in both 1993 races—New Jersey and Virginia.) Moreover, in style and numbers that will be as exciting as they are empowering, women will run with new confidence that they can make a difference as women, for women, simply by running—win or lose.

As her first Senate race drew to a close in 1974, Barbara Mikulski, trying to move up from Baltimore's city council, realized, "I became afraid—afraid of losing and afraid of winning. . . . I had known it was an uphill fight from the very beginning and so I had prepared myself for losing," she told *Ms.* magazine.

"At the same time, I was really gaining on Mathias during the last days. Victory was very much in the air. Suddenly I got scared of winning. Suppose I'm the only woman in the Senate? How will I meet all those demands, fulfill the expectations? Could I make good on my promises? Suppose I don't and they don't reelect me?

"Reelect me? To the U.S. Senate? What a fantastic idea—I kept on running."

She was to lose that first race for the U.S. Senate, but it seemed "nip and tuck," she said, until early the next morning.

At 11:00 P.M. election night, she climbed atop a desk at her headquarters and roused staffers with an "I will not concede" speech. Her mother got up beside her and shouted into the microphone, "To me, she'll always be a winner."

When the returns turned bad, a reporter asked what she'd do if she lost.

"I'm a household word, just like Brillo or Borax," Mikulski replied. "I'm going to be around for a long time." On November 3, 1993, Barbara Mikulski was elected to her second term in the U.S. Senate.

11

What Difference Does Difference Make?

During Ann Richards's first year as the governor of Texas, one of her male constituents expressed disappointment in her administration, wondering aloud whether she was just "Bubba in drag." He didn't question her capacity to govern, or her toughness, just whether she was any different from the men who had been governors.

At a time when women are finding electoral opportunities in their status as outsiders, they are also being pressed to demonstrate, usually in less parochial prose, that their presence makes a difference. Women themselves often expect to be different. Tune in to any discussion about increasing the number of women in politics and you will hear an exchange similar to one that occurred during a Women's Campaign Fund (WCF) breakfast in San Francisco in early 1992. A woman from the floor asked how to increase financial support for women candidates.

Mary Hughes, campaign consultant and former director of the California Democratic party, suggested that there were limits to supporting women candidates on the basis of "gender affinity" or because "it's the right thing to do." Prospective donors want information and access, she said. "We just haven't had that many political patrons or wealthy benefactors who would join a 'winner's circle' for Gerry Ferraro or Elizabeth Holtzman because they'll be on the Senate Finance Committee and they might benefit your brokerage firm."

"Ugh," murmur women from the floor, "that's just what we don't want to do."

"We wouldn't have deficits if women were in charge," shouted another.

This feeling that elected women should "do it differently," that they must not become part of the system, represents, in the Ginger Rogers analogy, one more intricate set of dance steps for elected women. The demand that women remain outsiders while transforming American politics is not a modest one. Women are not only expected to change policies, ranging from health care to deficits, but to transform the very manner in which political decisions are made. Richards wasn't called a "Bubba in drag" because of her policy accomplishments. She was being held to an illusive and unspecified standard of "difference."

The argument that women's voices and values are different from men's has emerged as a powerful new factor in American culture and politics as familiar female attributes have been revived, revalued, and pronounced preferable to masculine attributes. Women are perceived to be more caring, peace-loving, nurturant, compassionate, ethical, attentive, and collaborative than men. In the past, the assignment of these qualities justified confining women to familial roles and slowed their entrance into politics. Today, women are arguing that these qualities are desperately needed in the public realm.

"Men have killed this planet," proclaimed novelist Alice Walker, as she kicked off Congresswoman Barbara Boxer's annual fund-raising lunch. Walker's opening comment brought a roaring and approving response from the nearly 800 women who attended Boxer's "Women Making History" event.[1]

Former congresswoman Barbara Jordan (1973–79), who once rejected the idea of a women's caucus in Congress, surprised a mostly female audience in 1991 by expressing similar sentiments: "I believe that women have a capacity for understanding and compassion which a man structurally does not have . . . does not have it because he cannot have it. He's just incapable of it." More women in Congress, Jordan argued, would "break many of our political deadlocks."[2]

In 1992 the profound antipathy voters felt toward "politics as usual" lent itself readily to campaign slogans that stressed the theme of difference. Even before the Thomas/Hill hearings, Celinda Lake's polls showed that voters were giving women candidates an advantage because they were not considered part of the system that so angered voters. As Lake put it, "Women are the quintessential outsiders."[3] Using an outsider strategy to gain an election advantage is not unusual in American politics; however, women candidates have rarely found it viable. Previously, women needed to emphasize their experience in order not to raise or reinforce voter questions about their potential effectiveness. How could they accomplish their agenda or implement their platform if they were outsiders? Even Geraldine Ferraro and Elizabeth Holtzman, both of whom could be called veteran politicians, sparred over which woman was the authentic outsider. Ferraro stressed her role as a homemaker, rather than her congressional career or historic vice presidential nomination, and portrayed Holtzman, who had held elective office for more continuous years than Ferraro, as the true insider. While this was not the central skirmish of this four-candidate Senate primary race, the irony of two of the most senior political women in the country competing for outsider status did not go unnoticed.

The climate in 1992 allowed them to go one step further and argue that they could be *more* effective in office, since by definition women would not be "one of the boys." Candidates implied, and sometimes said directly, that they were more trustworthy than men on women's issues, such as child-care policy or family leave and especially abortion. Some candidates credited their difference from men to their experience, particularly the experience of raising children. Other candidates based their claims on the growing list of positive female attributes.

While "difference" had multiple meanings, wordy explanations have no place in campaign themes. The slogan "in a different voice" seemed to capture all meanings—outsider, guardian of women's issues, and possessor of certain qualities. The phrase required no explanation of why a woman's voice might be different; its truth was simply asserted.

Elizabeth Holtzman summed up the attractiveness of the "difference" strategy to an audience of women considering running for Congress. "Women," she said, are finally "benefiting from female stereotypes—whether they bear any relationship to the truth is another question."[4]

Holtzman's comment raises the question of whether it is good strategy to appeal to stereotypes whenever they benefit women, or whether too great an emphasis on women's difference can backfire in the long run. Supreme Court Justice Sandra Day O'Connor is among those who are skeptical of the new claims for women's virtue. "The gender differences cited currently are surprisingly similar to stereotypes from years past [:] They recall 'the old myths we have struggled to put behind us.'" O'Connor examined the application of the traits to women lawyers. "For example, asking whether women attorneys speak with a 'different voice' than men do is a question that is both dangerous and unanswerable. . . . It threatens, indeed, to establish new categories of 'women's work' to which women are confined and from which men are excluded." In her view, "there is no difference between a wise old woman and a wise old man."[5]

O'Connor's arguments are not dominant today. Beliefs about women's difference have emerged in the last decade, facilitated in part by women scholars who have documented the persistence of sex differences between men and women. For instance, the slogan "in a different voice," used in the 1992 campaigns, is taken from psychologist Carol Gilligan's *In a Difference Voice*, a study that found young girls reason differently from young boys and reach different conclusions about what is moral behavior.[6] No matter how cautious scholars are in discussing *why* these differences exist, the implication is increasingly drawn, and popularized, that women, simply because they are women, will think and act in a certain way.

However, for a growing number of advocates, the way women think and act is superior to the way men think and act. That is the thread that runs through the question of whether Ann Richards is really "Bubba" and the discussion at the Women's Campaign Fund breakfast, and the ubiquitous use of "a different voice" implies that women's performance in office will be, or should be, not only different but better than men's.

Veteran officeholders, such as former governor Madeleine Kunin, have worried that an overemphasis on difference might cause voters to hold individual women to a different standard of performance. "We cannot expect the few women in political life to change the values and the rules of the game alone, although that is sometimes precisely the expectation."[7]

Democratic strategist Wendy Sherman is even more emphatic than Kunin in her belief that these expectations are unreasonable. "There is not a critical mass of women yet to form their own cohesive power base; women are just not part of the institution [Congress] in important ways." After the November elections, columnist Ellen Goodman saw the danger of putting individual women back on a pedestal: "The higher a woman rose on the helium of moral superiority, the faster she could fall."[8] Several women candidates "suffered a precipitous slide in support when they came up short of the high standards—whether they were tardy on taxes or too quick with negative ads." Echoing Kunin and Sherman, Goodman asks, "How long before we read the first story asking why six women in the Senate haven't yet changed the institution?"

Both Kunin and Sherman implicitly point to a relationship between the number of women in office, and their ability to achieve change. They leave open the possibility that a larger number of women, *if they share a similar platform,* might be able to transform institutions in the future.

The failure to distinguish between particular women's platforms and generic female stereotypes frequently results in criticism when female elected officials fail to vote in unison or conform to the stereotypes. Women are said to be more peace-loving than men. Yet in 1991, for instance, while Democratic Senator Barbara Mikulski opposed the Gulf War, Republican Senator Nancy Kassebaum supported it. Women's votes in the House of Representatives were also divided along partisan lines. "A waste of woman power," said feminist critic Suzanne Gordon. Male-identified, not true women, charged others. No one criticized the men who voted against the war on the grounds that they were not true men, or that they were "really women in men's clothing."[9]

The confusion generated by the persistence of female stereotypes, favorable or negative, and the expectation that women will exercise power differently from men is considerable. It suggests that American women are undergoing an immense, and complex, transition. On the one hand, women have been engaged in an effort to rescue female traits from derision, and are vigorously protesting the tendency to undervalue women's work and women's activities. On the other hand, women are also attacking the privileged position that male traits or values have occupied in American political life. Women are questioning the standard of "toughness" as a sole criterion to enter politics, pointing out that this is a male standard against which women in public life have been measured and found wanting. The writer Antonia Fraser, who has studied the exercise of power by women monarchs, points to the vice presidential debate between Ferraro and Bush in 1984 as an example of how women are forced into male frameworks and definitions. When Geraldine Ferraro was asked during the vice presidential debate whether she was tough enough to push the button, a question not asked of male candidates, she began "Oh sure. . . . " Fraser writes, "[a]nother legitimate question—to candidates of both sexes—might be: Are you strong enough *not* to push the button?"[10] The question is should you do it, not could you do it.

The proliferation of campaign slogans that described women candidates as tough and caring partly reflects the rejection of exclusively male standards. Senator Barbara Mikulski characterizes some of these changes in the following way: Women are learning that "[their] private values are good enough to be public ones."[11] "But to assign values such as "caring" to all women candidates reduces the focus on what specific women will do once in office. As important, relying on female qualities or attributes to bring about political change subtly shifts the dialogue away from the strategies needed to bring about specific changes to a nonstrategic hope that the presence of more women in politics will bring about a general transformation.

When one or just a few women enter a predominantly male institution, and have little power, they are not likely to have much policy impact however courageous their individual actions might be. Frieda L. Ghelen studied congresswomen and a sample of congressmen in the 88th and 91st Congresses (1963–64) and (1968–69). There were twelve congresswomen in the first period, and there were ten in the second. Ghelen asked the same question we ask today: Does having women present make any difference? Her answer was "very little."[12] She studied their votes, their attendance, their attention to constituents, the number of women they hired as top aides on their congressional staffs, and their partisan loyalty. There were no significant differences between male and female Congress members on all these measures. She did find greater support for women's rights among the elected women, foreshadowing the findings of more recent studies. All but one woman had supported the major civil rights bill in 1964, and several had introduced the Equal Rights Amendment (ERA). Ghelen noted that this support for equality did not translate into more work opportunities for women in congresswomen's offices: only 20 percent of either sex had hired a woman for their chief position.

In reporting her conclusions, Ghelen refers specifically to the expectations placed on these women: "For those who would argue that increasing numbers of women ought to be elected to political office because of their unique contributions and their moral superiority, this paper offers little in the way of support." At the same time, she reassured those who feared women's increased participation: "For those who fear that too many women would mean too much tampering with the system, too many do-gooders who don't understand the realities of life, there is little support either."[13]

Her remarks remind us how long such hopes and fears have dominated the discussion of women's performance in politics. Ghelen's findings are not surprising when the historical period and minuscule number of women are considered. Excluded from the leadership and assigned to minor committees, there were few strategies women could use to achieve legislative success. When their numbers are very small, as they are in Congress to this very day, elected women have found it hard to find strategies that would help them just to function on an everyday level, let alone craft legislation, find allies, and build political coalitions.

Geraldine Ferraro, like Jeannette Rankin before her, described how intensely she felt the pressure of being one of the few women in the House of Representatives in 1977. "There were traps everywhere, even on the most insignificant details, and I made sure I fell into as few of them as possible.

"When I first went down to Washington I overheard a male member say about a new female member: 'She walked off the floor of the House and couldn't even find her way to the ladies' room.' No one was ever going to be able to say that about me, I decided. So before I walked out of any door, I mentally walked to wherever I was going, mapping out my exact route.

"Silly, right?" Ferraro continues. "And totally inconsequential. But you have to look as if you know where you're going—and nothing is worse than looking as if you don't."[14] Numerous studies confirm Ferraro's observation. It is difficult for women, or members of any minority, to adapt to a situation in which the dominant norms are alien to their experience. In these situations difference is exaggerated and women are often viewed as members of a group, not as individuals, and their behavior is seen as representative of all women. As recently as 1991, Barbara Mikulski characterized her experience in the Senate as the only Democratic woman in a similar way: "You feel that you are speaking for every woman in the world who has ever lived in the past, who currently lives today, and who will live into the third millennium."[15]

Sociologists have developed the concept of "critical mass" to describe what happens in an institution when a minority population grows to 20 or 30 percent of the total. The first noticeable changes are in the day-to-day atmosphere. Women feel "less like insurgents," and more like they really belong in the corridors of power, says former Vermont Governor Madeleine Kunin, describing the changes that she witnessed when women became a majority of her eight-member staff.[16] Today, at 10 percent of the congressional representation, women are still far from constituting a critical mass in Congress. Shortly after the November elections of 1992, Lynn Martin, former congresswoman and retiring secretary of labor, was asked whether or not more women in Congress meant more influence. "You can't talk about power without talking about position," she said making an obvious but frequently overlooked distinction.[17]

Hints of what the future might hold for a Congress comprised of more women may be found in state legislatures where women frequently have been elected in sufficient numbers to achieve a critical mass. In the six states of Arizona, Maine, New Hampshire, Vermont, Washington, and Colorado, women now comprise over 30 percent of elected legislators. Scholars have found a correlation between whether or not a legislative seat is considered prestigious, as it is in states with full-time professional legislatures that pay their members a salary, and the number of women elected. For instance, Vermont and New Hampshire have "citizen legislatures" that meet infrequently and for no pay. Women have done very well in these bodies. The growth has been much slower in California, where legislators are paid handsomely. How the newly enacted term limits will affect future elections is not yet known; however, most observers expect that more open seats will encourage more women to run. After the 1992 elections, women in the California legislature constituted 23 percent of the total.

Whether or not elected women organize formal caucuses within their legislatures as their numbers increase does not seem to follow a predictable path. Frequently, women form friendships with one another regardless of party affiliation to help them overcome feelings of isolation. Sometimes these informal networks have evolved into a more formal women's caucus, as they did in the California legislature. In the late 1970s, the eleven women who were serving in the California legislature got together for supper once a month. Nervous about threatening their male colleagues, or even being seen together, the legislators met in private homes and adamantly rejected forming a caucus. Belittled during the day, and left out of informal gatherings during the evening, the women developed friendships that crossed party lines.

In 1985 the support group became a women's caucus in response to an event typical of the day-to-day indignities women had endured in the legislature. Senator Diane Watson, a member of the judiciary committee, was speaking against the death penalty when the chairman suddenly interrupted, telling her to stop her "mindless blather." The first act of the newly formed women's caucus was to demand an apology. From this moment on, the women in the legislature began to construct an agenda of women's issues.

Veteran assemblywoman Sally Tanner says that before the caucus was formed, "women . . . did not dare carry controversial bills on women's issues such as sexual harassment," even if they were personally supportive. She includes herself: "I would have hesitated to carry that kind of bill then, not because I wouldn't believe in it, but because there would be very little support [from men] for it." Tanner thinks the spark was ignited in 1985 not just because there were more women in the legislature but because more women considered themselves feminists and were advocates for women's issues.[18]

A feminist bent appears important to whether or not informal groups turn into an organized caucus. Women's caucuses are less likely to be formed where legislatures are highly partisan, or in states where the women feel, as the California women felt earlier, that such an action would anger their male colleagues.

The Florida caucus remained an informal coalition until the last few years. And, while the caucus will not take a stand on any controversial issue, in the mid-1970s eleven women, both Republicans and Democrats, decided to demonstrate the power they could have if they were united. The women secretly picked an issue, no-fault insurance, on which they had no strong position. They decided to vote against the position supported by the insurance lobby, in part because not a single female legislator had been taken seriously enough to be approached by a lobbyist. On the day of the vote, the majority leader was sworn to secrecy but was told he had eleven sure votes. Then the no-fault measure passed by a three-vote margin. The women in the legislature were never so neglected again. Unpaid women's lobbyist Nikki Beare, who helped orchestrate this "show of force," said the legislators deliberately chose an issue not identified as a women's issue, and did not "care which way the vote went."[19]

A formal caucus was formed just a few years ago. With twenty-nine members, it is co-chaired by long-time Democratic representative Elaine Gordon and Republican minority leader Sandra Martham. In the spring of 1993, the women were able to pass a "gender balance" bill, urging that all state appointments "where possible" reflect the percentage of women in the population. Only one member of the Senate voted against the bill, and it passed the House with a 74–9 margin. Nevertheless, Democratic governor Lawton Chiles vetoed the bill on May 13, 1993, saying he did not want a "Noah's Ark."[20] Whether or not the women have enough clout to override this veto is the next test of their strength.

The tremendous increase in the number of elected women in the Oregon legislature led to the accidental recognition that they could, if they chose, act as a bloc. On International Women's Day, the speaker of the lower house refused to declare a recess so the assemblywomen could attend a ceremony in the state senate. The speaker's ruling was rendered moot when everyone realized there were enough women in the state house to constitute a quorum. If the women left the room, the legislature could no longer do business. Said one female legislator: "And the rest of the session, that was really recognized. [It] was the first time men ever knew we could take the quorum away from them."

Yet this numerical increase in the Oregon legislature did not lead to a greater reliance on a caucus strategy to introduce women's issues. As more women moved into leadership positions within the legislature, and became chairs of legislative committees, they relied more on ad hoc coalitions comprised of men and women to pass specific issues. Building such coalitions, of course, is a time-honored way to organize and move an issue through a legislative body.

The California, Florida, and Oregon cases suggest a complex relationship between numbers, feminism, partisanship, and institutional power. Systematic studies of how these factors affect legislative priorities and achievements are just beginning.

The Eagleton Institute's Center for the American Woman and Politics at Rutgers University recently announced the results of several studies it commissioned. In general, these studies have found that, despite women's lack of parity or majority status, they have been using what power they have to push for changes on issues of importance to women, defined as those issues that emerged as a result of the women's movement, as well as more traditional ones arising from a woman's role as caregiver. Sexual harassment, absentee fathers, breast cancer, abortion, child care, support for single mothers, domestic violence, rape, hiring practices, and pay equity are but a few examples.[21]

Political scientist Michelle Saint-Germain is among those scholars who have found that women legislators are more likely than men to make women's concerns their top priority.[22] Women who carried the most legislation affecting women and children were those who had close ties to organized women's groups.[23] Worth noting in some of these studies, however, are the exceptions. In the California legislature, more men than women had women's issues as their highest priority. This finding was attributed to the existence of liberal men in the California legislature whose policy positions reflected their ideology and presumably their recognition of the power of women's votes. Women are in fact changing the policy agenda by introducing new issues or taking up those that have been long ignored. The success or failure of specific legislation depends on majority support from men's votes.

Ironically, some state-level elected women believe they may be facing real competition from men over women's issues. Says Nancy K. Kopp, the speaker pro tem of the Maryland House of Delegates: "The traditional issues we were steered into—child care, health care, and education—have now become the sexy issues of the decade."[24] For some women, the niches they have established without much competition may now become contested. When the significance of women's votes is remembered, as explored in Chapter 7, the desire of men to demonstrate concern or legislative achievements in these areas may be seen simply as good politics.

In some cases, major policy shifts have been created by this competition between male and female officials. In Iowa, Attorney General Bonnie Campbell, widely thought to be a gubernatorial candidate in 1994, has made a top priority of child support and the tracking down of fathers who do not pay it. She has published pictures of the ten most wanted absentee fathers. She has run ads in city and small-town newspapers alike that graphically depict what financial support means to a child. The ad shows a child who needs clothing and school supplies; the cost of each item is listed. The incumbent governor, Terry Branstad, has been trying to outdo Campbell's aggressiveness. Branstad is emphasizing an enforcement plan to collect child support payments, which he claims will "have a bigger impact than just putting pictures on 'wanted' posters."[25]

Sometimes women have used their increase in numbers to force a more systematic examination of gender bias, as they have in the judicial branch of many states. Over thirty-five states have conducted such reviews and issued reports that delineate those biases in excruciating detail. Differential treatment was found in every corner, from the atmosphere of the courtroom and how women are addressed in court, to the decisions reached in divorce and child custody cases. The long, slow process of implementation is now under way. In 1982, New Jersey became the first state to establish a task force. After three years of study, the chief justice of the New Jersey Supreme Court appointed an implementation task force. Lynn Hecht Schafran, director of the National Judicial Education Program, and sociologist Norma J. Wikler evaluated the state's progress and concluded, "The Task Force's greatest accomplishment in the state is also its most subtle: creating a climate within a court system in which the nature and consequences of judicial gender bias are both acknowledged to exist and understood to be unacceptable in the New Jersey Courts." While this was good news for professional women, the evaluators also found that the law itself was the most resistant to change, especially family law (laws governing divorce proceedings and child custody cases) and domestic violence laws. Yet changes were occurring in these areas as well.[26]

Little examination has been conducted on the difference women have made by being elected to city councils, even though they frequently serve in numbers equal to men, or even, in a few cases, have a majority. Janet Flammang studied decision-making in the Santa Clara Valley, particularly in the city of San Jose, which she dubbed the "feminist capital of the world."[27] Women held a majority on the city council. The mayor was a woman. Key positions were filled by women. San Jose was the first American city to negotiate a comparable-worth settlement, an agreement that attempted to rectify the historical pattern of lower pay for women.

Yet San Jose, like other cities, has not been able to transcend the financial problems rampant in most states simply because more women are in charge. While women have gained legitimacy for new programs, such as battered women's shelters or rape crisis centers, they have had to confront dwindling revenues, and in some cases have had to eliminate funding support for these programs. Some observers worry that the sharp increase of locally elected female officials reflects the unpaid, relatively unprestigious nature of local positions compared with state or federal ones. Many city councils are also nonpartisan, thus running for local office synthesizes women's long-standing tradition of voluntary activity with nonpartisan politics.

Some states are acting affirmatively to reach parity in female representation and are enacting mandatory requirements that public appointments be equitably distributed between men and women. Iowa has adopted such a law despite the fact that the voters in 1992 rejected an Equal Rights Amendment to the state's constitution. The concept of parity often invokes a debate over the controversial issue of quotas associated with affirmative action, as it did in Feinstein's 1990 campaign. Some observers believe the lack of controversy surrounding the parity measure in Iowa was due to the state's relatively homogeneous population.

However, numerical increase in women's presence does not ensure their power within an institution, nor does it mean that women will share the same values or policy goals once inside. Parity does not lead inevitably to major changes in the political system. Parity won't change the committee system in Congress. Parity is not a guaranteed of campaign reform. If anything, a greater numerical presence of women in politics tends to highlight differences among women.

In Berkeley, California, Loni Hancock has served over fourteen years on the Berkeley City Council, six of them as mayor. "I've served with a majority of African-Americans, and another time with a majority of women. In each of these instances, both the most conservative and the most liberal member of the city council came from these majorities." Platform and personal values are what matter in her eyes. Hancock points out that when dozens of women are running in a local election directly against each other, it makes little sense to campaign "in a different voice." "Voters want to know what you propose to do."[28]

Some of the questions about the difference women make in politics cannot be answered until women occupy positions of power similar to men's. Those individual women who hold executive positions and who are sympathetic to women's issues have been using authority to implement a variety of changes. Governor Ann Richards, for instance, has used her power of appointment to fill half of all state-appointed positions with women or minorities, thus giving her a chance to influence the agenda and the atmosphere of numerous institutions. With a single stroke of her pen, San Francisco attorney Louise Renne established on-site child care for her staff as one of her first official acts. Such acts can help create a climate for working women that is profoundly different from predominantly male environments where no recognition has been given to the fact that working women with children remain their primary caretakers.

At the federal level, congressional women face a very different environment and set of choices. Until the 1992 election, women were roughly 5 percent of the House of Representatives. Now at 10 percent, they are still far from constituting a critical mass. The atmosphere remains profoundly male, and many congresswomen privately agree with the characterization of the legislature as a "jock-o-cracy," although they are more circumspect publicly. Their strategies for legislative success are much more limited in this environment.

Each congresswoman has to decide whether she will play an insider or an outsider role within the institution. This can be a tough decision. A congresswoman who remains an outsider may risk further marginalization, while those who try and become insiders risk becoming beholden to the same set of pressures as men. The insider route, however, is very difficult for women when their numbers are still so meager. "The trick for these women, if they want to play in this institution [Congress] is how to do that and not lose their integrity," says Wendy Sherman, former chief aide to Senator Mikulski. Sherman argues that "what these women understand is that they have no power within the institution."[29]

Sherman points to Congresswoman Pat Schroeder, "who works very hard for her constituents and plays an effective role nationally as an outsider" but who is reduced to "beating on the doors" of institutional power.[30] Schroeder herself says she has asked the leadership "whether they spend as much time yelling at the Republicans as they do me."

Political scientist Irwin Gertzog, who wrote one of the first books on women in politics, and who has continued to study women's performance in Congress, argues that "Pat Schroeder plays to an outside audience. She galvanizes the interests and goals of feminists, but that route doesn't make you effective inside Congress."[31]

Although she has been a member of the Armed Services Committee since her arrival, Schroeder is most identified with her support for women's issues. But in order to get legislation passed, Schroeder must depend on women's organizations to help mobilize support and to put pressure on other members of Congress. She expresses both appreciation and enormous frustration with women for failing to use the clout they do have.

Congresswoman Barbara Kennelly of Connecticut, who has tried to play a more insider role, agrees with Gertzog. "It's fine to be outside, but you don't get much done."[32] Congresswoman Jolene Unsoeld of Washington worries about the consequence of campaign strategies that emphasize women's outsider status. She argues that women running for Congress by definition are running to be part of it. She advises women candidates: "Try to express your freshness, your uniqueness and your energy as change. But don't bash the institution."[33]

In order to move a policy agenda, women must master legislative processes and build coalitions that will ensure at least majority votes. Regardless of the issue, legislative success often depends on the support of the leadership and always on the votes of men. Congresswomen who have tried to play by the rules and increase their power within the institution are also dependent on the men who hold powerful positions. Just getting a toe in the door, or receiving an important committee assignment, has been tough for women members.

"I've tried to get on Appropriations [committee] three times, and each time I've been nicely told that the woman's slot is already filled on that committee," Congresswoman Marcy Kaptur of Ohio told a *Washington Post* reporter in 1990.[34] Mary Rose Oakar, also from Ohio, says she camped outside Speaker Tip O'Neill's office morning after morning before he gave her a coveted position on the committee on aging.[35]

With the spotlight on the four new Democratic female senators elected in 1992, the newcomers won some important victories in their first committee assignments. In the House, veteran women pushed hard to help the new congresswomen win important committee assignments. If winning choice committee assignments is rough, getting elected to the leadership is even tougher. Leadership positions are crucial to the ability to move legislation forward. In 1993, one woman, Barbara Kennelly, holds a leadership position among Democrats in the House of Representatives. Former congresswoman Lynn Martin, who was secretary of labor under President George Bush, is the only Republican woman who has ever been in the House leadership. She was vice president of the Republican Conference.

In very recent years, women have begun to protest more vigorously their exclusion from power, particularly from the leadership. Like the march to the Senate over Anita Hill, these protests have been increasingly bold, and represent a more frontal assault on the institution. A tale less well known than the Anita Hill episode occurred among the Democratic congresswomen in 1991.

The all-male Democratic leadership in the House of Representatives agreed to a series of compromises on the civil rights bill to accommodate Republicans. Among their agreements was the limit on damages women could receive in a sex-discrimination case. Angry Democratic women approached the leadership, arguing such compromises—singling out women as less deserving than other victims of discrimination—would not have happened had they been in the room as decision-makers. As a result of the women's protests, Majority Leader Tom Foley quietly expanded the leadership circle in the House to include one woman, Barbara Kennelly.

Not all of the difficulty involved in playing insider roles can be laid at the doorstep of male resistance. The legacy of nonpartisan attitudes may also be inhibiting women's effectiveness in legislative bodies. Alan Ehrenhalt, editor of the *Congressional Quarterly*, recently studied the Colorado legislature, where women are thirty-four percent of the total and part of the leadership. He found male legislators in Colorado critical of their female colleagues. Great campaigners, they said, but not so great as legislators.[36]

The finding seemed surprising, since so many women claim to care more about policy than partisan matters. "Not so surprising," says strategist Sherman. The problem is that a lot of women think putting policy first means "having a good idea. . . . Passing legislation is an organizing task and must be seen as such. . . . "

In a recent study of women and their attitudes toward power, researchers found most elected women spoke about exercising power "on behalf of others." They frequently made statements about how they feared power and its corrupting influence.[37]

Manhattan borough president Ruth Messinger thinks some of these attitudes, so reminiscent of those from an earlier time, inhibit women's willingness to enter politics and their capacity to be successful politicians. Messinger, who spent nearly thirteen years on the New York City Council, moving slowly from being an outsider to becoming a powerful borough president, believes women do have the potential to change the fundamental rules of politics, but they must first get over the traditional view that politics is corrupt. "We have to break through the idea among issue and community groups that politics is a dirty business. If we . . . treat politicians with contempt, then we will get contemptible politicians."[38]

The election of more women to Congress, along with the development of an explicit agenda on women's issues, has forced Congress to deal with such issues. Newly elected women have often been surprised to find that a foremother had taken up certain issues ten, twenty, or even thirty years before. When Mary Rose Oakar came to Congress in 1977, she was amazed to find the last woman to represent Ohio in the House of Representatives, Frances Bolton, had fought for a greater recognition of breast cancer as Oakar was now fighting.[39]

While many congresswomen have shunned women's issues, the behind-the-scenes efforts by previous congresswomen are barely visible and largely undocumented. Preliminary evidence, however, suggests that from the time of Margaret Chase Smith and Helen Gahagan Douglas, women from both parties took up issues of importance to women, regardless of how they felt about feminism. When one woman retired or was defeated, another woman took her place. When Congresswoman Catherine May Bedell came to Congress in 1959, she remembers Katharine St. George telling her, "I have spent so many years now in this battle [on women's issues]. I know you are very interested in this field of legislation for women. Now, I'm going to ask you to share the load."[40] St. George, who served in Congress from 1947 to 1965, was the first woman to introduce the Equal Rights Amendment; it had previously been introduced by men.

Congresswoman Patsy Mink, who entered Congress for the first time in 1965, remembers that she and a few others felt they had "to voice the concerns of the *total* population of women in the country. [M]any women in Congress *refused* to voice these concerns, and that made it even more difficult for Edith Green, Martha Griffiths, and myself."[41] Those who were sympathetic could be easily named.

The formation of the Women's Caucus in 1977 made these differences among women more visible. Conflict plagued the young caucus. Some women refused to join, and its initial efforts ran afoul of partisan issues and infighting. A name change, and the admission of male members in 1982, rescued the caucus from extinction.[42]

Renamed the bipartisan Congressional Caucus for Women's Issues, the current ground rule requires a consensus in order to support legislation. This ground rule, while it has reduced partisan fighting, has ensured that nothing controversial will be supported. The caucus could not reach a consensus, for instance, on day-care legislation and therefore had no position. Those who expect women to agree on child care on the grounds that it is a quintessential women's issue, once again ignore that women hold different values and beliefs about the role government should play.

At the same time, when a consensus can be found, the power of the congressional caucus has been enhanced by its larger membership. In recent years the caucus has made a concerted effort to take up issues concerning women's health, and has played a pivotal role in raising public consciousness about the neglect of diseases that mainly affect women, such as breast cancer. Individual congresswomen helped alter the priorities on funding research and pressured the National Institutes of Health to revise the way they commissioned research. For the first time, in 1993, the Caucus was able to take a pro-choice stand.[43] Male members have used their membership in the caucus, and their support for such issues, to gain credibility with women voters.

Schroeder, who has a twenty-year perspective, sees a change in the Democratic leadership's attitude toward women's issues. "It used to be women were told by the leadership, pick one issue, one that doesn't cost a lot of money, and we'll try to move it for you. Now the leadership is being very good about bringing up our agenda year after year."[44]

Gertzog, who has studied the activities of the caucus, agrees: "The caucus will determine what's being talked about and the agenda that's being voted on."[45] Placing new items on the public agenda is a necessary and important step in building a strategy for legislative success.

As new policy items are introduced, there are glimmers that the old debate over women's nature is slowly giving way to a more complex formulation. Historically, the debate has been conducted as if there were only two ways to characterize women's "nature" as distinct from men's nature: women were either the "same" as men, or they were "different." This dichotomy has plagued women throughout their scant political history.

During the long drive for suffrage, most arguments for the vote rested on woman's difference from men, particularly her moral vision and virtue, although there were flashes of a more egalitarian argument based on men's and women's common humanity. In Chapter 2, we saw how the explicit egalitarianism—that men and women should have the same rights—contained in the Equal Rights Amendment to the Constitution in 1923 divided women activists for more than fifty years. The impasse ended in part because meticulous research demonstrated how protecting women's "difference" in the workplace was depressing women's wages and their capacity to earn a livelihood. The year before discrimination based on gender (sex) was banned by the 1964 Civil Rights Act, the Pay Equity Act of 1963 reflected new assumptions of similarity or "sameness." In rapid succession, and without the ratification of the ERA, a renewed women's movement, committed to egalitarian notions, led to the dismantling of an entire edifice of laws based on older assumptions of coverture, based on women's difference. New laws enabled women to obtain credit, keep their family names, or establish their own domiciles on the same basis as men.

Some scholars, such as Joan Tronto, argue that historically women's lack of power has affected the debate itself, particularly the tendency to remain stuck in the old dichotomies of "sameness" or "difference." Tronto argues that women need power to reframe the issues involved.[46]

There are hints that along with women's increased political power this reframing has begun. It can be heard in Feinstein's comment that running as a woman in politics is "no longer a disadvantage." It can be seen in the new freedom women have to run as the individuals they are, no longer required, as consultant Clint Reilly put it, to "ape men." It can be seen in sexual harassment laws and in public challenges to individual harassers, irrespective of whatever political, economic, or social power they might exercise. And it can be seen in some policy changes.

Congresswoman Pat Schroeder is one elected official who seems very conscious that her effectiveness is limited by these old dichotomies of sameness or difference. She praises women's organizations, her major allies, for being "great ceiling punchers," and for "opening doors," but says "We don't have a group organized around the fact that 'equal' does not mean 'same.'"[47] Schroeder has combined her feminism with advocacy for American families. She then asks "[w]hy are we not recognizing their care-giver role the way we do in every other society?"

In according more weight to activities and values associated with women, care must be taken not to confuse the need for these values with the belief that only women may exercise them.

While it is valid to say that women are more likely to bring to bear certain values, it is an empirical question as to whether particular women really do. Mary Hughes, who upset some of the women with her suggestion that "gender affinity" was an insufficient basis to support women candidates, also argued that "a case can be made that *this* woman, as opposed to *that* man, would not run up a deficit, manage a budget or bounce checks in her Congressional bank account." It may even be valid to give the woman candidate a presumptive edge on certain issues; however, presumption should never rule out examination. The trick is to bring more women into politics, and to bring more of the values traditionally associated with them into the political arena, without establishing a permanent link between the two.

The next generation of female politicians may make this distinction easier. The very bases for arguing that women have special needs or unique experiences may be undercut by women's greater integration in the work force and in political life. Will investment banker Mary Jones or public utilities lawyer Sally Smith share the womanly traits that are being advanced today? Or is a more plausible case for "difference" to be found between the candidacies of Jane Jones, homemaker and mother, and Sarah Smith, single woman and carpenter. Will child care be a "woman's issue" or an issue of concern to parents?

This book began with Patricia Schroeder's reframing of the issue of whether or not a woman candidate is running as a woman. We end with the hope there will come a time when the very question is moot. A time when to know a candidate is female is to remain ignorant of her political positions. A time when elected women will feel comfortable echoing Pat Schroeder's declaration when she entered Congress that she was "going to be me, Pat Schroeder." A time when both men and women will make decisions regarding war and peace, and will share responsibility for raising children and preserving the planet.

12

The Elections of 1994: A Work in Progress

In 1994 Democratic U.S. Senator Dianne Feinstein of California survived the fight of her political career to win reelection against Representative Michael Huffington and the $30,000,000 war chest he had amassed mostly from his own fortune. In a Republican year she had to struggle mightily to prevail, while popular Democratic governor of Texas, Ann Richards, went down to defeat—as did eight of the Democratic congresswomen, most of whom had served only one term. The incumbent Democratic governor of Oregon, Barbara Roberts, did not run for reelection, and neither did Democrat Joan Finney, governor of Kansas. None of the women who challenged incumbent governors achieved victory, so that the country went back to having only one woman governor, Republican Christine Todd Whitman of New Jersey.

Does this brief and gloomy summation of the results of 1994's election prove that the so-called "Year of the Woman" in 1992 was so much media hype? Are we in the grips of a profound backlash against women? Was this the "Year of the Angry White Male" as some have asserted?

The 1994 election cycle was hardly gloomy for newly elected Senator Olympia Snowe or for reelected Kay Bailey Hutchinson, or for Senator

Nancy Kassebaum, who is the first woman to chair a major Senate Committee. Or for the seven new Republican and four new Democratic congresswomen. Or for Republican women at the state legislative level, who won a record number—66 percent—of their races.[1] If any bumper sticker slogan is warranted to describe this last November, it should read "Year of the Republican Woman."

Reducing either the election cycle of 1992 or 1994 to bumper sticker slogans, even if they contain a grain of truth, however, does a profound disservice to understanding the political progress of women. The goal of achieving political equality entails profound societal changes, and like most powerful changes, such goals are not reached in a neat, step by step fashion. Social changes of this magnitude can not be gauged by a single election cycle. We feel as strongly about this assertion now as when we began this book and argued that history has tremendous explanatory powers. It is essential to put women's political progress in an historical context if we are to understand its dimensions. Calling this chapter "A Work in Progress" is one way to emphasize the need to separate one election cycle's characteristics from long-term trends that are more likely to be manifested by fits and starts in any given year. Journalist Linda Ellerbee, in December 1994, gave the concept of a work in progress a visual image. Now in her fifties, Ellerbee says her generation "graded the road," and that it is younger women who will "pave the road."[2]

The 1994 election cycle, for instance, helps us clarify what we can attribute to gender and what more appropriately should be attributed to party affiliation in women's electoral success or failure. Since a disproportionate number of women office-holders have been Democratic, there has been a tendency to equate their characteristics with all women. At the same time, to focus just on the partisan aspects of 1994 would be to miss the new thresholds that women crossed or the future challenges they face. To use just one example of a new benchmark, a record number of women decided to become candidates for national office, more than decided to run in the "Year of the Woman."

In this chapter, while reporting on the outcomes specific to 1994, we will go beyond the numbers and keep our eyes focused on deeper trends and new benchmarks. For instance, on the one hand, *we now can confidently assert that women candidates are no longer disadvantaged by either voter beliefs or in campaign contributions.* On the other hand, Americans exhibit a variety of complex feelings about women's roles, ranging from enthusiastic support at one end of the spectrum, to fear and anger, which is sometimes virulent, to milder forms of ambivalence. These feelings are evident in a range of issues, from the demonizing of Hillary Clinton, to the controversy over welfare proposals that advocate children be placed in orphanages, to the debate over abortion rights, and to the argument over family values.

Victors and Vanquished

The U.S. Senate now has eight women out of 100 members, up from two in 1990. Nationally, no Republican incumbent of either gender lost a race. Democratic incumbents in the House lost 34, of whom 8 were women. Nevertheless, the number of women in the House of Representatives will remain largely unchanged (47), since the net result is that eight new women will replace the eight Democratic women who lost. Three of the new Republican women ran as challengers; two of these three challengers defeated incumbent Democratic women.

Congresswoman Jolene Unsoeld (D–WA) was one of those defeated incumbents, whose defeat illustrates how much difference the character of one's district makes to winning or losing. Unsoeld's district was never solidly Democratic. Thus, as a Democrat in a conservative district, Unsoeld had had a tough time winning her two previous times. In her first election, 1990, Unsoeld squeaked by in a recount. The second race in a competitive district is a critical race for a newcomer. In 1992, Unsoeld won again, slightly increasing her margin. Early in 1993, however, Republican millionaire Tom Mayer announced his intentions to oust Unsoeld, and spent $2 million dollars of his own money. Mayer pummeled Unsoeld for months with a barrage of negative advertising, linking her to an increasingly unpopular president, to actions taken by the Washington state governor, and even to Illinois congressman, the indicted Dan Rostenkowski. According to Unsoeld, the relevance to Rostenkowski was the contention that the "courts can take care of Rosty; only you [the voters] can get rid of her."

Late in the primary season, Mayer ran into problems of his own over the failure to pay Washington state taxes. In a last minute write-in during the primary campaign, State Senator Linda Smith captured the Republican nomination but continued the thrust of Mayer's attack. Both Mayer and Smith used "wanted posters" to attack Unsoeld, a tactic designed to hint at wrongdoing. Smith is identified with the religious right, considered an extremist even among her own party members. In the general election, Unsoeld lost to Smith by approximately four points (52–48). Her gender was not an issue. Unsoeld attributes her defeat to a combination of factors, including Clinton's unpopularity, the strength of the religious right, the extensive drubbing she took from Mayer, and talk show hosts who broadcast torrents of criticism "16 to 24 hours a day."[3]

With the exception of Unsoeld and Congresswoman Jill Long (D–Indiana), most of the Democratic women incumbents who were defeated were freshman congresswomen in districts that were most frequently represented by a Republican. They were helped into office in 1992 by a Democratic bump. Examples include Congresswomen Karan English (D–AR), Karen Shepherd (D–Utah), Lynn Schenk (D–CA), and Majorie Margolies-Mezvinsky (D–PA). Margolies-Mezvinsky had attracted wide press coverage in 1993 after she cast a deciding vote in favor of President Clinton's budget bill. Coverage emphasized both her courage and her probable defeat as a consequence.

Whether Republican or Democrat, most of the newly elected Congresswomen conformed to the patterns discussed earlier in the book; for example, all but three women had office-holding experience. Newcomer Enid Greene Waldholtz was an attorney, and Sue Kelly (R–NY) had a business background. Helen Chenoweth (R–ID) was a Republican party consultant and a former national director of Young Republicans. What does distinguish 1994's class of Republican women is their position on abortion. All but one of the seven are anti-choice. Among Republican women, only New York's Sue Kelly considers herself pro-choice.

While no Democratic women were able to successfully challenge a Republican incumbent and win, four Democratic women captured open seats. Republican women won an equal number of the coveted open seat races. (Open seats are coveted because they are easier for any candidate, male or female, to win. For example, in 1992, twenty-two of the twenty-four newly elected women to the House of Representatives won in open seats. The flip side of this fact, however, is that the field of candidates is usually crowded. Later in this chapter, we will discuss in depth how several of these victors won over their male opponents.)

While these statistics seem like meager increases in women's representation, there is additional significance in the record number of candidates who ran. Incumbency is the key to understanding why women's representation in the House and the Senate has changed so slowly. In 1994, the House had 54 seats open out of 435; in the Senate, only eight seats out of thirty-five were open. More House seats (ninety-one) were open in 1992, primarily as a result of reapportionment: the once-a-decade redesign of House districts to keep them in line with population changes and the constitutional principle of one man, one vote. Several unexpected retirements bumped up the number of open seats in both 1992 and 1994. Despite all the rhetoric about anti-incumbent sentiment, however, most incumbents are still reelected.

One conclusion, then, about 1994 is that, in addition to competing for open seats, large numbers of women were ready to risk their political careers by taking on incumbents. More women candidates, for instance, announced they would run for governor of their state than ever before, and many of them won their party's nomination. When these women threw their hats in the ring, they joined a very select group of women who had been major party gubernatorial nominees. Many of the women who ran—Myrth York in Rhode Island, Dawn Clark Netsch in Illinois, Bonnie Campbell in Iowa, and Kathleen Brown in California— had to beat male candidates to win their party's primary. In York's case, she defeated the incumbent governor in the party—a nearly impossible feat. All the women who won their party's nomination were considered viable candidates, not flukes. Despite growing evidence of a Republican sweep toward the end of the campaign, some of these races were deemed too close to call before election day. While none of these Democratic challengers won the general election, their party affiliation and their challenger status were more important factors in their defeat than their gender.

Women who ran in 1994 for governor or Congress are just the visible ripple in an ever-growing pool of women who are gaining electoral experience in local councils and state legislatures, and who are positioning themselves to run for higher office. If, for instance, we look just one level down from gubernatorial positions, we see that women ran for and won a record number (nineteen) of lieutenant governor races. In Oklahoma, for example, where voters had never elected a woman to state-wide office, both parties nominated women and the Republican candidate won. These women, along with those who gained the positions of secretary of state, or attorney general, or treasurer, are most likely to be future gubernatorial candidates.

While the pool is growing, we cannot emphasize enough how small it remains, and how that affects the speed at which women are able to win seats. Despite the record number of candidates at the national level, for instance, the percentage of candidates who were women did not exceed 12 percent. One of the reasons to emphasize these factors—the size of the pool and the difficulty of beating incumbents—is because they are the primary factors driving incremental change. Voter bias is not the culprit—and that is dramatic news.

Studies by scholars and activists now confirm that *women candidates are not disadvantaged when they run. Women's success rates are equal to or better than men's success rates.*[4] Journalists, candidates, and women's activists alike have had trouble believing these assertions. Yet, these conclusions are based on a careful examination of over 50,000 candidates over several election cycles, and hold true for both state and federal levels of government.

Jody Newman, Executive Director of the National Women's Political Caucus (NWPC), undertook the painstaking work of examining 50,563 candidates for office. NWPC researchers did what any good scholar would do: they compared female incumbents to male incumbents, women running for open seats with men running for open seats, and female challengers to male challengers. In other words, the researchers compared like to like, apples to apples, and didn't mix races and candidates (apples and oranges) together. Their conclusion: *"The success rates for male and female candidates were virtually identical at every level of office."*

Figure 1 graphically illustrates these conclusions. In each of the three

FIGURE 1
Success Rates, State House (1986–92)
Source: NWPC

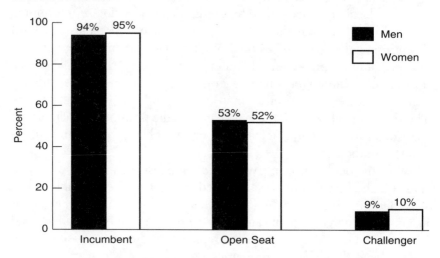

types of races, only 1 percent divides the success rates for men and women. The figure also dramatically illustrates the meaning of the phrase, "incumbent advantage." Neither men nor women won very many of these challenger races. With the odds only one in ten that a challenger will win, candidates are up against tremendous disadvantages.

The same pattern of comparable success rates held for candidates who ran for state senate seats (see Figure 2). The following illustration (Figure 3) differs from the first two in only one way: the researchers measured the success rates for a full twenty-year period, from 1972–1992. The results follow the pattern of success at the state level.

The longer timeline demonstrates how important it is to separate one election cycle, with all its "spin" from longterm trends. Whatever residual stereotypes remain in the body politic, voters are not wielding them as weapons against women. For far too long, activists did not distinguish between open seats and challenger races. They lumped them together, looked at the total number of women candidates, looked at those few who won, and concluded—erroneously—that women could not succeed in politics. When these two different kinds of races are considered separately, and they must be if conclusions are to be valid, success rates are even. In some cases, women's success rates are better. In no case, are they significantly worse than men's.[5]

FIGURE 2
Success Rates, State Senate (1986–92)
Source: NWPC

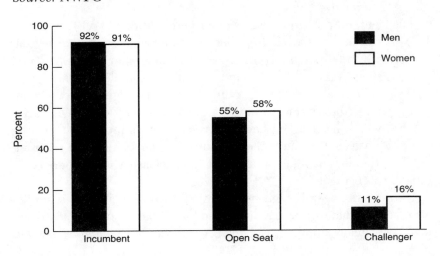

FIGURE 3
Success Rates, U.S. House (1972–92)
Source: NWPC

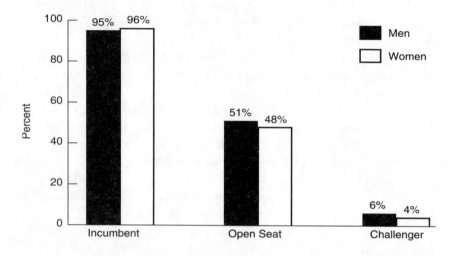

The overall results of 1994 have not been fully analyzed as of this writing. However, NWPC did publish their findings of women's success rates in the 1994 primaries. Not only did they follow the same pattern as before, but in races for the U.S. House, Senate, and governor, women's success rates were slightly better than men's (see Figures 4, 5, 6). For example, in open seat races for the House, women won 48 percent to men's 42 percent.

The Center for the American Woman and Politics (CAWP) at Rutgers University found that, while Republican women running for state legislative seats won 66 percent of their races, Democratic women had a 54 percent success rate. Republican women at the state level won 25 percent of their challenger races, setting an all-time high record. Democratic women, by contrast, won just 4 percent of their challenger races. CAWP, which has tracked and analyzed women's progress in politics more extensively than any other organization, concluded that partisanship was the dominant factor, and that "no backlash against women candidates was evident."[6]

If this were not sufficiently good news for women candidates, studies also showing that women candidates no longer have monetary disadvantages are equally stunning. *The dollar gap between men and women has*

FIGURE 4
Success Rates, U.S. House (1994 Primaries)
Source: NWPC

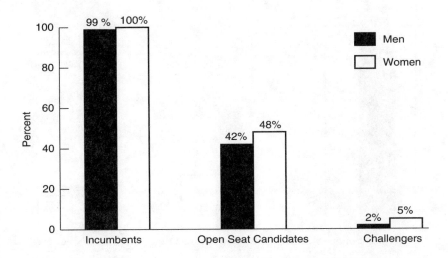

FIGURE 5
Success Rates, U.S. Senate (1994 Primaries)
Source: NWPC

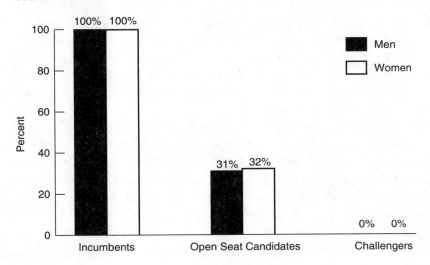

FIGURE 6
Success Rates, Governor (1994 Primaries)
Source: NWPC

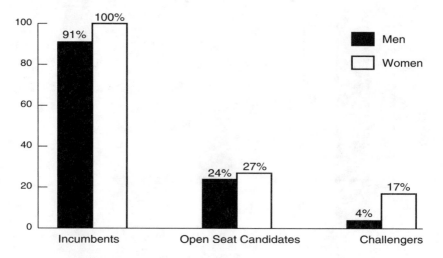

been closed.[7] Once again, the studies carefully distinguished among incumbent, challenger, and open seat races.

The breakthrough year for women and money was 1988, not 1992. In that year women candidates for Congress for the U.S. House raised 119 percent of what male candidates raised. Incumbent women equaled or surpassed men, challengers had no more difficulty than men, and in open seat races, since 1984, Democratic women have consistently raised more money than men. These data are a striking example of how misleading a focus on one election cycle can be. Many observers, including ourselves, thought the real story in 1992 was the flood of money going to women candidates. Instead, as these figures indicate, 1992 was the year when women's gains became *visible.*

We reported earlier that women feel particularly disadvantaged in raising money from Political Action Committees (PACs). Yet, since 1988, women have raised as much money as men from these committees. Women had a slight advantage in 1988, and in 1992, received on an average $54,000 more in PAC money than male candidates. This does not mean, of course, that every woman has adequate funding, but it does mean that the old shibboleths about women and politics are simply outdated.

Women's organizations rightly share a large portion of the credit for making financial support for women candidates a high priority. The capacity and willingness of women to donate money to candidates is part of a more fundamental change in American society.

EMILY's List, a Democratic PAC which supports pro-choice women, attracted extensive attention in 1992 when it gave nearly $6 million. In 1994, EMILY's List donations to candidates and to get out the vote campaigns reached a little over $9 million dollars. WISH List, modeled after EMILY's List for pro-choice Republican women but which has been operating for only a few years, raised $700,000 in this cycle. The PAC landscape for Republican women reflects the fact that the division over abortion runs much deeper in the Republican Party. For instance, the Susan B. Anthony List raises money for Republican candidates who are "pro-life."[8]

The Wall Street Journal recently reported that there are 48 women's PACs in the country, and that experts say that women's giving to all causes, not just politics, is on the rise. The Independent Sector studied women's giving and found a nearly 10 percent rise in charitable contributions between 1989 and 1991. During the same period men's giving fell 22 percent. Lawrence Katz, a Harvard professor who previously was the chief economist at the Department of Labor, explained, "Any way you cut the data, women have gained on men."[9]

With the proliferation of women's PACs has come a greater political diversity. Money is now available for women who do not share a feminist agenda or who decline to support abortion.

Beyond the Numbers

The most fascinating changes for women entering political life are not captured by the data on success rates or campaign contributions. These less tangible changes identified in the previous chapter, lie in trends that have developed over time, and which became *even more visible* in November of 1994. Increasingly, women candidates can run as the women they are—the fundamental meaning of the book's title, *Running as a Woman*. Regardless of whether their policy positions are liberal or conservative, women candidates are increasingly free from the old adage to be as "like-male as possible." The three elements that comprised the advice to "not run as a woman" bear repeating: 1) don't call attention to yourself as female; 2) don't mobilize women voters; and 3) don't pitch women's issues. While these constraints are not entirely absent from contemporary campaigns—indeed plenty of vestiges remain—their previous potency is truly a thing of the past.

Women candidates are increasingly able to present themselves to voters without cloaking themselves in male authority. As California campaign consultant Mary Hughes put it: "Women no longer have to pose behind large desks, and be backlit by booklined shelves. Campaign literature now pictures them as they are in their every day lives."[10]

This year women candidates offered plenty of those images to the voters. Campaign literature and television ads pictured women in station wagons, often with a full complement of children, as a way of saying they were in touch with daily life, not removed from it. Male candidates also had to convince voters they could understand everyday concerns—some men wore jeans or drove pickup trucks to emphasize their affinity with voters. The difference between male and female candidates lies in the liberation from past proscriptions. A station wagon full of kids, for example, is a quintessential female image. Most women candidates feared such images would make them look "unprofessional," or would fail to project the kind of stature and authority voters seek in their elected leaders. The ability to be placed in one's familiar context, even one that might emphasize women's traditional roles, and still be elected is new. Policy outcomes may or may not be affected as a result, but it sure does make the political arena a more comfortable place for women when they can be themselves.

In the 1994 election cycle, former Congresswoman Olympia Snowe helped widen the opportunity for another group, however small in number, of political women: she won her election to the U.S. Senate by a substantial margin, despite the fact that her husband was just finishing a term as the not-so-popular governor of Maine. Voters were clearly capable of distinguishing her record and her skills from those of her very public husband.

Conversely, in 1994, a wife's character and behavior became central in a man's campaign. Congressman Michael Huffington (who challenged Senator Feinstein) found himself defending his wife, Arianna, over everything from her religious beliefs to her ambition to the originality of her books. A long profile of Arianna, for example, in *Vanity Fair,* entitled "Arianna's Virtual Candidate," quotes her former literary agent as saying, "My illustration for them is 'Driving Michael Huffington': Arianna wearing a top behind the wheel and Michael sitting in the backseat looking bewildered."[11] Lurking behind these attacks were vestiges of ancient archetypes—images of the powerful but invisible seductress able to manipulate her man, a kind of modern-day Mata Hari. The same Democrats who expressed glee that such publicity helped defeat Republican Huffington despair when similar images are evoked over Hillary Clinton's political role. Yet, campaign strategy based on attacking a spouse's behavior or beliefs is increasingly rare and increasingly condemned when it occurs.

Another group of political women set records in 1994—lesbians. California voters elected Sheila Kuehl, a candidate from Santa Monica who was openly lesbian, to the State Assembly. Also in California, Teri Schwartz was elected to the Los Angeles Superior Court, and Bonnie Dumanis, was elected to the San Diego City Court. Lesbian women have broken through electoral barriers previously on the local level, and have been elected to city councils and boards of supervisors, but this year more aimed at state level or even state-wide races.

In New York, Democrat Karen Burstein, also a lesbian, ran for attorney general. Burstein was expected to win until, at the last moment, she was swamped by the Republican tidal wave. When Republicans tried to make an issue of her sexuality, the normally staid *New York Times* condemned the attack and argued that Burstein's sexual identity had no place in the race.

William Waybourn, of the Gay and Lesbian Victory Fund, a political action committee which supported seventeen candidates nationwide, twelve of whom were successful, quipped: "It's the first election I've ever been in where it was more hazardous to be an open Democrat than an open gay."[12] We do not mean to suggest that a candidate's sexuality no longer affects his or her political viability. Many women candidates still experienced attacks on their sexuality, whether lesbian or not. Still, the successful election of openly gay candidates, and the defeat of several antigay rights initiatives in Utah and Oregon, when considered in the light of history, indicate that the political environment has opened up a bit for all women.

Women candidates, whatever their sexual orientation, party affiliation, or policy positions, cannot be considered apart from the voters who elected them. This last election cycle provides additional evidence for several propositions identified in Chapter Seven: (1) although women voters do not automatically prefer women candidates, their votes—since they are a majority of the electorate—can determine the outcome of a woman's election; (2) male candidates can, and have, successfully mobilized women voters; (3) the Democratic party has a slight edge among women voters, but it is a benefit more likely to matter during primary contests than in general elections; (4) the key to understanding how to mobilize women voters resides in looking at differences among women rather than at their similarities; and (5) when a gender gap—a difference between men and women's votes—does materialize, it is rarely based on women's rights issues.

In 1994, the sheer size of the gender gap between women's and men's votes, especially white men, provided the fodder for 1994's slogan: "Year of the Angry White Male." Overall, women preferred Democratic candidates, while men preferred Republican candidates 54 to 46, an eight point difference between the sexes. A bare majority of men (51 to 52 percent) have consistently preferred the Republican party since about 1980. In 1994, the percentage of white men voting Republican, however, jumped to roughly 62 percent, giving the election cycle its moniker: "The Year of the Angry White Male." Despite women's greater allegiance to the Democratic party, however, they produced neither victories nor defeats for Democratic women candidates in any consistent fashion. At the same time, women voters put *some* male and female candidates over the top.

Texas Governor Ann Richards has experienced winning with women (1990), and losing them (1994). In her first race for governor, Republican and independent women voters crossed over and joined with large numbers of Democratic women to create her victory. In 1994, women divided their votes fairly evenly between the governor and her challenger, Republican George W. Bush. Governor Richards received 50 percent of their vote, while George W. Bush captured 49 percent; worth noting is the fact that women in Texas outnumbered the men who went to the polls, 52 percent to 48 percent. White voters, who comprise roughly 76 percent of the population preferred Bush by significant margins, whether they were women or men. White women gave 40 percent of their vote to Richards, and 59 percent to Bush. White men voted for Richards even less, 31 percent; they gave 67 percent to Bush.[13]

Candace Windel, director of the Texas Poll, believes several dynamics were at work. In 1990, when many Republican and independent women crossed over to vote for Richards, the Republican candidate, Clayton

Williams, embarrassed many of the women in his party. This year, Republican women felt comfortable with their candidate, George W. Bush, the ex-president's son.

In addition, Windel thinks both gender and race were involved in a series of issues that she labels "equal employment" issues. "A vociferous element of white, especially white-collar, men was negative . . . rolling into one ball of wax Richards, her appointments of women and minorities, women above them in the workplace, affirmative action and race." By contrast, "blue-collar white men focused on Richards's veto [of a bill which would permit carrying a concealed weapon] almost exclusively."

Both national and local reporters printed some of Richards's speeches, which so endear Richards to feminists, but which may have helped crystallize men's sentiments against her. At one Dallas campaign event, Richards compared George W. Bush to an ungrateful husband: "Every single one of you in this room knows what it's like to work like a dog to move things forward and then have some whiner come in there. How many of you have stood over a stack of white shirts—you know the kind I mean—and you've sprinkled 'em down real good the night before and you iron them and when he gets home he has plenty of nice white shirts folded in his drawer, and he comes in and he says, 'There's a wrinkle right here,' and he says, 'Why did you fold 'em and put 'em in the drawer? I like 'em on the hanger.'"

Warming to her topic, Richards continued, "And how many of you have had a real busy day at work or doing some volunteer job or getting everything ready at school for the big P.T.A. meeting, and you come home, and man, it's like a house afire. You run in there and you get that piece of meat and you salt it and season it and get it ready to put in the broiler. And you toss the salad and put the beans on and the potatoes get soggy. You're scurrying and scurrying and doing your damndest. And when he finally comes home, he tells you he's already eaten—in this case, off a silver platter."[14]

In a similar vein, she delivered a speech to a group of young women from Girls State who visited the capitol as part of their program, a speech that came to be known as the "Prince Charming Speech." "I cannot tell you what a pitfall it is to count on Prince Charming to make you feel better about yourself and to take care. Prince Charming may be driving a Honda and telling you you have no equal, but that's not going to do much good when you've got kids and a mortgage. And I could add he's got a beer gut and a wandering eye."[15]

Wayne Slater, the Austin Bureau Chief of the *Dallas Morning News,* heard the "ungrateful husband" speech, which he describes as droll and funny, and without the edge of anger that news stories convey. He noted, however, that some of Richards' operatives "went ballistic" immediately after the speech. Later, Slater came to understand its significance, and says that George W. Bush understood it as well. After the campaign was over, Slater and Bush traveled together to a meeting in Virginia. Bush told Slater that he knew when he heard these speeches "that he was in better shape than he thought with women," knowing his voters would not identify with this "I hate men aspect of feminism."

Slater echoes Windel's belief that affirmative action was important. While Texas governors have few real powers, they have an unusually large number of appointments to make. Richards, true to her campaign pledge that her appointments would reflect the diversity of the Texas population, named women to at least half of the more than 3,000 positions. "Every time she would tout these figures, they would be reinterpreted to reinforce Bush voters." Richards, understandably proud of her record of appointing "your sons and daughters," claimed a positive achievement. Bush voters, however, heard "quota." Slater says he now understands why Bush operatives kept goading him to write stories on her appointments. "Her claims may have reassured liberals but they raised a whole series of issues with moderates and conservatives." Slater says that by now most people have had some experience with affirmative action, or "think they do," and believe they or someone they know has lost a job to a minority or a woman.[16]

This dynamic, by no means the only dynamic operating for Bush— Texas has been growing more Republican for years—is eerily reminiscent of the 1990 governor's race in California between Pete Wilson and Dianne Feinstein, when polls showed Republican who were women thinking about voting for Feinstein "went home" to Wilson after she made a pledge that her appointments would similarly reflect California's diverse population. She called it opening up government; he quickly labeled it quotas.

In a contrast with Richards' electoral fate, California women voters saved Democratic Senator Dianne Feinstein by giving her the winning margin. But, the same female electorate simultaneously gave the majority of their votes to Republican Governor Pete Wilson rather than challenger Kathleen Brown. All four candidates involved in these two races tried to mobilize women voters.

The governor's race between Wilson and Brown illustrates a real difference in conceptualizing how to mobilize women voters. Governor Wilson, for instance, stressed from the beginning of his campaign three major themes of significance to women: economic opportunity, health care, and personal security or crime. In addition to these specific issues, the general Republican message against government intrusion was adapted for different segments of women, such as small businesswomen, especially those who chafed against governmental regulations.

Wilson's challenger, Kathleen Brown, by contrast, targeted women based on their voting history rather than developing a generic message that could be adapted to women voters. Over 800,000 "occasional women voters" were identified: these were women who voted Democratic in 1992 but who did not vote in the 1994 primary. These voters were presumed to be loyal Democrats who, if they could be persuaded to vote, would choose Democratic candidates. Campaign operatives regard the effort as successful in its own terms: 140,000 or so of the targeted women did vote in November 1994. However, the effort didn't help Brown, who lost to Wilson by 13 points. (It may have helped Feinstein in her much closer race.)

Brown's campaign manager, Clint Reilly, believes the coalitional nature of the Democratic constituency dictates this targeting strategy. For instance, the Brown campaign, fearful of losing men, particularly blue-collar men, also targeted them with television ads and mailings. The effort was singularly unsuccessful. Reilly describes blue-collar men as "unmovable," unable to get past a set of facts about Brown as a liberal Democrat. A focus group tactic, moreover, asking participants to assign an animal to each candidate, elicited strong gender bias. Wilson was described as a "lion, a tiger, or a bear." By contrast, the images of Brown were of "a kitten, kitty cat, rabbit, or lamb." Reilly contends that, with such voters, "any gender-based message would be counterproductive." "It's easier to mobilize women from the right [Republican] because the coalition is not so contradictory—you almost have to appeal separately to get them [Democratic constituencies] to vote." [17]

Yet, in the final analysis, campaigns must be considered as a whole, inseparable from candidate, message, district, and quality of campaign. Four vignettes, featuring candidates who ran for open congressional seats, and won, help to capture the flavor of women's campaigns in this election cycle—and show how diverse women candidates have become.

Newcomers Zoe Lofgren from San Jose, California; Barbara Cubin from Wyoming; Sue Kelly, from Katonah, New York; and Sue Myrick from Charlotte, North Carolina, all ran for open seats. As previously noted, open seats are coveted opportunities, often unleashing pent-up ambition in candidates who have invested a life time preparing themselves for such an opportunity. Each of these women faced one or more such ambitious men in their party primaries. Each woman is different from the other, but each campaign offers us a glimpse of the new freedom women have to run as themselves, as women, despite fierce competition and despite the profound differences in the character of their districts.

Democrat Zoe Lofgren of San Jose won election to California's 16th District, replacing Don Edwards, a much revered congressman who was retiring after 32 years. In the substantially Democratic district, Lofgren's achievement lay not so much in her overwhelming victory in November—she won 65 percent of the vote—but in her win in the June primary, a race in which she came from far behind to defeat the former mayor of San Jose and odds-on favorite Tom McEnery.

How did her victory happen? In a post-primary interview Zoe Lofgren, now 46, described her lifelong involvement with politics:

> I had always worked in campaigns. I didn't realize until high school that other people really didn't. My mother was the precinct captain for our block in South Palo Alto, and I walked my first precinct in 1952 . . .
>
> I got a scholarship to Stanford and majored in political science. My father was a truck driver, and my mother worked in a school cafeteria. When I graduated in 1970, I was the first in my family to go through college.
>
> I knew four kids who were going East right after graduation. They all had family connections for internships, that kind of thing. They had room for a fifth person in the car, so I went along. When I got to Washington, I talked my way into a job with Don Edwards and worked for him for eight and a half years.[18]

Lofgren went on to explain that, while trying to draft a bill, it suddenly came to her that law school would be useful. Returning to California, she attended the University of Santa Clara Law School, where she subsequently taught part time. She then practiced law briefly before running for public office, first for the community college board and then, in 1980, for the Santa Clara County Board of Supervisors. She served on that body until her successful race for Congress. In the late 1970s she married a fellow lawyer.

Tom McEnery is one of the best-known politicians in Santa Clara County. He remade the face of San Jose during his two terms as mayor with his active pursuit of redevelopment, but Lofgren is no slouch. She has been involved with politics in some form since early childhood and has been professionally involved therein almost all of her adult life. Nonetheless McEnery was seen as the heir apparent to Don Edwards, holding an early double-digit lead among likely voters. McEnery was endorsed by most of the significant local politicians, including incumbent San Jose Mayor Susan Hammer. The two most prominent figures in the area, retiring Edwards and Congressman Norm Mineta, also a former San Jose mayor, from the adjacent district remained neutral.

Yet Lofgren won the primary. How did she do this? First, Lofgren turned to women. She mobilized support from well-known women outside the district, including Senator Barbara Boxer and Congresswoman Anna Eshoo from nearby Palo Alto, along with a number of feminist organizations. An endorsement letter from Senator Boxer, for instance, was sent to women voters in the district. EMILY's List sent her major financial support, $30,000. Lofgren was also able to mobilize leaders of the minority communities whose programs she had sought to protect in her years on the board of supervisors. Support from these constituencies earned her ballot box dividends on election day. Her campaign media adviser Bill Carrick underscored that this was no accident when he told the *San Jose Mercury News:* "We loaded it [advertising] up on daytime TV and on shows where we knew there would be a lot of women viewers."[19]

In the second place, her campaign decided to play up her status as mother. Professional politician that she is, she has borne two children while a supervisor, caring for them in her office in their infancy—with help from her mother. Indeed, she even got her board of supervisors colleagues to time votes around her nursing schedule. She now says:

> The most important thing in my life in terms of understanding the world was having my children—the major shaper . . . I don't need to prove that I'm a professional person. Is that why I'm running for Congress? No. All the things I'd want to change I learned not at law school, but at the elementary school.[20]

Thus her campaign attempted to get her listed on the ballot as a county supervisor/mother. When the California Secretary of State issued the opinion that this would be illegal, a firestorm of publicity—free media coverage—ensued. "I hoped to raise a stink—I never expected to be on the Today Show and CNN." She received attention beyond her wildest dreams and high-priced publicity well beyond the limits of what her campaign could have afforded. San Jose State University political scientist Larry Gerston, the person who collected the data for the exit polls after the primary, calls this ploy a brilliant strategy.[21]

Finally, her campaign took a gamble on going negative, something most consultants agree is dangerous for women candidates to do. Television ads depicted McEnery as excessively pro-development. After the election, the San Jose Mercury News quoted "key members" of McEnery's staff as saying that "Lofgren defined herself as Saint Zoe and him as the Redevelopment Devil." McEnery refused to reply in kind and even lost the downtown city council district where both he and Lofgren reside. Says Bill Carrick: "In all honesty, it's easy to second-guess this stuff. But the truth is, you're sitting there and you have a 20-point lead, that's a tough call. Are you going to counterpunch with a negative ad?"[22]

McEnery saw his twenty-point lead evaporate. Exit polls and other post-election analysis reveal that her strategies paid off. The composition of her majority included women, and voters from minority and blue-collar precincts. Women gave her 58 percent of their votes, 38 percent to McEnery. Long service to blue-collar voters gave Lofgren a credibility in reaching out to them in the primary that other Democratic women candidates—most notably, Kathleen Brown—lacked in the 1994 election cycle. Her blue-collar support was all the more impressive in that McEnery was not only endorsed by all the major media, including the San Jose Mercury News, but by the unions.[23]

Like Lofgren, Republicans Sue Kelly of New York, Sue Myrick of North Carolina, and Barbara Cubin of Wyoming all won primaries with elements of surprise, indeed with elements of David going against Goliath. With no previous office-holding experience, for example, Sue Kelly won the right to succeed 26-year incumbent Hamilton Fish in New York's 19th District. Kelly defeated six men in the primary, two of them millionaires, and then defeated Hamilton Fish, Jr. in November. The younger Fish, who early on departed from the family's long-term affiliation with the Republican party (his grandfather was also a congressman), has been known to laugh off his Democratic liability in this Republican district with the quip "it's a family seat." Fish's family lineage, however, was not strong enough to withstand the anti-Democratic tide in New York.

Sue Kelly's most impressive credential is her experience in the business world. Mother of four and wife of a Westchester County real estate developer, she has been in the health-care field and has also worked in real estate herself. She decided to enter the primary late and received no help from the establishment. Nor did any important party figures come forward to support her, although she did receive help behind the scenes from Congresswoman Susan Molinari, who represents Staten Island.

Her campaign consultant, Jay Townsend, explains the thinking behind the September primary victory.

> What worked for the Democratic women in 1992 wasn't necessarily going to work again this time around. I told her, "Don't play up gender." She ran on the issue of jobs and of being tough as nails on crime. "You're a woman, and voters will be able to figure that out without your discussing it," was my advice.
>
> Mail is the most important tool in this district, because the TV comes out of New York City. We featured her six male opponents in every piece of campaign literature we sent out. We cornered the market on the female side, and we let her opponents deal with a fragmented male market. I estimate that she got about 65 percent of the female voters in the primary.
>
> At least four of her opponents outspent us. We spent smart. We figured we'd never get the older folks to vote for a woman, and we figured that people under 35 don't vote as much. We had 105,000 possible Republican voters and we defined the likely electorate out of that number and then defined her natural constituency within that. Other candidates mailed to the whole universe and wasted money. We didn't.[24]

Political novice Kelly had established an office for Congressman Fish in her city about twenty years ago and had volunteered there briefly, her sole political experience of any kind going into the primary. She demonstrated considerable political skill in the race, however, positioning herself as pro-choice in the primary against all the men and then moving to consolidate her position with party insiders after receiving the nomination. Says WISH List founding member Candy Straight, who gave Kelly both moral and financial support: "I knew Kelly was viable when I saw who she hired as a campaign manager," referring to a New Jersey political operative.[25]

During the general election, Kelly signed Newt Gingrich's Contract with America—although she told her home town newspaper the *North County News* that she doesn't support all of the Contract's provisions, such as the one calling for restrictions on abortion counseling at federally funded clinics.[26] At least one feminist organization, however, withdrew support and endorsed Fish as a result.

If Sue Kelly represents the "left wing" of the incoming class of Republican Congresswomen—she is the only one to be pro-choice—then Wyoming's Barbara Cubin represents the right, or more precisely, the religious right. Elected at large as the sparsely populated state's only House member, Cubin had been a state senator before her successful run for Congress. According to University of Wyoming historian Michael Cassity, Cubin was known derisively as "the prom queen" of the state legislature.[27] Cassity believes that gender operated in her favor in the primary in that she was the only woman in the five-way race. Wyoming had an open seat in both the House and the Senate, brought about by Senator Malcolm Wallop's retirement. Cubin's male opponents included the speaker of the legislature and Wallop's chief aide, who was seen as the candidate destined for the House seat. As in New York's 19th District, a plethora of male candidates left the only woman in the field triumphant—although by a plurality and not a majority.

Cubin's November victory also constituted a considerable achievement. The Democratic candidate, Jackson attorney Bob Schuster, outspent her by a significant margin. Indeed, according to Cassity, on a per capita basis, Schuster's spending was second only to Michael Huffington's in California. Wyoming's only statewide newspaper, the *Casper Star-Tribune,* refused to endorse either major party candidate, suggesting instead that the name of the former Wallop aide Rob Wallace, who had lost to Cubin in the primary, be written in. And, most surprising of all, the anti-choice Cubin endorsed an initiative measure that would have banned abortion, an initiative which went down to defeat—while Cubin won. Cassity ascribes this turn of events to the rage voters felt against President Clinton. Cubin is more conservative than the electorate, but Wyomingites were so eager to repudiate range reform, a policy initiated by Secretary of the Interior Bruce Babbitt, that they voted for her anyway. Barbara Cubin herself publicly thanked radio talk show host Rush Limbaugh a few weeks after the election for helping to create the climate for her victory.

Like Kelly and Cubin, North Carolinian Sue Myrick won the Republican primary against a large field of male opponents—four, to be exact, one of whom was the minority leader of the state legislature. A prominent political figure herself by virtue of being mayor of Charlotte, Myrick was a credible candidate in the heavily Republican 9th District, which includes only part of the city (and not its center) as well as surrounding rural and suburban areas.

In 1992, Myrick unsuccessfully challenged Lauch Faircloth in the Republican Senatorial primary, and is quick to point out that she found it much easier to raise money in 1994 for an open seat than she had in 1992 as a challenger. During her campaign against Faircloth, she had to contend with an underground telephone campaign of vilification in which it was alleged that she had had abortions, that her son is homosexual, that she had lived with men other than her husband, and that she is "New Age."

Ironically, the media and Democratic opponents have identified *her* with the religious right, she believes unfairly. In fact, Myrick considers the religious right the "most dangerous influence in America today." This identification stemmed from a remark she made during her initial foray into electoral politics. "My first mayor's race was very tight. I gave glory to God." Ever since then, Myrick said, "I've been tagged with it. I'm just a plain old Methodist."[28] While she is pro-life, she sees herself as somewhat moderate in that she is willing to accept abortions for reasons such as rape, incest, and the health of the mother, a position for which she has drawn fire from the religious right.

A fiscal conservative, Myrick is an advocate of small government and believes in allowing the churches and other private organizations to deal with controversial social issues. One to watch in the future, she has been elected freshman class liaison with the leadership. "I'm ready to go up front."

These women all illustrate the different ways women are being freed from the imperatives to mimic men. Lofgren, for instance, had the "like-male" credentials but chose to emphasize her concern for children and families. In lieu of office-holding experience, Kelly was able to utilize her business background to establish appropriate credentials. Despite Kelly's campaign consultant's advice that she "not run as a woman," her entire campaign was based on carefully targeting women voters. Cubin, like Kelly and Lofgren, defeated men who believed they were destined to win. Myrick won this year despite a recent campaign filled with attacks on her sexuality, her family, and her lifestyle.

These women also espouse very different political positions, even as members of a single political party. Running as a woman should not be construed as synonymous with running as a feminist, although running as a feminist may in fact work for some candidates in some elections. Candidates must not equate the capacity to run as a woman with a license to engage in sharp-edged anger against men. The anger so apparent in the 1992 campaign tended to be directed against the absence of women in legislative bodies, especially the U.S. Senate, and was expressed in such slogans as "Two percent is not enough," not against men per se.

All of the newly elected women, despite their diversity, succeeded in exciting women about their campaigns without claiming a gender advantage and without alienating male voters. Because women's entrance into politics is still a work in progress, however, each candidate will have to carefully negotiate the fine line between running comfortably as a woman, freed from the imperative to be "like-male," and running a campaign which flaunts gender. Women candidates must neither neglect women voters nor rely too heavily upon them. There is no formulaic answer, since districts and states can vary widely in voter attitudes. Failure to understand or analyze these fine lines, however, may sink more than a few campaigns.

Toward the Twenty-first Century

In the preceding eleven chapters we identified the ways in which the trajectory, or direction, of historical change for all American women has carried women politicians along with it, including those who oppose feminism or other issues involving women's rights. That trajectory started with married women who were without citizenship rights, "covered" by their husbands' identities for all public purposes, advanced to the formation of a political identity of their own in the nineteenth century based on women's altruism, nonpartisanship, and claims of moral superiority, and has reached the point where many women—frequently with a long-term commitment to employment—see themselves as having interests parallel to those of men, interests with an impact on public policy and on politics.

This several hundred-year-old current of change has gathered a tremendous velocity in the last few decades. Between Helen Gahagan Douglas's unsuccessful attempt in 1950 to capture one of California's U.S. Senate seats, and today's representation by Senators Barbara Boxer and Dianne Feinstein, lies a sea change that has left few people unaffected. In the 1950s, for instance, hundreds of thousands of young women went to college, but few expected to use their education for personal professional advancement. Rather, they expected to marry an appropriate mate and provide cultural enrichment to the home. In the 1990s, not only has the number of women attending college changed, but their aspirations are profoundly different. High percentages of women go to graduate school. In the last twenty years alone, women have more than tripled their presence in the nation's law schools.

In 1950 few, if any, major institutions were headed by women. Few women were found in corporate hierarchies. Women journalists were by and large consigned to the women's pages—there were no female counterparts to Edward R. Murrow. Women college professors were largely confined to teaching at women's colleges. Women politicians were a rarity, even at the local level. A married woman found it difficult, if not impossible to get credit in her own name. Few women had financial independence. Being competitive was seen as unfeminine, and there were few women athletes to give the lie to this belief. In short, few women could offer young girls images of female authority.

In 1995, two women sit on the U.S. Supreme Court. A woman is president of an Ivy League university (the University of Pennsylvania) for the first time. Not only are law school classrooms filled with young women but one woman, Herma Hill Kay, heads a prestigious law school, Boalt Hall at the University of California, Berkeley. Young women can realistically aspire to attend college on an athletic scholarship, where their competitiveness will be rewarded along with their intellectual achievements, and where sports programs required by federal law will give them equal opportunity. In numerous workplaces, women are now bosses. Women entrepreneurs outnumber men in small business startups, and have access to credit even if they are married. As a consequence of the growth in the number of businesswomen, there are now female heads of local Chambers of Commerce as well as woman presidents of local Rotary Clubs, until quite recently all-male bastions that bitterly resisted becoming open to both sexes. Increasing numbers of women are being ordained as Protestant clergy, and some have become rabbis. Women, although still in the minority on college faculties, have substantially increased their numbers, even at elite universities, and they have mounted a formidable challenge to the traditional curriculum.

In short, women are representing and exercising authority throughout society in roles unimagined by their mothers and grandmothers. These are developments that far transcend the partisan labels of Republican or Democrat, that go to the core of family structure and the global economy and will not be reversed by any one election cycle.

Certain episodes are especially telling. For example, in the summer of

1994 Americans following the preliminary hearing to determine whether famed athlete O. J. Simpson should stand trial for murder could watch a woman judge preside, while a woman prosecutor presented her arguments. Then they might listen to a female anchor interview a female criminal law expert about what to expect next. Not a single one of these authority figures would have likely been female forty years earlier.

These same changes have profoundly affected the climate in which top level women leaders exercise power. No woman senator, for example, has ever had a debut on the national stage like that of Dianne Feinstein. In chapter eleven, we discussed how little power women have within legislative bodies, once they arrive. Senator Feinstein's first two years in office were exceptional by any measure. Elected to fill a two-year term in 1992 because Pete Wilson had resigned to run successfully for the California governorship, Feinstein benefited from her party's stake in helping her create a high profile so as to position herself for a second race very soon after the first. Thus, her committee assignments—Appropriations and Judiciary—represented plums that don't often go to newcomers. This said, the politician herself must be given credit for maximizing her opportunities. Whether working to expedite relief for stricken Southern California after the Northridge earthquake of January 1994 or going to bat for California farmers, Feinstein convinced a broad range of Californians, including certain members of the business community, that she could effectively represent the state's interests—as witness, the prominent Republicans such as Peter Ueberroth and Los Angeles mayor Richard Riordan who endorsed her campaign for reelection in 1994.

Twice during the first two years, she put herself on the line for major pieces of legislation. More prominently than anyone else in the Senate, she fought to get a ban on assault weapons included in the Crime Bill of 1994. A dramatic moment occurred during a debate on the bill when Idaho Senator Larry Craig implied that, because she is a woman, she could not understand gun-related issues. She icily informed him that in 1978 assassinated San Francisco Mayor George Moscone had died in her arms after being shot, thus providing her with a first-hand experience of the tragic toll taken by firearms. This was a front page story, with Feinstein clearly seen as getting the best of the exchange in most accounts.

Even more remarkable was her leadership in shepherding the California Desert Protection Act to final passage in the waning days of the session immediately prior to 1994's election—legislation, it must be pointed out, that former senator Alan Cranston had labored for in vain. Having negotiated nineteen separate compromises with Republicans, she was able to get fourteen Republicans to vote with Democrats and thus break a threatened filibuster at a time when Republicans in the Senate were holding hostage many other pieces of Democratic-sponsored legislation. She won reelection narrowly, despite these achievements. On the other hand, it is remarkable that she won at all, given the nature of this election cycle and given the massive assault against her. Says Mark di Camillo of the California Poll: "I don't know of another politician in California who could have survived a six-months-long campaign of defamation like she did."[29]

In 1950 young girls could read about Senator Margaret Chase Smith standing up to Senator Joseph McCarthy. Brave though she was, however, Smith was not in the legislative trenches negotiating compromises, and neither were other women politicians at that time, except in rare instances. In the 104th Congress, Senator Nancy Kassebaum of Kansas chairs a committee, having become the second woman senator to do so.[30] (Only six women have ever served as chair of a standing committee in either the Senate or the House. Three have served in the House on a single issue, or select committee: of the three, two—Yvonne Brathwaite Burke and Martha Wright Griffiths—have served as chair of the "Committee on the House Beauty Shop," now blissfully defunct.[31] Young girls now have role models not only of courage, like Smith, but also of highly publicized political effectiveness, like Feinstein and Kassebaum.

These breakthroughs are happening so fast that they may appear commonplace. The same trajectory that women applaud, however, men may fear. Shortly after the elections, commentator Milton Viorst wrote an essay in which he explored the anger of white men. "The numbers tell us that something is going on in our society that is troubling white men but not white women—or at least is troubling women less—and it clearly lies beneath the surface of everyday political grievances." Viorst points to the "whirlwind of cultural and economic change that they [men] cannot control," likening it in intensity to the "dissolution of the feudal system and the rise of the Industrial Revolution." He identifies the culprit ". . . in the globalization of the workplace, unprecedented in human experience."[32] These are perhaps the workers, mostly men, that Secretary of Labor Robert Reich calls "the anxious class." The most anti-Democratic male voters in the electorate are those who lack a high school education and who have seen their income steadily decline over the last fifteen years, along with most employment opportunities.

The velocity of change in women's roles has even carried women along in its wake who are profoundly opposed to the women's movement or a feminist agenda. Twenty years ago, for example, advocates of the religious right might well have spurned women who traded homemaker roles for political ones. Today, as we have seen, women who espouse the views of the religious right are running for and winning office.

Sometimes ambivalence over women's roles is evident in an individual woman. Noteworthy is the post-1992 behavior of Marilyn Quayle, wife of the former vice-president Dan Quayle. In the summer of 1992, lawyer Marilyn Quayle addressed the Republican national convention and gave a rousing call to arms on behalf of traditional family values for women. Following the defeat of the Bush–Quayle ticket for reelection, she moved back to Indiana with her family, joined a law firm, and announced that she was Marilyn Tucker Quayle for professional purposes.

Tension over gender issues lies at the heart of most of today's critical electoral issues. In the same year (1994) that the movie *Disclosure,* which features a female boss's harassment of a male subordinate, is depicted as male backlash, exhibit A, all seven women Senators, regardless of party, closed ranks to try and deny two stars and full retirement funds to Admiral Kelso, the Navy official with responsibility for handling the sexual harassment scandal known as "Tailhook." While the Senate ultimately voted to allow Kelso to keep his rank and pension—after a rancorous debate—54 to 43, the women succeeded in mobilizing support from nearly half the senators, including support from some of the most ardent defenders of Supreme Court Justice Clarence Thomas against Anita Hill's allegations of sexual harassment. The literal definition of backlash is "a violent and usually hostile reaction to some event." In other words, backlash is a resistance to change, not a reversal of it.

In the Republican party, pro-choice women combat anti-choice women. Democrats worry about how they can reconcile support from women voters with men's defection. Tension over gender roles pervades most institutions of our time, whether they are economic, social, religious, or political. The Roman Catholic Church, for instance, struggled for several years to craft a new statement on women's roles. After becoming mired in controversy, the church abandoned the effort. The same tension is reflected when newly installed Speaker of the House Newt Gingrich creates an advisory committee on Family Quality of Life to reconcile Congressional and family demands, and his Majority Leader Dick Armey simultaneously declares that in order to accomplish an ambitious agenda, Republicans may have to "work seven days a week if necessary, even 20 hours a day if necessary."[33]

Whether one points to breakthroughs or to backlash, the deeper story behind the 1994 election cycle is that as women have entered public life, a profound shift has taken place. The era when women had to prove they were as capable as men of exercising power or authority is drawing to a close, as witnessed by electoral success rates and the ability to finance campaigns. As Linda Ellerbee might say: "that road has been paved." Still under construction is the work of reshaping American political institutions so that women can enter them on their own terms, exercise power comfortably, and design policies that include their needs and concerns. However haltingly or painstakingly, that road is now being graded.

NOTES

Chapter 1. Breaking Ground

1. The figure of 213 was cited in the *Los Angeles Times*, April 30, 1992, reportedly based on information from the Federal Election Commission. The precise figure for women running in primary elections is difficult to calculate. The FEC could not confirm the number of 213. Lucy Baruch, of the Eagleton Institute's Center for the American Woman and Politics (CAWP), told the authors that the figure is imprecise partly because the gender of many candidates' first names is difficult to determine from reading state ballots. Also, some women announce exploratory committees to consider running and then decide not to do so.

2. This slogan, which gained such prominence in 1992, was first used to describe the election cycle of 1974, when forty-four women won nominations for the House and three women won nominations for the Senate. (Eighteen of those women nominated for the House won their seats, while none of the three women won her Senate race.) It had been foreshadowed during Congresswoman Bella Abzug's reelection campaign in 1972. *Life* magazine did a feature story on Abzug, whose picture was on the front cover. Although Abzug's reelection bid was in trouble, she was viewed as a symbol of a women's movement in transition from "empty rhetoric and bra-burning fulminations" to the "tougher work of organizing to get what they want." The story opened with the sentence, "It may not quite be the Year of the Woman." The slogan was frequently applied to the 1990 election cycle, when women ran for governor in the important states of Texas, California, and Oregon, and in several high-profile House and Senate races. For instance, Congresswoman Lynn Martin challenged veteran incumbent Senator Paul Simon, and Congresswoman Claudine Schneider challenged longtime chair of the Foreign Relations Committee, Senator Claiborne Pell of Rhode Island. In each instance, the "Year of the Woman" was said to have not materialized.

3. The figure for the House of Representatives varies, depending upon whether District of Columbia delegate Eleanor Holmes Norton is counted, since delegates to the House do not have full voting privileges. When she is counted, the figure of women in the House of Representatives is listed as forty-nine.

315

4. Speech given by Susan Yoachim to the Women's Campaign Fund Breakfast, September 22, 1992, in which she quotes from her interview with Steinem at the 1992 Democratic National Convention.

5. Charen's syndicated column appeared in the *Rocky Mountain News* on October 29, 1992.

6. Author's interview with Ellen Malcolm, October 19, 1992.

7. See, for example, Celinda Lake, "Campaigning in a Different Voice," report prepared after the 1988 elections, and "Challenging the Credibility Gap," report prepared after the 1990 elections. Both reports are available from EMILY's List.

8. Remarks by Michael Berman at the Women's Campaign Fund Seminar, Institute of Politics, Kennedy School of Government, Harvard University, October 12, 1989, transcript p. 103.

9. Presentation by Celinda Lake at the Forum for Women State Legislators, sponsored by CAWP, San Diego, November 15, 1991.

10. Author's interview with Sharon Rodine, former executive director of the National Women's Political Caucus, January 19, 1991.

11. Author's interview with Mervin Field, August 21, 1991.

12. Quoted in a Sunday magazine story by Linda Witt, "Two Women," *San Jose Mercury News,* May 31, 1992.

13. Wire service copy, *New York Times,* August 20, 1992.

14. Feinstein and Boxer fund-raising event, Davies Symphony Hall, October 19, 1992.

15. The Kaptur and Morella comments were quotations from a special feature on women in *USA Today,* April 1, 1992.

16. Geraldine Ferraro, speech during a breakfast meeting sponsored by the Women's Campaign Fund, San Francisco, August 16, 1991.

17. Quoted in the "Getting It Gazette," published by an ad hoc watchdog group that monitored women's campaigns in 1992.

18. Wire service copy, *New York Times,* September 11, 1992. For examples of the historical debate over women's nature, see Aileen Kraditor, *The Ideas of the Woman Suffrage Movement: 1890–1920* (New York: Columbia University Press, 1965). Kraditor argues that the nineteenth-century movement made a transition from a rights-based argument, emphasizing equality and similarity, to one based on women's capacity to give service to others, thus playing up their difference.

19. For an in-depth account of women's changing economic roles, see Barbara R. Bergmann, *The Economic Emergence of Women* (New York: Basic Books, 1986), and Julie A. Matthaei, *An Economic History of Women in America* (New York: Schocken, 1982).

20. Cited in Leo Kanowitz, *Women and the Law* (Albuquerque: University of New Mexico Press, 1969), p. 35. On the concept of coverture, see also

Linda Kerber, *Women of the Republic: Intellect and Ideology in Revolutionary America* (Chapel Hill: University of North Carolina Press, 1980), and Nancy Cott, *The Grounding of Modern Feminism* (New Haven: Yale University Press, 1987). Kerber is currently completing a major study on women and citizenship.

21. Kanowitz, p. 59.
22. Kanowitz, p. 38.
23. Quoted in the "Getting It Gazette."
24. Hillary Clinton described this sequence of events at a fund-raising event in San Francisco, March 25, 1992.
25. This debate continues. Two months after President Clinton named Hillary Rodham Clinton to chair a task force to restructure the health care system, Republican Senate Minority Leader Robert Dole let it be known that he would be sympathetic to a change in the anti-nepotism statute to allow Hillary Clinton to be appointed to a cabinet position. Such a change would subject Hillary Clinton to Senate confirmation hearings, should she receive such an appointment, thereby answering the charge that she is somehow "unaccountable."
26. See Glenna Matthews, *The Rise of Public Woman: Woman's Power and Woman's Place in the United States, 1630–1970* (New York: Oxford University Press, 1992), which details how many centuries it took for women to establish their authority in public.
27. According to author Glenna Matthews, public buildings or monuments named after Frances Willard exist in forty states, testifying to the breadth of the nineteenth-century temperance movement and Willard's role in it. For further reading on the temperance movement, see Ruth Bordin, *Women and Temperance: The Quest for Power and Liberty 1873–1900* (Philadelphia: Temple University Press, 1981). For more analysis of how women extended their domestic roles and pioneered the development of voluntary and charitable associations in the nineteenth century, see Paula Baker, "The Domestication of Politics: Women and American Political Society, 1780–1920," *American Historical Review* 89 (June 1984): 620–47; and Anne Firor Scott, *Natural Allies: Women's Associations in American History* (Urbana: University of Illinois Press, 1991).

Chapter 2. Creating a New Tradition

1. There is beginning to be a literature on women's political culture in the nineteenth century. A pioneering article is by Paula Baker, "The Domestication of Politics: Women and American Political Society, 1780–1920," *American Historical Review* 89 (June 1984):620–47.
2. For a further discussion of these issues see Glenna Matthews, *The Rise of*

Public Woman: Woman's Power and Woman's Place in the United States, 1630–1970 (New York: Oxford University Press, 1992).

3. As an example of the altruism mode of arguing for suffrage, Jane Addams published an article entitled, "Why Women Should Vote" in the January 1910 issue of the *Ladies' Home Journal*. In this she argued that the American city was in a bad way because it lacked "domesticity" and that American women could serve a redemptive role as voters. Despite such seemingly naive ideas, it is important to acknowledge that many women did achieve a substantial impact on welfare policy in these years. Robyn Muncy contends that they set up a female domain in the settlement houses, and then very successfully carried this influence into the federal government by lobbying for the formation of the Children's Bureau. See Muncy, *Creating a Female Dominion in American Reform, 1890–1925* (New York: Oxford University Press, 1991). See also Theda Skocpol, *Protecting Soldiers and Mothers* (Cambridge: Harvard University Press, 1992).

4. Kevin Giles, *Flight of the Dove: The Story of Jeannette Rankin* (Beaverton, Ore.: Touchstone Press, 1980), pp. 70, 71.

5. Robert A. Caro, *The Power Broker: Robert Moses and the Fall of New York* (New York: Vintage Books, 1975), p. 91.

6. Elizabeth Israels Perry, *Belle Moskowitz: Feminine Politics and the Exercise of Power in the Age of Alfred E. Smith* (New York: Oxford University Press, 1987), p. 156.

7. *Outlook and Independent*, January 23, 1929, p. 126, as quoted in Martin Gruberg, *Women in American Politics* (Oshkosh, Wis.: Academia Press, 1968), p. 121.

8. There is substantial literature on the subject of the Sheppard-Towner Act, which Congress passed in the early 1920s under threat of an imminent "women's vote." The act set up an elaborate maternal and child health program and represented the most ambitious federally sponsored public health program to date in American history. When the women's voting bloc failed to materialize, Congress refused to renew funding for the program. See William Chafe, *The American Woman: Her Changing Social, Political and Economic Roles, 1920–1970* (New York: Oxford University Press, 1972) for a discussion of this act and of the schism among the ranks of organized womanhood that developed in the 1920s.

9. Blanche Wiesen Cook, *Eleanor Roosevelt: A Life*, vol. I (New York: Viking Press, 1992), p. 329.

10. See Susan Ware, *Beyond Suffrage: Women in the New Deal* (Cambridge: Harvard University Press, 1981).

11. Susan Ware, *Partner and I: Molly Dewson, Feminism, and New Deal Politics* (New Haven: Yale University Press, 1987), p. 204.

12. Helen Gahagan Douglas, *A Full Life* (Garden City, N.Y.: Doubleday and Company, Inc., 1982), p. 262.
13. Ingrid Winther Scobie, *Center Stage: A Biography of Helen Gahagan Douglas* (New York: Oxford University Press, 1992), pp. 211–13.
14. Ibid., p. 241.
15. Ibid., p. 169.
16. Transcript of oral history interview with Rosalind Wiener Wyman, "'It's a Girl': Three Terms on the Los Angeles City Council, 1953–1965" (Bancroft Library, University of California, Berkeley, 1979), p. 11. It should be noted that Wyman has the unique perspective of having worked for Douglas in 1950 as a college student, then having run for office herself plus having been an important fund-raiser for the California Democratic party, and finally of having played a significant role in electing Boxer and Feinstein in 1992.
17. These generalizations are based on an all-too-brief, but eye-opening, trip to visit her papers, which are housed at the Carl Albert Center, University of Oklahoma, Norman.
18. Her predecessors had all been widows of male senators. Rebecca Felton of Georgia served for only one day and Hattie Caraway of Arkansas, while actually running for reelection after her initial term, earned the nickname of "Silent Hattie."
19. Author's interview with Barbara Boxer, July 1991.
20. Linda Witt interview with Margaret Chase Smith, March 7, 1990.
21. A Republican was likelier than a Democrat to be pro-ERA at this juncture, because the Democrats had an important alliance with organized labor, and the unions staunchly opposed the ERA.
22. Martha Griffiths's speech to the National Press Club, Fall 1990.
23. Chafe's *The American Woman* is excellent on this subject. See also Glenna Matthews, *"Just a Housewife": The Rise and Fall of Domesticity in America* (New York: Oxford University Press, 1987), Chapter 8.
24. See Linda Gordon, *Woman's Body, Woman's Right: A Social History of Birth Control in America* (New York: Penguin Books, 1977); James Mohr, *Abortion in America, 1800–1900)* (New York: Oxford University Press, 1978).
25. We believe that neither sex should be encouraged to be wholly self-sacrificing, as neither should be encouraged to be wholly self-seeking. We further believe that it is regrettable that male careers have been normative for establishing credibility: for example, women's volunteer work has not been seen as the valuable preparation for a politician that it, in fact, is.
26. Fern S. Ingersoll, "Former Congresswomen Look Back," in *Women in Washington: Advocates for Public Policy*, Irene Tinker, ed. (Beverly Hills: Sage Publications, 1982), p. 195.

27. Cynthia Harrison, *On Account of Sex: The Politics of Women's Issues, 1945–1968* (Berkeley: University of California Press, 1988), p. 216.
28. Ibid., p. 137.
29. Ingersoll, p. 197.
30. Harrison, pp. 176–182. Democrat Edith Green of Oregon was the sole holdout, and this was because she, a staunch liberal, was afraid to do anything to dilute the strength of the proposed remedy for racial injustice.
31. Shirley Chisholm, *Unbought and Unbossed* (Boston: Houghton Mifflin, 1970), p. 75.
32. As will be discussed later, there are new divisions over the nature of woman's nature. On this subject see Wendy Kaminer, *A Fearful Freedom: Women's Flight from Equality* (Reading, Mass.: Addison-Wesley Publishing Company, Inc., 1990).
33. See Susan J. Carroll, "Women Candidates and Support for Feminist Concerns: The Closet Feminist Syndrome," *The Western Political Quarterly* 37 (June 1984):307–23.
34. Ethel Klein, *Gender Politics: From Consciousness to Mass Politics* (Cambridge: Harvard University Press, 1984), p. 143.
35. On this debate see Kristin Luker, *Abortion and the Politics of Motherhood* (Berkeley: University of California Press, 1984).
36. This was the burden of remarks delivered by Frank Greer at the session "Choice and Your Campaign: Providing the Margin of Victory," National Women's Political Caucus Convention, Washington, D.C., July 1991.
37. Susan M. Hartmann, *From Margin to Mainstream: American Women and Politics Since 1960* (New York: Alfred A. Knopf, 1989), p. 77.
38. *New York Times,* January 11, 1981.

Chapter 3. Emerging from Jezebel's Shadow

1. Martin Gruberg, *Women in American Politics* (Oshkosh, Wis.: Academia Press, 1968), p. 232.
2. Ibid.
3. *Atlantic,* March 1964, p. 64, as quoted in ibid.
4. Ruth B. Mandel, *In the Running: The New American Woman Candidate* (Boston: Beacon Press, 1981), p. 33.
5. Charles Belch, 4th District Democratic chairman, May 1990.
6. Author's interview, 1992.
7. Congressional Record, Wednesday, October 9, 1991.
8. Celia Morris, *Storming the Statehouse: Running for Governor with Ann Richards and Dianne Feinstein* (New York: Charles Scribner's Sons, 1992), p. 17.

9. Irwin N. Gertzog, *Congressional Women: Their Recruitment, Treatment and Behavior* (New York: Praeger, 1984), p. 66.
10. Author's interview, 1992.
11. For a more complete discussion of Anne Hutchinson's case, see Glenna Matthews, *The Rise of Public Woman: Woman's Power and Woman's Place in the United States, 1630–1970* (New York: Oxford University Press, 1992), pp. 3–31.
12. Mackey Brown, *Montana Business Quarterly*, Autumn 1971, p. 24.
13. Gertzog, p. 234.
14. Gruberg, p. 153.
15. *National Directory of Women Elected Officials 1991*, National Women's Political Caucus, pp. 13–18.
16. U.S. Congress, Congressional Record 1947, pp. 631–32. Cited in Gertzog, pp. 61–62.
17. Gertzog, p. 243.
18. Author's interview, June 1991.
19. Patricia Yollin, "Painting the Town Lavender," Image magazine, *San Francisco Examiner*, March 10, 1991, p. 21.
20. Maryon Pittman Allen, "Free at Last!," *Washington Post* Magazine January 21, 1979, pp. 7–12.
21. Gertzog, p. 243.
22. National Women's Political Caucus panel discussion, Washington, D.C., July 1991.
23. Authors' interview, July 1991.
24. Conversation with Abzug during NWPC twentieth-anniversary festivities, July 1991.
25. Bella Abzug, *Bella! Ms. Abzug Goes to Washington* (New York: Saturday Review Press, 1972), p. 19. In the receiving line at the White House, Abzug lectured Richard Nixon on the need to withdraw from Vietnam. The president "pushed me on to Pat," Abzug wrote. The First Lady "chirped, 'I've read all about you and your cute little bonnets.'"
26. Ann Richards's Keynote Address to the 1988 Democratic National Convention (as per her book *Straight from the Heart: My Life in Politics and Other Places* (New York: Simon & Schuster, 1989).
27. Howard Schneider, *Washington Post*, January 16, 1991, p. C3.
28. Mandel, p. 67.
29. Dorothy Bradley, "Sexual Deviance in the Montana House of Representatives: Remembrances of the Past Session by Montana's Youngest Lady Politician," *Montana Business Quarterly*, Autumn 1971, pp. 27–30.
30. Morris, p. 25.
31. Author's interview, January 1991.

32. Mandel, pp. 64–65.
33. Gertzog, p. 70.
34. *PACs & Lobbies,* March 4, 1992, p. 10.
35. *Boston Phoenix,* April 20, 1990, section one.
36. For a further examination of the 1950 Douglas/Nixon race see Ingrid Winthur Scobie, *Center Stage: A Biography of Helen Gahagan Douglas* (New York: Oxford University Press, 1992), chap. 12.
37. Gertzog, p. 58.
38. Authors' interview, July 1991.
39. Gruberg, p. 124.
40. Ibid.
41. Office of the Historian (Dr. Raymond Smock), U.S. House of Representatives, *Women in Congress 1917–1976* (Washington, D.C.: U.S. Government Printing Office, 1976), p. 15.
42. Gertzog, p. 70.
43. Mary Anderson, *Women at Work* (Minneapolis: University of Minnesota Press, 1951), p. 64, as quoted in Gruberg.
44. Gertzog, p. 58.
45. Maryon Pittman Allen, "Free at Last," pp. 4–12.
46. Ibid.
47. Gertzog, p. 64.
48. Ibid., p. 66.
49. Charles Truehart, *Washington Post,* September 20, 1990.
50. Ibid.
51. Ibid.
52. Authors' interview, July 1991, and follow-up conversation with Linda Witt at Journalism and Women Symposium (JAWS), September 1991.
53. Bruce Lambert, "Millicent Fenwick, 82, Dies; Gave Character to Congress," *New York Times,* September 17, 1992.
54. Louise M. Young, "The American Woman at Mid-Century," *American Review,* December 1961, p. 73, as quoted in Gruberg.
55. *Woman's Journal,* February 5, 1870.
56. *Literary Digest,* September 4, 1920, as quoted in Gruberg.
57. Frank Graham, Jr., *Margaret Chase Smith* (New York: John Day, 1964), p. 32, as quoted in Gruberg.
58. *The Woman Citizen,* October 30, 1920, p. 598, as quoted in Gruberg.
59. *Literary Digest,* September 4, 1920, as quoted in Gruberg.
60. David Mananiss, "Where the Good Ole Boys Make Good Ole Laws," *Washington Post,* July 19, 1990.
61. Martha Griffiths, speech at the National Press Club, Washington, D.C., 1990.
62. Aileen C. Hernandez, "E.E.O.C. and the Women's Movement 1965–1975,"

p. 4. Paper delivered at the Symposium on the 10th Anniversary of the United States Equal Employment Opportunity Commission, Rutgers University Law School, November 1975.
63. Authors' interview, July 1991.
64. Ibid.
65. JAWS remarks, September 1991.

Chapter 4. Squaring the Personal and the Political

1. Frances Perkins, correspondence, National Women's Hall of Fame, Seneca Falls, New York.
2. Ibid.
3. Center for the American Woman and Politics, Rutgers University, New Brunswick, N.J., 1991.
4. *Washington Post*, August 4, 1986.
5. Ruth B. Mandel, *In the Running: The New American Woman Candidate* (Boston: Beacon Press, 1981), p. 90.
6. Quoted by the Associated Press in an August 25, 1992, story datelined Des Moines.
7. *Wall Street Journal*, October 6, 1987.
8. As he admitted in his memoir, *Shout It from the Housetops* (Plainfield, N.J.: Logos International, 1972).
9. Geraldine Ferraro files.
10. Dan Balz, "Careers, Families Obscure the Lure of Campaign Trail," *Washington Post*, July 7, 1991.
11. *New York Times* (national edition), February 6, 1992, p. A10.
12. Philip Wylie, *Generation of Vipers* (New York: Rinehart and Company, 1955), pp. 199–200.
13. Angus Campbell, Philip E. Converse, Warren E. Miller, and Donald E. Stokes, *The American Voter* (New York: John Wiley and Sons, 1960), p. 490, as quoted in Martin Gruberg, *Women in American Politics* (Shkosh, Wis.: Academia Press, 1968).
14. Madeleine M. Kunin, "Why Move On?," remarks to the Strategic Leadership 1990 Conference, October 12, 1989, the Women's Campaign Research Fund and the John F. Kennedy School of Government, Harvard University.
15. *National Business Woman*, January 1958, p. 16, as quoted in Gruberg.
16. Ann Richards, *Straight from the Heart: My Life in Politics and Other Places* (New York: Simon and Schuster, 1989), pp. 145–46.
17. Helen Markel, "Twenty-four Hours in the Life of Margaret Chase Smith," *McCall's*, May 1964, p. 161 as quoted in Gruberg.
18. Bella Abzug, *Bella! Ms. Abzug Goes to Washington* (New York: Saturday Review Press, 1972), p. 45.

19. Gruberg, p. 238.
20. Dorothy Cantor and Toni Bernay with Jean Stoess, *Women in Power: The Secrets of Leadership* (New York: Houghton Mifflin, 1992), p. 127.
21. Ann Richards, p. 138.
22. Ibid., pp. 143–44.
23. Author's interview, April 1992.
24. Celia Morris, *Storming the Statehouse: Running for Governor with Ann Richards and Dianne Feinstein* (New York: Charles Scribner's Sons, 1992), p. 24.
25. Margaret Mead, *Male and Female: A Study of the Sexes in a Changing World* (New York: William Morrow, 1949), p. 234, as quoted in Gruberg.
26. As quoted in *Life,* June 1992, p. 40.
27. Alvin Toffler, *Ladies' Home Journal,* June 1964, p. 26, as quoted in Gruberg.
28. Richards, pp. 182–83.
29. Morris, p. 24.
30. Gruberg, p. 229.
31. *Time* magazine, September 4, 1964, p. 101, as quoted in Gruberg.
32. Mandel, p. 80.
33. Ibid.
34. Cantor and Bernay, p. 124.
35. Susan Yoachum, *West* magazine, *San Jose Mercury News,* January 14, 1990, p. 23, as excerpted in *California Votes: The 1990 Governor's Race,* edited by Gerald C. Lubenow (Berkeley: IGS Press, Institute of Governmental Studies, University of California, Berkeley, 1991).
36. Abzug, p. 45.
37. Mandel, p. 82.

Chapter 5. Crossing the Credibility Threshold

1. Author's interview with Rosa DeLauro, July 10, 1991.
2. Marcia M. Lee, "Why Few Women Hold Public Office," in *Portrait of Marginality* (New York: Longman, Inc., 1977).
3. Bella Abzug, with Mim Kelber, *Gender Gap* (Boston: Houghton Mifflin Company, 1984), p. 161.
4. Ibid., p. 161. In 1970, Abzug defeated a machine-backed seven-term Democratic incumbent in the primary before winning the general election. She left Congress in 1976 to run for the U.S. Senate and was defeated in the Democratic primary.
5. Raisa B. Deber, "The Fault, Dear Brutus: Women as Congressional Candidates in Pennsylvania," *Journal of Politics,* vol. 44, no. 2 (1982).

6. Irwin Gertzog, *Congresswomen: Their Recruitment, Treatment, and Behavior* (New York: Praeger, 1984).
7. See, for example, Susan Welch et. al., "The Effect of Candidate Gender on Electoral Outcomes in State Legislative Races," *Western Political Quarterly,* vol. 38, no. 3 (1985); Robert Bernstein, "Why Are There So Few Women in the House?," ibid., vol. 39., no. 1 (1986); Susan J. Carroll, *Women as Candidates in American Politics* (Bloomington: Indiana University Press, 1985).
8. Bernstein, p. 157.
9. Fact sheet, "Women Moving Into State Legislatures 1974–1993," Eagleton Institute's Center for the American Woman and Politics (CAWP), Rutgers University, January, 1993.
10. In political science terminology, such new profiles are part of a larger shift in who runs for office. "The shift from a recruitment pattern that places a high value on achievement at the expense of ascribed characteristics both reflects and presages a democratization of the recruitment process." Therefore, the opportunity structure "is accessible to a wider range of women than it was in the past." Gertzog, p. 45.
11. San Jose, California, was the first sizable city to have a majority of women on the council. The mayor also was a woman, Janet Gray Hayes. See Janet A. Flammang, "Female Officials in the Feminist Capital: The Case of Santa Clara County," *Western Political Quarterly,* vol. 38, no. 1 (1985). In 1992, the small town of Pacifica, located south of San Francisco, attracted national attention when the voters elected an all-female city council.
12. Author's interview with Jane Danowitz, January 17, 1991.
13. Kunin's remarks from the Women's Campaign Fund Seminar, Institute of Politics, Kennedy School of Government, Harvard University, October 12, 1989, transcript 27.
14. Author's interview with Rosa DeLauro, July 10, 1991.
15. Gertzog, p. 37.
16. Although she never again ran for elected office, she became the first woman U.S. ambassador, appointed ambassador to Denmark in 1933. She had to resign from the position, however, when she married a Norwegian man. Later in life she devoted herself, like Eleanor Roosevelt, to supporting the United Nations. See brief biographical sketch, *Women in Congress: 1917–1990* (Washington, D.C.: U.S. Government Printing Office, 1991).
17. Author's interview with Nancy Kassebaum, July 12, 1991.
18. Author's interview with Barbara Kennelly, July 10, 1991.
19. Author's interview with Nancy Pelosi, April 11, 1992.
20. Ibid. She had not planned to run for Congress until former congresswoman Sala Burton, ill with cancer, pleaded with her to run for Burton's seat. Pelosi

says that Burton said to her, "I want you to do this. Promise me you will do this. Why would you not do this? You love the issues." Sala Burton had won the seat as a result of the death of her husband, notorious kingmaker John Burton. In this passing of the mantle to Pelosi, Burton's seat became one of the first to go from widow to political daughter.

21. Dorothy Cantor and Toni Bernay with Jean Stoess, *Women in Power: The Secrets of Leadership* (New York: Houghton Mifflin Company, 1992), p. 4.
22. Author's interview with Mary Rose Oakar, July 10, 1991.
23. Cantor and Bernay, p. 204.
24. Ibid., pp. 204–205.
25. Judy Mann, "The Gender Gap from the Reagan Camp," *Ms.*, March 1984, p. 74, cited in *Women Leaders in American Politics*, James David Barber and Barbara Kellerman, eds. (Englewood Cliffs: Prentice-Hall, 1986), p. 350.
26. Betty Friedan, *It Changed My Life* (New York: W. W. Norton Company, 1985), p. 174.
27. Fernando J. Guerra, "Emergence of Ethnic Office-Holders in California," in *Racial and Ethnic Politics in California*, Byron O. Jackson and Michael B. Preston, eds. (Berkeley: Institute of Governmental Studies, 1991), pp. 117–131.
28. Author's interview with Gloria Molina, September 27, 1991.
29. Author's interview with Anita Perez Ferguson, November 2, 1991.
30. DiVall's remarks quoted in *Campaigns and Elections*, Aug./Sept. 1990, p. 52.
31. CAWP fact sheet, "Women Moving Into State Legislatures 1974–1993."
32. Author's interview with Evelyn Murphy, March 20, 1991.
33. Barbara Roberts, speech to the Women's Campaign Fund breakfast, June 21, 1991.
34. Remarks by Elizabeth Holtzman, "Leadership 2000: Investing in our Future," co-sponsored by the Women's Campaign Fund and the LBJ School of Public Affairs, Austin, Texas, September 27, 1991.
35. Author's interview with Jane Danowitz, January 17, 1991.
36. Fact sheet, "Statewide Elective Executive Women 1993," Center for the American Woman and Politics, Rutgers University.
37. Remarks by John Deardourff, Women's Campaign Fund Seminar, Institute of Politics, October 12, 1989, transcript p. 83; Celinda Lake, "Crossing the Credibility Gap," paper prepared for EMILY's List.
38. Remarks by Celinda Lake, Women's Campaign Fund Seminar Institute of Politics, October 12, 1989, transcript p. 407.
39. Remarks by Michael Berman, ibid, transcript p. 93.
40. Speech by Governor Barbara Roberts at the San Francisco City Club, sponsored by the Women's Campaign Fund, June 21, 1991.

41. Author's interview with Anita Perez Ferguson, November 2, 1991.
42. Paper prepared by Irene Natividad, "Women of Color and the Campaign Trail." Natividad was the former head of the National Women's Political Caucus.
43. Author's interview with Barbara Mikulski, March, 1991.
44. Timothy Bledsoe and Mary Herring, "Victims of Circumstances," *APSR*, vol. 84, no. 1, 1990. These researchers added a *caveat* to the entire study, saying they could not untangle whether the difference in ambition was a "response" problem (women are more reluctant to admit to ambition) or a "sex role" problem (women see themselves as marginal).
45. Author's interview with Barbara Mikulski, March, 1991.
46. Informal discussion with Max Sherman, dean of the LBJ School of Public Affairs, September 27, 1991.
47. Author's interview with Barbara Mikulski, March, 1991.

Chapter 6. Raising the Ante

1. Common Cause press release, November 6, 1992, indicated that the average cost of a House campaign was $3,009,836. However, these were averages for winners. The average figures are higher, if both winners and losers are taken into account. Rough calculations indicate an average House race would be $550,000, and an average Senate race $4,025,000.
2. *Campaigns and Elections* editorial, May/June 1991.
3. Ruth Mandel, *In the Running: The New American Woman Candidate* (Boston: Beacon Press, 1981), p. 190.
4. Thomas Edsall, *Power and Money: Writing about Politics, 1971–1987* (New York: W. W. Norton & Company, 1988), p. 139.
5. Author's interview with former Vermont governor Madeleine Kunin, March 18, 1991.
6. Author's interview with Josie Heath, March 19 and 20, 1991.
7. Mandel, p. 201.
8. Robin Toner, "California Showdown," *New York Times Magazine*, September 30, 1990, p. 98.
9. *Congressional Quarterly*, vol. 40, no. 41, Special Report (October 9, 1982), p. 2523.
10. Informal conversation with Unsoeld after a Women's Campaign Fund event, San Francisco, November 30, 1989.
11. Author's interview with Jolene Unsoeld, Washington, D.C., July 11, 1991.
12. Author's interview with Joan Kelly Horn, August 13, 1991.
13. Mandel, p. 182.
14. Ronna Romney and Beppie Harrison, *Momentum* (New York: Crown Pubs., 1988), p. 90.

15. Author's interview with Nancy Johnson, November 26, 1991.
16. *National Journal,* June 16, 1990, p. 1466.
17. Edsall, p. 193.
18. Carole Jean Uhlaner and Key Lehman Schloztman, "Candidate Gender and Congressional Campaign Receipts," *Journal of Politics,* vol. 48 (1986), p. 36.
19. Ibid., p. 33. Candidates running for open seats where their party was used to winning raised an average of $258,907. Those candidates associated with the "out party," raised an average of $159,932.
20. Mandel, p. 188.
21. Ronna Romney and Beppie Harrison, p. 93.
22. *National Journal,* June 16, 1990, p. 1470.
23. Ibid.
24. Geraldine Ferraro, with Linda Bird Francke, *My Story* (New York: Bantam Books, 1985., pp. 195–96.
25. Ibid., p. 196.
26. Author's interview with Harriett Woods, November, 1991.
27. Author's interview with Barbara Mikulski, March, 1991.
28. Marilyn Quayle is quoted in "It Happened One Night," *Campaigns and Elections,* November 1992, p. 18.
29. Interview with Nina Rothchild of Minnesota $$ Million was conducted by research assistant Jennifer Steen, January 4, 1993.
30. Research on May's List was conducted by Jennifer Steen.
31. Interview with Debbie Campbell from the American Nurses Association was conducted by research assistant Jennifer Steen, January 15, 1993.
32. Interview with Kim Moran from the American Federation of Teachers conducted by research assistant Jennifer Steen, January 15, 1993.
33. Jane Danowitz, quoted in the *San Francisco Examiner,* December 2, 1992.
34. Interview with Darien Leung of NARAL conducted by research assistant Jennifer Steen, January 28, 1993.
35. This exchange took place at seminar co-sponsored by the Women's Campaign Fund and the LBJ School of Public Affairs, Austin, Texas, September 27, 1991.
36. Author's interview with Anita Perez Ferguson, November 2, 1991. EMILY's List did support Ferguson when she ran again in 1992. The huge flow of contributions in 1992 enabled EMILY's List to relax some of its requirements.
37. Author's interview with Pam Fleischaker, June 24, 1992.
38. Ibid.
39. Author's interview with Jane Danowitz, January 17, 1991.
40. Both Ruth Messinger and Elizabeth Holtzman were quoted in *New York Times,* March 14, 1992.

41. Comments by Jane Danowitz at a Women's Campaign Fund breakfast meeting, San Francisco, September 22, 1992.
42. "Boxer Shows Strength in Race for Funds," *Los Angeles Times,* May 28, 1992.
43. Ibid.
44. Ibid.
45. Author's interview with Evelyn Murphy, March 20, 1991.
46. Ibid. It is precisely this reliance on the same donor constituencies that poses a particular problem for Democrats, since their sources of financial support are increasingly divorced from their traditional voting base of people without wealth. See both Edsall, 1988, and Robert Kuttner, *The Life of the Party* (New York: Viking Penguin Books, 1987).
47. Analysis of donor categories by the *San Francisco Chronicle,* October 6, 1990.
48. Author's interview with Rosa DeLauro, July 10, 1991. According to DeLauro's campaign office in Connecticut, in 1992 she beat Scott 66 to 34 percent.
49. The authors are indebted to Sherry Kenne Osborne, Colorado correspondent for *Newsweek,* for this material, including interviews with both Swanee Hunt and Merle Chambers.
50. The figure was reported in *New York Times,* March 26, 1993.
51. Reported by Jim Drinkard of AP Wire Service, January 10, 1993.
52. Geraldine Ferraro's remarks were made at a Women's Campaign Fund breakfast, San Francisco, August 16, 1991.
53. Ellen Miller, quoted in *Common Cause Magazine,* Winter 1992, p. 11.

Chapter 7. Mobilizing Women's Votes

1. The precise number of women in the population and in the eligible electorate changes slightly in each election cycle, and of course may vary in particular states and congressional districts.
2. E. J. Dionne, Jr., *Washington Post,* March 8, 1992. Dionne cites exit polls from the Voter Research and Surveys, which indicated that Bush was favored by women in primary contests in New Hampshire, South Dakota, Maryland, Georgia, and Colorado.
3. Exit poll, conducted by *Los Angeles Times* and reported on June 4, 1992.
4. Celia Morris, *Storming the Statehouse: Running for Governor with Ann Richards and Dianne Feinstein* (New York: Charles Scribner's Sons, 1992). Morris writes that women started to "come home" one month before the election, especially pro-choice women. "The pro-choice movement turned out to be the political equivalent of several hundred cruise missiles." Texas Abortion Rights Action League pledged $250,000 for 250,000 voters, and targeted independent, Republican, and young women (p. 147).

5. Linda Witt interview with Margaret Chase Smith, March 3, 1990.
6. Jane S. Jacquette, *Women in Politics* (New York: Wiley, 1974); also cites Martin Gruberg, *Women in American Politics* (Oshkosh, Wis.: Academia Press, 1968), p. 57.
7. Nancy Cott, "Across the Great Divide: Women in Politics Before and After 1920," in *Women, Politics, and Change,* Louise A. Tilly and Patricia Gurin, eds. (New York: Russell Sage Foundation, 1990), p. 171.
8. Ibid.
9. The Sheppard-Towner Act was discussed in Chapter 2. Also see William H. Chafe, *The American Women and Politics* (New York: Oxford University Press, 1972), pp. 28–29, or Sheila M. Rothman, *Woman's Proper Place: A History of Changing Ideals and Practices 1870 to the Present* (New York: Basic Books, 1978), pp. 136–52.
10. Cott, p. 30.
11. Virginia Shapiro: "Feminism: A Generation Later," *Annals of the American Academy* (May 1991):36.
12. Betty Friedan, *It Changed My Life* (New York: W. W. Norton & Company, 1985), p. 171.
13. Ibid., p. 170.
14. Shapiro, p. 14. She cites the work of Arthur Miller et al., "Group Consciousness and Political Participation," *American Journal of Political Science* vol. 25 (August 1981): 494, 511.
15. In the presidential election years of 1980, 1984, and 1988, Blacks gave 85, 89, and 86 percent of their vote to the Democratic nominee. Percentages in congressional races are similar, ranging from a high of 92 percent in 1984 to a low of 79 percent in 1990. See Harold W. Stanley and Richard G. Niemi, *Vital Statistics on American Politics* (Washington, D.C.: Congressional Quarterly Press, 1992).
16. Shapiro, p. 15.
17. Cott, p. 170.
18. Ibid., p. 171.
19. Laurie E. Ekstrand and William A. Eckert, *Western Political Science Quarterly,* vol. 34, no. 1 (1981): 78–87.
20. Ibid., p. 79.
21. Kathy Bonk, "Discovery and Definition," in *The Politics of the Gender Gap: The Social Construction of Political Influence,* Carol M. Mueller, ed. (Newbury Park: Sage Publications, 1988), pp. 85–100.
22. Jane Mansbridge, *Why We Lost the ERA* (Chicago: University of Chicago Press, 1986), p. 15, 226. Mansbridge argues that if the rest of the data had been published, it would have shown that "in the population as a whole . . . men supported the ERA almost as much as women and voted against Reagan on the basis of their ERA support just as much as women did. Con-

trary to the activists' beliefs, therefore, the ERA had only a very small effect on the gender gap in the 1980 presidential election. See also her article, "Myth and Reality: The ERA and the Gender Gap in the 1980 Election," *Public Opinion,* vol. 73 (1985): 305–317.

23. Bonk, pp. 95–99.
24. Women's Trust material in Paget's 1984 personal files.
25. Ibid.
26. See, for example, Judy Mann, "Gender Clout," *Washington Post,* February 17, 1984.
27. Geraldine Ferraro with Linda Bird Francke, *My Story* (New York: Bantam Books, 1985), p. 79.
28. Ibid., p. 93.
29. Bonk, p. 98.
30. Author's interview with Linda DiVall, January 17, 1991.
31. Judy Mann, "The Gender Gap from the Reagan Camp," *Ms.* Magazine, March 1984, pp. 74ff.
32. Ethel Klein, *Gender Politics: From Consciousness to Mass Politics* (Cambridge: Harvard University Press, 1984), pp. 36–37.
33. Ibid.
34. Author's interview with Geraldine Ferraro, January 15, 1991.
35. Ethel Klein, "The Gender Gap: Different Issues, Different Answers," *The Brookings Review* vol. 3, no. 2 (Winter 1985), p. 37.
36. Conversation with Paul Tully, May 20, 1991, Berkeley, California.
37. This charge of capitulating to special interests would so terrify the Dukakis campaign in 1988 that it refused to have any organization that might connote such captivity; thus, national campaign staff were organized by region, making it virtually impossible to find a point person for, say, environmental, labor, or women's issues.
38. Different analyses of whether Ferraro helped or hurt the Mondale ticket depend, in part, on different measurers. Tracking polls, taken throughout the campaign period for Mondale, showed that she was hurting him. Exit poll data show that she neither helped nor hurt Mondale. Her own, positive, assessment is that she helped, particularly by bringing in new contributors. Ferraro cites as evidence statements made to her by DNC officials.
39. Klein in *Brookings Review,* p. 34.
40. Author's interview with Ethel Klein, October 3, 1991; For a comprehensive analysis of the gender gap, see Martin Gilens, "Gender and Support for Reagan: A Comprehensive Model of Presidential Approval," *American Journal of Political Science,* vol. 32 (1988):19–49; see also Robert Y. Shapiro and Harprett Mahajan, "Gender Differences in Policy Preferences: A Summary of Trends from the 1960s to the 1980s," *Public Opinion Quarterly,* vol. 50 (1986):42–61.

41. Author's interview with Kathleen Frankovic, CBS, October 3, 1991.
42. Susan Yoachum, "Complaints of a Double Standard in Gender Politicking," *San Francisco Chronicle,* July 18, 1990.
43. Authors' interview with Rollin Post, KRON-TV, San Francisco, August 21, 1991.
44. Authors' interview with Mervin Field, director California Poll, San Francisco, August 21, 1991.
45. Authors' interview with Linda DiVall, January 17, 1991.
46. Ibid.
47. Ibid.
48. Barbara G. Farah and Ethel Klein, "Public Opinion Trends," in *The Elections of 1988: Reports and Interpretations,* Gerald M. Pomper et al., eds. (Chatham, N.J.: Chatham House Publishers, 1988), pp. 122–24.
49. American Viewpoint, Inc., and Hickman-Maslin Research, "The New Political Woman Survey," August 1987, prepared for the National Women's Political Caucus, p. 2.
50. Authors' interview with Nikki Heidepriem, January 17, 1991.
51. Frank Greer, panel presentation at the twentieth anniversary of the National Women's Political Caucus, Washington, D.C., July 12, 1992.
52. Authors' interview with Nancy Kassebaum, July 12, 1991.
53. Ethan Geto quoted in *New York Times,* May 1, 1992.
54. Quoted in a column by Jack Anderson, "Women Serve Notice to Congress," *Oakland Tribune,* June 24, 1992.
55. Ann F. Lewis, "Return of the Gender Gap—Just in Time for November," *Ms.* magazine, January/February 1992, p. 88.
56. Ibid., p. 88.
57. Author's interview with Bill Carrick, February 6, 1993.
58. Authors' interview with Linda DiVall, January 17, 1991.
59. Author's interview with Ethel Klein, October 3, 1991.
60. Pamela Johnston Conover, "Feminists and the Gender Gap," *Journal of Politics* vol. 50, no. 4 (November 1988):1004.
61. Ibid.
62. Celinda Lake quoted in Judy Mann, "It's Courting Time," *Washington Post,* October 2, 1992.

Chapter 8. Decoding the Press

1. *Washington Post,* August 26 and 27, 1992, as quoted by M. Junior Bridge (Unabridged Communications), in "The News, As If All People Mattered . . . ," a report of the research organization Women, Men and Media, UCLA School of Journalism, December 1992, pp. 5–6.

2. Isabel Wilkerson, "Black Woman's Senate Race Is Acquiring a Celebrity Aura," *New York Times*, July 29, 1992, p. 1.
3. *Boston Phoenix*, April 20, 1990, section 1.
4. *New York Times*, April 6, 1917, p. 1.
5. Kevin Giles, *Flight of the Dove: The Story of Jeannette Rankin* (Beaverton, Ore.: Touchstone Press, 1980), p. 76.
6. Ibid., p. 76.
7. Ibid., p. 82.
8. Ibid., p. 77.
9. Ibid., p. 83.
10. Ibid., p. 79.
11. Ibid., pp. 83–85.
12. Ibid. *New York Times*, April 6, 1917, as quoted by Giles.
13. *New York Times*, April 7, 1917.
14. Ibid.
15. *Giles*, p. 103.
16. Ibid., p. 98.
17. For a longer discussion of Harriet Beecher Stowe see Glenna Matthews, *"Just a Housewife": The Rise and Fall of Domesticity in America* (New York: Oxford University Press, 1987), p. 57.
18. Ibid., p. 50, quoting Stowe's correspondence of January 20, 1853, Huntington Library, San Marino, California.
19. Maurine Beasley and Sheila Gibbons, *Women in Media: A Documentary Source Book* (Washington, D.C.: Women's Institute for Freedom of the Press, 1977), p. 28.
20. Kay Mills, *A Place in the News: From the Women's Pages to the Front Pages* (New York: Dodd, Mead & Company), p. 24.
21. Ishbel Ross, *Ladies of the Press* (New York: Harper, 1936), pp. 65–66, as quoted by Mills.
22. Madelon Golden Schlipp and Sharon M. Murphy, *Great Women of the Press* (Carbondale, Ill.: Southern Illinois Press, 1983), p. 135, as quoted by Mills.
23. Ibid., pp. 149–50.
24. Giles, pp. 110–11.
25. The Office of the Historian (Dr. Raymond Smock), U.S. House of Representatives, *Women in Congress, 1917–1990* (Washington, D.C.: U.S. Government Printing Office, 1991), p. 110.
26. *New York Times*, August 24, 1893.
27. *New York World*, September 17, 1893.
28. Mills, p. 36.
29. *Spy* magazine, February 1993.

30. Kathy Bonk and M. Junior Bridge (Unabridged Communications) in a report for the annual conference of the organization Women, Men and Media, April 1990.
31. Ibid.
32. Linda Witt, "Facts Made Chauvinist Swine Equal," *Muskogee Oklahoma Phoenix,* April 20, 1990, p. A11.
33. *USA Today,* August 20, 1992, as referred to by M. Junior Bridge (Unabridged Communications), in "The News As If All People Mattered . . . ," Women, Men and Media report, December 1992, p. 4.
34. NWPC's national survey of 1,502 randomly selected voters also looked at how well women are accepted at three other national, five statewide, and four local offices—down to school board member. Hickman-Maslin Research Inc., a Democratic firm, and American Viewpoint, Inc., the Republican firm run by Linda DiVall, conducted the survey.
35. Dru Riley Evarts, "Newspaper Headlines About the Possibility of Having a Woman President: A Descriptive Study," Dru Riley Evarts, Ohio State University. Paper presented before the Association for Education in Journalism, and Mass Communication Convention in Minneapolis, Minnesota, August 1990, p. 27.
36. *San Jose Mercury News West* magazine, July 15, 1984, p. 14.
37. Christopher Matthews, "Crashing the Senate 'Men's Club,'" *San Francisco Examiner,* May 31, 1992, p. A13.
38. Associated Press, dateline San Francisco, Thursday, July 19, 1984.
39. Pat Louise, "Politics vs. Family Life: U.C. Audience Hears Ferraro Tell All," (Utica, N.Y.) *Observer-Dispatch,* October 23, 1990, p. 3A.
40. "Challenging the Credibility Gap," study conducted for EMILY's List by Celinda Lake of Greenberg-Lake, The Analysis Group, Inc., 1991, p. 23.
41. Martin Gruberg, *Women in American Politics* (Oshkosh, Wis.: Academia Press, 1968), p. 17.
42. Louise, p. 3A.
43. Author's interview, April 1992.
44. *Boston Phoenix,* April 20, 1990, Section 1.
45. Office of the House Historian, p. 71.
46. Stephen Shedagg, *Clare Booth Luce: A Biography* (New York: Simon & Schuster, 1970), p. 121.
47. Ibid, p. 122.
48. Helen Gahagan Douglas, *A Full Life* (Garden City, N.Y.: Doubleday and Company, Inc., 1982), p. 198.
49. Shedagg, p. 123.
50. Douglas, p. 201.
51. Harold Rogers, "Mrs. Douglas Uses Food Basket to Argue Case for Rent Control," *Washington Star,* March 14, 1947.

52. "Congress's Week," *Time,* March 24, 1947.
53. *New York Post,* as quoted by Linda DeMers Hunnel in (Baltimore) *Evening Sun,* September 9, 1991.
54. *Christian Science Monitor,* as quoted by Philip E. Jenks in *The American Baptist,* January-February 1988, p. 48.
55. Gerri Javor, Cook's Corner, Valley Page, *Marin Independent News,* August 7, 1974, p. B.
56. "Campaigning in a Different Voice," study conducted for EMILY's List by Celinda Lake, 1990.

Chapter 9. Delivering the Message

1. Geraldine Baum, "A Shock to the System," *Chicago Sun Times,* March 29, 1992, p. E1.
2. Ibid.
3. "As Women Step Up, Hillary Steps Back," *Chicago Tribune,* July 14, 1992, pp. 1 and 12.
4. Richard Shingles, a scholar at Virginia Polytechnic Institute, quoted on the Ann Richards–Clayton Williams 1990 race in *Time,* September 10, 1990.
5. There had been, prior to the thirty-one women in the 102nd Congress, just ninety congresswomen and fourteen women senators. Another senator, Joyce Burdick of North Dakota, was appointed to fill her late husband's term in the 102nd's last days, bringing the Senate total to seventeen. But because both Margaret Chase Smith and Barbara Mikulski served in both houses, the grand total before the 1992 elections was 134 women.
6. Celinda Lake, "Campaigning in a Different Voice," study conducted for EMILY's List, 1990, p. 7.
7. Ibid., p. 8.
8. For a further discussion, see Ruth B. Mandel, *In the Running: The New American Woman Candidate* (Boston: Beacon Press, 1981), chapter 2, "The Right Image."
9. Geraldine Ferraro with Linda Bird Francke, *My Life* (New York: Bantam Books, 1985), p. 147.
10. Linda Witt, "A Military Experience Quiz," *Chicago Tribune,* October 22, 1984, p. 13.
11. "The Mikulski Papers: How We Lost the Election but Won the Campaign," *Ms.* magazine, July 1975, p. 59.
12. "Heath Criticizes 'Insider' Pressure," *Denver Post,* June 17, 1992, p. 1.
13. Gerald C. Lubenow (ed.), *California Votes: The 1990 Governor's Race,* (Berkeley: IGS Press, Institute of Governmental Studies, University of California, Berkeley, 1991), p. 64.
14. Ibid.

15. Ibid., p. 80.
16. Ibid., p. 172.
17. Ibid., p. 164.
18. Ibid., p. 153.
19. Ibid., p. 162.
20. Ibid., p. 165.
21. Ibid., p. 163.
22. Ibid.
23. Ibid., p. 165.
24. Ibid., p. 166.
25. *Wall Street Journal,* October 5, 1992.
26. "The Mikulski Papers," p. 59.
27. "Values," Sherry Harris campaign piece, written by Cathy Allen, Campaign Connection, Seattle, Wash.

Chapter 10. Losing

1. Geraldine Ferraro with Linda Bird Francke, *My Story* (New York: Bantam Books, 1985), p. 306.
2. Ibid., p. 310.
3. Ibid., p. 312.
4. Ibid., p. 306.
5. Joanne Jacobs, *San Jose Mercury News,* March 29, 1975, p. 7b.
6. Office of the Historian (Dr. Raymond Smock), U.S. House of Representatives, *Women in Congress 1917–1990* (Washington, D.C.: U.S. Government Printing Office, 1991), pp. 199–200.
7. Mackey Brown, *Montana Business Quarterly,* Autumn 1971, p. 25.
8. Office of the Historian (Dr. Raymond Smock), U.S. House of Representatives, *Congressional Women 1917–1976* (Washington D.C.: U.S. Government Printing Office, 1976), p. 67.
9. Ibid.
10. Congressional Record, May 17, 1984 (S6002) as quoted in Office of the Historian, U.S. House of Representatives, *Congressional Women 1917–1976.*
11. Ibid.
12. Martha Griffiths, speech before the National Press Club, 1990.
13. *Independent Woman,* February 1947, p. 34, as quoted in Martin Gruberg, *Women in American Politics* (Oshkosh, Wis.: Academia Press, 1968).
14. Perle Mesta with Robert Cahn, *Perle: My Story* (New York: McGraw-Hill, 1960), p. 180, as quoted in Gruberg.
15. Gruberg, p. 60.
16. Dorothy Cantor and Toni Bernay with Jean Stoess, *Women in Power: The Secrets of Leadership* (New York: Houghton Mifflin, 1992), p. 180.

17. *Detroit News*, September 2, 1990.
18. Speech to Women's Campaign Fund audience, John F. Kennedy School of Government, Harvard University, October 1989.
19. For a closer look at the memories of all the players in Mikulski's 1974 campaign, see "The Mikulski Papers: How We Lost the Election but Won the Campaign," *Ms.* magazine, July 1975, p. 59, from which this and the following quotes are taken.

Chapter 11. What Difference Does Difference Make?

1. Alice Walker's remarks at the Boxer fund-raiser were made on April 24, 1992 in San Francisco.
2. Remarks by Barbara Jordan were made during a seminar, "Leadership 2000: Investing in our Future," co-sponsored by the Women's Campaign Fund and the LBJ School of Public Affairs, Austin, Texas, September 26–28, 1991.
3. Remarks by Celinda Lake, ibid.
4. Remarks by Elizabeth Holtzman, ibid.
5. Sandra Day O'Connor, James Madison Lecture at the New York University Law School, October 29, 1991.
6. Carol Gilligan, *In a Different Voice* (Cambridge: Harvard University Press, 1982).
7. Remarks by Madeleine Kunin, Women's Campaign Fund Seminar, Institute of Politics, Kennedy School of Government, Harvard University, 1989. Transcript, p. 25.
8. Ellen Goodman, "Where Does Year of the Woman Lead?," *Des Moines Register*, December 26, 1992.
9. Suzanne Gordon, "Women's Vote Wasted in Congress," *Oakland Tribune*, February 15, 1991.
10. Antonia Fraser, *The Warrior Queens* (New York: Vintage Books, 1990), p. 306.
11. Author's interview with Barbara Mikulski, March, 1991.
12. Frieda L. Ghelen, "Women Members of Congress," in *A Portrait of Marginality*, Marianne Githens and Jewel L. Prestage, eds. (New York: Longman, 1977), p. 317.
13. Ibid., p. 318.
14. Geraldine Ferraro with Linda Bird Francke, *My Story* (New York: Bantam Books, 1985), p. 43.
15. Author's interview with Barbara Mikulski, March, 1991.
16. Madeleine Kunin, "Why Move On?," remarks to the Strategic Leadership 1990 Conference, October 12, 1989, Women's Campaign Research Fund and John F. Kennedy School of Government, Harvard University.

17. Lynn Martin, interview on Newsmaker Sunday, CNN, January 24, 1993.
18. "Women: Caucus of Female Lawmakers Gaining Clout in Sacramento," *Los Angeles Times*, November 6, 1991.
19. Author's interview with Nikki Beare, May 14, 1993.
20. Ibid.
21. Susan J. Carroll, Debra L. Dodson, and Ruth B. Mandel, *The Impact of Women in Public Office: An Overview*, report published by the Center for the American Woman and Politics, Eagleton Institute of Politics, Rutgers University, 1991.
22. Michelle Saint-Germain, "Does Their Difference Make a Difference? The Impact of Women on Public Policy in the Arizona Legislature," *Social Science Quarterly*, vol. 70, no. 4 (1989).
23. Janet K. Boles, "Local Elected Women and Policymaking: Movement Delegates or Feminist Trustees." Paper delivered at the American Political Science Association, 1991.
24. Nancy Kopp quoted in *New York Times*, November 18, 1991.
25. Branstad's remarks were quoted in a *Washington Post* wire story, *Oakland Tribune*, January 4, 1993.
26. Author's interview with Lynn Hecht Schafran, May 4, 1992. See also Lynn Hecht Schafran, "Overwhelming Evidence: Reports on Gender Bias in the Courts," *Trial* (February 1990): 28–33.
27. Janet A. Flammang, "Female Officials in the Feminist Capital: The Case of Santa Clara County," *Western Political Quarterly*, vol. 38, no. 1 (1985).
28. Author's interview with Loni Hancock, January 15, 1993.
29. Author's interview with Wendy Sherman, September 29, 1991.
30. Ibid.
31. Irwin Gertzog, quoted in "Crashing the Ultimate Men's Club," by Lyric Wallwork Winik in *San Francisco Chronicle*, December 20, 1992, This World, p. 9.
32. Interview with Barbara Kennelly, July 17, 1991.
33. Interview with Jolene Unsoeld, July 18, 1991.
34. Lois Romano, "On the Hill, The Gender Trap," *Washington Post*, March 6, 1990.
35. Author's interview with Mary Rose Oakar, July 18, 1991.
36. Alan Ehrenhalt, *The United States of Ambition* (New York: Times Books, 1991).
37. Dorothy W. Cantor and Toni Bernay, *Women in Power: The Secrets of Leadership* (New York: Houghton Mifflin Company, 1992).
38. Author's interview with Ruth Messinger, September 29, 1991.
39. Author's interview with Mary Rose Oakar, July 18, 1991.
40. Fern S. Ingersoll, "Former Congresswomen Look Back," in *Women in*

Washington, Irene Tinker, ed. (Beverly Hills, Calif.: Sage Publications, 1983), p. 195.

41. Ibid., p. 192.
42. Interview with Louise Lorenzen, acting director of the Congressional Caucus for Women's Issues, January 17, 1991.
43. Conversation with Lesley Primmer, executive director, Congressional Caucus for Women's Issues, May 14, 1993. In the wake of the 1992 elections, the caucus lost approximately 41 members. Primmer said approximately 115 men belong to the caucus, and that all but two of the newly elected women had joined after the 1992 elections.
44. Author's interview with Pat Schroeder, July 20, 1991.
45. Gertzog, p. 9.
46. Joan Tronto, Seminar discussion, Berkeley, California, March 11, 1992. See also Berenice Fisher and Joan Tronto, "Toward a Feminist Theory of Caring," in E. Abel and M. Nelson, eds., *Circles of Care: Work and Identity in Women's Lives* (Albany: State University of New York Press, 1990), pp. 35–62; or Joan Tronto, "Beyond Gender Difference to a Theory of Care," *Signs,* vol. 12 (1987):644–63.
47. Quoted in *Los Angeles Times Magazine,* February 2, 1992, p. 38.

Chapter 12. The Elections of 1994

1. Democratic women won 54 percent of their state legislative races, indicating continued high success rates, discussed later in the chapter. Data courtesy of the Center for the American Woman and Politics, Eagleton Institute of Politics, Rutgers University. Press release, December 1, 1994.
2. Linda Ellerbee, quoted during remarks made at the National Women's Health Coalition dinner, December 1994.
3. Interview with Congresswoman Jolene Unsoeld, December 12, 1994. Unsoeld said the final margin figure of 4 percentage points was rough, due to absentee ballot counts. She had seen figures lower than 52 percent for Smith, but never higher.
4. Barbara Burrell, *A Woman's Place Is in the House: Campaigning for Congress in the Feminist Era* (Ann Arbor: University of Michigan Press, 1994).
5. Jody Newman, "Perception and Reality: A Study Comparing the Success of Men and Women Candidates," National Women's Political Caucus, September 1994.
6. Op. Cit., CAWP, Rutgers University, December 1, 1994.
7. Barbara Burrell, "Money and Women's Candidacies for Public Office," Paper prepared for Research on Women and American Politics Conference, CAWP, April 1994.

8. EMILY's List Newsletter, "Notes from Emily," December 1994.
9. Rick Wartzman, "Women are Becoming Big Spenders in Politics and on Social Causes," the *Wall Street Journal*, October 17, 1994.
10. Interview with Mary Hughes, December 2, 1994, San Francisco, California.
11. Maureen Orth, "Arianna's Virtual Reality," *Vanity Fair*, November 1994.
12. Quoted in the *Los Angeles Times*, November 10, 1994.
13. Exit poll information from interview with Wayne Slater, Austin Bureau Chief, *Dallas Morning News*, December 16, 1994.
14. Quoted in the *New York Times*, November 2, 1994.
15. Interview with Texas Poll director Candace Windel, December 12, 1994; See also the *New York Times*, June 22, 1994.
16. Op. Cit., Wayne Slater.
17. Interview with Clint Reilly, December 22, 1994.
18. Interview with Zoe Lofgren, July 13, 1994.
19. Bill Carrick quoted in the *San Jose Mercury News*, June 9, 1994.
20. Ibid., July 13, 1994.
21. Interview with Larry Gerston, June 20, 1994.
22. Op. Cit., *Mercury News*, June 3, 1994
23. Gerston, June 20, 1994.
24. Interview with Jay Townsend, December 12, 1994.
25. Interview with Candy Straight, December 2, 1994.
26. *North County News*, November 2–8, 1994.
27. Interview with Michael Cassity, University of Wyoming, December 11, 1994.
28. Interview with Sue Myrick, December 8, 1994.
29. Interview with Mark di Camillo, December 2, 1994.
30. Op. Cit., CAWP.
31. Ibid.
32. Quoted in the *Los Angeles Times*, December 2, 1994.
33. Quoted in the *New York Times*, November 15, 1994.

INDEX

Abortion issue, 15, 47, 159–60, 171, 294, 307
  HWPAC and, 141
  male flip-flopping over, 16, 219–20
  men's appropriation of, 226–27
  polling data on, 16
  press coverage of, 192
  as quintessential women's issue, 16
  Republican women's division on, 233
  running because of, 255
  as "wedge" issue, 172
  young women voters and, 172
Abrams, Robert, 19, 176
Absentee fathers, 17, 275
Abzug, Bella
  campaign slogan, 110–11
  decision to run, 101
  elderly parents of, 94
  entry into politics, 85
  on hats, 59
  mother's support of, 84
  New York State Democratic party and, 261
  Nixon and, 321n25
  NWPC launching and, 47–48
  on press coverage, 208
  reelection campaign of ('72), 315n2
  response to stereotypes of women, 215
  Schroeder, Patricia, and, 97
  unseating of, 250
Abzug, Helene, 94
Abzug, Liz, 63
Achtenberg, Roberta, 58
  Helms, Jesse, attack on, 58
Activism
  altruistic political service and, 30
  nonpartisan, 26–27

  rationale for, 26
Adams, Brock, 70, 234
Addams, Jane, 190, 318n3
Affirmative action laws, 220,299–300
African-American voters, 158, 175, 176, 330n15
Ahab, 54
Aides, legislative, 111–12
Alatorre, Richard, 111–12
Alioto, Joseph, 212–13
Allen, Cathy, 230–31, 232
Allen, Maryon Pittman, 58, 59, 66
Allred, Gloria, 67
Altruism, 29–34, 221
  evolution away from, 35–37
  as mode of entry into politics, 85–86
  partisan politics and, 34
  power and, 30
  reproductive rights issue and, 43
  stereotypical expectation of, 214
  suffrage and, 318n3
  value to public activism, 30
  women journalists and, 187
  women's issues and, 72–73
Ambition, political, 119–20
  Jezebel legacy and, 61
American Federation of Teachers (AFT), 136, 140
American Nurses Association (ANA), 136, 140
American Teachers Association, 140
"American Women" (report), 44–45
Anthony, Susan B., 25
Anti-abortion activists, 23
Anti-incumbent sentiment, 8, 12
Apple, R. W., Jr., 177
Aquino, Corazon, 101

on "difference" strategy, 268, 269
on fear and loathing of political system, 104
on fund-raising, 129
journalist background of, 187
on political ambition, 86, 247
on stereotypical roles expected of women, 81–82
on support after loss, 258
on women's reluctance to enter politics, 108
Kuwait, 222, 225

Labor force, women's entry into, 20–21
Labor laws, 26
Labor movement, 40
Labor unions, opposition to ERA, 44
Lagomarsino, Robert, 112, 143
LaGuardia, Fiorello, 186
Laidlaw, Harriet, 186
Lake, Celinda, 199, 207
  assessment of '90 elections, 223
  on credibility, 116–17
  on economic concerns of women, 179
  on "feistiness," 237
  on fund-raising, 133
  on gender differences in campaigning, 9
  Head Start question, 238
  on husbands' effect on campaigns, 200
  on outsider status of women, 267
  on power for women, 219
  on press coverage of women, 208
  on superiority of women, 224–25
  Unsoeld and, 120
  on viability, 239
  on voter acceptance of women, 113
  on voters' presumption of women's competence in women's issues, 227
Landon, Alf, 106, 174
Landrieu, Mary, 105
Landrieu, Moon, 105
Laurie, Annie, 189
Law career, running and, 258–59
Laws
  campaign reform, 134

discriminating against women, 22
labor, 26
Leadership position in Congress, 279
Leadership traditions for women, 25, 104
League of Women Voters, 156, 254–55
Lesbian politicians, 58, 63, 103, 296–97
Levine, Mel, 122–23, 145–46, 176, 235
Lewis, Ann, 145, 147, 178, 230
Lewis, Eleanor, 162
Lewis, William, 77
Life-style, political, 59–60, 61
Lincoln, Abraham, 81, 187, 200
Lincoln, Mary Todd, 200
Lindsay, John, 101
Livesay, Beverly, 261
Lloyd, Marilyn, 73
Lloyd-Jones, Jean, 4
Local political level, experience from, 112–13
Lockwood, Marjorie, 109
Lofgren, Zoe, 301–2, 307
  blue-collar support for, 304
  and image as mother, 303
  and negative ads, 303–4
  and women and minority leaders, 303
Long, Dee, 140
Long, Jill, 51, 71, 260, 288
Losing, 241–63
  career after, 257–61
  Clagett, 255–57
  Eshoo, 241–42
  Ferraro, 242–46, 261–62
  gender differences in experience of, 246–49
  as pause in struggle, 253–54
  Pyle, 250–52
  Rankin, 249–50
  as rite of passage, 247–48, 252–54
  support after, 254–55, 258
  in unwinnable races, 252–54
Louisiana legislature, 71–72
Luce, Clare Boothe, 203–4, 252
Luckovich, Mike, 55
Lynch, Dotty, 165

Morella, Connie, 19, 97
Morris, Celia, 329*n*4
Moscone, George, 94, 117
Moseley-Braun, Carol
   advantage as incumbent in next race,
      148
   campaign strategy of, 239
   campaign turnaround for, 209–10
   as federal prosecutor, 260
   Head Start issue and, 238
   on personal-political balance,
      82–83
   press coverage of, 181
   Republican strategy against, 238–39
   support from African-American voters,
      175, 176
   support from working women, 178
   use of family name, 80
Moskowitz, Belle, 32–33, 36
Mother(s)
   candidate's image as, 116–17
   of political women, 84
Motherhood, 95–96
   activism as extension of, 26
   authority from, 81
   as campaign liability, 9, 10
   Ferraro on, 244
"Mother Mary" model, 102
Motivations for entering politics, 247
Mott, James, 25
Mott, Lucretia, 25
"Ms." title, 192
Muir, John, 10
Muncy, Robyn, 318*n*3
Murphy, Evelyn, 64, 94–95, 113,
   146–47, 183, 202–3, 208
Murray, Patty, 7, 95, 176, 207, 210,
   211
   advantage as incumbent in next race,
      148
   groundbreaking campaign of, 234
   press scrutiny of, 59
   women's votes and, 173, 174–75,
      178
Murray, Rob, 95
Myrick, Sue, 301, 304, 306–7

Name, family (or "maiden"), 79–80
National Abortion Rights Action League
   (NARAL), 136, 142
National Institutes of Health (NIH), 68,
   73
National Organization for Women
   (NOW), 45, 145, 159–60, 167,
   210
National Woman's Party, 34
National Women's Political Caucus
   (NWPC), 145, 158, 159, 254–55,
   290, 292
   financial support from, 135–36
   founding of, 47–48, 111, 157
   moral and psychic support from, 120
   study of voting behavior, 171–72, 196
   Thomas/Hill hearings and, 4
Natividad, Irene, 118–19
Nature of women, debate over, 47,
   282
Netsch, Dawn Clark, 289
Networks. *See also specific names of orga-
   nizations and networks*
   financial, 133–34
   of high-dollar donors, 149–50
   support, 120–21
New Deal, 37
New Jersey task force on gender bias,
   276
Newman, Jody, 290
New York Post, 205
New York Times, The, 181, 184, 185–86,
   193, 297
Nineteenth Amendment, 29
Nixon, Richard M., 15, 39, 59, 64, 80,
   156, 247–48, 321*n*25
Nolan, Mae Ella, 31–32
Nomination, obtaining party's, 119
Nonpartisan legacy, 280
Noonan, Peggy, 221
Norbeck, Peter, 251
Norton, Eleanor Holmes, 131, 201, 202,
   315*n*3
Norton, Mary, 33, 36, 66
Nunn, Sam, 16, 125
Nurturing role of women, 94–95

San Jose city council, 276
Santillo, Peggy, 262
Sarbanes, Paul, 138
Sargent, Claire, 20, 177
Saunders, Marion K., 105
Savage, Gus, 238
Scalia, Antonin, 220
Schaefer, Robert, 122
Schaefer, William D., 61
Schafran, Lynn Hecht, 259, 276
Schenk, Lynn, 288
Schneider, Claudine, 169, 218, 222, 260, 315n2
  on being politician, 69
  Ferraro and, 121
  husband's influence on, 87–88
  on marriage and politics, 89
  1978 loss of, 253
  on political ambition, 85, 92
  press coverage of, 182
Schoettler, Gail, 58, 85, 90, 91, 92, 259–60
Schroeder, James, 87
Schroeder, Patricia, 48, 73, 111, 124, 177, 220, 260
  on balancing personal and political life, 96–97
  on Democratic leadership's attitude change toward women's issues, 282
  entry into politics, 87
  on Harvard Law School, 259
  on high-dollar donors, 150
  on Hill/Thomas assault up Senate steps, 3
  on lack of power within House, 278
  on men's fears of women's sexuality, 72
  mother's support of, 84
  NIH sexual discrimination and, 67–68
  presidential candidacy of, 49–50, 93, 196, 215
  press coverage of, 205
  on running as a woman, 12, 284
  on same-equal distinction, 283
Schuster, Bob, 306

Schwartz, Teri, 296–97
Schwegmann, Melinda, 12
Scott, Tom, 148
Seattle Post-Intelligencer, 232
Seawell, Marjorie, 150
Self-interest, 37–48
  Bolton and, 41
  Douglas and, 37–40
  economic, 36–37
  Griffiths, Martha, and, 41–44
  Rogers and, 41
  St. George and, 41
  Smith, Margaret Chase, and, 40–41
Selflessness. *See* Altruism
Senate, average cost of race for, 127
Senate candidacies, Hill/Thomas hearings and, 4–5
Senate Judiciary Committee, 3
Senators, use of Hill/Thomas hearings by women, 1–2
Sergeant, A. A., 69
Serious Women, Serious Issues, Serious Money (fund-raising event), 149–50
Settlement house movement, 26
Sex, power and, 51–53, 62, 68–69
Sex differences. *See* Gender differences
Sex discrimination, 72
  President's Commission on the Status of Women and, 44–45
  Title VII of the 1964 Civil Rights Act and, 45
Sex equity issues, women's leadership on, 96
Sexism. *See also* Gender gap
  denial of, 255
  in press coverage, 199–202
  reverse, 225
Sex scandals, 70
Sexual behavior, double standard about, 53
Sexual confrontation, 50
Sexual etiquette, male-determined, 50
Sexual harassment, 51, 72, 229, 273, 312. *See also* Hill/Thomas hearings
Sexual innuendo, 26, 56–57